A Critical Study on T. F. Torrance's Theology of Incarnation

European University Studies
Europäische Hochschulschriften
Publications Universitaires Européennes

Series XXIII
Theology

Reihe XXIII   Série XXIII
Theologie
Théologie

Vol./Band 869

PETER LANG

Bern · Berlin · Bruxelles · Frankfurt am Main · New York · Oxford · Wien

Man Kei Ho

A Critical Study on T. F. Torrance's Theology of Incarnation

PETER LANG

Bern · Berlin · Bruxelles · Frankfurt am Main · New York · Oxford · Wien

Bibliographic information published by Die Deutsche Bibliothek
Die Deutsche Bibliothek lists this publication in the Deutsche Nationalbibliografie;
detailed bibliographic data is available on the Internet at
‹http://dnb.ddb.de›.

British Library Cataloguing-in-Publication Data:
A catalogue record for this book is available from *The British Library*, Great Britain

Library of Congress Cataloging-in-Publication Data

Ho, Man Kei.
A critical study on T. F. Torrance's theology of incarnation / Man Kei Ho.
p. cm. -- (European university studies. Series 23 vol. 869)
Includes bibliographical references.
ISBN 978-3-03911-678-2 (alk. paper)
1. Torrance, Thomas F. (Thomas Forsyth), 1913-2007.
2. Incarnation.
3. Jesus Christ--Person and offices. I. Title.
BT220.H58 2008
230'.044092--dc22
2008034088

ISSN 0721-3409
ISBN 978-3-03911-678-2

© Peter Lang AG, International Academic Publishers, Bern 2008
Hochfeldstrasse 32, Postfach 746, CH-3000 Bern 9, Switzerland
info@peterlang.com, www.peterlang.com, www.peterlang.net

Printed in Germany

This book is dedicated to my wife Ellen.

Acknowledgements

I would like to express my gratitude to Professor Tom O'Loughlin of University of Wales for his guidance and supervision in my studies.

Table of Contents

1. Introduction

T. F. Torrance, probably the most well known theologian of our times, advocates strongly the incarnational theology of his teacher, Karl Barth, that God himself is the content of his revelation, and that God is not revealing something other than himself. The unity of God and his revelation form the very essence of the Gospel. Grace is not something detached from God; the gift of God and the giver are essentially one and the same.[1] That is to say, the Act cannot be detached from the Being of God, and the Being cannot be detached from the Act of God.

Though Torrance is known as a theologian who has a vast knowledge of many different subjects which cover both ancient period and modern era, he also deeply engages in natural science by arguing that science and theology share similar methodology in its inquiry of objective truth. To Torrance, the ultimate objective truth lies in the incarnation. The theology of incarnation serves as the heart of his overall theology that we may not know God apart from the incarnate Son. The purpose of this book is to explore and examine various themes of his incarnational theology. Some of the subjects examined may be quite controversial, others are less so. An introductory chapter will review various theological methods employed by Torrance to formulate his theology, and subsequent chapters will explore major subjects of Christology, Trinity, Revelational Epistemology, and Kenosis. The book plays special attention to the internal coherence of Torrance's writings and discovers that in many instances, Torrance's arguments lack consistency. This is evident is his rejection and later accommodation of natural theology.

In his theology, Torrance tries to make a careful balance between patristic tradition and modern novelty. He tries to remain loyal to the teachings of patristic fathers and various confessions of the early church councils, at the same time, he insists on the infinite mobility of God's revelation that there is always newness in theology. This is particularly

---

1   A Walker, 'Interview with Professor Thomas F. Torrance', in *Different Gospel* (London: Hodder & Stoughton, 1988), 48.

true in his theological science that new scientific theories are brought into the realm of theology.

Dialectics and theological science are two important tools employed by Torrance to formulate his theology. Dialectics allows him to pull two opposite ideas together to form a unified concept without having to address its discrepancies or mismatches, and theological science gives him a modern scientific platform for his unitary structure. However, his frequent use of dialectics or employment of dialectics without limits create some disturbances as whether he is addressing profoundest truth or simply absurdity. Torrance was honored with the Templeton award for his contribution of theological science, but there still remains the age-old question that whether religion and science indeed belong to the same category, and whether science can in reality lead people to the ultimate truth. In fact, Torrance's theological science is not really about science but about faith. He is using the scientific structure to address the intricacy of theology.

Torrance employs the patristic doctrine of *hypostatic union* to affirm the dual nature of Christ that he is fully divine and fully human, the doctrine of *homousion* to affirm the divinity of Christ that he is consubstantial with the Father, and doctrine of *perichoresis* to affirm the equality and interrelationship of the three divine persons in the Being of God. The Son is the only linkage between God and humanity; thus, Torrance believes that unless we know the Son, we do not know the Father. We cannot know God behind the back of Jesus Christ. He regards the incarnation as the supreme and ultimate divine revelation in which God reveals himself to us through the Act and Being of himself in the incarnate Son. Through the salvific activities of the incarnate Son, we may have the knowledge of the Trinity, the inner relationship in the Being of God. Apart from the Son, we may not really know God. Thus, the supreme revelation of the incarnation relativizes all other so-called revelations which include natural theology and the Old Testament revelation.

Kenosis, due to its paradoxical nature, is not well addressed by Torrance. He argues that the truthfulness of Christ's kenosis can only be understood in accordance with the assumption of humanity rather than the subtraction of divinity. He affirms the patristic position and rejects modern kenotic theories of depotentiation of Christ's divinity. However, the mechanism of the integration of divinity and humanity as it is reflected through one unitary act in the person of Jesus Christ is not well addressed. Torrance gives a good analysis on the distinction between *person* and *being* but unfortunately, he fails to give any distinction among *nature, person*, and *being*. At times, there are confusions between *nature* and *Being, hypostatic union* and *perichoresis*. Torrance is only able to address kenosis from the aspect of *nature* rather than of *person*.

There are many books today examining Torrance's thoughts and ideas, most are praiseworthy of his work. The only exception may be his epistemological approach of the revelational knowledge of which it draws a few dissenting voices. This book, however, would provide a wider range of criticism, all constructive in nature, of Torrance's theology of incarnation, and may serve as a platform for further discussion.

2. Theological Method

Torrance establishes his theology mainly on the foundation of Nicene-Constantinopolitan confessions. In the formulation of his theology, he favors Greek fathers more than Latin fathers, and relies heavily on the teachings of Athanasius in the patristic period, Calvin and Barth in the modern era. Christology is the centre of Torrance's theology, and incarnation is the heart of his Christology. Torrance considers that his theology is dynamic and open, and rejects any idea of a mechanistic universe in containing God. His theology of incarnation is objectively oriented in the living God and is thus constantly renewed by the self-revelation of God.[1] Torrance plays a particular role in the scientific community in bringing science and theology together to form a scientific theology by arguing that theology is no different than science in studying the object in accordance with its proper nature. Both disciplines employ the same methodology though one moves towards the creaturely object while the other moves towards the divine object. In additional to theological science, hermeneutics, natural theology, dualism and dialectics form the basis of Torrance's theological method. These ideas are not independent from each other, but rather related to each other to give an integral form of his overall Christian dogmatics.

2.1. Hermeneutics

Under the influence of Karl Barth, Torrance's hermeneutics is undoubtedly more theological than biblical. The hermeneutic style of Barth traces back to his father who on one hand accepts the Scripture as the Word of God and on the other hand, believes that the Scripture is im-

---

1   T. F. Torrance, *Reality and Evangelical Theology* (Downers Grove: InterVarsity Press, 1999), 49–50.

perfect.[2] Monsma argues that Barth's father champions a faith based on the life of Jesus rather than a system of doctrine. Barth inherits his father's belief by accepting the Scripture as the Word of God but denies its full equality with the Truth.[3] Separating the human aspect of the word of God from that of the divine is not unique to Barth and Torrance, Hendry shares similar idea on the authority of the Scripture, he says,

> The Bible is the Word of God, but it is the Word of God only by the inspiration of God, not by virtue of any property inherent in itself. In itself the Bible consists of human words, which like all such are subject to error. Like all human words, however, they have their significance, not in themselves, but in that which they signify, in the object to which they point; and they can only be interpreted aright by reference to this object.[4]

The Scripture is only divine when it is interpreted in accordance with its object reference. By itself, it is simply human words. Thus, Barth says that dogma is not found in the biblical text because dogma is an interpretation of the text.[5] However, if Scripture is inspired by the Holy Spirit only in the things that it signifies, then, all exposition of Scripture is in fact allegorical[6]. Hendry says,

> I have never yet listened to an exposition of any text of Scripture in which the text was not invoked to say other things, and sometimes very other things indeed, from the plain literal sense of the words... I know this is dangerous. But then all interpretation of Scripture is dangerous.[7]

If Hendry's idea is correct then the interpretation of Scripture is like taking a chance, and is indeed a very dangerous undertaking. Torrance

---

2   P. H. Monsma, Peter Halman, *Karl Barth's Idea of Revelation*, (Somerville, N.J.: Somerset Press, 1937), 10.
3   Ibid.
4   G. S. Hendry, 'The Exposition of Holy Scripture', *Scottish Journal of Theology*, 1 (1948), 36–37.
5   K. Barth, *Church Dogmatics*, tr. G.T. Thomson, 1/1 (Edinburgh: T & T Clark, 1963), 475.
6   Allegorical, according to Hendry, means simply saying other things. See Hendry, 46.
7   Hendry, 46.

avoids this pitfall by rejecting allegorical interpretation[8] and sees it as a product of dualist modes of thought which caused damage to the biblical interpretation of the early and medieval church.[9] Instead, Torrance uses typological interpretation of which he sees as having its proper place in early church exegesis because it reflects a deep connection between the Gospel and the ancient past in the Old Testament.[10] Through typological interpretation, all redemption events in the Old Testament such as that of the Exodus, according to Torrance, could be Christologically interpreted; and this reflects the influence from his mother in his early age.[11] Torrance says, 'the shadowy prefigurements of redemption under the old covenant have now given way to the final truth of redemption through the sacrifice of Christ in the new covenant.'[12] That is to say, the Old Testament serves only as a shadow of the things to come, and the final truth is realised in the incarnate Son.

Torrance admits that he does not have a hermeneutical theory or method,[13] and rejects the validity of any such method because he believes that theology is open-ended in its speech about God.[14] However, he nevertheless provides some principles in approaching the Scripture. He says that it is important for us to dwell in the Scripture as a whole by going through all books and passages, and allow the messages of the Scripture to dwell in our mind so that we can be drawn into God's revelation of himself through himself. This indwelling is done through faith, devotion, meditation, prayer and worship, so that we are given the

---

8   Torrance sees two types of allegorical interpretation. The first one is that God speaks to us mythologically within a framework of abstraction between idea and phenomenon, timeless reality and contingent happening. The second one is that God is utterly unknowable and unspeakable that we can have no conceptual knowledge of him, but we may still have some kind of symbolic knowledge of God gained in hidden ways. See T. F. Torrance, *Divine Meaning* (Edinburgh: T&T Clark, 1995), 34.

9   T. F. Torrance, *Space, Time and Resurrection* (Edinburgh: T&T Clark, 1998), 44–45.

10   Torrance, *Divine Meaning*, 101.

11   A. E. McGrath, *T.F. Torrance, An Intellectual Biography* (Edinburgh: T&T Clark, 1999), 25.

12   T. F. Torrance, *Theological Science* (Edinburgh: T&T Clark, 1996), 172.

13   T. F. Torrance, 'Thomas Torrance Responds', in *The Promise of Trinitarian Theology*, ed. Elmer M. Coyler (Landam, Md.: Rowman & Littlefield, 2001), 329.

14   Ibid.

access to the inner communion of the Triune God.[15] Unless we are led by the Holy Spirit which inspired the Scripture, we are unable to understand its deep spiritual meaning.[16] That is to say, we cannot undertake the task of interpreting the Scripture without having a personal relation with the Truth. And through constant prayer we may be illuminated by the Truth in the understanding of his word.[17] The knowledge that we receive from God by itself is a grace because we possess no faculty in the interpretation of the Scripture, it is only by the grace of God that we may understand.[18] Torrance suggests that if one does not believe in the divine reality revealed through the Scripture, then one may simply give up the claim of the knowledge of God rather than interpreting the Scripture apart from the living God.[19] Thus, the right of interpretation of the Scripture belongs to the believers because interpretation has to be preceded by the work of the Holy Spirit.

The divine revelation, according to Torrance, is given to us not in a visual form but in an auditory form that it is through the hearing the word of God that people respond. He further illustrates that nowhere in the Gospel did the eye-witnesses tell us anything of what Jesus looked like, because they knew Christ primarily through the hearing of his words.[20] Therefore, Torrance says that we are shifting away from the visual mode of thought to an auditive form of hearing God. As a way of interpreting the Scripture appropriate to the distinctive nature of God's self-revelation, we are required to listen to God's living voice through the Gospel witness.[21] However, in reality, David Siemens argues that the visual experience is not that different from the auditory experience, they are so automatic in our human growth; it is the communication rather than the primacy of audit mode over visual mode that serves the relevancy of theology.[22] Thus, the visual element of the Scripture should

---

15   T. F. Torrance, *The Christian Doctrine of God* (Edinburgh: T&T Clark, 2001), 37–38.
16   Ibid.
17   Torrance, *Reality and Evangelical Theology*, 136.
18   Torrance, *Divine Meaning*, 96–97.
19   Torrance, *Reality and Evangelical Theology*, 97.
20   Torrance, *The Christian Doctrine of God*, 38–39.
21   Torrance, *The Christian Doctrine of God*, 39.
22   D. F. Siemens Jr., 'Two Problems With Torrance', *Perspectives on Science and Christian Faith*, 43/2 (June 1991), 112–113.

not be underestimated or degraded to a secondary place as what is suggested by Torrance. It is true that the New Testament witnesses do not provide any physical description of Jesus Christ, however, the prophet Isaiah does describe him as a man of no beauty or majesty, there is nothing in his appearance that we should desire him. (Isaiah 53:2) In several Scriptural passages, visual experience tends to give a much deeper level of communication than that of auditory experience. This experience is clearly reflected in the life of Job, he says, 'My ears had heard of you but now my eyes have seen you.' (Job 42:5) That is to say, seeing achieves a higher level of communication with God than listening. And Jesus himself also uses the metaphor of spiritual blindness (John 9:37-41) to illustrate the importance of visual aspect of the truth. Nonetheless, Torrance's auditory hermeneutics is commendable because it emphasizes the necessity of our obedience[23] which it is fundamental to our relation with the living God.

The correct interpretation of the Scripture, according to Torrance, is to allow the texts to witness to us, and to let them impress upon us the appropriate frame of reference for our understanding of them, so that we may interpret the texts from within its own coherent structure.[24] That is to say, the Scripture has to be interpreted in accordance with its own self-witness. The scientific procedure of interpretation of the Scripture should only be taken within its own distinctive framework, on its own intelligibility based on what it has to say about God and the world and his saving activity in history without any alien framework of thought such as the exclusion of supernatural events and messages.[25] Torrance says that only when this scientific approach is exhausted, may we interpret the Scripture in terms of a different set of axioms.[26] Historical critical methods, according to Torrance, are not scientific in themselves because the realities that the Scripture signifies are rejected, and no attention has been paid to its intelligibility. Thus, theologians should not be concerned with the historical criticism which strips clear all later additions of the church to the basic layer. Torrance argues that these additions in the New Testament are exactly what the primitive church

---

23 Torrance, *Thomas Torrance Responds*, 325–326.
24 T. F. Torrance, *Space, Time and Resurrection* (Edinburgh: T&T Clark, 1998), 4.
25 Ibid., 5.
26 Ibid.

took in its rise and shape.[27] In other words, if the church is founded on the Gospels, then one cannot get to the historical reality of the Gospels without honoring the integrity of the primitive church. By rejecting the apostolic tradition and the written words of the Scripture, one is unable to reach the so-called basic layer of a stratified structure of the Gospels. Thus, Torrance suggests a holistic approach that the interpretation of the Scripture has to be based on the ontological and epistemological ground on which they are produced in the light of God's unique Trinitarian self-revelation. All books of the New Testament are to be understood not only as historical documents derived from the primitive church but also the revelation by which God addresses his living Word to us through his Spirit.[28] The contemporary biblical critics, according to Torrance, tie up with an observationalist and phenomenalist approach that the Scripture is interpreted apart from its intrinsic relations and structures. Thus, they tend to regard the Scripture in terms of expressing the subjects of the authors or the mind of the community in which the documents arose.[29] Torrance argues when we interpret the text such as the Gospel of Mark, we do not seek to go behind the text into the soul of Mark to interpret what he is saying,[30] because the text actually reflects the reality to which it bears witness.

There are two ways of presenting the truth in the Scripture and Torrance sees that the *concerning of the truth* is more important than the *on behalf of the truth*. The former is illustrated by the example of Paul's missionary address to the Athenians on the Areopagus (Acts 17:16-34) which owing to its nature, provides necessary knowledge of the actual subject-matter such as 'The God who made the world and everything in it is the Lord of heaven and earth and does not live in temples built by hands.' (Acts 17:24) The latter is illustrated by Paul's address to the Athenians the worship of the unknown god (Acts 17:22-23)[31] which is regarded of secondary importance because it does not establish the truth but lays the path by removing false and hostile opinion. The

---

27   Ibid., 10.
28   Torrance, *The Christian Doctrine of God*, 36–37.
29   Torrance, *Reality and Evangelical Theology*, 63–64.
30   T. F. Torrance, *God and Rationality* (London: Oxford University Press, 1971), 37–38.
31   Torrance, *Divine Meaning*, 40; T. F. Torrance, 'Phusikos Kai Theologikos Logos, St Paul And Athenagoras At Athens', *Scottish Journal of Theology*, 41 (1988), 11.

interpretation of the Scripture, according to Torrance, consists of two levels. The first level is empirical, literal, denotative or semantic, and the second level is theological, connotative or syntactic.[32] The first level is related to the obvious moral and social aspects of our daily existence, and the second level carries a deeper theological meaning in the light of the incarnation.[33] Thus, parables would quickly lose their distinctive significance if they were restricted to the first level because their truth value lies in their theological dimension referenced through the incarnation.[34] The second level controls the correct interpretation of the first level. However, without the text, there is simply no second level. Torrance understands that the first level is the subject-object relation between the interpreter and the text, and the second level is within the text. It would be wrong, according to Torrance, for an interpreter to interpret the Scripture as if he himself is the biblical writer because it would come to a delusion that he can understand the author better than that of the author himself. And this destroys the whole objective frame of reference within which the Scripture presents and interprets itself to us.[35] The objective reality of God himself must control the interpretation of the object in the object-object relation in hermeneutics.[36] That is to say, the subject is indeed controlled by the object, the subject-object relation in the interpretation of the Scripture is in fact an object-object relation that God (object) reveals himself (object) to us. Apparently, Torrance is arguing in a circular fashion that the validity of the objective reference is perceived from a subjective belief, and the subjective belief is grounded in objective reference. Torrance admits that he is arguing in a circular procedure because his presupposition of the ultimate realities[37] cannot be validated outside of itself.[38] However, it is still a correct procedure because similarly, according to Torrance, the laws of logic cannot be

---

32   Torrance, *Reality and Evangelical Theology*, 106.
33   Torrance, *Theological Science*, 275–276.
34   Ibid., 276.
35   Torrance, *Reality and Evangelical Theology*, 104.
36   Ibid.
37   Torrance sees incarnation and resurrection as two important pillars and ultimates in the understanding of the revelation through the Scriptures that cannot be challenged, as they cannot be tested or validated outside the ultimates. See Torrance, T.F., *Space, Time and Resurrection*, 20–22.
38   Ibid., 15.

11

proved by others except by its own.[39] Colyer comments on Torrance's circularity,

> There is a circularity to this hermeneutical activity in which exegesis and interpretation of Bible is guided by a theological articulation of the realities and truths which the Bible mediates, though those realities and truths are only accessible to us through our ongoing exegesis of the biblical witness.[40]

Torrance denies that his hermeneutic circle 'is a vicious circularity artificially intruded into the ground of knowledge' [41] because his hermeneutic circle is properly inherent in a coherent system of objective ultimate facts which are the very ground of our experience and knowledge of it.[42] The Scripture is ontologically controlled by the realities that it signifies, however, at the same time, the sign has to be differentiated from the reality that it signifies because it does not possess the truth in itself but in the reality that it serves.[43] That is to say, interpretation of the Scripture cannot be established or defended simply by appealing to biblical texts or passages or even biblical concepts, but only through listening to the truths they signify or attest and allowing our minds to be objectively determined by them.[44]

Torrance suggests that in order to affirm our interpretation of the Scripture, we should clarify and check ours in accordance with the *canon of truth*.[45] That is to say, we need to employ the patristic conceptions such as *hypostatic union* and *homoousion* as guidance to interpret the Holy Scripture because these conceptions are developed out of hard exegesis and interpretation of biblical statements. Thus, they serve as the interpretative lenses of God's self-revelation in Jesus Christ. And this *canon of truth* becomes an irreversible reference and forms the basis of the subsequent interpretation of the Scripture and the formulation of the Christian doctrines.[46] In other words, the *canon of truth* is based on the

---

39   Ibid., 15–16.
40   E. M. Colyer, *The Nature of Doctrine in T.F. Torrance's Theology* (Eugene: Wipf and Stock Publishers, 2001), 66.
41   Torrance, *Space, Time and Resurrection*, 15.
42   Ibid., 15, 38.
43   Torrance, *Reality and Evangelical Theology*, 66.
44   Ibid., 119.
45   Ibid., 101.
46   Ibid., 112–113, 117–118.

biblical interpretation, and the biblical interpretation is based on the *canon of truth*. Torrance in essence is creating a vicious circle, which he denies, in hermeneutics without a fixed point of reference.

Regarding the constant newness of God's revelation, on one hand, Torrance seeks the *canon of truth* as produced by the patristic fathers as the basis of our Christian doctrines, on the other hand, he claims that theological statements are basically open concepts that are wide open to God's infinite objectivity and inexhaustible intelligibility.[47] It is difficult to understand how to make a static historical doctrine open to new dynamic inexhaustible intelligibility. No wonder many people think that Torrance is reading modern scientific ideas back into the patristic writings.[48] Morrison comments, 'it seems that Athanasius becomes an occasion, something of a mouthpiece for a particular view of God and the world that may not be fully his own.'[49] That is to say, Torrance sees that his modern ideas and conceptions are actually part of the patristic formulations because theological statements by itself is dynamic in nature and open to divine intelligibility. Unfortunately, many feel that Torrance is force-feeding his ideas into the minds of patristic fathers.

Torrance's hermeneutics rejects any possibility of dualism as it restricts theological idea to what is logically derived from observations or appearances, and disconnects the ontological relation of the statements to the realities that they refer to.[50] If the reference is disconnected from its ontological objective, Torrance argues, either the biblical statement is referenced to the subject or to other statements; however, both would simply collapse on itself by breaking off their ontological reference.[51] Torrance says,

> our thoughts and statements then derive from no objective source and point to nothing beyond ourselves – they are ultimately no more than autobiographical statements, and theology inevitably degenerates into anthropology.[52]

---

47   Torrance, *Divine Meaning*, 347–348.
48   Ibid., 1.
49   J. D. Morrison, review of T.F. Torrance, *The Trinitarian Faith* (Edinburgh: T&T Clark, 1988), in *Calvin Theological Journal*, 25/1 (April 1990), 119–122.
50   T. F. Torrance, *The Ground And Grammar of Theology* (Edinburgh: T&T Clark, 2001), 33–34.
51   Ibid.
52   Ibid., 36–37.

According to Torrance, the meaning of the statement does not lie in itself but rather in its objective reference. Thus, Torrance believes that we should not focus myopically on the words and statements but rather see the truth and reality that lie beyond them. The Scripture serves only as the spectacles through which we are brought to know God in his self-evident reality.[53] That is to say, the Scripture is not the Word of God in itself, it is not divine, it serves as the only media through which we may know God. Torrance's hermeneutics is both realist and asymmetrical, it is realist because the text carries a real meaning beyond itself. The knowledge of divine truth lies in what the words and statements signify, and is independent of the Scripture.[54] It is asymmetrical because in the two-way relation between the Scripture and the divine revelation, the ontological priority and authoritative primacy of the divine revelation takes precedence over the Scripture.[55] Torrance argues that if

> words or signs are to do their job properly, they must have some measure of detachment or incompleteness or even discrepancy to allow them to point away from themselves to the realities intended, in the light of which their truth or falsity will be judged.[56]

Words and statements are related to the ultimate realities, but they themselves are not the realities that they signify because the knowledge of the reality is independent of the language. Torrance says the 'words and statements are understood only when we come to know through them what is being indicated apart from them.'[57] Torrance does not deny the necessity of employing linguistic and grammatical methods in the rigorous exegesis of the Scripture.[58] However, in the interpretation of the Scripture we may not treat the words as linguistic symbols detached from their objective content in divine revelation, that is to say, we cannot detach the word from his Being and activity because it is the very Being of God who is speaking to us and acting upon us in a personal way.[59] Kurt Richardson says that 'the atoning act of sacrifice cleanses the text

---

53   Torrance, *Reality and Evangelical Theology*, 64–65.
54   Ibid., 22.
55   Ibid., 96–97.
56   Ibid., 65–66.
57   Ibid.
58   Torrance, *The Christian Doctrine of God*, 39.
59   Ibid., 42.

of Scripture as well as the people who hear its word of reconciliation.'[60] Torrance takes note of Richardson's saying and argues that the Scripture itself has to come under the cleansing of the atoning blood of Christ.[61] That is to say, for all its greatness, the Scripture does not share the same divine glory of the reality it signifies. The Scripture is a dim mirror and a partial testimony to the reality.[62] In seeking support from Athanasius, Torrance says, 'Athanasius was thus no Biblicist - he does not need to prove all his theological statements by the citation of texts'.[63] According to Torrance, Athanasius' main concern is to get inside the coherent structure of the Scripture and draw out its statements constructively in the light of the saving grace of the incarnate Son.[64] Torrance thus undercuts the very Scriptural foundation of Athanasius' arguments. In fact, none of the patristic fathers are able to argue apart from the text of the Scripture, otherwise, it would be philosophical ideas instead of onto-logical references. Though it is true that some may utilize more Scriptural texts than others, the Scripture nonetheless forms the very basis of their theological arguments and statements. Torrance also violates his own presentation of the main feature of Athanasian inter-pretation, which says that

> interpretation must give careful attention to the whole context of each passage, noting especially the circumstances of time and place, the person to whom the statements refer, and the subject-matter in question.[65]

That is to say, theological statements are the product of a close exami-nation of the biblical text because the text is the sole source of all theological statements. Torrance argues that Christian doctrines cannot be defended simply by appealing to biblical texts, but by the objective reference that the text signifies.[66] If that is the case, the objective refer-ence perceived would be indeed a subjective reference because each

---

60 K. A. Richardson, 'Revelation, Scripture, and Mystical Apprehension', in *The Promise of Trinitarian Theology: Theologians in Dialogue with T.F. Torrance*, ed. Elmer M. Coyler (Landam, Md.: Rowman & Littlefield, 2001), 191–192.

61 Torrance, *Thomas Torrance Responds*, 325–326.

62 Richardson, 'Revelation, Scripture, and Mystical Apprehension', 190.

63 Torrance, *Divine Meaning*, 274.

64 Ibid.

65 Ibid., 272–273.

66 Ibid., 284.

person may have different perception of the objective reference. If the objective reference cannot be approved by the biblical text, there is simply no mechanism to claim its validity.

Even though Torrance does not see himself a biblicist, he pays close attention to the words used in the Scripture. He says that in all coherent rational writing, statements have a primary reference which is denotative or semantic, and a secondary reference which is connotative or syntactic. However, neither function is meaningful without the other.[67] This is particularly obvious in his doctoral dissertation *The Doctrine of Grace in The Apostolic Fathers*, of which he spends a significant portion in the study of the word grace *(charis)*.[68] Actually, Torrance makes an extensive study of the word *charis,* which covers extra-biblical literatures in both classical Greek and Hellenistic Greek, Philo's usage, biblical texts of Old Testament, Gospels, Paul's writings and other New Testament writings. Thus, he comes to the conclusion that Christ himself is the content of grace in the light of a singular event that the Word of God became man in the human history.[69] There are also many instances[70] when he employs word studies in his hermeneutics. By doing so, Torrance indicates that the text itself is of great importance, unless we understand the words of the text fully, we may not be able to grasp the theological meaning that it signifies. And this clearly violates his own theological approach to the hermeneutics that the text by itself is somehow imperfect compared to the realities that it signifies. Torrance sees the ultimate truth does not lie in the Scripture but rather in the objective reference that it signifies. He regards the Scripture as a faithful witness to the realities it intends, yet itself may be to a certain degree imperfect and inaccurate.[71] Scriptures are not the Word of God, but rather they witness to the Word of God, they themselves are not the ultimate

67   Torrance, *Reality and Evangelical Theology*, 113.
68   T. F. Torrance, *The Doctrine of Grace In the Apostolic Fathers* (Eugene: Wipf and Stock Publishers, 1948) 1–35.
69   Torrance, T.F., *The Doctrine of Grace In the Apostolic Fathers*, Wipf and Stock Publishers, 1948, p. 21.
70   Word studies on verbs *anistemi* and *egeiro*. See Torrance, *Space, Time and Resurrection*, 32–33; Word studies on verbs *anabainein, kathizein, analambanein, hupsoun*. See *Space, Time and Resurrection*, 107.
71   Colyer, Elmer M., *The Nature of Doctrine in T.F. Torrance's Theology* (Eugene: Wipf and Stock Publishers, 2002), 67.

realities, but they point to the ultimate reality. According to Torrance, the Scripture is regarded a human book, yet we hear God's Word in and through the Scripture. [72] Torrance says, 'The words of the Bible themselves are not the Words of God, but they are the vehicles of the Word, but *really* the vehicles of the Word.'[73] The human words of the Scripture are not equal to the divine Word of God. Torrance says that the Scripture by itself

> is imperfect and inadequate and its text may be faulty and errant, but it is precisely in its imperfection and inadequacy and faultiness and errancy that God's inerrant Holy Word has laid hold of it that it may serve his reconciling revelation and the inerrant communication of his Truth. Therefore the Bible has to be heard as Word of God within the ambiguity of its poverty and riches, its weakness and power, and heard it such a way that we acknowledge that in itself in its human expression, the Bible comprises the word of man with all the limitations and imperfection of human flesh, in order to allow the human expression to fulfill its divinely appointed and holy function for us, in pointing beyond itself, to what it is not in itself, but to what God has marvellously made it to be in the adoption of his Grace.[74]

That is to say, the Scripture is both human and divine in the sense that it is human and imperfect by itself and it is divine and inerrant only when it points to the realities beyond itself. The Scripture remains a faithful witness to the historical event of the Gospels, yet the witnesses themselves and their writings may be full of errors. Torrance is in fact creating a dualism by separating the identity of the Scripture from the reality that it signifies, thus he disintegrates the very nature of the Scripture which is fully human and fully divine. Unless the Scripture itself is divine, it cannot point beyond itself to the divine reality. The Scripture cannot bridge the gap between human and divine, unless it itself is both human and divine. Brunner rightly speaks of the Scripture that it 'does not only speak of the revelation; it is itself the revelation.'[75] Thus, Torrance violates the very fundamental belief of Reformed doctrine that the Scripture is by itself inerrant because all our faith and belief are based on the very text of the Scripture. This also contradicts

---

72   Torrance, *Divine Meaning*, 6–7.
73   T. F. Torrance, *The Doctrine of Jesus Christ* (Eugene: Wipf and Stock Publishers, 2002), 100.
74   Torrance, *Divine Meaning*, 10.
75   E. Brunner, *Revelation and Reason* (London: Student Christian Movement Press Ltd., 1947), 21.

Torrance's own emphasis on word studies. If the text is errant, there is no need to emphasize the meaning of the words used in the Scripture because it may well be incorrect. Mackey argues that if the authority of the Scripture is not taken seriously and regarded itself as the Word of God,

> we are wondering about the origin of or the authorization for a particular doctrine, and someone points us to the Word behind the words, the Spirit within the letters, it never does any harm to ask what precisely these very inspiring phrases are intended to denote. What is this Word behind the words? What Spirit is thought to be within the letters? Answers to the former question in terms of a 'gospel within the Gospels', or a resume of the teaching of the Bible are too obviously invitations to arbitrary selectivity.[76]

If the reality is detached from the Scripture, the reality becomes arbitrary. There is no place to settle our differences in theology or to affirm our theology if the text is regarded as anything less than perfect and divine. Gunton observes that Torrance's theology is more patristic than biblical, he says, 'it is remarkable how little exegesis of Scripture, as distinct from the Fathers, is to be found in the major treatments of Trinitarian themes.'[77] By disregarding the validity of any hermeneutic principles, Torrance interprets the Scripture theologically based on his own so-called patristic ideas. Richardson calls Torrance's hermeneutics a mystical interpretation which is based on a unique relational knowing of God by creature.[78] Torrance's Christ-centered hermeneutics is also questioned by Langford, 'Does Torrance take all of Scripture as equal?'[79] Clearly, Torrance tends to treat New Testament more important than the Old Testament, because the incarnate Son in the New Testament embodies both the Act and Being of God, and there is no ultimate revelation other than that as revealed by the Son. Morrison comments, 'Diem[80]

---

76   J. P. Mackey, *The Christian Experience of God as Trinity* (London: SCM Press, 1983), 44.

77   C. Gunton, 'Being and Person', in *The Promise of Trinitarian Theology: Theologians in Dialogue with T.F. Torrance*, ed. Elmer M. Coyler (Landam, Md.: Rowman & Littlefield, 2001), 130.

78   Richardson, 186–187; Torrance, *Thomas Torrance Responds*, 327.

79   J. D. Morrison, *Knowledge of The Self-Revealing God in The Thought of Thomas Forsyth Torrance* (New York: Peter Lang, 1997), 259-260.

80   Hermann Diem

found that Barth did not provide for adequate interaction between dogmatic work and scriptural exegesis. That is even more applicable to Torrance.'[81] The weakness of Torrance's hermeneutics is his detachment of the word of God from the Word of God, creates a dualism that undercuts the very foundation of his own dogmatic work.

2.2. Theological Science

It is widely recognized that one of the great contributions of Torrance is his theological science that he positions theology in the category of science. He sees that both theology and natural science operate within the same premise of time and space and both serve as the bearers of the contingent order. It is important to know that the word *science* has a slight different meaning as understood by the general population. The meaning as employed by Torrance is reflected by the German usage of the word *wissenschaftlich* which carries a meaning of truthful undertaking of a rigorous and disciplined inquiry of the object according to its unique nature.[82] The inquiry would also engage in the search of elemental form and basic order out of which the complexity and multiplicity of knowledge develop.[83] In natural science, the knowledge operates in three logical levels, the first level is the knowledge of things according to what they are; the second level is to formulate this knowledge through some coherent calculations; and the highest level is to interpret these formulations and determine its mode of connection and consistency.[84] Similarly in theology, according to Torrance, there are three different levels of knowledge, the basic level is the level of knowledge that is acquired through our daily worship and communion with God through prayer, fellowship, and the interpretation of the Scripture.[85]

---

81 Morrison, *Knowledge of The Self-Revealing God in The Thought of Thomas Forsyth Torrance*, 259–260.
82 Torrance, *Theological Science*, 116–117; T. F. Torrance, 'Science, Theology, Unity', *Theology Today*, 21/2 (July 1964), 149.
83 Torrance, *Theological Science*, 116–117.
84 Ibid., 259–260.
85 Torrance, *The Christian Doctrine of God*, 88–90.

The next level is the theological level that we learn the saving act of Christ and the Person of Christ as Lord and Savior in his incarnate economy through our experiential apprehension and worship of God. Our knowledge at this level is distinctively theological that we know more fully the economic[86] and ontological structure of the Triune God as he is presented to us in the Gospel. This is also the conceptual level of knowledge of the economic Trinity in which the dynamic reality of God in his triune being is brought into clearer and more explicit formulation in terms of his differentiated yet unitary personal self-presentation as Father, Son and Holy Spirit.[87] The third level is the ontological level that we learn of God in his own Being. Thus we move from a level of economic trinitarian knowledge of what God is towards us in his saving grace to the level of knowing the intrinsic relations that are immanent in God himself.[88] Torrance sees that the understanding of the Trinity can be achieved through a progression of various levels of investigation,[89] and the ontological level forms the basic order of the revealed knowledge. The very purpose of Torrance's theological science is to seek a convergence of creation and redemption in Christ because the true knowledge of God and the world cannot be apart from the incarnate Son, theological knowledge is always a partnership to natural science.[90]

According to Torrance, the revolution of science and the development of theology cannot be disconnected,[91] and he ties theology closely to science and treats it as a special branch of science in its investigation and epistemological thinking. Torrance always appeals to modern day scientific theories in his pursuit of theological science and sees that his theological science is indeed a logical reconstruction of a conceptual system by a radical change of mind to face to the objective reality that is laid in

---

86   According to Torrance, the word 'economy' is a patristic expression developed by St. Paul to indicate Christ's redemptive activity in his incarnate condescension. See Torrance, *The Christian Doctrine of God*, 92.
87   Torrance, *The Christian Doctrine of God*, 91–92.
88   Ibid., 98–99.
89   McGrath,168–169.
90   K. A. Richardson, 'Foreword: Introducing Torrance', in *Reality and Evangelical Theology* (London: InterVarsity Press, 1999), xviii; J. D. Morrison, review of T.F. Torrance, *The Trinitarian Faith*, 119–122.
91   T. F. Torrance, *Kingdom and Church* (Eugene: Wipf and Stock Publishers, 1996), 1–2.

front of us. It is a kind of conversion, according to Torrance, reflected in the transition from the Newtonian principles to that of relativity and quantum theory. The old system becomes the limiting case of the new.[92] Torrance affirms the teaching of Aristotle that each branch of science need its own distinctive method appropriate to its inquiry.[93] However, disregarding all differences in different branches of scientific investigation, there is a formal procedure that is universal in its range. Thus, there is a procedure common to every discipline of science, however, in each particular branch, a modification of its formal procedure is required to reflect its distinctive nature of the object.[94] The modification, according to Torrance, does not constitute two independent procedures, but he sees it as two modes of one scientific procedure.[95] Theological science shares with other science a generally recognized scientific procedure which is based on the principle of objectivity, and its inquiry is determined by the unique nature of its particular object.[96] Regarding the unique procedure of scientific theology, the primary element is its devotion to the proper object. It will not be genuine knowledge if it does not correspond to the given reality. In the field of natural science, knowledge has to be wrested from nature, but nature does not intend to deceive us. Unreality lies not in the object but rather in ourselves, thus, Torrance sees that true questions of inquiry are a form of self-criticism.[97] In order to have a successful theological inquiry, we must operate in a dialogical relation with the Object and let the Object to break through the monologue of reason with itself.[98] That is to say, we must let the Object to reveal its own intelligibility instead of dictating the outcome of the inquiry from our own reasoning.

Though it is correct to say that science has shifted its paradigms from Newton to Einstein, according to Muller, it is a mistake to assume that theology operates on Newtonian premises. Muller claims that theology

---

92   Torrance, *Space, Time and Resurrection*, 16–17.
93   Torrance, *Theological Science*, T&T Clark, 108.
94   Ibid., 112.
95   Ibid., 113.
96   Ibid., 112.
97   Ibid., 121.
98   Ibid., 133.

never followed Newton.[99] From a historical perspective, Newton's contribution is restricted to his scientific theories, discoveries, and formulations; he has a limited contribution to the development of theology. In other words, Newtonian science has nothing to do with theology. Similarly, Barth denies that natural theology or science and its methodology have anything to do with theology.[100] Muller says that 'The divergence of ways of knowing leaves theology free from science and science free from theology.'[101] That is to say, according to Muller, theology and science are independent from each other. However, from the historical perspective, interference does exist between theology and science, and it is evident in the criticism of Galileo's findings by the Roman Church. On the other hand, in justifying his theological science, Torrance, as observed by McGrath, is selective in his use of natural science, in that he focuses exclusively on a certain kind of physical science.[102]

One of the commonalities between theological science and natural science, according to Torrance, is that both are regarded as human inquiry, and both presuppose that its object is intelligible and thus open to rational investigation. [103] Natural science is concerned with the structures of the creaturely existence while theology pursues the knowledge of the Creator. Both acquire their knowledge in accordance with the nature of their objects, one is created, the other uncreated. Thus, Torrance sees that theologians and scientists live and work side by side within the same orderly created world in pursuing the knowledge of the object.[104] In both cases, though man is the inquirer of his knowledge of God or knowledge of nature, he is not the master in his inquiry, but rather he acts under the compelling claims of his object.[105] In the theological science, God plays a unique part in our understanding of himself

---

99   R. A. Muller, review of T.F. Torrance, *Transformation and Convergence in the Frame of Knowledge: Explorations in the Interrelations of Scientific and Theological Enterprise* (Grand Rapids: Eerdmans, 1984), in *The Westminster Theological Journal,* 47/1 (Spring 1985), 137–138.
100 Ibid.
101 Ibid.
102 McGrath, 198.
103 Torrance, Theological Science, 286.
104 Ibid., xx.
105 Torrance, Reality and Evangelical Theology, 30–31.

because our knowledge of him is revealed by him and through him. In the inquiry process, God takes control over us and becomes the sole master of our knowing.[106] Torrance employs conceptions developed by Martin Buber in differentiating the relation between *I and It* and *I and Thou*. In the *I and It* relationship of the natural science inquiry, the subject takes an active role in acquiring the knowledge of a passive object. However, in the *I and Thou* relationship, the subject encounters an active Object and itself is transformed by the encounter of the objective reality.[107] Thus, when God enters into our subject-object relationship, he reverses our relation of knowing.[108] In this epistemological inversion, according to Torrance, we know only as we are known[109] because our knowledge is only made possible under the commanding majesty of the object which controls the real knowledge appropriate to us.[110] Torrance argues that God is the Lord of our knowledge even though it is we who know, thus, our knowing is taken under the command of the God.[111] This real knowledge is objectified in the person of Jesus Christ, so that we know him as the Way, the Truth, and the Life, and in him and through him alone that we can go to the Father, and thus he serves as the only reference that we have true knowledge of God.[112] There is no factual knowledge of God except through the self-giving and self-revealing incarnate Son. We cannot know God behind his objectivity. Thus, we can only know God through the person of Jesus Christ.[113] Torrance believes genuine theology is never a speculative thinking or a priori thought, but of a posteriori knowing in the revelation through the encounter of the reality in the Incarnation[114] because the knowledge does not come from the centre in ourselves but from a centre in the Object.[115] That is to say, we seek to acquire knowledge which

---

106 Ibid., 47.
107 Ibid., 33.
108 Ibid., 47.
109 Ibid., 131.
110 Ibid., 47.
111 Ibid., 131–132.
112 Ibid., 51–52.
113 Ibid., 55.
114 Ibid., 33.
115 Ibid., 281.

exists ontologically independent of us, and this is regarded as the essence of Torrance's theological science that epistemology follows ontology.

Both Torrance and Barth have been consistent in maintaining that man is passive in his inquiry of the knowledge of God, and Macquarrie agrees that in any revelatory experience, man cannot be other than submissive before the objective reality. Macquarrie says,

> when man begins to reflect on such an experience – and only at this point does theology begin – he must question the revelation itself. Was it indeed a revelation or only an illusion? And this question must be done by the light of reason and such human wisdom as the man may possess.[116]

That is to say, the essential element in assessing the truthfulness of the revelation depends on the subjectivity of the subject rather than the objectivity of the object, thus one can eliminate illusions from genuine revelation. Unfortunately, this subjective reasoning is lost in Torrance's theological science because human endeavour always remains passive when it comes to the discernment of the revelatory experience. In fact, Torrance's whole theological science is founded on a few implicit and explicit presuppositions. All these presuppositions cannot be validated by human reasoning or scientific proof. In the subject-object relation, the knowledge of God is not controlled by the inquirer but by God who becomes the Master of our knowing. Thus instead of playing an active and leading part, the inquirer takes on a passive role in his understanding of God who is the Lord of our knowing and faith in him entails the opening up of our subjectivity to the Subjectivity of God through his Objectivity. Faith is thus necessary to know that the centre of knowing is in God and not in us, so that we know because we are known by him.[117] Torrance says,

> We still believe that God is reliable and faithful, and that form and order belong to the fabric of the universe, and that behind creation and fall there remains God eternally and infinitely loving and wise.[118]

---

116 J. Macquarrie, *Twentieth-Century Religious Thought* (London: SCM Press, 1963), 333.

117 Torrance, *Theological Science*, 131–132.

118 Ibid., 264.

The belief that God is reliable and faithful is paramount in Torrance's theological science, unfortunately, this presupposition is by no way scientifically proved. It is true that one has to inquire in accordance with the nature of the object, and if the object is the ultimate reality, the true knowledge of God is controlled by the God himself instead of the inquirer. Torrance's strong Christian cultural background inevitably paints the picture that the ultimate reality is the Triune God of the Scripture, thus his theological inquiry will lead inquirers to this God instead of other gods. Many would question by using the same approach, can a Hindu or a Buddhist come to see that their ultimate reality lies in their gods?[119] In today's world, there are many so-called revelations or ultimates, unfortunately, no mechanism is offered in Torrance's theological science to eliminate false presuppositions, revelations, or experiences. Macquarrie says,

> whenever any person or institution or sacred book prefaces its utterances with the formula, 'Thus said the Lord', we have immediately to ask whether this expression may not be a veiled but impressive way of saying, 'I'm telling you.' We can do this only by testing the alleged revelation by the light of that human wisdom and philosophy which is so despised by some of our theologians. One consequence of unquestioning acceptance of revelation and the exclusion of human wisdom is that no way remains of discriminating among the many revelations. Mohammed claimed to have divine revelations, so did Kawate Bunjiro and so did Joseph Smith. Perhaps in varying degrees they did have them. But we would want to discriminate among them.[120]

Every religious faith can employ Torrance's theological science to secure its own claim of reality. Unless we can somehow uphold the human reasoning in the discernment of these presuppositions, there is simply not much ground for accepting or rejecting these claims and Torrance's theological science is simply another fancy name for a personal belief which is totally independent of science. Macquarrie thus

---

119   Norris gives an example that Buddhism can also form an important part of human understanding of science. See F. W. Norris, 'Mathematics, Physics and Religion: A Need For Candor and Rigor', *Scottish Journal of Theology* 37 (1984), 467; Battaglia says that the modern physicist's view of the world is surprisingly like that of the Chinese and Indian mystics. See A. Battaglia, review of T.F. Torrance, *Transformation and Convergence in the Frame of Knowledge* (Grand Rapids: Eerdmans, 1984), in *Theology Today*, 41/1 (April 1984), 492.

120   Macquarrie, 334–335.

argues that we must test presuppositions in accordance with our reason and conscience.[121] Torrance is well aware that there are many presuppositions, antecedent ideas and theories. He claims that when we engage in theological thinking, we must renounce all these presuppositions and concentrate on the object because he sees that genuine theology must be a posteriori in thinking rather than a priori dogmatism.[122] Torrance argues that the detachment from presuppositions does not mean detachment from the object to be inquired, but rather on the contrary, it indicates a firm attachment to the object.[123] In other words, Torrance is suggesting to reject all presuppositions other than the presupposition that is revealed through the incarnate Son. He says,

> To commit ourselves to God in faith in this way means that we let ourselves be called so radically in question that we are stripped of all our presuppositions and prejudgments.[124]

However, this important presupposition is not well addressed in Torrance's writings as he keeps on arguing that the ultimate reality cannot be validated outside of itself. Without addressing this particular presupposition through apologetics as a preamble to his theological science, people would have a problem to see how theology can be part of science, because to certain extent, all religious faiths are claiming their own ultimate realities. Torrance provides few apologetic arguments other than that of the presuppositional. In fact, Torrance is taking an a priori presupposition in his a posteriori mode of thinking, that is to say, his presupposition overrules all other presuppositions. Science is not simply presupposition without reason and proof, thus, Torrance sadly admits that the science community in general is moving away from theological science by seeing that theology is incompatible with science. Unfortunately, Torrance argues that this phenomenon is due to the dualistic nature of western thinking.[125] In fact, the real problem lies in the presuppositions used in his theological science by presupposing the

---

121 Ibid.
122 Torrance, *Theological Science*, T&T Clark, 34–35.
123 Ibid., 35.
124 Torrance, *Reality and Evangelical Theology*, 122–123.
125 A. Walker, 'Interview with Professor Thomas F. Torrance', in *Different Gospels* (London: Hodder & Stoughton, 1988), 43.

existence of the objective reality that cannot be scientifically proven, and presupposing that the objective reality is indeed the Christian God as revealed in the Scripture. There is simply no scientific way to validate any of these presuppositions because it lies beyond the scope of scientific capability to approve or disapprove. Thus, by positioning personal faith as a branch of science, and yet detaching it from scientific validation, Torrance is creating a paradox that is difficult to comprehend. However, this type of paradox occurs frequently in his dialectical theology. In Thiemann's *Revelation and Theology*, Thiemann argues that revelation is no revelation unless it is preceded by grace, reality is no reality unless it is seen by faith endowed by God's grace.[126] Since the knowledge of reality is given and not acquired, the theological science inquiry will lead to nowhere without prevenient grace in the form of faith. Thus, what Torrance is really saying in his theological science is that faith is absolutely necessary in order to encounter the objective reality. Thus, theology itself is not scientific in its inquiry because in a science such as chemistry, everyone who follows the same inquiry will come up with the same conclusion. In theology, it depends solely on the prevenient grace of God. Faith is not a monopoly of intellects, there is no scientific procedure that can lead people to realize the objective reality, however, at the same time, both the educated and the illiterate, the poor and the rich, the old and the young could come to realize the reality through God's grace despite the fact that some may not even be able to comprehend a simple logic or mathematical equation. Torrance's theological science, according to Yeung[127], is actually talking about faith rather than science.

It is clear that in Torrance's theological science, his basic presuppositions cannot be questioned, thus, Thiemann sees that he is under the influence of theological foundationalism.[128] Though Torrance rejects any foundationalist label,[129] his theological science nonetheless is based on some presuppositions which are regarded as basic and fundamental. Of which the existence of God is implicitly assumed in his theological

---

126 R. F. Thiemann, *Revelation and Theology* (Notre Dame, Ind.:University of Notre Dame Press, 1985), 92.

127 Personal communication with Professor Jason Yeung of China Graduate School of Theology, Hong Kong, Feb 17, 2005 email.

128 Thiemann, 40.

129 Torrance, *Thomas Torrance Responds*, 331.

inquiry. However, according to Plantinga and Wolterstorff, it is not among the propositions that are considered properly basic[130] that can be unquestionably accepted by the general population. They say, 'hence a person is rational in accepting theistic belief only if he has evidence for it.'[131] Unfortunately, there is no evidence or any scientific data to prove the existence of God, and Torrance has no intention to prove the existence of God by any scientific means. Thus, presuppositions are the only tools for both Barth and Torrance, according to Langford, to affirm the primacy and sovereignty of God in their dogmatics.[132] Achtemeier says,

> Torrance's claim, that true knowledge represents genuine disclosure to the mind of that which is objectively real, seems to me an indispensable presupposition for the church's proclamation of the Gospel.[133]

The only argument that Torrance provides is his so-called circular argument in regarding the ultimates that he sets in the objective references. He argues that although these ultimates cannot be proved, however, their validity and existence cannot be denied. There is no possible proof of the laws of logic, according to Torrance, nonetheless we have to presuppose those laws in our logical reasoning. Similarly in physics, we have to presuppose that there is an order in the universe if we are to have a science of physics.[134] Torrance believes that in each special science, pre-scientific knowledge presupposes the reality and

---

130 According to Plantinga and Wolterstorff, the basic propositions are those that are self-evident, evident to our senses. They say that 'Since the proposition that God exists is none of the above, it is not properly basic for anyone; that is, no well-formed, rational noetic structure contains this proposition in its foundations.' See A. Plantinga and N. Wolterstorff, *Faith and Rationality* (London: University of Notre Dame Press, 1986), 59.

131 Ibid., 48.

132 T. A. Langford, 'T. F. Torrance's Theological Science: A Reaction', *Scottish Journal of Theology*, 25 (1972), 155.

133 P. M. Achtemeier, 'The Truth of Tradition: Critical Realism in The Thought of Alasdair MacIntyre and T.F. Torrance', *Scottish Journal of Theology*, 47/3 (1994), 355.

134 Torrance, *Space, Time and Resurrection*, 15–16; T. F. Torrance, 'The Framework of Belief', in *Belief in Science and in Christian Life: the Relevance of Michael Polanyi's Thought for Christian Faith and Life*, ed. T.F. Torrance (Edinburgh: Handsel Press, 1980), 19.

accessibility of its own proper object and the possibility of knowing it further. This presupposition, according to Torrance, is justified by the object's own positive content and inner rationality.[135] Thus, circular argument could still be a proper and valid argument, according to Torrance, if it is internally consistent with the conclusions reached according to those anticipated in our basic presuppositions.[136] Unfortunately, this very argument is immediately rejected by Torrance himself as he claims that even the system is completely consistent within itself, it still could conceivably be false.[137] That is to say, there exists no rational reference at all to validate the very presupposition that the system is based on. In Torrance's theological science, he first presupposes with the actual knowledge of God, then seek to clarify this knowledge by careful inquiry into the relation between our knowing of God and God himself in his being and nature. Through the disciplined obedience of our mind to God as he reveals himself to us that we advance our knowledge of him. Torrance rejects the question in our inquiry of *How can God be known*?[138] Because this will challenge the very presupposition that he employs. Instead, Torrance says, we must seek to know God through his act of self-revelation. He argues,

> We cannot begin by forming independently a theory of how God is knowable and then seek to test it out or indeed to actualize it and fill it with material content. How God can be known must be determined from first to last by the way in which He actually is known.[139]

Thus, the best we can do, according to Torrance, is to passively acquire the revealed knowledge. And our knowledge of God is fully rational because Torrance believes that the communication and response between God and man are fully rational.[140] Though theological inquiry is a human endeavour in the quest of the Truth, it is nonetheless the Truth which makes itself known to us.[141] Thus, according to Torrance, it is not the inquirer who is able to acquire the knowledge of the Object, it is the

---

135 Torrance, *Theological Science*, 3.
136 Torrance, *Space, Time and Resurrection*, 15–16.
137 Ibid.
138 Torrance, *Theological Science*, T&T Clark, 9.
139 Ibid.
140 Ibid., 11.
141 Ibid., 281.

Object who makes the inquirer known of him. Unless the Object reveals, we cannot know, or unless God wants himself to be known, the inquirer is unable to know him. This seems to contradict Torrance's other claim that theological science follows proper scientific procedure in its inquiry, and the inquiry itself consists both of learning and reasoning,[142] and at the decisive moments, the inquirer will exercise his personal and rational judgment.[143] That is to say, the human person takes initiative in the inquiry, and if he follows the proper scientific procedure, he will come to the same reality by proper reasoning. This formulation unfortunately does not apply to the knowledge of God because it is given rather than acquired. It is through faith that one comes to the realization of the ultimate reality, and faith by itself does not follow any scientific procedure or even validated by any scientific formulations, and cannot be regarded as an act of rationality in the community of science in general. According to Barth, faith is 'always a leap into the darkness of the unknown.'[144] Science does require a certain degree of faith or taking a certain degree of risk, however, it does not claim this risk or faith as scientific or rational because it may turn out wrong. Torrance admits that we can only seek to apprehend the Object as far as we may,[145] and this means that our human endeavour by itself has a limit to acquire the knowledge of the Object. Unfortunately, this important aspect is not well emphasized in Torrance's theological science. Torrance's usage of Einstein is a good example to reflect this deficiency. Einsteinian theory of relativity plays a prominent role in Torrance's argument of theological science that a proper way of inquiry will lead to a sound knowledge of the Object. Unfortunately, Einstein's scientific inquiry of the universe can only lead him to the admiration of the unlimited range of intelligibility of the universe,[146] he himself is still detached from the knowledge of the Creator. Torrance admits that even though Einstein regularly reads the Bible, he does not have a personal faith and religious commitment. Einstein, according to Torrance, is a typical loner with

---

142 Ibid., 286.
143 Ibid., 303.
144 K. Barth, *The Epistle to the Romans*, tr. Edwyn C. Hoskyns (London: Oxford University Press, 1975), 96.
145 Torrance, *Theological Science*, 281.
146 Torrance, *The Christian Doctrine of God*, 86.

deep religious awe without any religious belief.[147] Einstein himself also admits that he only has cosmic religious feeling, and does not have any conception of God corresponding to it.[148] He claims it a lie to assume him to have any religious conviction because he says,

> I do not believe in a personal God and I have never denied this but have expressed it clearly. If something is in me which can be called religious then it is the unbounded admiration for the structure of the world so far as our science can reveal it.[149]

Einstein at best is a deist and his theory of relativity and unitary outlook does not by itself lead him to the ultimate reality – his Creator. What does this leave with Torrance's argument that theology is itself a scientific inquiry? If Torrance's hypothesis of theological science is correct, at least, Einstein should be the ideal candidate to validate his argument that proper inquiry would lead us to the knowledge of the object. Ironically in Torrance's theological science, Einstein, the person he admires so much in his quest of the objective knowledge, does not believe in the personal God; Newton, the person he detests so much for his dualist thinking and mechanistic space and time, proclaims his Christian belief. There are simply no facts on the ground to support Torrance's argument that theology is indeed science because the ultimate reality has nothing to do with the way it is acquired whether it is scientific or not. Mullers comments,

> Torrance's approach hardly represents a scientific consensus. There is also considerable doubt in the mind of this reviewer that even the most resolute Einsteinian who accepts both Einstein's physics and his metaphysics would accept their merger with Torrance's rather nonscientific and basically a priori declaration that Christ as incarnate Logos is the key to understanding the order of the universe and to overcoming a dualistic separation not only of form and being but also of God and man.[150]

---

147 T. F. Torrance, *Einstein and God*
    <http://www.ctinquiry.org/publications/torrance.htm> accessed 1 Mar 2005.
148 A. Einstein, 'Religion and Science', *New York Times Magazine*, (9 November 1930), 1–4.
149 A. Einstein, *The Human Side*, ed. Helen Dukas and Banesh Hoffman (n.p.: Princeton University Press, 1979).
150 R. A. Muller, *Transformation and Convergence in the Frame of Knowledge: Explorations in the Interrelations of Scientific and Theological Enterprise*, 139.

Torrance indeed applies a priori declaration to justify his theological science. Even though his a priori declaration may be acceptable to all Christians, it is by no means scientific. In other words, commitment to God in faith is the presupposition that Torrance uses to override other presuppositions that he thinks are impeding us for our inquiry of the knowledge of God. There is simply no scientific way to validate that his presupposition is better than any other presuppositions that he rejects. Though Torrance clearly identifies that some features of the inquiry of theology are similar to that of science, however, it is still not sufficient to position theology in the category of science. It is like that chimpanzee shares 98% of the common genes with human being, it still cannot be positioned as a human being. It is a mistake that Torrance develops his theological science solely on a few common features between theology and science because if it is valid, then Islam and science could make similar claims.

2.3. Natural Theology

Natural theology is an interesting topic to Torrance because on one hand he objects to the idea of natural theology which operates with a deistic disjunction between God and the universe, and on the other hand, he sees a proper place for rational argumentation within the active interrelation between God and the universe that empirical and theoretical operate inseparably together.[151] Torrance's earlier rejection of natural theology is heavily influenced by Karl Barth, however later, under the immense impression of the wonders of nature and the Einsteinian unitary theory, Torrance comes to realize that natural theology is part of the revealed theology.

---

151   Torrance, *Space, Time and Resurrection*, 1.

2.3.1. The Influence of Karl Barth

Karl Barth plays a major role in Torrance's understanding of natural theology in his earlier days by instigating an idea that natural theology is no theology.[152] According to Barth, natural theology means

> every (positive or negative) formulation of a system which claims to be theological, i.e. to interpret divine revelation, whose subject, however, differs fundamentally from the revelation in Jesus Christ and whose method therefore differs equally from the exposition of Holy Scripture.[153]

Natural theology is regarded by Barth as something which is fundamentally different from God's revelation, and could not be used in the exegesis of the Scripture. Brunner offers a slight different conception of its meaning, he sees that natural theology comes with two different senses, one is objective which he accepts and the other is subjective which he rejects. The former means that the knowledge of God in his creation can be acknowledged by the faithful, and the latter means that the knowledge of God can be accessed by the ungodly.[154] Brunner suggests that to avoid confusion, it is better to substitute *natural theology* with *general revelation*. That means, natural theology deals with the topic of general revelation. In the discussion, these two terms are used interchangeably and inseparably from each other.[155]

Natural theology, according to Barth, undermines the necessity and uniqueness of God's self-revelation in Christ. According to Berkouwer, Barth does not believe that we are able to perceive general revelation prior to the special revelation in Christ; on the contrary, one must know Christ first in his special revelation in order to know anything about revelation.[156] That is to say, without the special revelation, there is no possibility that we can know God anywhere. Thus, the focus of Barth's theology is that God's revelation is exclusively in Christ, there is simply no room for general revelation. According to McGrath, Barth regards the

---

152 K. Barth, 'No! Answer to Emil Brunner', in *Natural Theology* (Ann Arbor, Mich.: University Microfilms, 1959), 75.
153 Ibid., 74–75.
154 E. Brunner, 'Nature and Grace', in *Natural Theology* (Ann Arbor, Mich.: University Microfilms, 1959), 9.
155 G. C. Berkouwer, *General Revelation* (Grand Rapids, Mich.:Eerdmans, 1955), 33.
156 Ibid., 22.

natural knowledge of God as an element of sinful human tendency towards self-affirmation in the face of God.[157] If the knowledge of God can be achieved independently apart from his self-revelation in the incarnate Son, then humanity can dictate the place, time and means of its knowledge of God.[158] Torrance highlights Barth's argument that if the God we come to know through Jesus Christ is really Father, Son, and Holy Spirit in his own eternal being, then what are we to make of an independent natural theology which terminates only in an abstract God.[159] That is to say, if we can know God through natural theology, there is no need for the incarnation. Torrance comments,

> Natural theology by its very operation abstracts the existence of God from his act, so that if it does not begin with deism, it imposes deism upon theology. If really to know God through his saving activity in our world is to know him as Triune, then the doctrine of the Trinity belongs to the very groundwork of knowledge of God from the very start, which calls in question any doctrine of God as the One God gained apart from his trinitarian activity – but that is the kind of knowledge of God that is yielded in natural theology of the traditional kind.[160]

Natural theology cannot provide any knowledge of the Triune God, at best it can provide us some ideas about an abstract deity. Barth sees that natural theology represents a human attempt to 'understand itself apart from and in isolation from revelation, representing a deliberate refusal to accept the necessity and consequences of revelation.'[161] And if God could be known through nature, then his self-revelation can be disregarded. Thus, to 'concede the legitimacy of natural theology would thus be to compromise the entire principle of the priority and necessity of God's self-revelation.'[162] Instead of relying on God's self-revelation, humanity runs its own autonomy. Barth's rejection of natural theology is reflected in his commentary on Romans. Brunner charges that the first

---

157   McGrath, 175–176.
158   T. F. Torrance, *The Ground And Grammar of Theology* (Edinburgh: T&T Clark, 2001), 89–91.
159   Ibid.
160   Ibid.
161   McGrath, 179.
162   McGrath, 175–176.

two chapters of Romans are not well treated by Barth,[163] and is agreed with by Monsma who comments,

> This suggest once more that Barth's procedure is apparently not what he would have it be – a thinking based on some part of the Bible which has become the Word of God for him; but is rather a philosophical procedure which interprets the Bible to suit its needs. His basic assumption is apparently not taken directly from the Bible but rather read into it.[164]

Monsma has clearly highlighted a mistake that Barth makes in his hermeneutics that he is reading into the Scripture with his own pre-determined theology instead of honest exegesis of the Scripture. This is particularly evident in his exegesis of Romans 1:19-21, instead of the things that Paul claims that may be known of God, Barth interprets the exact opposite that we do not know God because of our ignorance.[165] Paul says that the 'invisible things of God are clearly seen' by man, Barth claims that Paul's statement is only applicable to the past, because we have long forgotten those clear signs due to our lack of humility, recollection and fear in the presence of God.[166] Barth says,

> can *since the creation of the world* be clearly seen *through the things that are made* by God. By calm, veritable, unprejudiced religious contemplation the divine 'No' can be established and apprehended.[167]

In fact, Barth is challenging Paul's very claim because in Barth's mind, he believes that man cannot know God except through the incarnate Son, simple observation of the imperfect world by no means being a sub-stitute.[168] This runs against Torrance's evaluation of Barth's commentary on the Romans by saying that 'True interpretation involves the deter-mination to face up to what the text is actually saying whether we like it or not, and whether it agrees with our presuppositions or not'.[169] Barth's

---

163 P. H. Monsma, Peter Halman, *Karl Barth's Idea of Revelation*, (Somerville, N.J.: Somerset Press, 1937), 198.
164 Ibid.
165 Barth, *The Epistle to The Romans*, 45.
166 Ibid., 46.
167 Ibid.
168 Ibid., 47.
169 T. F. Torrance, *Karl Barth: An Introduction To His Early Theology, 1910–1931* (London: SCM Press, 1962), 48.

presupposition is clearly manifested in his interpretation of the passage. Berkouwer comments,

> Barth's entire interpretation of Romans I is conditioned by his fear that in addition to the revelation in Christ there be accepted another independent source of knowledge of God, one preceding the cross. Such a second source of knowledge would, he thinks, be in sharp conflict with the redemptive character of God's revelation.[170]

The whole discussion of natural theology in Romans, according to John Baillie, rests on the word 'inexcusable' (Romans 2:1). Baillie claims that the first two chapters clearly deal with the responsibility of the ungodly for their ungodliness, and argues that the ground of this imputation of responsibility lies in the doctrine of natural theology.[171] The logic of Paul's argument is simple, because they know, thus they are inexcusable. It would be difficult to argue if they do not know, how can they be inexcusable? In the article *Nature and Grace*, Emil Brunner says that the world is the creation of God, and in every creation, the creator must have his imprints in his works, that is why Psalmists praise God for his creation. In order to be faithful to the Scripture, Brunner argues that general revelation has to be respected. The imprint of God in nature is indeed a revelation, a self-communication of God.[172] The reason why men are inexcusable because God manifests himself so clearly to them through his creation.[173] In fact, according to Brunner, there are two revelations: the special revelation in Christ and general revelation in nature, however, they are not detached but related to each other.[174] Through the Scripture, natural revelation is both clarified and complemented because the Scripture serves as a lens for natural revelation.[175] The revelation in nature by itself is not sufficient to know God in such a way to bring salvation, thus, only the Christian who stands within the revelation in Christ has the true natural knowledge of God.[176] Brunner

---

170 Berkouwer, 32.
171 J. Baillie, *Natural Theology* (Ann Arbor, Mich.: University Microfilms, 1959), 10.
172 Brunner, *Nature and Grace*, 25.
173 Ibid.
174 Ibid., 26–27.
175 Ibid., 39.
176 Ibid., 26–27.

also appeals to Calvin that his natural theology is indeed a Reformed tradition.[177]

Calvin is taking a more moderate approach in treating natural theology in his exegesis of Romans. He comments that although God is invisible, his majesty shines forth in his creation; the world acts as a mirror to reflect the reality of the invisible. Men are inexcusable because the manifestation of God and his glory in his creation is sufficiently clear, however, due to our own account of blindness, it is not found sufficient. Nonetheless, we are not blind enough to claim our ignorance as an excuse. We know there is a God, however, according to Calvin, our reason fails to identify what sort of Being God is.[178] That is to say, even though nature does not make us to see clearly, it does allow us to see, so that there is no excuse for us to deny God's presence. Thus, Calvin does allow natural theology to play a part in the overall revelation of God which is manifested through both his creation and redemption.

Unfortunately, Brunner's article draws a fierce reply from Barth arguing theologically that grace is revelation and revelation is grace,[179] and natural theology is never considered to be part of the formulation of God's grace. Barth says, ''natural theology' does not exist as an entity capable of becoming a separate subject within what I consider to be real theology – not even for the sake of being rejected.'[180] Barth does not provide a good response to Calvin's exegesis of the Romans by claiming that he is not a Calvin scholar and asks his brother, Peter Barth, to do the work.[181] Barth argues that though Calvin claims the possibility of a real knowledge by natural man through God's creation, however, Barth argues, it is only a possibility, a possibility that is not recognized by him.[182] Barth insists that there is no cooperation, according to evangelical doctrine, of reason in the acquiring of the knowledge of God because human reason by itself is blind to the truth of God and human is unfree to do what is right, light and freedom can only be found

---

177 Ibid., 36.
178 John Calvin, 'Commentaries on The Epistle to The Romans', in *Calvin's Commentaries*, 19 (Grand Rapids, Mich.: Baker, 2003), 70–71.
179 Barth, 'No! Answer to Emil Brunner', 71–72.
180 Ibid., 75.
181 Ibid., 100.
182 Ibid., 106.

exclusively in faith.[183] By treating natural theology as the great enemy of faith,[184] Strawbridge charges that Barth is fundamentally a fideist because there exist no proofs to provide a rational foundation for faith in his theology.[185] Barth is also incoherent in upholding the authority of the Scripture because he basically disregards the teaching of God's revelation in nature.[186] Strawbridge sees that the reformed doctrine of *Sola Scriptura* may give Barth an unnecessary impetus to this incoherence that 'if there is another revelation other than Scripture, then there is not another revelation other than Scripture.'[187] However, the Scripture does indicate natural theology as what is proclaimed by Paul in Romans. In essence, the argument of natural theology is not driven by logical or philosophical thinking apart from the Scripture, but rather it is firmly based on the hard exegesis of the Scripture. Strawbridge firmly believes that Romans 1:19-20 state clearly the Scriptural argument of general revelation.[188] Barth on the other hand, denies that there exists any connection between general revelation and special revelation. The essence of Barth's argument is that he does not want to create a second revelation even at a subsidiary level because it would jeopardize the very claim of his revelational theology in Christ.

According to Torrance, Barth's objection to natural theology has nothing to do with deistic dualism between God and the world, that God does not interact with the world, but on the contrary, Torrance says that Barth puts an immense emphasis on the concrete activity of God in space and time, in both creation and redemption. Thus, Barth is more of interactionist than a dualist because Barth believes that there exists a close interaction between God and the world of nature and human history.[189] In opposition to the fusion of creation and redemption into na-

---

183   Ibid., 97.

184   Berkouwer, *General Revelation*, 21.

185   G. Strawbridge, *Karl Barth's Rejection of Natural Theology or An Exegesis of Romans 1:19–20* <http://www.wordmp3.com/gs/barth.htm> accessed 3 Jan 2005.

186   Ibid.

187   Ibid.

188   Ibid.

189   T. F. Torrance, 'The Problem of Natural Theology in The Thought of Karl Barth', *Religious Studies*, Vol. 6 (1970), 121, 123.

tural theology, Torrance says that Barth tries to tear apart the synthesis by creating a *diastasis*[190] between God and man that God

> could really be recognised as God in the sheer majesty of his divine nature and in his absolutely unique existence and power, while man, disenchanted of his pretended divinity, could be free at last to be truly and genuinely human.[191]

However, in doing that, Barth is somehow creating a dualist idea that creation and redemption are two separate entities. Indeed, Torrance charges that Barth has a deep problem of Augustinian and Lutheran dualism in his theology,[192] and which is manifested in his understanding of sacraments.[193] Comstock sees that Barth takes a radical dualistic approach of separating Christ from culture in order to demolish the independence of culture in seeking of truth about the world.[194]

Torrance later argues that Barth is not really denying the existence of a natural knowledge of God, but rather Barth sees that natural theology by itself stands in opposition to the Word of God, however, natural theology has its proper place within the ambit of revealed theology.[195] Barth, according to Torrance, in his later years has changed his position on natural theology that he no longer rejects the existence of natural knowledge but regards its as something that is 'impossible' but nonetheless 'exists'.[196] Thus, Barth finally comes to the terms of natural theology similar to that of Emil Brunner of which he fiercely opposed in 1934.

---

190 'the separation of normally joined parts, as in the dislocation of bones, without fracture.' See <http://www.infoplease.com/dictionary/diastasis> accessed 7 Sep 2005.
191 Torrance, *The Problem of Natural Theology in The Thought of Karl Barth*, 121.
192 Ibid., 122.
193 Ibid., 123.
194 W. R. Comstock, review of T.F. Torrance, *The Ground and Grammar of Theology* (n.p.: University Press of Virginia, 1980), in *Journal of The American Academy of Religion*, 52/1 (March 1984), 190.
195 McGrath, 184–185; Torrance, *The Ground And Grammar of Theology*, 89–91.
196 Torrance, *The Problem of Natural Theology in The Thought of Karl Barth*, 121, 125.

2.3.2. Torrance's Rejection of Natural Theology

Barth's strong negative view on natural theology is evident in Torrance's theology in his earlier days. Torrance believes that we cannot know God behind the back of Jesus Christ, there is simply no alternative to know God other than the incarnate Son. The wonderful works of God in nature does not and cannot make us to know him. Torrance's earlier view on natural theology suggests that nothing of any significance can be known of God in nature.[197] Torrance says,

> it is most important to remember that nature is mute. It does not utter any voice, or talk to us. The voices we hear in nature are not the voices that we hear out of it, but the voices we put into it. It is our own voice that we hear echoing in nature, but when we want another voice to speak to us, to comfort us or to strengthen us, nature fails us, for nature by itself is quite dumb. If a man's conscience cries out against him because of some shameful deed, and his soul is in desperate need of forgiveness, he does not go to nature to get pardon.[198]

Torrance believes that the beauty of nature cannot offer us forgiveness, what we can hear is only the echo of our guilty conscience from the nature. Thus, he says that to worship God in nature is to worship a dumb idol.[199] Torrance's Auburn lectures (1938-39) further reflect his criticisms on the notion of natural theology[200] that the nature does not provide any ground for salvation. Natural theology may offer the greatest hindrance to science and theology because the purer theology is, the more strictly that it behaves in terms of the nature of its Object which is revealed in the incarnate Son through God's grace. Justification by grace sets aside any natural goodness, and this includes natural theology because it belongs to the life of natural man.[201]

In additional to Barth's influence, Torrance also has a deep personal experience of the absolute necessity of a theology that cannot separate God from Jesus. There was a particular incident happened on the October 17, 1944 when Torrance was serving as a stretcher bearer in an

---

197 McGrath, 188.
198 T. F. Torrance, *When Christ Comes and Comes Again* (Eugene: Wipf and Stock Publishers, 1957), 88.
199 Ibid.
200 McGrath, 188.
201 Torrance, *Reality and Evangelical Theology*, 102.

attack on the hamlet of San Martino in Italy. He came across a young soldier who was dying and he asked Torrance, 'Padre, is God really like Jesus?' Torrance assured him that he was. This incident left an indelible impression on Torrance.[202] Jesus Christ, according to Torrance, is the only God, and there is no God other than the one who is revealed in the incarnate Son. Thus, nature cannot provide us a God separated from the one who can only be known through the incarnate Son.

Torrance refuses to accept natural theology as foundation of scientific theology onto which positive theology can be made to rest.[203] At best, natural theology may be recognized as a sort of mixture pursued by men of faith reasoning with the natural realm. Torrance does not see that natural theology can stand on natural grounds because faith belongs to faith and nature belongs to nature, that nature cannot lead us to faith.[204] Torrance argues,

> that nature by itself speaks only ambiguously of God, for while it may be interpreted as pointing intelligibly beyond itself to God, it does not permit of any necessary inferences from its contingence to God. Thus the fact that the immanent rationality of the universe is unable to give any final account of itself is the obverse of the fact that the rational connection between the creation and God is grounded in God alone, and does not rest partly in God and partly in the creation.[205]

Nature by itself can only give us an abstract idea about God, it cannot identify whom this God is and how he could be approached. It could point us to the reality, unfortunately, it itself cannot offer us that reality. Torrance believes that the connection between creation and God is grounded in God alone because he is the only being that can provide the immanent rationality of the universe. Torrance's position on natural theology is not much different than that of Barth as both insist that there is no divine revelation other than the revelation in Christ.

---

202 McGrath, 74.
203 Torrance, *Theological Science*, 104.
204 Ibid.
205 T. F. Torrance, *Space, Time and Incarnation* (London: Oxford University Press, 1969), 59–60.

2.3.3. Torrance's Acceptance of Natural Theology

When Barth's idea is put aside, one has to admit that the wonders of nature do intuitively point to its Creator. In the beautiful mountainous area of New Hampshire in the United States, there is a human-faced rock (old man of the mountain) on the top of a mountain at the Franconia Notch, of which poet Daniel Webster once said, 'Men hang out their sign indicative of their respective trades; shoemakers hang out a gigantic shoe; jewelers a monster watch, and the dentist hangs out a gold tooth; but up in the mountains of New Hampshire, God Almighty has hung out a sign to show that He makes men.'[206] Torrance, under the immense majesty of the wonders of nature, finally comes to the agreement that 'Natural theology is not a phenomenon that can simply be brushed aside, for it has a strange vitality in virtue of which it persists in the history of human thought.'[207] Instead of treating nature as mute in his Auburn days, Torrance takes up a more positive view on natural theology, he says,

> the more the created universe unfolds its marvelous symmetries and harmonies to our scientific inquiries, the more it is bound to fulfill its role as a theater which reflects the glory of the Creator and resounds to his praise.[208]

Though natural theology is regarded as a foreign body in scientific theology which calls for strict conformity with the nature of its object, according to Torrance, it is only methodologically but not metaphysically rejected by scientific theology.[209] Torrance argues that just as theology by its nature excludes natural science from the body of its knowledge, scientific theology acts similarly in excluding natural theology in its methodology. Natural science has its starting point that does not include God and moves in the opposite direction to theology in accordance to its nature, however, natural theology starts from the same premise and seeks to move toward God, and in doing so, it brings itself into conflict with both science and theology, proving itself a confusion in the progress. However, Torrance says, we cannot deny at the same time

---

206 <http://www.neguide.com/nh/index.htm#symbol> accessed 17 Oct 2005.
207 Torrance, *The Problem of Natural Theology in The Thought of Karl Barth*, 121, 125.
208 Torrance, *Reality and Evangelical Theology*, 11.
209 Torrance, *Theological Science*, 103.

there is indeed a form of natural knowledge that the reality of God presses upon us everywhere in nature.[210] Thus, Torrance argues on one hand natural theology is methodologically different from that of theology, yet on the other hand, its intuitive presence cannot be denied.

Torrance wisely re-positions natural theology within his theological science because he sees that human inquiry involves a triadic relation of God, world, and man, and the world serves as a medium in which God makes himself known.[211] Natural theology is no longer detached from science and theology, but rather lies within the overlap of both,[212] and natural theology has its proper place in the dialogue between science and theology.[213] His acceptance of natural theology is regarded by McGrath as a significant theological achievement in relocating natural theology within the tradition of Reformed theology[214] in general.[215] However, instead of treating natural theology as an independent conception by itself, he suggests that natural theology should be incorporated into the revealed theology of which the incarnation plays the pivotal role. It is true that nature points to the right direction, however, with the help of the God's self-revelation in the incarnate Son, it reveals the ultimate reality.

In addition to a realistic view on the role of nature, the modern development of science also provides Torrance an impetus in the understanding of natural theology. According to Einsteinian relativity theory, Torrance sees that geometry does not necessarily stand apart from physics but rather within the unitary structure of physics.[216] Einstein, according to Torrance, insists that geometry can no longer function on its own and be immune from the modification of empirical reality, but rather be integrated with physics as a four-dimensional geometry.[217]

---

210 Ibid.
211 Torrance, *Reality and Evangelical Theology*, 27.
212 Ibid., 31.
213 Torrance, *The Ground And Grammar of Theology*, 94.
214 'In the sixteenth century, the emerging Reformed tradition developed a highly sophisticated theory of natural theology, which on the one hand stressed its subordinate role to divine revelation, while on the other noting its not insignificant apologetic implications and possibilities.' See McGrath, 176.
215 Ibid., 175–176.
216 Torrance, *Space, Time and Resurrection*, xi–x.
217 Torrance, *Reality and Evangelical Theology*, 33.

Instead of swallowed by physics, Torrance sees that geometry becomes the epistemological structure in the heart of physics though it is incomplete without physics.[218] Thus in a similar way, natural theology cannot function independently apart from revealed theology, but rather the former functions as a theological geometry within the latter.[219] Barth, according to Torrance, only rejects natural theology as a preamble of faith or an independent system capable of acquiring actual knowledge of God, not in its value of philosophical analysis.[220] Torrance finally seeks Barth's approval in affirming his revised understanding of Barth's position on natural theology. Torrance admits that natural theology has its proper place and status within the area of overlap between natural science and theological science.[221] This contradicts his earlier sayings in his pursuit of theological science that natural theology offers the greatest hindrance to natural science and scientific theology,[222] because natural science and scientific theology operate through a methodological exclusion of one another and move in opposite directions, while natural theology confuses these two together.

By accepting natural theology, Torrance also accepts its apologetic values and sees that many early Christian theologians used it to address unbelievers in convincing them that by turning themselves to the order of the universe, they were already on the way to the objective God.[223] For those apologetic arguments, Torrance says,

> No attempt was made there to find a way of reaching God by logical reasoning, but rather to point out a way of communing with the regulative and providential activity of God in the rational order of the universe, in which our minds come under the force of the truth of God as it bears upon us in its own self-evidence and shines through to us in its own light. This order pervading the universe does not derive from some immanent cosmological reason, or *logos*, such as the philosophers envisage, but from the uncreated and creative *Logos* of God.[224]

---

218 Ibid.
219 Torrance, *Space, Time and Incarnation*, 69–70.
220 Torrance, *Space, Time and Resurrection*, xi–x.
221 Torrance, *Reality and Evangelical Theology*, 31.
222 Torrance, *Theological Science*, 102.
223 Torrance, *The Ground And Grammar of Theology*, 76–78.
224 Ibid.

Though reason alone cannot help us to access the knowledge of God, however, it could help to point to the right direction in realizing the rationality behind the universe. Thus, natural theological argument by itself is not sufficient to bring people to God, Athanasius' *Contra Gentes*, an apologetic writing, has to be paired with his *De Incarnatione* so that we are directed further to the incarnate Son who gave order to creation. Thus, both creation and incarnation have to be embedded in the argument of natural theology.[225] That is to say, creation points us to the existence of the Creator, and incarnation reveals that the Creator is the incarnate Son.

2.4. Dualism and Dialectic Theology

A major problem that hinders the development of the church for more than a millennium, according to Torrance, is the alien idea of dualism which does not have its origin in the Christian church but rather comes from Plato and Aristotle in the pre-Christian times. Plato separates the sensible world from the intelligible world, Aristotle separates event from idea, becoming from being, material from spiritual, visible from invisible, temporal from eternal.[226] Plato, according to Torrance, distinguishes real knowledge from empirical knowledge because only the noumenal world can give us true knowledge, while the phenomenal world can offer us only opinion or conjecture.[227] Torrance argues that the phenomenal experience would fall apart by dislocating itself from the ontological reality.[228] In the Christian era, Torrance says that Arianism as a typical form of dualism in the early Church, which creates a divide between the realms of divine and human, and they only touch each other tangentially at a mathematical point in the person of Jesus. Arians see the person of Jesus as ultimately belonging to the world of creature instead

---

225 Ibid.
226 T. F. Torrance, *The Trinitarian Faith* (Edinburgh: T&T Clark, 2003), 47.
227 Torrance, *Divine Meaning*, 17.
228 Morrison, *Knowledge of The Self-Revealing God in The Thought of Thomas Forsyth Torrance*, 28–29.

of the other world of divine Being.[229] In Gnosticism, the world of the divine and the world of the creature are so separated that any interaction between them has to be understood in a mythological way. Thus the acts of God in history such as incarnation, crucifixion, resurrection are regarded as myths, and only a gnostic or mythological interpretation can make any sense out of them.[230] Torrance criticizes that the dualist thought detaches not only Jesus from God, but also his message from his person. Thus, Jesus is uprooted from his ground in the Being of God, and his message from his intrinsic relation to the Being of God.[231] Origen, according to Torrance, develops his dualistic thought by thinking beyond the literal content of the Scripture to the divine realities signified, thus, the visible and corporeal things on earth are simply copies of the true things which are invisible and incorporeal in heaven.[232] Since the Reformation, Torrance sees that Cartesian-Kantian dualism splits the world into two disparate realms,

> a physical realm of external reality which is open to investigation and explanation in terms of hard causal connections, for which the appropriate procedures are developed in the mathematical and instrumentalist sciences, and a mental realm of internal reality which is open to investigation and understanding in terms of meaning, for which the appropriate procedures are developed in the historical and human sciences.[233]

Newton, further enhances the dualism in modern science by creating a mechanistic universe. He believes that the basic concepts and theories can be logically derived from the empirical data. The human reason has acquired a legislative role in reducing the understanding of nature to a coherent mechanical system. All rational explanation of natural phenomena can be achieved through the frame of absolute mathematical time and space.[234] In his rejection of Newtonian dualism, Torrance says that absolute time and space are not even derived from experience, and sees that Newton develops a notion of autonomous reason parallel to auto-

---

229 Torrance, *The Ground And Grammar of Theology*, 38.

230 Ibid.

231 Ibid., 37.

232 Torrance, *Theological Science*, T&T Clark, 35.

233 Torrance, *Space, Time and Resurrection*, 40.

234 T. F. Torrance, *The Christian Frame of Mind: Reason, Order, and Openness in Theology and Natural Science* (Colorado Springs: Helmers & Howard, 1989), 67.

nomous structure of nature,[235] and charges that the laws of nature are not reading out of nature but read into the nature.[236]

Within the Christian Church, according to Torrance, a dualist outlook would separate Christ's divinity from his humanity. Torrance says that in formulating a doctrine of Christ, we would either start from humanity and try to get across to his divinity as a bottom up approach, or from divinity to his humanity as a top down approach. However, Torrance warns that each approach will end up by denying itself and passing over into the opposite.[237] Torrance emphasizes that in upholding the truth we must formulate a unitary approach to the doctrine of Christ by recognizing Jesus Christ in his wholeness and integrity that he is both God and man.[238] The act of God in the person of Christ cannot be separated from the being of the Triune God. Gunton comments, 'It is not too much of an exaggeration to say that Torrance's Trinitarian theology is a sustained attempt to overcome that dualism.'[239] The Nicene concept of *homoousion* is the key to create such a unitary outlook in the theology of Torrance.

The term *dualism* used by Torrance in his writings is slightly different than that of the general definition. In general, *dualism* is defined as a reality that is consisted of two disparate parts, and an unbridgeable gap exists between these two parts,[240] or it is defined as a twofold classification which admits no intermediate degrees.[241] Aulen says that there are two types of dualism, absolute dualism and relative dualism. The former carries a meaning of absolute separation of two ideas, the latter is used to reflect the ideas constantly occurred in the Scripture of the opposition between God and his created world, between the divine love and human rebellion, and though good and evil are totally disconnected,

---

235 Ibid.

236 Ibid., 68.

237 T. F. Torrance, *The Mediation of Christ*, Exeter (Exeter: Paternoster Press, 1983), 63.

238 Ibid.

239 Gunton, *Being and Person*, 117–118.

240 R. Audi (ed.), *The Cambridge Dictionary of Philosophy* (2nd edn, Cambridge: Cambridge University Press, 1999), 244.

241 W. A. Elwell, (ed.), *Evangelical Dictionary of Theology* (Grand Rapids, Mich.: Baker, 1996), 334.

evil does not have its eternal existence.[242] However, in Torrance's definition of *dualism*, his emphasis is more on the disjunctive aspect than the holistic apprehension. Likewise, the same approach applies to his understanding of the unitary principle that relatedness is emphasized more than disconnection. Thus, dualism, according to Torrance, is not a total separation, but rather two ideas meet tangentially at a mathematical point in the worst case. In many cases, dualistic ideas overlap each other.

2.4.1. Origenian & Augustinian Dualism

In the dualistic thought of Clement and Origen, according to Torrance, the world operates with a disjunction between a sensible world and an intelligible world, a physical Gospel and a spiritual Gospel. The former Gospel is earthly and is a representation of the latter, and it will eventually pass away. However, the latter, the invisible church will last forever.[243] Torrance accuses Origen of creating two churches: a visible earthly church and an invisible heavenly church;[244] and claims that the visible and empirical church in time and space is the only church, the body of Christ.[245] Torrance argues that the Creed speaks only of a visible church.[246] In fact, the Creed speaks only of the catholic church, it carries no clarification whether this church carries a connotation limited only to the empirical church.[247] Torrance fails to realize that the visible church and the invisible church basically belong to the same group of people, the body of Christ. Origen sees that the word *church* carries both physical and spiritual meanings because the church is both physical and spiritual.[248] This clearly does not form a dualism because physical and spiritual cannot operate separately, but rather coherently in the theology

---

242 G. Aulen, *Christus Victor*, tr. A.G. Hebert (London: Society for Promoting Christian Knowledge, 1937), 20–21.

243 Torrance, *The Ground And Grammar of Theology*, 275–276.

244 Torrance, *The Trinitarian Faith*, 275–276.

245 Ibid. 276.

246 'The Creed is here speaking of the visible or empirical Church'. See Torrance, *The Trinitarian Faith*, 280.

247 Torrance, *Space, Time and Resurrection*, 156.

248 Origen, 'Against Celsus', in *Ante-Nicene Fathers*, ed. Alexander Roberts and James Donaldson, 4 (Peaboy, Mass.: Hendrickson, 1999), 595.

of Origen. The visible church, according to Torrance, is a mixed bag, it is a mixture of good and evil, saved and unsaved.[249] If that is the case, the empirical church cannot be regarded truly as the Body of Christ because unbelievers cannot be members of the Body. If Torrance holds firm to his belief that only empirical visible church is the body of Christ, then it would be extremely difficult to explain the existence of churches in persecuted places because there is simply no visible sign of its existence. Torrance's own experience and that of his father in China could witness that during the Communist persecution, the Chinese church was totally cut off from the outside world with no visible sign of its existence, however, the invisible church was growing. Regarding Luther's interpretation of the Church as a 'spiritual body', Torrance argues that spiritual does not mean only of spirit, but also mean that of the physical body.[250] Torrance says that a 'spiritual man' is no less man because he is spirit, thus even the church is spiritual, it is in reality an empirical body.[251] That is to say, a spiritual man is both spiritual and physical. There is no need to deny the dualistic nature of a man that he has soul and body. Thus, church is both spiritual and empirical.

While the church is empirical, Torrance says that it lives in two times, a worldly time and a spiritual time. The worldly time will decay into the ashes of death, the spiritual time is of the new creation through the *koinonia* of the Spirit. Thus the church lives and fulfils its mission in the overlap of these two times.[252] It seems there is clearly inconsistency in Torrance's thinking, on the one hand, he rejects the dualistic nature of church which is both visible and invisible, on the other hand, he accepts a dualistic reality of spiritual time and worldly time in which the church lives in. Klinefelter argues that Torrance is indeed converting dualism into a form of duality.[253]

When it comes to the theology of Augustine, Torrance charges that Augustine embodies a deep epistemological, sacramental and cosmo-logical dualism that God and world, heaven and earth, eternal and tem-

---

249   Torrance, *Space, Time and Resurrection*, 156.
250   T. F. Torrance, *Kingdom and Church* (Eugene: Wipf and Stock Publishers, 1996), 49–50.
251   T. F. Torrance, *Royal Priesthood* (London: Continuum T&T Clark, 2003), 44–45.
252   Torrance, *Space, Time and Resurrection*, 99.
253   D. S. Klinefelter, 'God and Rationality: A Critique of the Theology of Thomas F. Torrance', *The Journal of Religion*, 53 (1973), 129.

poral are so sharply divided and separated, there needs to be a great attempt to pull them together.[254] The radical Augustinian dualism between the *mundus intelligibilis* and the *mundus sensibilis*, according to Torrance, drives a wedge between a world of inward spiritual experience and an outward sensible world governed by rigid laws of cause and effect.[255] And this is evident in the symbolist concept of sacrament as an outward visible sign of an inward invisible grace.[256] The visible and invisible difference is so great that it can only be bridged by an intermediary realm of grace.[257] Augustine, according to Torrance, is in fact creating two kingdoms, one is eternal and invisible, the other is temporal and visible. These two kingdoms at best meet only tangentially at a mathematical point.[258] Torrance argues that we have to reject this dualist view of kingdom, in doing so, we can re-establish again the oneness of the church in the person of Jesus Christ who is both visible and invisible.[259] It is true that in Augustine's *City of God*, he portrays two different cities, the city of God and the city of the world, of which he provides an account on the origin, development, and destiny of these two cities. However, they are not two separate cities as Torrance suggests. Augustine says,

> In truth, these two cities are entangled together in this world, and intermixed until the last judgment effects their separation. I now proceed to speak, as God shall help me, of the rise, progress, and end of these two cities; and what I write. I write for the glory of the city of God, that, being placed in the comparison with the other, it may shine with a brighter lustre.[260]

These two cities, according to Augustine, overlap each other during the human historical span of time and space, they will however be separated at the last judgment. How would this full overlapping constitute a

---

254 Torrance, *The Ground And Grammar of Theology*, 22.
255 T. F. Torrance, *Theology in Reconciliation* (Eugene: Wipf and Stock Publishers, 1996), 46.
256 Ibid., 43.
257 Ibid., 122.
258 T. F. Torrance, *Space, Time and Incarnation* (London: Oxford University Press, 1969), 33–34.
259 Torrance, *The Trinitarian Faith*, 284.
260 Augustine, 'The City of God' in *Nicene and Post-Nicene Fathers*, ed. Philip Schaff, 2 (Peaboy, Mass.: Hendrickson, 1999), 21.

dualistic thinking? Would it be simply two different aspects of the same reality? How would this be different than that of Torrance's theological science that its unitary structure is based on a small overlap between theology and science. In fact, Torrance realizes that in the 'meantime in the world and history the Church is a mixed body, with good and evil, true and false, wheat and tares in its midst.'[261] That is to say, Torrance affirms both the earthly and heavenly aspects of the church. If the church is only a physical body, then no one can tell that there exists wheat and tares because these are not physical observables but rather spiritual properties. Thus, by telling the existence of wheat and tares in the church, Torrance inevitably accepts his so-called Augustinian dualism of which he rejects.

2.4.2. Newtonian Dualism

Newton is probably the most prominent figure criticized in Torrance's writings, and frequently criticized for both epistemological and cosmological dualism.[262] However, in presenting Newtonian dualism, one would inevitably find the dualist separation is indeed not at all separated. Newton, according to Torrance, sees that the rationality and stability of the universe rest upon the ultimate rationality and stability of God. However, Torrance argues that Newton attaches God to the universe in a grand synthesis which makes him through absolute time and space as the supreme regulative principle of the universe, however, at the same time, God is so transcendent that he is deistically detached from the creation in his eternal impassibility and immutability.[263] The Newtonian universe operates through mechanical natural laws with mathematical precision,[264] though the laws of nature do not apply to those creative processes by which nature came into being, but only applicable to those that are already in being.[265] Thus, the universe is a contingent order, however, at the same time, God is deistically detached from it, and the world

---

261 Torrance, *Space, Time and Resurrection*, 156.
262 Torrance, *Theology in Reconciliation*, 11
263 T. F. Torrance, *Divine and Contingent Order* (Edinburgh: T&T Clark, 1998), 8.
264 Ibid.
265 Ibid.

operates according the causal determination and all motions are subjected to the mechanical laws. [266] Torrance says that Newtonian dualism operates under the premise of disconnectedness between God and creation, between absolute time and space and the contingent events that take place within its embrace.[267] The Newtonian error of dualism, according to Torrance, is clearly reflected in the writings of Lessing that the necessary truth of reason is separated from the accidental truths of history, and of Wilhelm Herrmann that *Historie* is separated from *Geschichte*[268], that faith is detached from its objective historicity.[269]

Apart from the patristic appeal of his unitary outlook, Torrance sees that Maxwell provides him a dynamic platform to integrate matter, force and field; Einsteinian relativity theory helps him to close the gap between experience and mathematics in the logical structure of classical physics. Thus, he says that the rigid absolutes of the Newtonian idea fall apart, and a more open and objective based knowledge is developed.[270] However, Newtonian physics, is not totally rejected, it becomes a limiting case of an integrated field physics.[271] Thus, Torrance says that the universe now is finite yet unbounded, limited and not completely self-explanatory.[272] The universe does not stand on its own as a closed system of cause and effect, but has a close interaction with the divine. The primary point in Newtonian cosmology, according to Torrance, is that the universe cannot be reduced completely to a mechanical system, there is a need for some non-mechanical agency to provide sufficient

---

266 Ibid., 10.
267 Torrance, *The Ground And Grammar of Theology*, 23; T. F. Torrance, 'The Church in an Era of Scientific Change', *The Month*, 6/4 (April 1973), 136.
268 Cushman says that *Historie* carries a meaning of an objective history, while *Geschichte* is an historic event based on one's experience of faith. See R. E. Cushman, 'Is the Incarnation a Symbol?', *Theology Today*, 15/2 (Jul 1958), 167; Torrance says that *Historie* concerns with event which is rooted in objective empirical reality, while *Geschichte* concerns with event which is rooted in the inner life and experience of men, which is so spaceless and timeless that it has only tangential relation to the world of concrete historical events. See Torrance, *Space, Time and Resurrection*, 40.
269 Torrance, *The Ground And Grammar of Theology*, 23.
270 Torrance, *The Christian Frame of Mind*, 69–70.
271 Torrance, *Divine and Contingent Order*, 11.
272 Torrance, *The Christian Frame of Mind*, 69–70.

reason for its accessibility to scientific investigation.[273] Thus, Newton does not allow creation and creator to operate independently from each other, but rather the creation is contingent upon its creator for its intelligibility and existence. That is to say, Newton cannot be regarded as dualist since his cosmology does not separate creation from God, but rather creation is contingent upon God. On the one hand, Torrance highlights the disjunction in Newtonian dualist ideas, on the other hand, he admits that those disconnections are actually connected and related. This is also evident in his argument for Aristotelian dualism that there exists a huge divide between the empirical and the theoretical, the physical and the spiritual, the eternal and the temporal, the mortal and the divine,[274] however, at the same time he admits that Aristotelian philosophy and science create a synthesis such that theology and science are intimately connected with one another in a unified and rational outlook upon God and the world,[275] and also refuses to 'separate matter and form, for they are two aspects of one thing.'[276] He also credits that this unified concept provides a rationality of an ordered universe for the rise of modern science.[277] Thus, Torrance creates a sense that whether an idea is really dualistic depends on how it is looked at rather than the idea itself.

In his accusation of Newtonian dualism, Torrance claims that Newton creates a mechanistic cosmos of absolute space and time. However, not everyone agrees with Torrance that Newton creates an absolute space. Stephen Hawking, a British physicist, says, 'In fact, he (Newton) refused to accept absolute space, even though it was implied by his laws.'[278] Newton does not create an idea of absolute space, instead Hawking says that Newton's laws of motion put an end to the idea of absolute position in space.[279] Absolute space and absolute time, according to Torrance, would inevitably create a ultimate co-existence with the Creator and create an absolute infinite container that may restrict the transcendence of the Creator. Thus, he fervently rejects any dualistic notion of absolute

273 Torrance, *Divine and Contingent Order*, 9.
274 Torrance, *The Ground And Grammar of Theology*, 21.
275 Ibid., 22.
276 T. F. Torrance, 'Scientific Hermeneutics, According to St. Thomas Aquinas', *The Journal of Theological Studies*, 13 (1962), 260.
277 Torrance, *The Ground And Grammar of Theology*, 22.
278 S. Hawking, *A Brief History of Time* (New York: Bantam Books, 1988), 18.
279 Ibid., 33.

space and time. However, in his unitary structure through the Einsteinian relativity, Torrance establishes the absoluteness of light and the absoluteness of temperature.[280] Unfortunately, Torrance does not see that the absolute speed and absolute temperature would similarly create the same dualistic problem because the absoluteness itself is a direct challenge to the absolute Creator.

2.4.3. Dualism in Science and Natural Theology

In the arena of science, Torrance says that modern science through Einsteinian relativity theory in addition to the quantum mechanics provides a unitary frame in the understanding of science. However, physicist Stephen Hawking argues that it is very difficult to construct a complete unified theory of everything in the universe. He says that Einstein spent most of his life unsuccessfully searching for a unified theory, and criticizes Einstein's refusal to accept the reality of quantum physics,[281] or the randomness of particles in quantum physics. Hawking claims that the uncertainty principle is a fundamental feature of the universe that we live in.[282] In other words, there exists disjunctive laws in the universe, that randomness and the orderly co-exist. Instead of unitary structure, dualistic elements are evident in our understanding of nature.

Clearly, causality is the main reason why Einstein rejects randomness in the field of physics because randomness does not provide any rational approach to the understanding of the mechanism involved. Thus, Einstein is called a determinist who believes that the laws of nature are the determining factors in the causality of the world, however, Torrance rejects this idea and prefers to see Einstein as a realist.[283] It is obvious that if Einstein is a determinist, then, he is no better than Newton, and this would put Torrance in a dilemma. Nonetheless, in Einstein's unitary outlook of science, his main focus is on the mechanism of causality.

---

280 T. F. Torrance, *God and Rationality* (London: Oxford University Press, 1971), p. 56; The absolute zero is a theoretical temperature at which the molecules of a substance have the lowest energy. *Encyclopedia Britannica CD* (1998 standard edition).

281 Hawking, 155–156.

282 Ibid.

283 Torrance, *Divine and Contingent Order*, 44.

Torrance on the other hand refuses to accept the mechanistic cause and effect determined by natural laws and mathematics because he believes that God's interaction with the world cannot be constrained by mechanical causality. It is evident that Einstein cannot agree with Torrance on this issue because Einstein accepts no divine reality and believes that the world operates according to its own mechanism of causality. That is to say, the Einsteinian unitary structure destroys the very essence of Torrance's unitary outlook that God cannot be separated from his creation. In fact, Rey says that Einstein's theory is the final extension of the Cartesian dualism or of a dualism even older than Descartes'.[284] Lovejoy says,

> Numerous other philosophers and physicists have regarded the theory of relativity as proving, not that Galileo and Descartes were moving in the wrong direction, but only that neither moved far enough in the right direction – that, namely, of excluding the characters of our perceptual experience from a non-relative, independent, objective realm of being which is the physical world.[285]

Einstein's theory of relativity is by itself a scientific theory, it has certain applications, and it becomes muddled when it is used outside the community of science. In the development of modern science, Lovejoy says that Descartes' dualism has been dethroned that the subjective appearance and objective reality is a passed mode, however, at the same time, the same dualism is the corner-stone of the new physics. The abstractions and rigidity of the mechanical conception of cosmos have been overcome, yet a more abstract and rigid conception has been established.[286] That is to say, dualistic thinking always remains.

In the modern science, rigid Newtonian absolutes were replaced by a more profound objective, unitary dynamic structure. However, Torrance realizes that the unitary structure of modern science does not resolve the dualistic nature of particle and light.[287] It is a general knowledge in any science book that light has two unique natures or properties, namely particle and wave. Particles are discrete and bounded by a finite space,

---

284 A. O. Lovejoy, *The Revolt Against Dualism* (La Salle, Il.: Open Court Publishing, 1960), 5–6.

285 Ibid.

286 Ibid., 6–7.

287 Torrance, *Divine and Contingent Order*, 13.

they cannot exist at more than one physical location at any one time, and they travel from one location to the other according to the Newtonian law of motion. This particular aspect of light in the form of particles is championed by Newton. However, a wave cannot be considered as a finite entity, and it travels in all directions, and exists in many locations at the same time. Unlike Torrance's unitary doctrine, the theory of light is actually moving from unitary to dualist. Dutchman Christiaan Huygens in the seventeenth century argues that light does not travel as particle, it travels as wave. This introduces a long battle between particle theorists and wave theorists. On one side, Newton proves that light travels in a straight line, and so it must be particles. On the other side, Huygens demonstrates that light is bent in refraction, and so it must be in wave form. In the diffraction experiment, a larger scale would confirm Newtonian theory that a barrier does block the light which travels in straight line, while a smaller scale such as a light passing through a narrow slit, the light could scatter behind the barrier and which confirms its wave effect. English physicist James Clerk Maxwell suggests that light is like a wave which propagates under the deformation of electro-magnetic field, and at the same time, the German physicist Philipp Lenard observes the so called photoelectric effect that the electrons are displaced by the light wavelengths. The electrons escape from the metal-lic surface have energies that are dependent on the wavelength of light, and not its intensity, which contradicts the wave theory. Overall, light can be explained in reflection, refraction, interference, small scale di-ffraction, polarization by its wave property, while its particle property can be used to explain reflection, refraction, large scale diffraction and photoelectric effect. Though wave and particle are two different pro-perties, the way they behave when propagating and passing through media is very different, yet both characteristics are observed in ex-perimental results. In 1924 Einstein wrote,

> There are therefore now two theories of light, both indispensable, and – as one must admit today despite twenty years of tremendous effort on the part of theoretical physicists – without any logical connection.[288]

---

288 <http://www-groups.dcs.st-and.ac.uk/~history/HistTopics/ The_Quantum_age_begi ns.html> accessed 6 May 2005.

Torrance admits that this dualism, as expressed by Einstein, has yet to disappear. He says that 'it is doubtful whether in the nature of the case the duality between particle and field can ever be removed'.[289] As of today, the dualistic nature of light is universally accepted as the basis for scientific research. If the community of science is embracing the idea of the dualism of light, it does not seem that Torrance's unitary approach is the only option in the understanding of God's revelation. Torrance is trying to establish an epistemological reality, but at the same time refusing to accept the reality that science is developed dualistically in the pluralistic culture of the understanding of the cosmos.

In his earlier days, Torrance rejected natural theology simply because of its dualistic nature that it detaches the Act of God from the Being of God in the person of Jesus Christ. Torrance argues that natural theology is an excellent example of a theological discipline which reflects dualism.[290] Later, when Torrance comes to terms with natural theology, sees that it can be integrated into the overall revealed theology, natural theology is no longer regarded a dualist idea. Torrance says,

> If natural theology is to have a viable reconstruction even in something like its traditional form, it can be only on the basis of a restored ontology in which our thought operates with a fundamental unity of concept and experience, or of form and being, within a contingent but inherently intelligible and open-structured universe.[291]

That is to say, natural theology is a viable idea if it is liberated from a dualist mode of thinking.[292] However, an important point is missing from this re-alignment of thinking. If Torrance's argument is true, then, dualism rests on one's interpretation of the idea rather than the idea itself. The definition of natural theology remains the same, the basic concept has not changed. What has been changed is the interpreter's theological preference. Thus, in many cases, an idea is made dualistic by Torrance rather than by what it actually represents.

289 T. F. Torrance, 'Introduction', in *A Dynamic Theory of the Electromagnetic Field*, ed. T.F. Torrance (Edinburgh: Scottish Academic Press, 1982), 25.
290 McGrath, 143.
291 Torrance, *The Ground And Grammar of Theology*, 86–87.
292 McGrath, 193.

2.4.4. Dialectic Theology

In his struggle against the infusion of dualism, Torrance admits that dualistic thinking plays a prominent role in the development of ideas in both human history and church history. It is evident that dualistic ideas are imbedded in many fundamental and profound Christian doctrines. The life of Jesus, according to Tillich, is a good demonstration of this dualistic or paradoxical nature that the perfectly concrete is united to a perfectly absolute.[293] Ramsey says,

> while the human and divine natures of Jesus Christ were separate, the attributes of the one could be predicated of the other because of their union in the one person of Christ. Here is paradox indeed. Natures supposedly wholly separate are found to be united.[294]

The hypostatic union is a mystery, a paradox to many. This view is shared by Karl Barth when he argues that God is not man, God is wholly other, but Jesus is God and man. Dualism, according to Barth, is understood as one that must become two in order that it may be truly one.[295] We are unable to comprehend except by means of dialectics that theology has to be understood by using the method of statement and counter-statement.[296] Even the name Jesus Christ is dialectic because the two words belong to two separate spheres, one is human, the other is divine.[297] Ramsey argues that any talk about Jesus will be indeed paradoxical.[298] Since God is infinite and inexpressible, Prestige sees that even the method and result of the doctrine of Trinity is paradoxical, he says, 'How can the finite human mind sum up and describe the nature of the personal being of Almighty God?'[299]

---

293 P. Tillich, *Systematic Theology*, 1 (Welwyn, Herts: James Nisbet & Co., 1963), 167.

294 I. Ramsey, *Christian Empiricism* (London: Sheldon Press, 1974), 102–103.

295 H. R. Mackintosh, *Types of Modern Theology–Schleiermacher to Barth* (London: Nisbet and Co., 1937), 266.

296 Ibid.

297 Ibid., 267.

298 Ramsey, 113.

299 G. L. Prestige, *Fathers and Heretics* (London: Society for Promoting Christian Knowledge, 1940), 184.

However, paradox is no accident in Christian theology, according to Mackintosh, it belongs to the staple of doctrinal thinking.[300] And this is reflected in Karl Barth's and Torrance's dialectical theology which unite two opposite and separate dualistic ideas into one single undetachable proclamation. According to Tillich, theology as any other science depends on formal logic in its pursuit of real knowledge. In formal logic, yes and no, affirmation and negation exclude each other, however, in dialectics, opposites demand each other. Tillich does not see that there is any real conflict between dialectics and formal logic because in dialectics, it follows the thought or movement of reality through yes and no, it is dynamic in nature and describes it in logically correct term.[301] This is like H_2O which is soft at room temperature, and hard at freezing temperature. Thus, water can be both soft and hard depending upon its temperature. Tillich argues that it is not a contradiction when Hegel describes the identity of being and non-being by showing the absolute emptiness of pure being in reflective thought.[302] This also applies to the dogma of Trinity that it does not affirm the logical nonsense that three is one and one is three, it only describes in dialectical term of the inner movement of divine life as an eternal separation from itself and return to itself.[303] Tillich argues that incarnation, redemption, justification are all paradoxical events. However, dialectical theology cannot violate the principle of logical thinking, otherwise, it will simply be genuine logical contradictions.[304] Tillich warns that the term *paradox* should be defined carefully, he says,

> Paradoxical means "against the opinion," namely, the opinion of finite reason. Paradox points to the fact that in God's acting finite reason is superseded but not annihilated; it expresses this fact in terms which are not logically contradictory but which are supposed to point beyond the realm in which finite reason is applicable.[305]

The concern of Tillich is that when paradox is brought down to the level of genuine logical contradictions, and people are asked to sacrifice reason in order to accept senseless combinations of words as divine

---

300 Mackintosh, *Types of Modern Theology*, 266.
301 Tillich, 63–64.
302 Ibid.
303 Ibid.
304 Ibid.
305 Ibid., 64.

wisdom.[306] Thus dialectics can act both ways, it can be either a profound interpretation of the truth or a simple absurdity. Even though dialectical theology is paradoxical in nature, Torrance refuses to see paradox in a positive sense but as absurdities.[307] He argues that paradoxical theological statements sometimes are due to insufficient or inappropriate methods of interpretation. They appear paradoxical only to an alien framework.[308] That means, proper interpretation will harmonize these paradoxes. That does not mean that Torrance objects to paradox, rather he objects to the existence of genuine contradictions in the Scripture. Thus, Torrance is employing Hegelian dialectics that a synthesis can be obtained at a higher level. This is evident in his acceptance of Godel's theorem that a logical system cannot be both consistent and complete, it must open upwards for its explanation.[309] On the other hand, his teacher Karl Barth in his *Church Dogmatics* says that the Word of God alone fulfills the conception of paradox with complete strictness, while other paradoxes can be harmonized from some superior point of vantage.[310] That means, the paradox of the incarnate Son cannot be harmonized by our human wisdom, it has to be accepted by faith. And faith by itself is dialectical in nature. This complete paradox, according to Mackintosh, comes from Kierkegaard's theology of utter dualism between God and man, eternity and time.[311] Kierkegaard's dialectics is different than that of the Hegelian notion in which all contradictions can be ironed out in a higher synthesis.[312] In Hegel's dialectical theology, a thesis such as *being* would give rise to an anti-thesis *nothing*, and the reconciliation lies in the synthesis *becoming*.[313] However, there is no grand synthesis in Kierkegaard's dialectics, each pair of dualistic ideas, such as holiness and love, grace and responsibility, eternity and time, are negating yet resting on each other. Mackintosh says, 'Kierkegaard dwells on them

---

306 Ibid.

307 Torrance, *Theological Science*, 180.

308 Ibid.

309 Torrance, *Space, Time and Incarnation*, 88–89.

310 Mackintosh, *Types of Modern Theology*, 268.

311 Ibid., 258.

312 Ibid., 227.

313 B. Ramm, 'Dialectic', in *Wycliffe Dictionary of Theology*, ed. F. Everett Harrison, Geoffrey W. Broniley, and Carl F. Henry (Peaboy, Mass.: Hendrickson Publishers, 1999), 165.

with subtle vigour, protesting against the eager hunt for idyllic harmony.'[314] Kierkegaard, according to Schnucker, believes that propositional truths are not sufficient, and the theological assertions that the faith has to be paradoxical requires the believer to hold opposite truths in tension. Thus, 'reconciliation comes in an existential act generated after anxiety, tension, and crisis, and which the mind takes to be a leap of faith.'[315] According to Kierkegaard, faith is dialectical[316] and is itself a self-contradiction because we renounce the temporal realm in order to gain eternity, we gain eternity that we can never renounce. Kierkegaard says,

> it takes a paradoxical and humble courage to grasp the whole temporal realm now by virtue of the absurd, and this is the courage of faith. By faith Abraham did not renounce Isaac, but by faith Abraham received Isaac.[317]

The dialectical meaning of faith is best demonstrated by the story of Abraham, according to Mackintosh, that he was commanded to sacrifice Isaac, a morally wrong act, however, his personal relationship with God suspends all ethics. Mackintosh says,

> such a relationship, to be real, must be baffle reason and outstrip all interpretation; for what is faith, except a leap of despair?... Despair, as it has been put, is the condition of latent melancholy and doubt so impossible to endure that a man is driven back by it into the refuge of belief.[318]

Doubt and belief form the extreme opposites of the dialectical faith. Paradox in Kierkegaard, as regarded by Mackintosh, is far from nonsense, it is part of faith to hold that for God the paradox is resolved.[319] Faith is wholly opaque and irrational.[320] Thus, many are puzzled how to

---

314   Mackintosh, *Types of Modern Theology*, 227.
315   R. V. Schnucker, 'Neo-orthoxy', in *Evangelical Dictionary of Theology*, ed. Walter A. Elwell (Grand Rapids, Mich.: Baker,1984), 755.
316   S. Kierkegaard, 'Fear and Trembling', in *The Essential Kierkegaard* (Princeton, N.J.: Princeton University Press, 2000), 94–95.
317   Ibid., 98.
318   Mackintosh, *Types of Modern Theology*, 233.
319   Ibid., 234.
320   Ibid., 233.

distinguish between a genuine contradiction and the kind that is a vehicle of the profoundest truth.[321] Ramsey asks,

> can we do anything to distinguish illuminating and revealing improprieties from those which merely bewilder and confound us? It is a question which Hepburn himself raises early in his book: 'When is a contradiction not a mere contradiction, but a sublime Paradox, a mystery?'... If certain paradoxes preserve and reveal something, what do they reveal, and how? Can we give any clues by which to recognize illuminating improprieties, revealing absurdities?[322]

The answer to the question is clear that there exists no concrete mechanism to separate wheat from chaff. Thus, even Barth advises that dialectics has to be used sparingly.[323] There are several types of paradox as seen by Ramsey, first, he calls it avoidable paradox, because it is created by muddle that can be cleared up by retracting the steps of our argument, it may well be a mistake that one makes. The second is the Hegelian dialectic that a synthesis can be generated from a paradox of thesis and antithesis, that means a new assertion is arisen out of the two original assertions. The third is unavoidable paradox which permits no logical examination or assessment and thus logically inaccessible.[324] Ramsey offers two practical guidelines in the discernment of those unavoidable paradoxes. First, the unavoidable paradox could be defensible if it is structured as to be evocative of a disclosure situation comprising 'what is seen and more'. Second, it would be more acceptable if it can be explored based on personal relationship instead of wholly impersonal models or theories.[325] However, these guidelines are to a certain degree subjective, and by themselves cannot offer any objective reference. Unless the objective reference is based on the Scripture itself, there is no mechanism to separate chaff from wheat, or unless the dialectical doctrine is clearly reflected by the Scripture, it cannot be objectively validated.

In Torrance's theology, particularly in his doctrine of incarnation, all dualistic elements are somehow integrated into his unitary structure dialectically. Therefore, he can see himself totally detached from dual-

---

321   Ibid., 234.
322   Ramsey, 98.
323   Mackintosh, *Types of Modern Theology*, 268.
324   Ramsey, 99.
325   Ibid., 117.

ism through his dialectical theology which is characterized by duality in unity and unity in duality. From Torrance's perspective, there is no dualism in his theology because the separation has been bridged by his dialectic presupposition. In his discussion of natural theology, on the one hand, he claims that we cannot know the truth behind the back of Jesus, one the other hand, he says that natural theology has its significance in revealing the truth. Natural theology does carry a dualistic idea as Torrance claims, however, this dualistic idea is dialectically accommodated in his revealed theology. In his theological science, our inquiry of knowledge is initiated by the subject, however, the subjectivity of the subject is determined by the objectivity of the object. On the one hand, Torrance tells us how to make a proper rational inquiry that the inquiry has to be made according to its nature, on the other hand, he says that faith is given, not acquired, that means, without faith, no one can realize the objective knowledge. These two opposite assertions, through his presuppositional validation, are accommodated dialectically in his unitary structure of theological science. In his addressing of the body of Christ, Torrance rejects the spiritual notion of the church by seeing it as taking an Augustinian form of dualism in separating the spiritual realm from the physical realm, however, the body of Christ, manifested in the physical church, is in fact a spiritual body because the head of the body is spiritual. Thus, both are integrated dialectically in his doctrine that the church is ontologically related to the being of Christ.[326] Anhypostasia and enhypostasia, to be discussed later in chapter two, are two different and to certain degree opposite ideas in the clarification of the human nature of the person of Jesus Christ, Torrance simply adopts these two ideas in a dialectical way without ever addressing their incompatibility. He shares the benefits of both without ever addressing how to bridge the unbridgeable gap between these two ideas. There exists really a fine line between a genuine profound truth and an irrational dialectics. In fact, Torrance's dialectical theology is more of Kierkegaard's than that of Hegel's because he seldom argues apart from presuppositions.

---

326 Torrance, *Royal Priesthood*, 29–30.

3. The Incarnate Son

The Incarnate Son, according to Torrance, is both God and man. His divine nature and human nature form a perfect union in the Person of Jesus Christ. These two natures conjoined in the hypostatic union are not two *hypostases* indwelling in a person, but two unique and distinct natures forming an inseparable union in the Person of Jesus Christ. According to his divine nature, Christ is fully God; and according to his human nature, he is fully man.[1] The Nicene-Constantinopolitan Creed gives Torrance the primary doctrinal platform for his understanding of the Person of Christ.[2]

3.1 Human Nature

In the incarnation, the eternal Son takes up human nature into hypostatic union with himself, and in the assumption, Christ becomes not only real man and also a man,[3] he is the One and the Many.[4] That is to say, by becoming man, Christ shares all our human nature, acts as a representative of the whole human race; however, at the same time he also becomes one

---

1   T. F. Torrance, *The Mediation of Christ* (Exeter: Paternoster Press, 1983), 66–67.

2   T. F. Torrance, 'Introduction', in *The Incarnation: Ecumenical Studies in the Nicene-Constantinopolitan Creed A.D. 381*, ed. T. F. Torrance (Edinburgh: The Handsel Press, 1981), xi.

3   T. F. Torrance, 'The Atonement and The Oneness of The Church', *Scottish Journal of Theology*, 7 (1954), 245.

4   Torrance, 'The Atonement and The Oneness of The Church', 250. In his article, *The Mission of The Church*, Torrance explains that the One includes the Many, and the Many includes each one, thus, he acts both corporately and individually. See T. F. Torrance, 'The Mission of The Church', *Scottish Journal of Theology*, 19 (1966), 135.

of us, a real historical individual person.[5] Torrance employs Barth's idea that Christ's universality is revealed in his particularity that Christ is the One who became man for Many.[6]

Torrance argues that the incarnate Son has to assume human nature, otherwise his love falls short as he is not one of us, and his love is not ultimately love.[7] It is essential to realize that Jesus is man, otherwise, there is no bridge that can cross the gulf between God and man, and there is no representative or foundation on our side. Jesus as the Mediator must be wholly and fully man in order to make a full re-presentation of us.[8] By becoming one of us, and through the use of our human language, Christ reveals to us something of the innermost secret of his own divine life as the Son of God, that he is both human and divine.[9] Thus, the revelation is determined and shaped by the humanity of Christ. Torrance says,

> we know of no revelation of the Word of God except that which is given through Christ and in the form of Christ. Jesus Christ is the Truth, Truth as God is Truth, and that same Truth in the form of Man, Truth answering itself, Truth assuming its own true form from the side of man and from within man.[10]

According to Torrance, God's revelation is essentially bi-polar that God reveals himself to us in terms of what is not-God, that is to say, 'revelation is given to us only in terms of what it is not, in the humanity of those to whom it is given',[11] God reveals to us through his humanity. In other words, Christ becomes visible in order to reveal what is invisible, to become a mortal to reveal what is eternal. Thus, it is through his humanity, his eternal Being is revealed to us. To uphold the vital necessity of humanity as an integrated part of the Person of Jesus Christ,

---

5   T. F. Torrance, *The Christian Doctrine of God, One Being Three Persons* (Edinburgh: T&T Clark, 2001), 161.
6   K. Barth, Church Dogmatics, tr. G.W. Bromiley and T.F. Torrance, 4/1 (Edinburgh: T&T Clark, 1957–1981), 167.
7   T. F. Torrance, The Trinitarian Faith (Edinburgh: T&T Clark, 2003), 7.
8   Ibid., 8.
9   Ibid., 55.
10   T. F. Torrance, Theology in Reconstruction (London: SCM Press, 1965), 130.
11   Ibid.

Torrance rejects any possibility of a docetic view[12] in the understanding of Christ, and warns that the heresy would undermine the objective and historical reality of Christ.[13] The assumption, as insisted by Torrance, cannot have a dualist conception of separate body and soul, but rather Christ assumes the whole man that consists of both body and soul. It is not soul without body nor body without soul or mind.[14]

In Torrance's theology, he pays special attention to the heresy of Apollinarianism which is seen as to minimize the humanity of Christ. Apollinarius, is a strong defender of Nicene orthodoxy against the heretic Arianism, yet he maintains that when the Logos becomes flesh he takes the place of the rational human soul in the Person of Christ.[15] Torrance argues that if the Logos replaces the human soul of the Person of Christ, then, Christ is merely an instrument in the hand of God and the integrity of his humanity is demolished.[16] By eliminating a human soul from the Person of Christ, there is simply no vicarious humanity left in him for our salvation.[17] Torrance charges that Apollinarianism also

---

12   Torrance sees Docetism as a 'Christology from above' because the docetic Christology does not see that Christ assumes a real human body, and treats the human nature and the suffering of Christ as unreal. See Torrance, *The Trinitarian Faith*, 60.

13   Ibid., 131.

14   Ibid., 150.

15   Harrison, F. Everett, Geoffrey W. Broniley, and Carl F. Henry, *Wycliffe Dictionary of Theology* (Peaboy, Mass.: Hendrickson Publishers, 1999), 55; Angel says that the essential attribute of Christ's flesh is its capacity to experience, and not for initiative. Thus, Christ has one active principle because Apollinarius sees no volitional conflict in Christ's life. See G. T. D. Angel, 'Apollinarius: Apollinarianism', in *The New International Dictionary of The Christian Church*, ed. J.D. Douglas (revised edn, n.p.: Regency Zondervan, [1986]), 56.

16   T. F. Torrance, *Theology in Reconciliation* (Eugene: Wipf and Stock Publishers, 1996), 116.

17   Torrance says that by eliminating human rational soul from Jesus, Apollinarius deprives Jesus of fully human experience. By saying that Christ does not share with us in the wholeness of our human being of both body and soul, Apollinarius damages the complete economy of salvation because the whole man is not taken up in the Incarnation. Christ has not really come all the way to us, and His death was merely of his own and not our death made His own by the vicarious action that He became truly man. By avoiding taking up fallen human nature, Apollinarius is preaching another Gospel which does not cope with original sin or the root of sin in the rational constitution of man. By making the human body of Christ as an

violates the principle of the reconciling exchange of Christ that a ransom is paid in exchange for a different thing instead of body for body and soul for soul.[18] Torrance appeals to Cyril of Alexandria in his objection to Apollinarianism that if the incarnate Son does not assume a human soul, the redemption would not reach the directive principle of human life. If Christ does not assume a human mind, he is unable to act authentically as man in offering atoning obedience and sacrifice from the side of humanity towards God, and he cannot act as our human priesthood as a human mind has no essential place in the vicarious humanity of Christ.[19] In essence, Torrance is taking a view by accommodating both the objective atonement that God reconciles with us through satisfaction and the subjective atonement that Jesus as man fulfils the justice demanded by God.

The human nature of Christ is not a pre-existent reality, it is created by God for his salvific mission.[20] That is to say that the incarnation has its beginning in human space and time, it involves a true man in the salvation of mankind. However, the humanity of Christ is not only manifested in his earthly sojourn, it is also actualized in his resurrection and ascension. Torrance insists that if Christ was not risen in body, then salvation is not actualized in reality, and we are still in sin. If Christ was not ascended in the fullness of his humanity, then, we have no anchor within the veil and we are still outside of the salvation.[21] Our salvation is so integrated in the humanity of Christ, according to Torrance, that the humanity of Christ will remain in existence forever. Torrance argues that,

It is his endless self-oblation. In the humanity of the ascended Christ there remains for ever before the Face of God the Father the one, perfect, sufficient Offering for mankind. He presents himself before the Father as the Redeemer who has united himself to us and has become our Brother.[22]

---

instrument in the hands of God, salvation is conceived only as an act of God upon man's phyiscal being and bypasses the intellectual nature of his constitution as man. See Torrance, *Theology in Reconciliation*, 147–149.

18   Ibid., 149–150.
19   Ibid., 112.
20   T. F. Torrance, *Trinitarian Perspectives Toward Doctrinal Agreeement* (Edinburgh: T&T Clark, 1999), 62.
21   T. F. Torrance, *Royal Priesthood* (London: Continuum T&T Clark, 2003), 43.
22   T. F. Torrance, *Space, Time and Resurrection* (Edinburgh: T&T Clark, 1998), 115.

Though the human nature of Christ is created and has a beginning in human history, according to Torrance, it extends forever into eternity. Torrance basically says that the incarnation is an open-ended activity which embraces our humanity in his humanity. In other words, the eternal Christ is no longer purely a Being of divine nature, he forever carries with him a human nature - a created identity. This implies that the mission of the incarnation is open-ended, the eternal Son becomes the incarnate Son and remains as the incarnate Son forever. This triggers a serious issue of how is this humanity positioned in the understanding of the immanent Trinity. It will be addressed later in the thesis.

According to Torrance, the church or the Body of Christ is identified with the humanity of Christ. It is through the humanity of Christ that all who believe are humanized and restored to the true and perfect humanity.[23] God is Truth, but this same Truth is also in the form of Man, and the Truth assumes its own true form in the humanity of Christ.[24] Torrance observes that the humanity of Christ has long been neglected in theology, and argues that revelation is not solely based on the subjectivity of the religious experience or faith, but also on the objective reality of the Truth.[25] In other words, it is not only our own subjective experience of Christ's saving grace that forms the basis of his revelation to us that he is the ultimate Truth, but also the historical reality of the Person of Christ who walked on earth as a human being among us. The former is a subjective experience, however, the latter is an objective event. Thus, the Truth is both objectively and subjectively fulfilled in the humanity of Christ. Torrance says,

> The subjective reality of this Truth can never be made a separate theme for theology any more than the Humanity of Jesus in abstraction from the Incarnation. That Humanity as the subjective reality of the Truth is already enclosed in the objective reality of the Truth: that is precisely the significance of the Humanity of Christ for the procedure of dogmatics.[26]

---

23   Torrance, Royal Priesthood, 44–45.
24   Torrance, Theology in Reconstruction, 134.
25   Ibid.
26   Ibid.

Thus, the humanity of Christ is the very substance of revelation.[27] There is no revelation of the Word of God except that which is given through Christ in the form of man.[28]

3.1.1. Corrupted Human Nature

In maintaining the fullness of his incarnation, the whole Christ had become a curse for us. Torrance adopts the idea from Barth that Christ took upon himself the fallen Adamic humanity from the Virgin Mary,[29] which is our perverted, corrupted, degenerated, diseased human nature. Baillie comments that Barth knows very well that both Catholics and Protestants affirm the traditional belief that Christ assumed only the unfallen human nature.[30] Calvin in his *Institutes* says that Christ was sanctified by the Holy Spirit in conception, thus he assumed a human nature as that of Adam's before the Fall.[31] But Barth insists that the fallen human nature is the only nature that we know in ourselves.[32] Barth says, 'it is the situation of sinful man in its totality which Jesus Christ has made His own, and for which He has accepted responsibility before God.'[33] The totality of sinful man cannot be apart from his fallen human nature. This is not a new idea, in his *Exposition of the Orthodox Faith*, John of Damascus says,

> as soon as He (Jesus) was brought forth into being, was deified by Him, so that these three things took place simultaneously, the assumption of our nature, the coming into being, and the deification of the assumed nature by the Word.[34]

---

27   Ibid., 130.
28   Ibid.
29   T. F. Torrance, 'Justification: Its Radical Nature and Place in Reformed Doctrine and Life', *Scottish Journal of Theology*, 13 (1960), 231.
30   D. M. Baillie, *God Was In Christ* (London: Faber and Faber Limited, 1960), 16.
31   J. Calvin, John, *Institutes of the Christian Religion*, tr. Henry Beveridge, 2.13.4 <http://www.reformed. org> accessed 1 Sep 2005.
32   Baillie, *God Was In Christ*, 17.
33   Barth, *Church Dogmatics*, 4/1, 405.
34   John of Damascus, 'Exposition of the Orthodox Faith', *Nicene and Post-Nicene Fathers*, ed. Philip Schaff & Henry Wace, 9 (Peaboy, Mass.: Hendrickson, 1999), 3.12, 56.

The assumed nature has to be deified immediately by the Word because it was fallen and corrupted.[35] Deification does not mean that the assumed human nature was deified to become a divine nature, it means that Christ human nature was sanctified and became holy and sinless. John of Damascus maintains that divine nature and human nature are two distinct natures, there is no confusion of two natures. In the modern era, the assumption of fallen human nature, according to Bruce, had been taught by Gottfried Menken of Bremen and Edward Irving in England.[36] Menken insists that in order to do justice to the humanity of Christ, he must have taken upon a body of sin, and sinfulness has its rightful place in the natural earthly humanity. A being free from original sin does not belong to that humanity.[37] Menken's view was further expanded by the Scottish preacher Edward Irving that Christ took sinful human nature into connection with his own person. Irving argues that it is impossible to find any human nature other than the fallen human nature after the fall of Adam, thus, it is the only human nature that Christ has to assume in order to partake in the brotherhood of human being.[38] Irving says that Jesus was sanctified by the Holy Spirit at the moment of his conception, his soul was pure and had no evil suggestion, his flesh however was corrupted and was liable to all forms of temptations,[39] and he had to struggle with temptations throughout his life.[40] Since Jesus was born of Mary, he was taking the same substance of the fallen Virgin Mary, namely, the corrupted human flesh.[41] It is the work of the Holy Spirit that makes Jesus' soul sinless and holy. Irving goes further to say that the Person of Christ is actually a union of the Holy Spirit and a human soul,[42] Jesus' divine nature comes from the Holy Spirit, and his human nature comes from the Virgin Mary. Jesus' flesh is in a fallen state while

35   Ibid.
36   A. B. Bruce, *The Humiliation of Christ* (Grand Rapids, Mich.:Eerdmans, 1955), 250.
37   Ibid., 250–251.
38   E. Irving, 'The Methold is By Taking Up the Fallen Humanity', in *Collected Writings of Edward Irving*, ed. G. Carlyle, 5 (London: Alexander Strahan, 1865), 116.
39   Ibid., 126–127.
40   Ibid., 194.
41   Ibid., 117.
42   Ibid., 126.

his soul is sanctified.[43] Irving's view is regarded as extreme by Torrance. Torrance criticizes the idea that the sinlessness of Jesus Christ is upheld not by his own nature but by the indwelling of the Holy Spirit. While Torrance says that we cannot think of Jesus' flesh is different from us, yet he does not see that Jesus' flesh is as corrupted as is suggested by Irving.[44] Torrance comments in his Auburn teaching notes,

> Thus while we must say that Christ entered into fallen and corrupt humanity, we cannot say that his flesh was created out of nothing and absolutely *de novo*, it was created out of fallen humanity, but without the will of fallen humanity. In this Union the flesh of Christ becomes Holy though it is a member of humanity under the curse of the law, under the ban of God's wrath. Thus we are to think of Christ's flesh as perfectly and completely sinless in his own nature, and not simply in virtue of the Spirit as Irving puts it.[45]

Torrance agrees with Irving that the corrupted human nature comes from the flesh through the Virgin Mary. At this early stage, Torrance has yet to put forward the idea of self-sanctification that Christ sanctifies himself in the incarnation. However, the assumption of fallen human nature through the flesh creates another problem, namely, does sin originate from the soul (mind, will) or from the body? Flesh by itself is just an organic matter, it is morally neutral, unable to sin. Without the will or soul, one is not able to sin. Tertullian says that it is absurdity to 'attribute sin and crime to that substance (flesh) to which you do not assign any good actions or character of its own!'[46] Flesh alone without the soul can do nothing. The nature of a person lies not in his earthly element but in the faculty of his soul.[47] By claiming the assumption of the fallen human nature is from the flesh, but without the will of fallen humanity, Torrance basically contradicts himself because flesh alone does not possess any sinful nature, it is the will that makes both thought and act sinful. If the soul is pure, the flesh must be equally pure. Otherwise, there exists a dualism that the body and soul can run separately on its own. Bruce sees

---

43   Ibid., 135.
44   T. F. Torrance, The Doctrine of Jesus Christ (Eugene: Wipf and Stock Publishers, 2002), 121–122.
45   Ibid., 122.
46   Tertullian,   'A Treatise on the Soul', in Ante-Nicene Fathers, ed. Alexander Roberts & James Donaldson, 3 (Peaboy, Mass.: Hendrickson, 1999), 220.
47   Ibid.

this type of approach to Jesus' human nature as simply another form of Adoptionism, he says, 'What is the worth of this theory of our Lord's humanity, held by the Adoptionists in the eighth century, and revived by Menken and Irving in the nineteenth?[48] By presenting the necessity of assuming the fallenness of human nature, many would naturally see that Jesus was actually a fallen man and became God by adoption. In Torrance's earlier days while he was teaching at Auburn, his thought on this issue was not particularly clear. He taught that sin does not make Christ more a man, but actually less.[49] Thus it is not necessary for Christ to assume a fallen human nature in order to make him more human, because fallenness actually makes him less human. Thus, Christ's assumption of a fallen human nature was not clearly reflected in Torrance's earlier teaching notes. However, in his later writings, Torrance did adopt Barth's idea and champion the theory that Christ did not only assume a human nature, he assumed a frail and corrupted human nature,[50] a fallen nature just like us in order to become one of us and to identify fully with us. The purpose of the genealogy of Jesus as recorded in the Gospel of Matthew is to show that he was incorporated into a long line of sinners, that he identified himself with our fallen and estranged humanity.[51] Torrance argues that the divine salvation and reconciliation have to do with the whole human reality, that it deals not only in the corruption of physical nature, but also in the depravity of spiritual nature. Torrance says,

> the Incarnation had to be understood as the sending of the Son of God in the concrete form of our own sinful nature and as a sacrifice for sin in which he judged sin within that very nature in order to redeem man from his carnal, hostile mind.[52]

If the Incarnate Son cannot penetrate deep into our fallen and sinful human nature, then, Torrance argues, his atonement and reconciliation can only be understood in terms of external relations between Jesus Christ and sinners. Thus, the atonement becomes an external forensic

---

48   Bruce, 254.
49   It is the teaching notes he quoted from H.R. Mackintosh. See Torrance, *The Doctrine of Jesus Christ*, 124.
50   Torrance, *The Trinitarian Faith*, 102.
51   Torrance, *The Mediation of Christ*, 50.
52   Ibid., 49.

relation as a judicial transaction in the transference of the penalty for sin from the sinner to the sin-bearer, instead of making it an ontological reality of expiation and propitiation internal to humanity.[53] These external and internal relations are expressed by McGrath as God acting in Christ instead of and in the place of all humanity.[54]

In supporting his argument, Torrance appeals to patristic writings that the doctrine could be found everywhere in the first five centuries. Unless the whole man is assumed by Christ, it is not saved. By adopting the principle of 'the unassumed is unhealed' from Gregory of Nazianzus,[55] Torrance argues,

> the whole man had to be assumed by Christ if the whole man was to be saved, that the unassumed is unhealed, or that what God has not taken up in Christ is not saved. The sharp point of those formulations of this truth lay in the fact that it is the alienated mind of man that God had laid hold of in Jesus Christ in order to redeem it and effect reconciliation deep within the rational centre of human being.[56]

If Christ assumes corrupted human nature, does this make him a sinner? Torrance says that even though Jesus assumes our fallen human nature, he remains sinless because he sanctifies himself in the incarnation. Torrance says,

> From his birth to his death and resurrection on our behalf he sanctified what he assumed through his own self-consecration as incarnate Son to the Father, and in sanctifying it brought the divine judgment to bear directly upon our human nature both in the holy life he lived and in the holy death he died in atoning and reconciling sacrifice before God.[57]

There exists a logical sequence between the assumption of fallen human nature and the self-sanctification in Torrance's writings. Torrance indicates clearly that Jesus' whole human life is holy and sinless.[58] Thus, the

---

53   Ibid., 50.

54   A. E. McGrath, T.F. Torrance, *An Intellectual Biography* (Edinburgh: T&T Clark, 1999), 157.

55   Gregory of Nazianzen, 'To Cledonius The Priest Against Apollinarius', in *Nicene and Post-Nicene Fathers*, ed. Philip Schaff and Henry Wice, 7 (Peaboy, Mass.: Hendrickson, 1999), 440.

56   Torrance, *The Mediation of Christ*, 49.

57   Ibid., 50.

58   Ibid.

incarnation by itself is holy and perfect. It was Latin theology, Torrance argues, which in the fifth century rejected this fallen human nature idea, instead it claimed that Christ assumed a humanity in its perfect original state prior to the Adamic fall. Torrance charges that this theology forced Roman Catholicism into the strange notion of immaculate conception.[59]

There are a couple of problems with Torrance's view on Christ's fallen human nature: first, Christ's full identification with humanity and second, the sanctification process of the assumed sinful human nature. In order to become a truly and fully human Being, Torrance insists that Christ has to assume a fallen human nature, a pre-fall Adamic human nature by itself is not sufficient for his identification with the fallen race. However, we can see that there is a huge diversity within the human race. A woman is as human as a man, yet a woman is different than a man. A black skin person is different than a white skin person, yet both are human beings. This mental or physical difference does not indicate the insufficiency to claim the full identification of the human race. A man who cannot experience the labor pain cannot use this physical difference to claim that he is more or less human than that of a woman. By the same argument, it is not necessary for Christ to assume the fallenness of human nature in order for him to identify with the human race fully. Torrance stresses so much on the fallenness of human nature that it would be difficult to explain how the pre-Fall Adam as a human person cannot fully identify with himself after the Fall.

The identification has many levels, and since each human being is unique, unless the identification reaches to the level of an individual, it cannot be regarded as truly and fully of that individual. Clearly, the humanity of Christ that is truly man and fully man excludes the notion that he is exactly identical with every detail of a human person,[60] but

---

59 Ibid., 49.
60 In modern science, Jesus' DNA, if any, would highly be doubtful to be the same as ours because our DNA traces back to our earthly parents. He who identifies Himself as a human being does not require to share the same element in all aspects of human anatomy. Professor Donald Macleod comments on this interesting anatomical issue, he says, 'He (Jesus) was a unique genotype precisely because she (Mary) contributed at least half his chromosomes [as any human mother would]. How the rest were contributed remains a mystery. The one certainty is that Mary could not herself have contributed the sex-determining chromosome, Y, which is

rather he is identical with us in all general human terms such as he takes a true body, a reasonable soul, he lives in our physical and social environment, shares our emotions, pains and sufferings. Torrance faces a similar situation in his dealing with 'Calvinist Extra' by rejecting Lutheran full identification criteria that the Word who became man born in Bethlehem cannot leave something behind or 'extra' in heaven.[61] Instead, Torrance believes it is not necessary to embody everything in the humanity of Christ in order to make his humanity fullest. By the same argument, it is not necessary for Christ to assume the fallenness of human nature to become the fullest possible human being.

The uniqueness of Christ's humanity was highlighted by Torrance in his Auburn lectures that Jesus Christ is someone who is absolutely unique. In fact, Torrance says, Jesus' humanity was never even associated himself with men on the same level.[62] That means, Jesus is not exactly identical with us on every physical and spiritual detail. No matter how much sameness of humanity we want from the person of Christ as that of us, we have to admit that humanly he is different from us that Christ was conceived by the Holy Spirit and born of the Virgin Mary. In reality, none of the human race has gone through a similar process of conception and birth. Unfortunately, this uniqueness is somehow dissipated by his later adoption of Barth's idea.

Torrance's insistence that Christ assumes all that is ours and sanctifies what he assumes[63] is actually putting Christ in a different human category than ours, as no human being is able to sanctify his own fallen nature and corruptions. If sanctification is accomplished through his divine capability, then, he is not after all as human as us. There is a lack of consistency in Torrance's arguments. Macleod criticizes Torrance's principle of 'the unassumed is the unhealed',

> It is quite perverse to suggest that 'the unassumed' in this statement is 'fallen human nature'. What Gregory has in his sights is the Apollinarian insistence that Christ did

---

always provided by the biological father.' See D. Macleod, *The Person of Christ* (London: InterVarsity Press, 1998), 162.

61 Torrance, *Space, Time and Resurrection*, 124.
62 Torrance, *The Doctrine of Jesus Christ*, 27.
63 Torrance, *Theology in Reconciliation*, 111.

not assume a human mind: 'If he has a soul,' he asks, 'and yet is without a mind, how is he man, for man is not a mindless animal?'[64]

Torrance is well aware that the expression 'the unassumed is the unhealed' is directed towards Apollinarius who suggested that two natures were united in the Person of Christ, yet Christ did not possess a rational human soul or mind. According to Apollinarius, by assuming a corrupted human mind, the Son would inevitably be corrupted, thus he replaced it by his own Spirit.[65] Since the human soul is the source of sinful human nature, thus, by assuming a human soul, Christ assumes a fallen human nature. In Torrance's earlier teaching, the corrupted humanity is limited to the flesh but not the will.[66] However, in his later writings, the corrupted humanity clearly refers to corrupted human mind.[67] Thus, 'the unassumed' is related to the 'fallen human nature' through the assumption of corrupted human mind. Macleod clearly misses this important linkage.

Torrance often cites his idea that the corrupted human nature is a patristic doctrine that was prevalent in the first few centuries. Macleod challenges the claim and its validity, he says,

> none of the fathers held that Christ took fallenness. Indeed, the pointers we have from the fathers are in the opposite direction. Cyril, for example, in his Answers to Tiberius declared: 'though he clothed himself, as they say, in Adam, he was not, as Adam was, of the earth earthly, but was celestial and so incomparably superior to what was earthly'. The Western fathers were of the same mind. 'For there was born,' wrote Augustine, 'not a nature corrupted by the contagion of transgression, but the one only remedy of all such corruptions.' Leo, in his Tome, expressed it more epigrammatically: 'Nature it was that was taken by the Lord from His mother, not defect.'[68]

In fact, both Torrance and Macleod make excessive claims. Evidences, from their own quotations and my examples, show that the assumption of both fallen and unfallen human natures are found in patristic writings. John of Damascus favors the assumption of fallen human nature, while in the writing of Athanasius, Torrance's favorite patristic father, there is

---

64 Macleod, *The Person of Christ*, 224.
65 Torrance, *Theology in Reconciliation*, 112.
66 Torrance, *The Doctrine of Jesus Christ*, 122.
67 Torrance, *The Mediation of Christ*, Exeter, 49.
68 Macleod, *The Person of Christ*, 224.

a strong indication that Athanasius does not see that Christ took our fallenness. Athanasius, in addressing incarnation, says that Christ 'takes a body of our kind, and not merely so, but from a spotless and stainless virgin, a body clean and in very truth pure from intercourse of men.'[69] Athanasius somehow presents that Virgin Mary was in a state of purity when Christ was conceived in her womb. If Mary is spotless and stainless, from whom can Christ assume a sinful human nature? In fact, it would be easier to argue that if Christ was born of impure Mary, naturally he assumed a sinful human nature and then he sanctified it. However, if Christ assumed the fallen human nature apart from the human womb which is pure, it would only mean that God is the creator of Christ's sinful human nature, and this clearly violates God's goodness and holiness as nothing evil can come from him.

One would wonder, if Christ assumes sinful human nature, does that make him a sinner like us? Even if he is sanctified, he is at best a sinner sanctified, he is then a sanctified sinner, not a sinless person. It seems Torrance especially put this logic in sequence that he assumed our sinful nature first, then he sanctified the sinful nature that he assumed. However, if sanctification happened after the assumption, as what Torrance suggests, then, Christ cannot be sinless at the time of assumption, there remains a possibility of the violation of the holiness of the incarnate Son. If sanctification happened at the same time, then the whole idea becomes meaningless, the effects simply cancel out each other. According to Torrance, human salvation is very much linked to the fallen human nature assumed by Christ, he says,

> If in Jesus Christ God did not really become one with us sinful men and women through taking our actual human nature upon himself, then all that Christ was and did on our behalf was finally empty of saving content.[70]

If Christ did not experience any effect of our fallen human nature since it was immediately cancelled out by his own sanctification, how does it effect our salvation? It is at best a symbolic gesture without any substance in it. If this idea of immediate sanctification upon assumption of fallen human nature is a valid proposition, then it will be difficult for

---

69   Athanasius, 'Incarnation of the Word', *Nicene and Post Nicene Fathers*, ed. Philip Schaff and Henry Wace, 4 (Peaboy, Mass.: Hendrickson, 1999), 40.
70   Torrance, *The Trinitarian Faith*, 4.

Torrance to ridicule the Roman Catholic idea of immaculate conception, as both share the same idea of conceptional sanctification.

3.1.2. Vicarious Humanity

In adopting the idea that God becomes incarnate within our fallen humanity, and in becoming incarnate, Christ does not only take what is ours to make it his, but also really takes upon himself our guilt and sin, so that through his atonement[71] he might deliver us from evil and sanctify our human nature from within us.[72] By taking upon himself the form of a servant, Christ transfers to himself our corrupted fallen human nature.[73] The importance of the Nicene theology, according to Torrance, is its immense concentration upon the vicarious humanity of the incarnate Son.[74] Thus, the vicarious nature of the atonement lies in the humanity of Christ. Torrance says, 'The *vicarious humanity* of Christ thus became integral to the doctrine of the "atoning exchange" effected by him and in him between God and man.'[75]Christ's vicarious humanity makes the atoning exchange[76] possible as he identifies himself fully with us and acts in our place, so that he ministers not only the things of God to man but also the things of man to God. Anderson understands that while Christ is revealing to us in his humanity, reconciliation happens simultaneously in a corresponding movement from humanity to God in Christ's vicarious humanity. Anderson says,

---

71 According to Torrance, atonement is not to be understood only in terms of what happened at the Cross, but also in terms of the whole incarnate life of Jesus that was sin-bearing and redemptive. Thus the atonement is to be understood as having taken within the inner depths of the incarnate life of Jesus Christ, and not just as an external judicial transaction in his death on the Cross. See T. F. Torrance, 'Thomas Torrance Responds', in *The Promise of Trinitarian Theology*, ed. Elmer M. Coyler (Lanham: Rowman & Littlefield Publishers, Inc., 2001), 310.

72 Torrance, *The Mediation of Christ*, 74.

73 Torrance, *The Trinitarian Faith*, 161.

74 Ibid., 62.

75 Ibid., 4.

76 It is an exchange that through God's love 'Christ took our place that we might have his place, becoming what we are that we might become what he is.' It is also termed as reconciliation. See Torrance, *The Trinitarian Faith*, 179.

> The twofold significance of the vicarious humanity means that through the person of
> Christ all that belongs to the innermost being of God is revealed to us through Christ
> and all that is demanded of God from humanity is fulfilled through Christ.[77]

Torrance commends that Anderson has put vicarious humanity of Christ in its right perspective.[78] Thus, both the demand for justice through revelation and the fulfilment of justice are accomplished by the vicarious humanity of the Person of Christ. The correct understanding of Jesus Christ, says Torrance, should not be understood as God in man, but rather God as man. The humanity of Christ is not merely instrumental in the hands of God, but rather it should be understood in a personal and vicarious way, thus the immediate focus of the incarnation is centered on the humanity of Christ in our actual human existence.[79] Torrance emphasizes the importance of Christ's humanity in his vicarious act, he says,

> It was the whole man that the Son of God came to redeem by becoming man himself
> and effecting our salvation in and through the very humanity he appropriated from us
> — if the humanity of Christ were in any way deficient, all that he is said to have done
> in offering himself in sacrifice 'for our sakes', 'on our behalf' and 'in our place'
> would be quite meaningless.[80]

Because Christ is truly man, thus, he can act on our behalf through his vicarious humanity. Unless what Christ did on the Cross was the vicarious act of God in the ontological depth of human existence, then what took place on the Cross would have been in vain.[81] What Christ did and suffered in his humanity, he did and suffered for our forgiveness.[82] As the Mediator of our human response to God, Christ's vicarious humanity carries both meanings of representation and substitution. He does not only represent us, but also substitutes for us. Torrance says,

---

77   R. S. Anderson, 'Torrance as a Practical Theologian', in *The Promise of Trinitarian Theology*, ed. Elmer M. Coyler (Lanham: Rowman & Littlefield Publishers, Inc., 2001), 166.

78   Torrance, *Thomas Torrance Responds*, 322.

79   Torrance, *The Trinitarian Faith*, 151.

80   Ibid., 152.

81   Ibid., 142.

82   T. F. Torrance, *The Christian Doctrine of God, One Being Three Persons* (Edinburgh: T&T Clark, 2001), 249.

It will not do to think of what Christ has done for us only in terms of representation, for that would imply that Jesus represents, or stands for, our response, that he is the leader of humanity in humanity's act of response to God. On the other hand, if Jesus is a substitute in detachment from us, who simply acts in our stead in an external, formal or forensic way, then his response has no ontological bearing upon us but is an empty transaction over our heads. A merely representative or a merely substitutionary concept of vicarious mediation is bereft of any actual saving significance. But if representation and substitution are combined and allowed to interpenetrate each other within the incarnational union of the Son of God with us in which he has actually taken our sin and guilt upon his own being, then we may have a profounder and truer grasp of the vicarious humanity in the mediatorship of Christ, as one in which he acts in our place, in our stead, on our behalf but out of the ontological depths of our actual human being.[83]

If the vicarious humanity of Christ means only a simple representation, Torrance does not see it as sufficient in the efficacy of Christ's atonement, because representation does not include the ontological iden-tification with those that are represented. Thus, it is important to have the substitutionary element which involves an ontological exchange that it is Christ's humanity substituting our humanity. Torrance embraces both complementary conceptions of representation and substitution as the full understanding of vicarious humanity of Christ in atonement that Christ is one of us and acts on behalf of us.

Christ is seen as the embodiment of all our necessary salvific ingredients. By embodiment, Torrance means that all these salvific elements cannot be achieved apart from Christ or even found outside of him. All these elements are intrinsic to the incarnate Son. God's act of justification[84] and our human appropriation of it are both embodied in Christ who is the Mediator from God to man and at the same time man to God. Thus, justification was fulfilled in Christ from both sides, from the side of the justifying God and also from the side of justified man through

83   Torrance, *The Mediation of Christ*, 90–91.
84   According to Torrance, justification has a meaning of both forgiveness of sin and the bestowal of a positive righteousness through our union with Jesus Christ. See Torrance, 'Justification: Its Radical Nature and Place in Reformed Doctrine and Life', 227. In justification, Torrance comments that the objective and subjective aspects are both realized in the vicarious humanity of Jesus Christ. Justification is an objective act of the redeeming God and a subjective actualization of it in our humanity that is taken place in Christ. See Torrance, *Theology in Reconstruction*, 157.

his vicarious humanity.[85] It is in his vicarious humanity that we share his faith and faithfulness. It is clear in Torrance's theology that our faith is not ours, but rather his faith on our behalf, thus, our faith is implicated in his faith.[86] Christ is the great Believer who believes vicariously in our place and in our name.[87] In other words, it is Christ who believes God on our behalf, it is his faith in God that justifies us instead of our own faith that acts in the process of reconciliation.[88] However, whether it is our faith in Christ or the faith of Christ it becomes an issue of discussion. Gabriel Hebert published an article on *"Faithfulness" and "Faith"* in 1955, in it Hebert argues that on the basis of the Old Testament that *pistis Christou Iesou* should be interpreted as the faithfulness of Christ. Hebert equates the Greek *pistis* to Hebrew *emunah* and claims that in the Old Testament it is repeatedly used to mean the faithfulness of God.[89] Torrance responded favorably to Hebert's idea of the Hebraic references and says that since Christ is not only the incarnation of the Divine *pistis*, but also the embodiment of man's *pistis*, thus,

> the *pistis Iesou Christou* does not refer only either to the faithfulness of Christ or to the answering faithfulness of man, but is essentially a polarized expression denoting the faithfulness of Christ as its main ingredient but also involving or at least suggesting the answering faithfulness of man, and so his belief in Christ, but even

---

85   Ibid.

86   Torrance, *The Mediation of Christ*, Exeter, 93–94.

87   Torrance, *Theology in Reconstruction*, 156–157.

88   Ibid., 159.

89   In Romans 3:22 and several similar passages, Hebert says that he does not understand why 'through faith in Jesus Christ' is immediately followed by 'Unto all them that believe', it seems redundant. The Authorized Version 'through faith of Jesus Christ' is not intelligble enough. Thus he goes to the Greek equivalent Hebrew word *emunah* to find its Hebraic meaning and found that it carries the meaning of 'the faithfulness of God', thus, he suggests *pistis Christou Iesou* means 'the faithfulness of Jesus Christ'. Hebert uses Psalms 36 to illustrate that the Hebrew word denotes steadfastness and firmness which apply properly to God and not to man who is repeatedly characterized as physically frail, such as Isaiah 40:6-8 that all men are like grass and the grass withers and the flowers fall, and who is also morally unstable as in Psalms 36 where ungodly man flatters himself with his own eyes and his words are wicked and deceitful. Thus, faithfulness is not a quality or virtue of man. See G. Hebert, '"Faithfulness" and "Faith"', *Theology*, 58 (1955), 373–374.

within itself the faithfulness of Christ involves both the faithfulness of God and the faithfulness of the man Jesus.[90]

Torrance enhanced Hebert's idea further by including both the faithfulness of God and our faith in Christ as a polarized expression of interpretation, and our faith in Christ is somehow implicated in the faith of Christ. Karl Barth in his commentary *The Epistle to the Romans* employs a similar subjective genitive interpretation that it is through the faithfulness of God that we meet the Christ in Jesus.[91] To Barth, faith is the faithfulness of God.[92] Thus, faith never originates from man, it is not acquired, but given. Barth says, 'We do not demand belief in our faith; for we are aware that, in so far as faith originates in us, it is unbelievable.'[93] This theological understanding of faith clearly has its influence on Torrance in his biblical understanding of *pistis Christou Iesou*. Torrance's unique interpretation of *pistis Christou Iesou* encountered many criticisms. Professor Moule was probably the first to criticize that Torrance was on a false trail. Moule comments that though *pistis* in the New Testament carries a meaning of faithfulness of God as that expressed in the Old Testament, however, to say that *pistis Christou Iesou* includes mainly the faithfulness of Christ is to ignore all biblical data. Moule did not agree that the grammar indicates subjective genitive instead of objective genitive, and *pistis* in some passages clearly means believer's faith instead of Christ's faith or faithfulness. Moule's concern is that Torrance by his interpretation of *pistis Christou Iesou* seriously reduced the necessary reference to man's act of will in response to God's approach.[94] What Moule means is that even though our faith is objectively endowed by God, it has to be subjectively executed by us. In

---

90 In coming to this conclusion, Torrance did some grammatical exegesis on related *pistis Christou Iesou* occurrences in the New Testament (2 Thessalonians 2:13; Romans 1:17, 3:3, 21–25; Galatians 2:16,20,22). See T. F. Torrance, 'One Aspect of the Biblical Conception of Faith', *The Expository Times*, 68 (October 1956 - September 1957), 113.

91 K. Barth, *The Epistle to the Romans*, tr. Edwyn C. Hoskyns (London: Oxford University Press, 1975), 96.

92 Ibid.

93 Ibid., 99.

94 C. F. D. Moule, 'The Biblical Conception of "Faith"', *The Expository Times*, 68 (October 1956 - September 1957), 157.

reply, Torrance held his position. Though Torrance agreed that *pistis* may be used sometimes unmistakably with Christ as object, yet,

> It is not enough, however, to interpret Paul's language merely out of the rules of Greek grammar without careful and exact reference to his Hebraic background and thought...one tempted to forget that Paul was a Hebrew of the Hebrews?[95]

Torrance insists that based on the Hebraic references, the word *pistis* carries the meaning of the faithfulness of God, and which is the primary meaning of the interpretation of *pistis Christou Iesou.* Moule refutes that Torrance's view would be

> only that to reduce emphasis upon our faith in Him reduces – emphasis upon our faith! It is not the fact of the necessary existence of the two together that I was questioning; only the elimination of primary reference to our faith in the passages in question.[96]

Moule's main concern is whether we have an active role in our faith in Christ or it is reduced to a passive role. Both Hebert and Torrance built their argument mainly on the foundation of Hebraic references of the word *emunah*. This had drawn severe criticism from James Barr. In his book *The Semantics of Biblical Language*, Barr says that he is not interested in the discussion whether the faithfulness of God is related to the faith of man, but is simply interested to examine the linguistic arguments of Hebert and Torrance as both based their arguments on the correctness of their assessment of the Hebrew usage.[97] Barr provides a strong linguistic argument that both Hebert and Torrance were not making a linguistic judgment but rather a theological argument. The Hebrew word *emunah* denotes 'steadfastness' and 'firmness' that apply properly only to God and not to man is linguistically incorrect. He says that the Psalmist is simply comparing God and man and expressing his thought that God, unlike men, is steadfast and faithful. In differentiating the theological judgment and linguistical judgment, Barr says,

> If I may coin an example, a theologian might disapprove of the phrase 'The Devil is good', as being an 'improper' use of the word 'good', i.e. inconsistent with what the

---

95   Torrance, 'One Aspect of the Biblical Conception of Faith', 221–222.
96   Moule, 222.
97   J. Barr, *The Semantics of Biblical Language* (Eugene: Wipf & Stock, 1961), 161.

Devil in fact is; but linguistically there is nothing 'improper' unless the phrase is linguistically unusable in the usage of the time and group under discussion. If a Moslem calls 'great', it is absurd to deduce that the word 'great' is not used 'properly' when applied to a bus or a camel. Such a statement about the word 'great' would not be true, even if the user of the word himself thought theologically that only God was really great and buses and camels were quite slight things in comparison with him.[98]

Barr highlights the fundamental problem in Hebert and Torrance's Hebraic references of the understanding of *emunah* that what is 'proper' in theological judgment is different from what is 'proper' in linguistic judgment. Barr further used examples of 2 Kings 12:15 and 22:7 that the group of men acted in fidelity or trustworthiness *(emunah)* to indicate that the usage is not 'proper' has absolutely no linguistic validity. Barr says, 'The conception that the "proper" meaning of this root is only with reference to God is both wrong in itself and supported by an illegitimate confusion of theological and linguistic methods.'[99] Barr says that none of the linguistic arguments advanced by Hebert or Torrance are valid linguistically. Regarding Torrance's unique polarized expression, Barr comments,

> I need only reiterate how extremely misleading the presentation of linguistic evidence in favour of this understanding has been and how completely wrong it is to suppose that the description of 'polarized expression' can be justified by the argument from Hebrew usage which has been made. At the point of identification of the 'polarized expression', which is in a way the summit of the article, as at so many other points linguistic discussion is simply abandoned and replaced by theological discussion.[100]

It is true according to the detailed semantic analysis of the Hebrew word *emunah* by Barr, Torrance's interpretation is more theological than linguistical.[101] Barr clearly points out the mistake that 'it is quite wrong to suppose that *emunah* is used properly *only* when used of the faithfulness of God.'[102] However, the issue still has not been settled without knowing whether *pistis Christou Iesou* is of subjective genitive or ob-

---

98   Ibid., 162–163.
99   Ibid., 163.
100   Ibid., 203-204.
101   Ibid., 204.
102   James Barr sides with Moule in his criticism that Torrance himself is making an inappropriate Hebraic reference. See Barr, 165–166.

jective genitive. This is probably an unsolved open issue, many[103] simply leave both possibilities open. Due to the fact that most of the modern translations other than the Authorized Version translate *pistis Christou Iesou* as 'faith in Christ Jesus' rather than 'faith of Christ Jesus' by using objective genitive, Torrance claims that these translations are inadequate.[104] D.W.B. Robinson suggests that the genitive after *pistis* is not objective on the ground of general Greek usage through his studies on the word *pistis* in the New Testament.[105] However, Professor John Murray in his book *The Epistle to The Romans* sees that the apostle is careful to define faith (Romans 3:22) as faith in Jesus Christ. Though the notion of the faithfulness of Christ is in view, there is no warrant it has to be the case here.[106] He says wherever there is faith, there is always the faithfulness of God and of Christ that faith is directed and from which it takes its origin.[107] Thus, Professor Murray says our faith always involves this so-called polarized situation, which differs from polarized expression of Torrance, that it does not carry two different meanings at the same time, our faith is originated from the faithfulness of Christ. However, *pistis Christou Iesou* only carries a meaning of our active faith in Christ. Murray argues that the

---

103 Joseph Fitzmyer says the sense of genitive is disputed, though he favors objective genitive. See R. E. Brown, J. A. Fitzmer, and R. E. Murphy (eds.), *The New Jerome Biblical Commentary* (Upper Saddle River, N.J.: Prentice Hall, 1990), 839–840. Witheringon simply comments that Romans verse 22 can be interpreted either as through faith in Christ or through faith/faithfulness of Christ, thus both subjective and objective genitives are offered as possibility of interpretation. See B. Witherington III, *Paul's Letter to the Romans* (Grand Rapids: Eerdmans, 2004), 101.

104 Torrance, 'One Aspect of the Biblical Conception of Faith', 113.

105 Bishop Robinson lists Gal. 2:16 (twice), 20,22; Rm. 3:22, 26; Phil 3:9; Eph 3:12 eight passages to investigate what he calls grammatical problem - what is the force of the genitive after *pistis*? Is it objective or subjective; the semantic problem - what is the meaning of the word *pistis*? and the theological problem - what is Paul talking about? Is he telling us the work of Christ, or the response of man, or, as Hebert and Torrance would have liked it, about both in the same breath? See D. W. B. Robinson, *Justification and the Faith of Jesus* <http://www.presenttruthmag.com/archive/XLIV/44-3.htm> accessed 1 Nov, 2004.

106 J. Murray, *The Epistle to the Romans* (Grand Rapids: Eerdmans, 1968), 111.

107 Ibid., 373.

faith that is directed to Christ cannot consist in any respect in the faithfulness of Christ himself... Therefore, once it is demonstrated that the faith of the believer is reflected on in the passages concerned, that means that the faithfulness of Christ is not included in the faith that is reflected on. In other words, it is one thing to say that our faith always involves a polarized situation; it is another thing altogether to say that faith is a polarized expression. It is this confusion that the argument has sought to expose.[108]

I think Professor Murray has correctly put the meaning of the faith of Christ and the faith of man in correct perspective according to the linguistic structure of *pistis Christou Iesou*. It is an objective genitive that we play active role of our faith in Christ which is expressed through *pistis Christou Iesou*, however, this faith actually originates from the faith and faithfulness of Christ which is not directly reflected by the phrase *pistis Christou Iesou* but is found in other passages. Torrance's theological view is well respected, the only issue is his biblical inter-pretation of the text, he tends to read into the text than read from the text with his theological spectacles, and this reflects his weakness in her-meneutics or his style of hermeneutics.

Faith of Christ certainly plays a vital role in our faith that we are not justified by our own initiated faith in Christ, but rather justified by the faith of Christ.[109] Since it is not our faith that makes us justified before God, Torrance argues that we are justified by the grace of Christ alone, as it eliminates any possibility of human credits such as natural goodness and knowledge that we may bring towards our own salvation. However, it does not mean that there is no natural knowledge, it simply means that natural knowledge is unable to earn us salvation, as no one can go to the Father but by Jesus Christ.[110] Christ's role as the high priest through his vicarious humanity forms the fundamental understanding of the in-stitution of sacraments.[111] As the high priest, he ministers not only things of God to us but also things of man to God.[112] Christ's baptism in the

---

108 Ibid.
109 Torrance, *Theology in Reconstruction*, 160.
110 Ibid., 162–163.
111 By becoming one of us, Christ's vicarious humanity takes on the role of priesthood. And through his priestly ministry on behalf of us, it becomes the focus of our worship of the Father. See Torrance, *Theology in Reconciliation*, 110–112, 175–176.
112 Torrance, *Theology in Reconciliation*, 156.

Gospel is seen by Torrance as a baptism 'into repentance', that he came to bear our sins not merely in a forensic way, but to bear our sins intrinsic in his humanity. Thus, Christ's baptism was a baptism of vicarious repentance for us.[113] According to Torrance, vicarious repentance is necessary because corrupted human beings are unable to repent. He says,

> As fallen human beings, we are quite unable through our own free-will to escape from our self-will for our free-will is our self-will. Likewise sin has been so ingrained into our minds that we are unable to repent and have to repent even of the kind of repentance we bring before God. But Jesus Christ laid hold of us even there in our sinful repentance and turned everything round through his holy vicarious repentance.[114]

Since human beings are unable to acquire repentance, and have faith in God, all these are given to us by Christ on behalf of us through his vicarious humanity. Torrance makes it clear that it is God's election, rather than man's selection that make us acceptable to him. Justification and faith are given by God, rather than acquired by man. In fact, according to Torrance, every aspect of our salvific requirements are embodied in the humanity of Christ, which include our new birth, our regeneration and our conversion in addition to our faith and subjective justification through Christ. We are sanctified, cleansed, and redeemed through his vicarious humanity in his incarnation. Thus, Torrance says,

> In other words, our new birth, our regeneration, our conversion, is what has taken place in Jesus Christ himself, so that when we speak of our conversion or our regeneration we are referring to our sharing in the conversion or regeneration of our humanity, brought about by Jesus in and through himself for our sake. In a profound and proper sense, therefore, we must speak of Jesus Christ as constituting in himself the very substance of our conversion, so that we must think of him as taking our place even in our acts of repentance and personal decision, for without him all so-called repentance and conversion are empty.[115]

Torrance takes a holistic approach that Christ embodies both the act and fact of our salvation in his own humanity,[116] and it is also embodied in

---

113   Torrance, *The Mediation of Christ*, Exeter, 94–95.
114   Ibid., 95.
115   Ibid., 97.
116   Torrance, *The Trinitarian Faith*, 156.

himself in a vicarious form our responses to God.[117] Thus, our whole being is assimilated in the vicarious humanity of Christ. The very purpose of Christ's vicarious humanity is to penetrate into our sinful past in our human existence and undo our sin.[118] In becoming one of us, Torrance says that Christ made human will as his very own, and bent it back into obedience to the will of God.[119] For what Christ did in his humanity was not for his own sake but for our sake, he was the Word of God given to man, but he was also man who responded to the Word of God in faith and obedience.[120]

Torrance's understanding of the vicarious humanity of Christ does not limit its meaning applicable only to the classical epistemology and soteriology, it also addresses contemporary social ethical issues. In responding to Anderson's question,

> Torrance has recently affirmed the practice of ordaining women for pastoral ministry in the church based on the 'new humanity of Christ.' Would he be equally affirming of the inclusion of gay Christians in the church, if not also for ordination? And if not, why not?[121]

Torrance says that the importance of the biblical moral requirements has to be respected, homosexual behavior is clearly condemned. However, through the unlimited love of his vicarious humanity, Christ died for them that they may be saved. So, Torrance does not have objection for the inclusion of gay Christians in the church if they have been like that from birth, but they should not engage in any homosexual practices. Torrance suspects that most of the gay people are not born with deviated genes but rather they become gay due to their sinful lust.[122] It is crucial to note that Torrance's theology is never far from his practical pastoral concern for the church.

It is clear that Torrance contributes most of the vicarious activities and functions to the humanity of Christ. However, what role does the divinity of Christ play in the vicarious act in the Person of Christ?

---

117 Torrance, *The Mediation of Christ*, 97.
118 Torrance, *The Christian Doctrine of God*, 215.
119 Torrance, *Theology in Reconstruction*, 157.
120 Ibid.
121 Anderson, 'Torrance as a Practical Theologian', 177–178.
122 Torrance, 'Thomas Torrance Responds', 323–324.

Torrance sees that the vicarious act is also divine, it is the vicarious act of God himself. He says,

> unless the atoning exchange effected through the suffering and death of Christ was indeed the vicarious act of God himself in order to bring about our salvation, then what took place in his crucifixion would have been in vain. Only if the Lord God himself were directly and immediately engaged in the vicarious passion of his incarnate Son could it be the vicarious means of redeeming and liberating the creation.[123]

That is to say, it is both the vicarious humanity and divinity of Christ that effect our salvation. If vicarious functions can be achieved by a man, then, God may simply create a perfect human being to save the world. However, because only God can save, thus, God has to be part of the vicarious act of Jesus. Torrance says,

> If he were not divine, he could not act divinely, and if he were not Creator, he would not be able to save and recreate humanity. 'No creature can ever be saved by a creature'.[124]

Though the emphasis is on the vicarious humanity of Christ, there is no denial of the importance of his divine vicarious act. The humanity and divinity form an indissoluble oneness in the Person of Jesus Christ.[125] Thus, the whole work of Jesus is referred to the Person instead of either of his two natures.

---

123 Torrance, *The Christian Doctrine of God*, 247.
124 Torrance, *The Trinitarian Faith*, 138.
125 Torrance, *The Mediation of Christ*, 78.

3.1.3. Anhypostasia and Enhypostasia

Anhypostasia[126] and *enhypostasia*[127] are two different ideas developed by the patristic fathers to conceptualize the role of human nature in the person of the historical Jesus Christ. Torrance says that these concepts were illuminated under the guidance of Cyril of Alexandria and further developed by Severus of Antioch and John of Damascus.[128] Macleod says that the concept of anhypostasia was implicit in the Apollinarian thesis that Christ did not have a human mind, and it was explicit in the Christology of Cyril of Alexandria that the Logos united himself only to the human nature but not to a man, and the term occurred during the sixth century and was employed by Leontius of Byzantium (485-543).[129] According to Torrance, *anhypostasia* is that, 'the human nature of Christ had no independent per se subsistence apart from the event of the Incarnation, apart from the hypostatic union.'[130] Torrance says that by anhypostatic, the human nature does not have independent hypostasis or subsistence apart from hypostatic union in the incarnation. He claims that this concept rules out any adoptionist error.[131] The purpose of the concept is to avoid any impression or possibility that a fourth person was created in the incarnation. Schaff explains:

---

126 Andrew Purves, student of Torrance, defines anhypostasia as a doctrine that asserts that Christ's human nature has its reality only in union with God, having no independent existence apart from the incarnation. See A. Purves, 'The Christology of Thomas F. Torrance', in *The Promise of Trinitarian Theology*, ed. Elmer M. Coyler, (Lanham: Rowman & Littlefield Publishers, Inc., 2001), 59. Donald Baillie understands anhypostasia as an ancient doctrine that Christ is not a human person, but a divine Person who assumed human nature without assuming human personality, Christ human nature is impersonal. See Baillie, *God Was In Christ*, 85.

127 Andrew Purves defines enhypostasia as a doctrine that asserts that Christ's human nature was nevertheless a real and specific existence in which Jesus has a fully human mind, will, and body. See Purves, Andrew, *The Christology of Thomas F. Torrance*, 59. Donald Baillie understands enhypostasia as proposed by Leontius of Byzantium that the humanity of Christ is not impersonal but is personalized in the Divine Logos, thus it is in-personal. See Baillie, *God Was In Christ*, 90.

128 Torrance, *The Christian Doctrine of God*, 160.

129 Macleod, *The Person of Christ*, 200.

130 Torrance, 'The Atonement and The Oneness of The Church', 249.

131 Torrance, *The Christian Doctrine of God*, 160.

> The divine nature is therefore the root and basis of the personality of Christ. Christ himself, moreover, always speaks and acts in the full consciousness of his divine origin and character; as having come from the Father, having been sent by him, and, even during his earthly life, living in heaven and in unbroken communion with the Father. And the human nature of Christ had no independent personality of its own, besides the divine; it has no existence at all before the incarnation, but began with this act, and was so incorporated with the pre-existent Logos-personality as to find in this alone its own full self-consciousness, and to be permeated and controlled by it in every stage of its development.[132]

Schaff understands that it was the Logos that assumed the humanity, therefore, there was no interruption of his divine nature before and after the incarnation. The same divine Logos now became the incarnate Son and still acted as he was before the incarnation in sharing the unbroken communion with the Father. On the other hand, the human nature of Christ did not have any existence prior to the incarnation, it cannot exist independently apart from Logos or his divine nature. Thus, the human nature does not have its own personality, and is incorporated with the pre-existent Logos' personality. There are different interpretations about the exact meaning of *anhypostasia*. According to Baillie, it simply means that 'in Christ there was no distinct human personality, but divine Personality assuming human nature.'[133] Baillie says that Cyril's position was that there was no man Jesus existing apart from the divine Logos, the human element in the incarnation was simply human nature assumed by the eternal Christ. The human nature of the Son is impersonal. This is the position that was accepted by the church and regarded orthodox.[134] This view has to be distinguished from Apollinarianism, which was condemned, that it does not deny the existence of human nature of Christ. It just explains that the human nature cannot exist independent of the incarnate Christ. Negatively, it repudiates Nestorianism that the divine nature is clearly prominent in Christ. However, some see it differently. Erickson criticizes,

> The major point of anhypostatic Christology is that the man Jesus had no subsistence apart from the incarnation of the Second Person of the Trinity. It supports this thesis

---

132   P. Schaff, *History of The Christian Church*, 3 (Grand Rapids: Eerdmanns, 1995), 757–758

133   Baillie, *God Was In Christ*, 85.

134   Ibid., 86.

by denying that Jesus had any individual human personality. The problem with this position is that to think of Jesus as not being a specific human individual suggests that the divine Word became united with the whole human race or with human nature; taken literally, this idea is absurd.[135]

Anhypostasia does indicate that Christ assumed only human nature but not a human. Mackintosh shares a similar understanding of the Christology of Cyril of Alexandria that Christ assumed human flesh, yet he was not an individual man.[136] This challenges Torrance's idea on the humanity of Christ that Christ became not only real man but also a man.[137] Though there is a danger in Cyril's theology which resembles the theory of Apollinarius by declaring Christ's human nature impersonal, Mackintosh says that Cyril escapes the danger by his insistence on the completeness of human nature assumed by the Logos.[138] The crucial point in the conception of *anhypostasia* is that it is not the conversion of the divinity into flesh, but the assumption of the humanity into God. Heppe says,

> In essentials all Reformed dogmaticians are agreed that the divinity of Christ is not really the divine nature but the person of the Logos,... and that the humanity of Christ is the human nature common to all human personalities.[139]

However, many would like to see a more significant role of human nature in the Person of Jesus Christ. They say that the human nature in *anhypostasia* is reduced to unconscious and impersonal. Mackintosh says, 'for no real meaning could be attached to a human "nature" which is not simply one aspect of the concrete life of a human person.'[140] To counteract the idea of impersonal Christ, the concept of *enhypostasia* was imported that the human nature of Christ, though not an individual, is individualized as the human nature of the Son of God.[141] Thus, the human nature of Christ is in-personal. Torrance says,

---

135   M. J. Erickson, *Christian Theology* (Grand Rapids: Baker, 1994), 732.
136   H. R. Mackintosh, *The Doctrine of The Person of Jesus Christ* (Edinburgh: T. & T. Clark, 1912), 205.
137   Torrance, 'The Atonement and The Oneness of The Church', 245.
138   Mackintosh, *The Doctrine of The Person of Jesus Christ*, 207.
139   H. Heppe, *Reformed Dogmatics* (Grand Rapids: Baker Book House, 1978), 414.
140   Mackintosh, *The Doctrine of The Person of Jesus Christ*, 207.
141   Macleod, *The Person of Christ*, 202.

By 'enhypostatic', however, it was given a real concrete hypostasis or subsistence within the hypostatic union – it was enhypostatic in the incarnate Son or Word of God – which ruled out any Apollinarian or monophysite error.[142]

By affirming the personality of the human nature of Christ, the doctrine rules out heresies of monophysitism and Apollinarianism. However, Torrance's definition creates an impression that Christ humanity is a concrete hypostasis, and it is this human hypostasis that is indwelling in the person of Christ. In reality, it is not a union of two persons, but a union of two natures in the hypostatic union of the incarnate Son. Torrance tends to personalize *nature* as *person*. It is evident that he employs the same word on Trinity, Torrance says,

> That is to say, our approach to the doctrine of the Holy Spirit must be from his inner '*enhypostatic*' relation to the triune being of God.[143]

> The Father and the Son coinhere in one another in the one being of God, but, as Epiphanius and Didymus would have it, coinhere 'enhypostatically', that is in respect of their distinct personal or hypostatic realities each of which is 'whole God'.[144]

Torrance extends the meaning of *enhypostatic* beyond the subsistence level of person. Apparently, the relationship between *nature* and *person* is similar to that of *Person* and *Being*, and this confuses the characteristics and uniqueness of *nature*, and creates an impression that God does not only assume a human nature but also assume a human person that it becomes a divine person uniting to a human person.

The whole spectrum of Christ's humanity, according to Torrance, rests on both conceptions of *anhypostasia* and *enhypostasia*, and these two different thoughts are inseparable.[145] Torrance thus applies this so-called patristic couplet[146] of *anhypostasia* and *enhypostasia* to both atonement and revelation. He says,

---

142   Torrance, *The Christian Doctrine of God*, 160.
143   Torrance, *The Trinitarian Faith*, 208.
144   Ibid., 233.
145   Torrance, 'The Atonement and The Oneness of The Church', 249; Torrance, *The Christian Doctrine of God*, 160.
146   Ibid., 144.

If anhypostasia alone were to be applied to the atonement then Aulen's view[147] would be right and proper, but that would mean that the deed of atonement would be a pure act of God over the head of man, and not an atoning act involving incorporation. Certainly the atonement is the act of God, supremely act of God, but that act of God is incarnated in human flesh, giving the human full place within the divine action issuing forth out of man's life. On the other hand, if enhypostasia alone were to be applied to the atonement without anhypostasia then atonement would have to be understood as a Pelagian deed placating God by human sacrifice. The inseparability of anhypostasia and enhypostasia in application to the death of Christ is thus supremely important for it means that while atonement is throughout act of God for us, we are to understand it as act of God done into our humanity, wrought out in our place and as our act.[148]

Here the doctrine of anhypostasia and enhypostasia applied to the incarnation applies equally to our understanding of revelation. Revelation is entirely God's action but within it, it is the concrete action of Jesus Christ that mediates revelation and is revelation. Revelation is supremely God's act but that act is incarnated in our humanity, giving the human full place within the divine action issuing forth our of man's life. The human obedience of Jesus does not only play an instrumental but an integral and essential part in the divine revelation.[149]

When Torrance employs these terms of *anhypostasia* and *enhypostasia* in his theology, he uses it simply to reflect the nature of *divine* and *human* without ever addressing the intricacy of these conceptions which

---

147 According to Professor Aulen, there are two commonly contrasted theories on atonement, one is 'objective' which is represented by Anselm, and the other is 'subjective' which is represented by Abelard. The objective atonement states that God is the object of Christ's atoning work, and is reconciled through the satisfaction made to His justice. The subjective atonement describes a doctrine that atonement as essentially in a change taking place in human being rather than a changed attitude from God. Aulen proposes another alternative that he calls 'dramatic' atonement that it carries the idea as a Divine conflict and victory. It is God who reconciles the world to Himself, and is at the same time reconciled. The difference between the dramatic atonement and objective atonement is that God takes active work continuously from first to last in dramatic atonement, while in the objective type, the act of Atonement has its origin in God's will, but is, in its carrying-out, an offer made to God by Christ as man and on man's behalf, and is regarded as discontinuous divine work. In dramatic atonement, God combats and prevails over the evil and God reconciles with the world. See G. Aulen, *Christus Victor*, tr. .G. Hegert (London: Society for Promoting Christian Kowledge, 1937), 18–22, 72.

148 Torrance, 'The Atonement and The Oneness of The Church', 250.

149 Torrance, *Theology in Reconstruction,* 130–131.

embody both divine and human natures. Torrance further expands the meaning of patristic couplet to the analogy between Christ and his Church. He says,

> Within the orbit of this whole relation between Christ and His Church and within the analogical form which it demands, we may seek cautiously to apply the conceptions of *anhypostasia* and *enhypostasia* to the Church. Anhypostasia would then mean that the Church as Body of Christ has no *per se* existence, no independent *hypostasis*, apart from atonement and communion through the Holy Spirit. *Enhypostasia*, however, would mean that the Church is given in Christ real *hypostasis* through incorporation, and therefore concrete function in union with Him.[150]

By using it on the relation between Christ and the church, Torrance breaks away from the traditional definition and uses it freely and subjectively. The relationship between Christ and the church clearly does not share the same essence in meaning as that of the human nature in the Person of Christ. The central issue of *anhypostasia* and *enhypostasia* rests not on whether Christ has only one nature or two unique natures, but rather which of the two natures is primary, and how does the created human nature fit with the eternal divine Person. Logically, the eternal has the primacy over the temporal, this is the Alexandrian thinking. However, Christ who walked on earth is clearly a historical person, his humanness is undeniable according to the Antiochene thinking. The Chalcedonian two nature formula seems to be a compromise to both parties by stressing Antiochene two unique natures and Alexandrian one Christ. However, the emphasis of the human nature in the Person of Christ remains a disagreement between the East and West since. Torrance tries to solve this dilemma by affirming that these two opposite thoughts of *anhypostasia* and *enhypostasia* are inseparable.[151] This approach is common in Barth's dialectical theology. Barth himself tries to embrace both *anhypostasia* and *enhypostasia*, he says *anhypostasia* asserts the negative that Christ's human nature has no existence apart from the divine Person, and while *enhypostasia* asserts the positive that Christ has his own human personality. However, Barth's definition of *anhypostasia* and *enhypostasia* does not provide a clear distinction of the

---

150 Torrance, 'The Atonement and The Oneness of The Church', 254–255.
151 Ibid., 249; Torrance, *The Christian Doctrine of God, One Being Three Persons*, 160.

uniqueness of these two conceptions.[152] Logically, Barth is holding an anhypostatic view that the manhood of Christ is not self-existent, and is only the predicate of his Godhead.[153] Though Barth does not want to speak of Christ being 'man' but not 'a man' as the doctrine of *anhypostasia* traditionally requires,[154] he is holding an impersonal view. He says,

> what the eternal Word made His own, giving it thereby His own existence, was not a man, but man's nature, man's being, and so not a second existence but a second possibility of existence, to wit, that of a man.[155]

Barth's impersonal view[156] is similar to what was taught by Torrance in his earlier years at Auburn. Torrance was teaching the doctrine of *anhypostasis* by emphasizing the Divine personality that the man Jesus has no existence apart from becoming flesh, because it is the Word who became flesh. It is God who is personally present in the flesh, and God is the subject of the actual human being and existence.[157] Torrance taught that humanity is the predicate of Christ's divinity,[158] and Christ's personality is divine.[159] Torrance even embraced in his teaching that Christ had assumed human nature, but not a human person, that he did not assume human personality.[160] Later, when Torrance began to emphasize the fullness of Christ's human identification with us, he adopted

---

152 K. Barth, *Church Dogmatics*, tr. G.T. Thomson, 1/2 (Edinburgh: T & T Clark, 1957–1981), 163.

153 Ibid. 162.

154 A. F. Buzzard, 'Some Questions About the Chalcedonian Christology of Karl Barth', *A Journal from the Radical Reformation*, 5/2 (Winter 1996), 33.

155 Barth, *Church Dogmatics*, 1/2, 163.

156 Barth understands that the true being of Christ is concealed in His human form. Christ's deity is His true being, and His humanity does not have the equivalency of a true being. See Barth, *Church Dogmatics*, 4/1, 163. Barth also does not agree that there are three personalities in the Godhead. There is only one personality of God, it is Father, Son and Holy Spirit. And this is the personality revealed by the Son of God. Three personalities according to Barth would imply three gods, or three independent entities. Thus, the person of Jesus Christ can have only one personality, which is divine. See Barth, *Church Dogmatics*, 4/1, 205.

157 Torrance, *The Doctrine of Jesus Christ*, 113.

158 Ibid., 114.

159 Ibid., 124.

160 Ibid., 125.

Kierkegaard's dialectical approach of accepting both views even though they are not complementary to each other. Instead of synthesizing two different views as that of Hegel's dialectical approach, he simply accepts the paradoxical theological assertions. It is clear that Torrance received strong influence from Kierkegaard in his use of dialectic interpretation of truth by promoting that theological assertions are paradoxical in character, and rejecting the synthesis of two contrarieties.[161] This, however, runs against Torrance's own idea of 'the logic of endorsement', that he adopts from Polanyi, which lies in the very heart of science.[162] Torrance argues that since belief arises within a context of commitment to reality, it entails a judgment that excludes a divergent belief. When one accepts one way of looking at things, he at the same time destroys other alternate conceptions.[163] *Anhypostasia* and *enhypostasia* are two different conceptions about the role of human nature in the Person of Christ, it should not be easily taken as two complementary conceptions without ever addressing its incompatibility and conflicts.

3.2. The Historical Jesus

In the twentieth century, few theologians or biblical scholars could avoid the discussion of the historical Jesus. The quest which started in the eighteenth century by Reimarus and had reached it height in the late nineteenth and early twentieth centuries. Torrance confronts this issue in his Auburn lectures and other writings such as *Space, Time and Resurrection* and *Reality & Evangelical Theology*. The historical Jesus plays an important role in Torrance's theology of incarnation because the historicity of the man Jesus is paramount to the Christian faith. Torrance claims that we cannot know the Truth if it is not historical, as the Truth

---

161 F. E. Harrison, Geoffrey W. Broniley, and Carl F. Henry (eds.), *Wycliffe Dictionary of Theology* (Peaboy, Mass.: Hendrickson Publishers, 1999), 166.

162 T. F. Torrance, 'The Framework of Belief', in *Belief in Science and in Christian Life: the Relevance of Michael Polanyi's Thought for Christian Faith and Life*, ed. T.F. Torrance (Edinburgh: Handsel Press, 1980), 15.

163 Ibid., 14.

intervenes decisively in our human existence. The Truth of God cannot be separated from the historical Jesus as history belongs to the essential nature of this Truth.[164] Christian faith is simply a myth if it is not solidly anchored in the fact that Jesus Christ is a historical reality according to the Gospels.

3.2.1. Background

At the beginning of the eighteenth century, the traditional unchallenged Christian faith had come under attack on two fronts: Pietism and Enlightenment. Pietism emphasizes one's own spiritual progression through a deeper personal and subjective experience with God and belittles the objective validity of the affirmations of faith. On the other hand, Enlightenment elevates the human reasoning to such a status that it becomes the only objective criteria to measure the Christian faith. It becomes an instrument to eliminate any doctrines that are incompatible with the scientific laws. This Cartesian-Kantian dualism, according to Torrance, separates the world into a physical realm of external reality and a mental realm of internal reality. The physical realm is open to investigation according to the laws of nature while the mental realm is open to investigation in terms of meaning.[165] Pietism takes up the mental realm and seeks only internal meaning, while Enlightenment seeks only empirical data in its investigation under the guidance of the natural laws. Each excludes the other in its pursuit of the quest of the historical Jesus. These conditions set the stage for the challenge of the traditional belief of the historical Jesus in the Gospels.

The quest for the historical Jesus was first proposed by Hermann Samuel Reimarus in his writings *On the Resurrection* and *On the Intention of Jesus and His Disciples* in the eighteenth century. These writings have since changed the landscape of the studies of the historical Jesus. Reimarus believes that the Apostles in writing down the acts of Jesus are presenting their own views and thoughts, he says,

---

164 T. F. Torrance, *Theological Science* (Edinburgh: T&T Clark, 1996), 208–209.
165 Torrance, *Space, Time and Resurrection*, 40.

they (Apostles) never claim that Jesus himself said and taught in his lifetime all the things that they have written. On the other hand, the four evangelists represent themselves only as historians who have reported the most important things that Jesus said as well as did.[166]

Reimarus questions the sources of the Gospels and believes that the Gospels are colored by the early church's own interpretation and he would accept only those genuine Jesus material that have escaped the church's redaction. He thus tries to separate the preaching of Jesus from that of the early church and finds that Jesus was preaching nothing more than moral ethics and duties intended to please God. The work of Christ to Reimarus is simply a continuation of the Judaistic tradition with no new revelation apart from the Old Testament. Christ is only human and he did not introduce any new doctrine or mystery.[167] The central theme in Reimarus' quest is that Christ wanted to be the Messiah, and that he wanted his message about the kingdom of heaven to be heard, thus persuaded people to help him to establish an earthly Jewish kingdom. The Messianic secret found in the Gospels simply arouses people to spread the Messianic news that Jesus is a worldly deliverer.[168] Reimarus says, 'Jesus did not project the purpose of his kingdom of God beyond the Jewish nationhood.'[169] Christ's divinity is thus denied, and his last supper is nothing other than a simple Passover meal.[170] How did a dead Christ become the founder of the new religion? Reimarus suggests that his disciples had a change of heart.[171] When the disciples saw their hope crushed, they turned their griefs into creating a spiritual figure and altered the entire historical event and made Jesus a suffering savior of all mankind. In further destroying the myth of Christian faith, Reimarus questions the historical validity of the resurrection of Christ. He argues,

For if that (resurrection) actually had taken place, it would have been able to effect an inner conviction of the truth of Jesus' resurrection both among the Jews and the

---

166 H. S. Reimarus, 'Concerning the Intention of Jesus and His Teaching', in *Reimarus: Fragments*, ed. Charles H. Talbert (Philadelphia: Fortress Press, 1970), 64.

167 Ibid., 88.

168 Ibid., 151.

169 Ibid., 102.

170 Ibid., 118.

171 Ibid., 129.

heathen of that day, and the apostles would not have needed to do anything else in proof of their testimony than refer everywhere to this event known by the whole city, or insist upon Pilate's letter and seal concerning the guarding of the tomb by soldiers until the third day.[172]

Reimarus sees that Matthew was the only Apostle who gave the account of Christ's resurrection, and it is not supported by other testimony.[173] Therefore, Matthew's account is untrustworthy. Reimarus suggests, 'It was entirely possible that Jesus' body was secretly stolen from the tomb at night and that it was buried in another place.'[174] The basis for rejecting supernatural elements is 'because miracles are unnatural events, as improbable as they are incredible, requiring as much examination as that which they are supposed to prove;'[175] In Reimarus' mind, the whole biblical account of Jesus is simply a fabrication by the early church. Later, Lessing attempts to separate the historicity of Christian origin from that of the truth of the Christian religion by rejecting the historical facts and at the same time maintaining Christian faith. Talbert summarises Lessing's position,

> Even if Reimarus's objections were unanswerable and the factual claims of the Christian religion unsupportable and the biblical accounts hopelessly contradictory, Christianity contains an intrinsic truth, immediately grasped by the believer, which retains its validity whether or not Jesus actually rose from the tomb after three days.[176]

In addressing these apparently contradicting positions, Lessing argues that the subjective personal experience is factual and Christianity existed before Evangelists and Apostles who wrote the events. This understanding is reflected in Lessing's dictum 'accidental truths of history can never become the proof of necessary truths of reason'[177] Torrance comments that the eternal truth which is part of history is regarded by Lessing as the picture book of reality.[178] Lessing also assumes that a

---

172 Ibid., 154.
173 Ibid., 155.
174 Ibid., 161.
175 Ibid., 230.
176 C. H. Talbert (ed.), *Reimarus: Fragments* (Philadelphia: Fortress Press, 1970), 30–31.
177 Ibid., 31.
178 Torrance, *The Doctrine of Jesus Christ*, 66–67.

Hebrew or Aramaic primitive gospel was lying behind all three Synoptic Gospels and regards that the Fourth Gospel belongs to an entirely different category and is not regarded as a historical source on the same level as Synoptic Gospels.[179] Schleiermacher, according to Torrance, in the nineteenth century concludes that the Christ of faith is not the Jesus of history, it is only the Christ-idea that lives on in human civilization and in the church,[180] and suggests that Christ appeared to be really dead when he was taken down from the cross, however, nothing can be certain in regard to it; and Christ's resurrection was only a reanimation after apparent death.[181]

Strauss tries to show that despite what Reimarus had taught Christianity was not the result of fraud. However, he downplays the supernatural elements in the Scripture.[182] Strauss believes that the individual stories and sayings in the Gospels were fragments that had received artificial treatment from the Evangelists.[183] Though Strauss favors the kind of criticism generated in the examination of the historicity of the Gospels, he is concerned that Scripture is losing its divine aspect and is dragged through dust and filth.[184] At the beginning

---

179 Talbert, 35.
180 Torrance, *The Doctrine of Jesus Christ*, 66–67.
181 A. Schweitzer, *The Quest of the Historical Jesus* (Minneapolis: Fortress Press, 2001), 61–62.
182 Talbert, 36.
183 R. E. Brown, Joseph A. Fitzmer, and Roland E. Murphy (eds.), *The New Jerome Biblical Commentary*, (Upper Saddle River, N.J.: Prentice Hall, 1990), 1135.
184 D. F. Strauss, 'Hermann Samuel Reimarus and His Apology', in *Reimarus: Fragments,* ed. Charles H. Talbert (Philadelphia: Fortress Press, 1970), 45; In the understanding of the historical account of the Scripture, Strauss said, 'If it was not God that caused thunder and lightning when the law was given on Sinai, who is to tell us that there was lightening and thunder at all? It is the same writer who tells us that it was God; and without further ado we believe him in one respect and refuse him in another. If Jesus did not rise miraculously on the third day, who will guarantee us that his corpse was sought in the tomb and not found? If the apostles on the first Pentecost did not speak in foreign tongues because of a supernatural capacity, how do we know at all that they spoke any differently from ordinary people? In this way, as soon as one becomes aware that he may not drop the miraculous character and retain the historical in a miraculous story, and that the miracle is not merely a husk that can be stripped away without further ado, but that a good deal of the history remains clinging to it;' See Strauss, 48. When one wants to remove the miracle from the history, Strauss realized that only a skeleton would

of the twentieth century, William Wrede published *The Messianic Secret* in which he insisted that Evangelist Mark did not give an objective account of the historical Jesus, and questioned why on several occasions in the Second Gospel that Jesus urged his disciples not to speak of his Messiahship to others. Wrede concluded that Jesus was not claiming the Messiahship. The Messiahship concept was not a Markan invention but was a tradition apparently present at that time which Mark wove it into his gospel.[185] The Second Gospel thus is not a simple biography but a theological presentation of Jesus.[186] At the same time, Adolf Harnack taught that Christ is our brother and teacher. The central point in Christian faith is not the Person of Christ, who is put aside when his work is done, but is the revelation of the Father.[187]

The landscape is further changed when Rudolf Bultmann teaches that it is almost impossible to know anything about the life of Jesus. However, to have faith in Christianity does not necessary demand any historical

---

remain. Reimarus and other critics advocated the use of agreement and contradiction in their Quest, yet they themselves embodied the same contradiction. Strauss said, 'No matter what contradictions he [Reimarus] conjures up without malice in other cases! Jesus is supposed to have preached with an irresistible enthusiasm the purest, most glorious, truly divine doctrine of morals and religion, the commandments of love of God and of one's neighbor, of purification of heart and of self-denial; yet he himself was an ambitious man concerned with earthly things. The apostles are supposed to have known best that there was not one single word of truth in the news of their master's resurrection, since they themselves spirited his corpse away; yet regardless of this they are supposed to have spread the same story with a fire of conviction that sufficed to give the world a different form.' See Strauss, 49. Strauss found that Reimarus's arguments were difficult to harmonize. It would not be possible for the Evangelists to imagine a thing, to believe it and to proclaim it to the world with conviction and enthusiasm without having it be historically valid.

185 Achtemeier, Paul J., Joel B. Green and Marianne Meye Thompson, *Introducing the New Testament: Its Literature and Theology* (Grand Rapids: Eerdmans, 2001) 57; Cranfield highlights that in Mark 1:34 & 3:12, the demons were silenced by Jesus. And in Mark 1:44, 5:43, 7:36, 8:26, silence was ordered after the miracles. Thus, Wrede exaplains that Jesus neither claimed to be the Messiah nor was recognized as such by his disciples during his life. See C. E. B. Cranfield, *The Gospel According to Saint Mark*, (Cambrigdge: Cambridge University Press, 1959), 78.

186 Brown, *The New Jerome Biblical Commentary*, 1135.

187 Torrance, *The Doctrine of Jesus Christ*, 66–67.

validity of Jesus. Bultmann believes that authentic faith can never be based on historical research, what is important is the personal encounter of the living Christ. The Gospels have to be demythologized in order to get to the roots of the historical facts.[188] According to Bultmann, many passages in the Scripture bear the mythological impressions. He says,

> To demythologize does not mean to eliminate these passages, but rather to make them understandable to modern thought. Demythologizing is not a process of subtraction, but a method of interpreting Scripture.[189]

In order to meet modern scientific requirements, many mythological passages in the Scripture have to be interpreted in such a way that they cause no conflict with modern science. The historical person of Jesus Christ, according to Bultmann is a combination of history and myth. Jesus is historical because of his human parents, he is mythical because he is the pre-existent Son of God. This combination clearly presents many difficulties to Bultmann.[190] Thus, he tries to emphasize the article of faith instead of the historicity of the event. Supernatural events can only be interpreted through the article of faith by removing its mythology. Thus, resurrection, according to Bultmann, is not a historical event, it is the first disciples who came to believe in the resurrection.[191] Bultmann's extremeness in divorcing the historical Jesus from the Christian faith disturbed his followers who initiated a New Quest by 'postulating the same authentic existence in response to the historical Jesus as to the kerygma.'[192] Prior to Bultmann, Albert Schweitzer produced a masterpiece of the development of *The Quest of the Historical Jesus* in early twentieth century. At the end of his quest, he concluded that the Jesus of Nazareth, who came as the Messiah, preached the Kingdom of God, and died, never existed. It is because the historical image of Jesus had been shattered by the concrete historical problems

---

188 G. E. Ladd, *A Theology of The New Testament* (Grand Rapids: Eerdmans, 1993), 10–11.
189 R. Bultmann, *Modern Theology: Selections from Twentieth-Century Theologians*, ed. E.J. Tinsley, (London: Epworth Press, 1973), 64.
190 Ibid., 69.
191 Ibid., 77.
192 Ernst Kasemann, Bultmann's student, started the New Quest in his 1954 essay on the *The Problem of the Historical Jesus*. See Ladd, 11.

which came to the surface one after the other.[193] Jesus is simply at our time a stranger and an enigma, at best he is a moralist.[194] Dodd says that old school of historical criticism such as that of Reimarus tries to seek the historical fact by eliminating the intrusive material of the early church without heeding the interpretation given by the early church. They are seeking facts in human history without its associated meanings and the facts are to be assured scientifically within the boundary of natural laws. The new school of criticism such as that from Bultmann, on the other hand, puts aside any historicity, and emphasizes only the religious aspects of the Gospels.[195]

3.2.2. Criticism of the Quest

One major problem, according to Torrance, of the historical criticism lies in the dualism between absolute space and time and the creaturely world, which leads to a deism in which God is seen as remote and passive.[196] The detachment of the created world from its Creator erects its own framework to receive and comprehend knowledge of God, and the result is that it projects its own thought upon God. As this dualism grows, its own independent frame of rationality further undermines the reality of history and makes the relation between Christian faith and history ambiguous.[197] Lessing's thesis that 'the accidental truths of history can never become the proof of necessary truths of reason', according to Torrance, means that even though we can apprehend the eternal truth within the space and time, it cannot be demonstrated historically.[198] Thus, Lessing creates a huge ditch between the historical fact and the Christian faith. Torrance says,

> Thus there grew up in modern Protestant theology a sharp antithesis between phenomenal status and eternal ideas, so that it came to be widely held that the spatial

---

193   Schweitzer, 478.
194   Ibid., 486.
195   C. H. Dodd, *History and the Gospel*, (London: Hodder & Stoughton, 1964), 9.
196   T. F. Torrance, T.F., *Space, Time and Incarnation* (London: Oxford University Press, 1969), 40.
197   Ibid., 41.
198   Ibid., 42.

and temporal ingredients in theological concepts must be entirely discarded if we are to succeed in jumping over the chasm between them. But to retain spatial and temporal ingredients in the structures of our thought, as D.F. Strauss taught, is to remain stuck in mythology.[199]

There is a wedge between phenomenal status and eternal ideas, and if one wants to retain temporal and spatial elements, faith simply becomes myth. Thus, Bultmann tries to demythologize all biblical myths and discard all the unhistorical elements in favor of personal faith, that is to say, one can speak about God only in the detachment from the creaturely and worldly content. The present is a timeless instant and the past has vanished forever and it bears no meaning for us, thus historical Jesus bears no significance and the future offers us no existence. Torrance sees that the whole emphasis of Bultmann in space and time is that it is 'for me' here and now,[200] the personal subjective spiritual encounter with Christ is all that matters. Torrance argues that it is not only our subjective experience of Christ's saving grace but also the historical reality of the Person of Christ who walked among us as a human being forms the basis of the revelation and our faith.[201]

Torrance criticizes that both Bultmann and Lessing employ dualist view in their understanding of history. Bultmann is only concerned with the inner life and personal experience which is spaceless and timeless, while Lessing puts his attention in the objective empirical reality in space and time. Torrance says that these two views have only tangential relation to each other.[202] However, the self-communication of God, Torrance argues, reveals to us through the concrete spatio-temporal events in the history, otherwise, 'God would not have established relations with *us*, and the Gospel would have no relevance at all for men and women of flesh and blood.'[203] Thus, Christian faith cannot act independently apart from the historical event of the Gospels, in other words, personal experience of God cannot be real unless the historical event of the life of Jesus Christ according to the Gospels is a reality.

---

199   Ibid., 42–43.
200   Ibid., 48–49.
201   Torrance, Theology in Reconstruction, 134.
202   Torrance, Space, Time and Resurrection, 40.
203   Ibid., 178.

Incarnation and resurrection, according to Torrance, are two ultimate events in the history of mankind, through which God interacts with man, and within which the whole Gospel is to be interpreted and understood.[204] Apart from these two pillars, no truth or faith can be attained. The self-revelation and self-communication of God are reflected through the incarnation and resurrection, and it provides the objective framework within which the Gospel is to be understood.[205] Both carry their own authority, and bear their own proof.[206] Torrance says, both incarnation and resurrection are acts of God within the natural structures of space and time, thus they could be open to rational examination within its own structures of natural and human sciences.[207] However, since they are acts of God, they are explicable only from the grounds in God. These ultimates are not open to verification within the natural structures in which they share. These ultimates constitutes the 'boundary conditions' that it can be open to higher and wider level of reality for explication. This is similar to various levels operated in natural science that each is open to the meta-level above it. Thus, incarnation and resurrection are rational historical events understood not in terms of natural laws and principles, but rather through a higher level of rationality based on the transcendent and creative reality of God.[208]

Theologians, according to Torrance, should disregard historical criticism, instead, they should focus their interest in the apostolic tradition incorporated in the New Testament which bears witness to the saving acts of God in Jesus Christ. The self-proclamation of Christ and the apostolic proclamation of Christ together create an impact on the historical memory of the primitive church, and these two cannot be detached.[209] The New Testament as a whole is a testimony to the historical event of the life and teaching of Jesus Christ, and carries a framework of objective meaning. When the writings of the New Testament are fragmented for various historical critical studies in isolation from one anther at the linguistic and phenomenal level, their conceptual coherence

---

204 Ibid., 20.
205 T. F. Torrance, Reality and Evangelical Theology (Downers Grove: InterVarsity Press, 1999), 105.
206 Torrance, Space, Time and Resurrection, 19–20.
207 Ibid., 22
208 Ibid., 22–23.
209 Ibid., 10–11.

with one another is disintegrated. And this destroys the basic unity in the New Testament and its meaning.[210] Torrance says that when we examine the New Testament, we examine not only purely the historical picture but also the witness of a living faith in Jesus. According to the witness, there is a complete agreement on the fact that Jesus is the Christ, the Son of God. Thus, in the New Testament, there is an interweaving of the Jesus of history and the Christ of faith. Torrance says,

> There is never in all the writings of the New Testament any disagreement or even hesitation in the matter of Christology. There is complete agreement on the fact that he is the Christ, the Son of the Living God, the Saviour or Redeemer... Thus we have in the New Testament inextricably woven together the Jesus of history and the Christ of faith, the Christ set forth under two aspects and with stress sometimes one more on one than the other, but never the one without the other.[211]

In refuting Bultmann's idea, Torrance says that the testimony of the apostles and the New Testament do not separate the Jesus of history from the Christ of faith, because, as far as the testimony goes, the Jesus of history is the Christ of faith. Thus, one cannot see the Jesus of Nazareth apart from the light of the whole New Testament. It is only through the people who encountered the risen Jesus Christ that he is presented to us. Torrance believes that it is not the historical fact that is made the primary judgment of the historical Jesus, but rather the fact in the interpretation through the witnesses that these historical facts are grounded. [212] Torrance teaches that we may not begin with the historical Jesus and proceed to apostolic Christ in our formulation of Christology, but rather we must take the Christ as understood by the apostles to interpret the Jesus of history. Only then the historical Jesus becomes intelligible, and the messages of the Synoptics can be properly understood. [213] The historical data for Christology could not shine on its own, it depends on the witnesses. To Torrance, the self-testimony of Jesus is not the same as the testimony to Christ which proclaimed and witnessed by his believers through the indwelling of the Spirit. Thus, the objective revelation is proclaimed through the subjective illumination,[214] such that

---

210 Ibid., 14.
211 T orrance, *The Doctrine of Jesus Christ*, 9.
212 Ibid.
213 Ibid.,11.
214 Ibid., 33.

the interpretation of the witness would become meaningful and of significance. Theological interpretation is important, Torrance says, 'The historical Jesus only can be theologically explained and understood, never just historically or psychologically.'[215] The Gospels are not dogmatic presentation of Jesus but rather a narrative from believers who witnessed him as the Messiah. It is not a historical report but the work of believers confirming their witnesses by pointing to the historical person Jesus. The Gospel of John is no different than the Synoptics, as both share essentially and materially the same message that Christ is the Object of the Christian faith.[216] It is the faith of the disciples rather than the self-consciousness of Jesus that brings forth the Christian religion.[217]

Regarding Wrede's *Messianic Secret*, Torrance says, Jesus reveals himself through the hiddenness of his life. Jesus reveals himself progressively, and is in step with his actual historical circumstances in his life. By doing that, according to Torrance, Jesus maintains his true historical humanity because any other way would destroy the full significance of his humanity, a humanity that is to be demonstrated through his atonement and the death on the cross. That is to say, a full and sudden declaration of his divine nature as Logos would hinder his identity as full human person. The double behaviour of Jesus to reveal himself explicitly through his concealment has much to do directly with his position as the Mediator because as a God-man, he is both hidden and revealed.[218] Torrance points to the fact that God makes himself known through both veiling and unveiling of himself to his people: proclaiming Jesus' identity from the house-tops would destroy this balance and preclude any actual revelation. Torrance says that although Jesus is God, his divinity has to be revealed through his humanity, which entails certain degree of hiddenness.[219]

Many critics charge that the life of Jesus is not mentioned by Paul's epistles. It is true that Paul's epistles seldom mention the life of Jesus, it is because, according to Torrance, Paul's interest centers in Christ's death and resurrection. Besides, for Paul, human life is a form which is

---

215 Ibid.,12.
216 Ibid., 24–25.
217 Ibid., 25.
218 Ibid., 33.
219 Ibid., 34.

inadequate to Christ's real being, thus instead of the full picture of the historical Jesus, Paul instead presents the risen and living Lord whose majesty is greater than the earthly life which is now past. The whole point according to Torrance is that the Apostles do not so much remember Christ as believe in him.[220]

Resurrection, as understood by Torrance, is a historical event because it is based on the New Testament witnesses. The evidence from these witnesses can be handled and tested appropriately.[221] Torrance uses Thomas as an example that he is very skeptical at first, but as soon as he encounters the resurrected Christ, he is lifted to a higher level of reality.[222] Two separate pictures of the historical Jesus and the risen Jesus together give a stereoscopic depth of the reality of the person of Jesus. If we remove the dimension of resurrection from the New Testament, the actual picture of the historical Jesus disintegrates because we remove the basic clue in the apprehension of Christ in his objective reality.[223] Since the resurrection has decisively molded the writing of the Evangelists, which gives rise to the tradition of the early church, it is impossible to dig beneath the evangelical presentation of Jesus Christ to get at the so-called *raw facts* upon which it relies.[224] This is to say, it is meaningless to search the real historical Jesus behind the back of the Gospels as presented by the Evangelists. There is simply nothing left in the life of Jesus by rejecting resurrection as a historical event because the content of the resurrection is Jesus Christ.[225]

Resurrection is an event in historical time. However, it is something from above that bursts through our limited structure of time and space, and it is not something that can be caught within these structures, and can be interpreted by secular historians who can only work within it. Resurrection is a new kind of historical happening, unlike ordinary historical event, it will not crumble away into dust, it overcomes and resists corruption and decay, it runs not backwards but forwards.[226] Thus, the event has to be interpreted apart from our existing natural structures, and

---

220 Ibid., 55
221 Torrance, *Space, Time and Resurrection*, 37.
222 Ibid., 164.
223 Ibid., 167.
224 Ibid., 168.
225 Ibid., 60.
226 Ibid., 87–89.

from a higher vantage point of view. The problem in understanding the resurrection event by the historical critics, according to Torrance, lies in the reductive analysis that causes the semantic disintegration into meaningless fragments, imposing an artificial framework in order to restore coherence. Torrance says,

> he is tempted further to tamper with the evidence, tailoring the data, to fit his theory – surely the one unforgivable sin in any kind of scientific procedure – as, for example, those scholars appear to do who are determined to make out that St. Mark's Gospel was not composed under the impact of the resurrection![227]

Thus, historical criticism has only limited validity. It can lead to the destruction of the Scriptural meaning, and tear the empirical and theoretical components of New Testament witness apart, and impose its own subjective interpretation upon the witness.[228] Torrance argues that in order to understand the Holy Scriptures, we must hear God speaking in person that we must constantly give ear to God's Truth. Since the Reformation, there is a revival by Luther, Calvin and Barth to interpret the language and statements of the Scriptures by restoring the connection between the Word written and the Word spoken. Torrance sees that the written and spoken Word become the battle ground of the historical criticism especially in the modern obsession with the linguistic and literary form analysis.[229] Torrance charges that historical critics operate with a disruption of the natural inherence of vision and hearing. He argues that the biblical revelation has come down in the form of written documents, and these documents cannot be torn apart by the oral traditions without its meaning being undermined.[230] That is to say, the written word is the final form of the revelation, it cannot be dissected by the oral traditions without its authority being challenged. The oral traditions, instead of upholding, basically take over the authority from the written form of the revelation, and this is against the visionary and auditory character of the biblical language. Oral tradition from our natural memory is a database, yet it is not organized. However, on the other hand, the written language is an organized in-depth structure of our

---

227 Ibid., 168.
228 Ibid., 169.
229 Torrance, *Reality and Evangelical Theology*, 77–78.
230 Ibid., 78.

natural memory.[231] The modern criticism of the Synoptics and the documentary hypothesis (such as Q document), Torrance says, depend more on the criteria of oral form which preceded the composing of the Gospels than the literary form, thus, they assign many empirical and theological elements to the creative working of the early Christian community instead of Christ himself.[232]

3.2.3. Critical Analysis

One major problem in Torrance's apologetical defense of the historicity of the events in the life of Jesus is that there exists no common ground between Torrance and the historical critics. Torrance presupposes incarnation and resurrection as two absolute ultimates that cannot be validated or proved, and unless it is seen from the perspective above the natural structures of time and space, one is unable to observe its reality. Other defenders of the Gospels are more willing to accommodate the weakness of human rationality. Frank Morison's *Who Moved the Stone?*[233] and Val Grieve's *Verdict on the Empty Tomb*[234] both use the existing recognized judicial system as the common ground to affirm the validity of the Empty Tomb that Christ had risen from the death. Unfortunately, due to the transcendental nature of the events, Torrance does not want to argue within the natural structure. Thus, most of his arguments are presuppositional in nature, and not many critics are willing to accept it as a valid argument. Coyler comments,

> And for Torrance, the fact and significance of resurrection have a quite literally unforgettable character that was indelibly impressed upon the memory of the Apostles and the early Christian community in such a way that, in spite of in-accuracies regarding the details, what is of real consequence has been faithfully and adequately preserved in the New Testament witness.[235]

---

231 Ibid.
232 Ibid., 80.
233 F. Morison, *Who Moved The Stone?* (Grand Rapids, Mich.: Zondervan, 1958).
234 V. Grieve, *Verdict on the Empty Tomb* (n.p.: Church Pastoral Society, 1976).
235 E. M. Colyer, The Nature of Doctrine in T.F. Torrance's Theology (Eugene: Wipf and Stock Publishers, 2001), 67.

It is true that Torrance does not bother to address the discrepancies of the narrative details of the resurrection because his interest lies very much in the theological significance of the event instead of the detailed historical sequence. According to Torrance, the Scripture may be faulty and errant,[236] however, what it witnesses remains truthful to the historical event as God is using an imperfect human tool for his inerrant revelation.[237]

There is a similarity between Torrance and Barth in their dealing with biblical historical criticism by avoiding the questions that the critics raise specifically about the narratives of the Gospels. Kent says that Barth uses a very vague description of the resurrection in the commentary on *Romans*, and a more traditional description in *Church Dogmatics* with bodily nature of the 'appearances' in place, and Barth asserts that these narratives described an event beyond the reach of historical research or description.[238] Kent says, 'This amounts to saying that the appearances of Jesus had a "non-physical physicality", and that the state of the tomb was that of a "non-empty emptiness".'[239] This is also true in Torrance's theology that he is not able to confront the critics on purely historical basis but tries to defend from a theological perspective, and argues that the historical Jesus can only be explained and understood theologically[240] instead of historically. Thus, form criticism and redaction criticism have no effect on the interpretation of the historical Jesus, this raises the eyebrows of many. Zahrnt makes the point bluntly, says,

The powerful stream of dialectical theology had swept past the problem of history, as though two hundred years of critical historical study of the Bible and the sources of Christianity had never taken place, and as though Gotthold Ephraim Lessing, Johann Salomo Semler, Ferdinand Christian Baur, David Freidrich Strauss, Julius Wellhausen, Johannes Weiss, Albert Schweitzer, Adolf von Harnack, and all the others had never lived or thought.[241]

---

236   T. F. Torrance, Divine Meaning (Edinburgh: T&T Clark, 1995), 10.
237   Ibid.
238   J. H. Kent, The End of The Line (London: SCM Press, 1982), 124.
239   Ibid.
240   Torrance, The Doctrine of Jesus Christ, 12.
241   H. Zahrnt, *The Question of God*, tr. R.A. Wilson (New York: Harcourt, Brace & World, 1969), 215.

Could the dialectical theology, which accepts paradoxical facts and ideas as a profound way of understanding the truth, of Barth and Torrance make the two hundred years of historical critical study worthless? Torrance clearly does not see its value, other scholars do not agree. Dodd disagrees strongly with those historical critics[242], however, disregarding all errors he finds in the historical criticism, Dodd still sees a value in historical criticism.[243] Martin Hengel realizes that the understanding of history is quite different now than that in antiquity, however, it would be a distortion to denounce the work of modern historians.[244] He says that there is no historiography without heuristic interests.[245] Thus, the problem of biblical historical criticism lies not in the critical methods or criticism itself, but rather in its presuppositions. The main presupposition of the Quest, according to Dodd, is that the Gospels are simply regarded as common secular literature that contains faults and contradictions. Dodd points out that Gospels were not only written with historical or biographical motives, they were written 'from faith to faith'. In other words, they were written primarily as confessions of faith in Jesus Christ, who died on the cross and was raised on the third day. The writings were direct witness accounts of this particular event in history. Thus, Gospels are not only religious writings but also historical in

---

242 The Gospels, Dodd claims, did not come from imaginaries of the early church but from an established Christian tradition based on the proclamation of what had been witnessed historically. It is a historical tradition presented in eschatological terms. Apart from the Gospels, one could still recover the historical tradition of Jesus occupied by the early Church. However, Dodd regards the Gospels as the primary source and the crystallization of the tradition in narrative form. See Dodd, 52. In addressing the influence of the early Church on Christian writings, Dodd challenges the assumption, which many critics had employed in the Quest, that the community created the kerygma. He suggests that it was the kerygma that created the community, and not the community created the kerygma. Dodd says that unless 'something happened of which the apostolic preaching gives an account, we can assign no adequate reason for the emergence of the Church.' See Dodd, 53.

243 Regarding the value of form criticism, Dodd says, 'it enables us to study our material in fresh groupings, which point to distinct strains of tradition, preserved from various motives, and in some measure through different channels, and to compare these strains of tradition, much as we compared Mark and 'Q', in search of convergences and cross-correspondences.' See Dodd, 63.

244 M. Hengel, *Earliest Christianity* (London: SCM Press, 1986), 52.

245 Ibid.

essence.[246] Torrance, by rejecting the whole historical criticism, is unable to appreciate the benefits of these criticisms in enhancing the understanding the Scripture.

3.3. Hypostatic Union

Hypostatic union is understood generally as a doctrine of the substantial union of the divine and human natures in the person of Jesus Christ. The doctrine was formally accepted at the Council of Chalcedon in 451, even though the phrase *hypostatic union* was not used, its concept was expressed in Cyril's third letter to Nestorius[247] and in the words 'the property of each nature being preserved and coalescing in one *prosopon* and *hypostasis*.'[248] The characteristics of the concept of two natures in one person are clearly reflected in the Tome of Leo, it says,

> For each of the natures retains its proper character without defect; and as the form of God does not take away the form of a servant, so the form of a servant does not impair the form of God…the Lord of the universe allowed his infinite majesty to be overshadowed, and took upon him the form of a servant: the impassible God did not disdain to become passible, and the immortal one to be subject to the laws of death.[249]

Thus, whatever the words said and deeds done by the person of Jesus, they must always be attributed to the whole person. Whatever the properties that belong to either nature, it must also be said that they belong to the whole person.

---

246 Dodd, 11.

247 In the letter, Cyril says that the Word of God was united to the flesh by hypostasis, that this person is both God and man. He rejects conjunction by dignity or authority or power, because it does not sufficiently indicate the union of two natures. See Cyril of Alexandria, 'The Third Letter of Cyril to Nestorius', in *Christology of the Late Fathers*, ed. Edward R. Hardy (Philadelphia: The Westminster Press, 1954), 349–358.

248 J. D. Douglas, *The New International Dictionary of the Christian Church* (revised edn, n.p.: Regency Zondervan, [1986]),.496.

249 Leo, 'The Tome of Leo', in *Christology of the Late Fathers*, ed. Edward Hardy (Philadelphia: The Westminster Press, 1954), 364.

3.3.1. Hypostatic Union and The Person of Christ

According to Torrance, it is the love of the Triune God towards his creature that actualizes the hypostatic union. In the union he gives himself to us in the person of Jesus Christ who is both God and man, and through his vicarious humanity, he assumes his mediatorial and re-conciling activities for us.[250] The doctrine of hypostatic union, Torrance says, is a belief that the divine nature and the human nature are being united in the person of the incarnate Son in such a way that both are neither separated from one another or confounded with one another. Thus neither nature suffers loss or change through relation to the other. That is to say, in the hypostatic union the human nature of Jesus Christ is taken up, established, secured and anchored for ever in its undiminished integrity in the Son of God.[251] It is also a union between uncreated rationality and created rationality, between uncreated and created word, so that it is through the rationality of the creaturely human word that the Son mediates God's Word to mankind.[252] Torrance maintains that the hypostatic union itself is the heart of the revelation, and it is only through the incarnate Son, the Truth is proclaimed and demonstrated. Christ does not come only to communicate the Truth to men, but to live as the Truth among men, and the Truth is enacted in the midst of our untruth.[253] He not only reveals the word from God, but also reveals himself as Word of God. In the hypostatic union, Christ acts as one of us and represents all of us before God, and also acts as God to us. Thus, Christ becomes a true Mediator as both divine and human are embodied in him. In Christ, God turns grace towards us and makes himself open to us, and summons us to be open toward him.[254] It is through hypostatic union that we may understand the Truth as God himself who communicates to us in the language that we can understand, as Christ did not come to us apart from his own self-revelation in his Act and Being. Christ reveals to us that his Being is his Act in his Being and his Act is his Being in his Act. His Act and Being dynamically inhere in one another.[255] Thus, one cannot regard

---

250 Torrance, *The Mediation of Christ*, 75–76.
251 Ibid., 80–81.
252 Torrance, *Reality and Evangelical Theology*, 91.
253 Torrance, *Theological Science*, 143.
254 Ibid., 143.
255 Ibid., 131; Torrance, *The Doctrine of Jesus Christ*, 4.

God's revelation to man in Christ or man's response to God in faith just in terms of what Christ does, but also in terms of what Christ is. The objectivity of the reality of Truth cannot be separated from the subjectivity of the reality of the Person of Jesus Christ.[256]

The identity of God's Word and Person is the central characteristic of the Truth, and the reception and understanding of this Truth must be analogous to its twofold nature. Yeung suggests that in accordance with Torrance's theology, 'the message is not received except in personal relation to the Truth, and personal communion with the Truth does not take place apart from the reception of the message.'[257] It is through the hypostatic union that the Truth is related to us and we are received by the Truth. Hypostatic union entails reconciliation such that we are justified and sanctified in Jesus Christ.[258] Torrance argues that in the hypostatic union, we are justified because the Son has made himself our brother, and by being our brother, he has made us sons of the Father. Through his Sonship, Christ reveals God to us and reconciles us to God. And as the Mediator, Christ takes upon himself the punishment due to our transgressions.[259] Not only does Christ stand in our place as our substitute and representative, he also lives an obedient life and fulfills the divine act of righteousness. Christ is not only the embodiment of God's act of justification, but also the embodiment of our human appropriation of it.[260]

The hypostatic union which is regarded as God's economic condescension, according to Torrance, becomes an eternal subsistence of the Son and that his union with humanity is eternal.[261] That is to say, Christ's temporal humanity becomes an eternal reality. Torrance speaks favorably of Rahner's idea[262] that he believes Jesus is not simply God in general, but the Son who is man and only he is man in the Trinity as the second divine person, God's Logos. Thus, it is the hypostatic union that

256 Torrance, *Theology in Reconstruction*, 134.
257 J. H. K. Yeung, *Being and Knowing: An Examination of T.F. Torrance's Christological Science* (Hong Kong: Jian Dao, 1996), 107.
258 Torrance, *The Mediation of Christ*, 75–76.
259 Torrance, 'Justification: Its Radical Nature and Place in Reformed Doctrine and Life', 229.
260 Torrance, *Theology in Reconstruction*, 157.
261 Torrance, *The Doctrine of Jesus Christ*, 190.
262 Torrance says that Rahner returns to the classical Greek view. See Torrance, *Theological Science*, 89.

defines Christ as the second Person, it is also his human nature that defines him as the second Person. Thus, it is in the economy that the Logos is revealed to us as the second Person, Rahner says,

> it is only through a hypostatic union as such that a single divine person, as distinct from the other divine persons, can have his own proper relation to the world. For only in such a union is there actualized what is proper to the person, the personality, the "outward" hypostatic function. Now there is only one hypostatic union, that of the Logos;[263]

That is to say that since the second Person is known through his hypostatic union, this hypostatic union will be part of the him in his relation with his creation and with his Being. And this hypostatic union, according to Torrance, is dynamic in nature that it is not a static relation but a dynamic union between God and man running throughout all Christ's historical life from birth to resurrection[264] and beyond. However, John Walvoord disagrees that Christ as the second person in the Trinity is only defined by his incarnation, he says that even before the incarnation, Christ had already distinguished himself from the Father and the Spirit. Walvoord claims that in the Old Testament, Christ appeared frequently in the character of the Angel of Jehovah even though he did not take up any human or angelic attributes, or involve in any change or addition in his nature.[265] Since the Scripture is the witness of the self-disclosure of God himself, thus, one cannot deny that the second Person must also be manifested in the Old Testament, though it may be less prominent than that in the New Testament.

3.3.2. Hypostatic Union and Trinity

In his writings, Torrance, though not explicitly but nevertheless implies two different understandings of the doctrine of hypostatic union. The concept is originally assigned to the understanding of the union of two distinct natures in the person of Jesus Christ, however, Torrance extends

---

263 K. Rahner, *The Trinity*, tr. Joseph Donceel (London: Burns & Oates, 1970), 23–25.
264 Torrance, *Theological Science*, 216.
265 J. F. Walvoord, *Jesus Christ Our Lord* (Chicago: Moody Press, 1969), 106–107.

the meaning to include the consubstantial relation within the Triune God. He says,

> The patristic concepts of a "consubstantial relation" or a "hypostatic union" between the incarnate Son and God the Father may properly be regarded as disclosure models in this sense, for they serve as conceptual lenses or as interpretative instruments for ever-deepening and ever-widening understanding of God's self-revelation in Jesus Christ.[266]

Thus, in Torrance's theology, the concept of hypostatic union is not limited to the understanding of the two natures of Christ, he also sees that the concept derives from the consubstantial communion within the Trinity. Torrance says,

> The hypostatic union is grounded in, derived from and is continuously upheld by what is called the 'consubstantial communion' within the Holy Trinity, that is, the mutual indwelling or coinhering of Father, Son and Holy Spirit as three Persons of one and the same Being in God. That is a union in which divine nature and human nature are united in Christ in such a way that there is no diminishing or impairing of his divine nature and no diminishing or impairing of his human nature.[267]

That is to say, the essence of the hypostatic union in the Person of Jesus Christ is actually a reflection of the consubstantial communion within the Holy Trinity. The two natures of Christ are each distinct by itself, so are the three Persons in Trinity. Thus, there is a strong implication in Torrance's theology that the relationship between *nature* and *person* is in essence similar to that of *Person* and *Being*. Hypostatic union is no longer restricted to the unique understanding the two natures in the Person of Christ, it extends from the understanding of the person of Christ to that of the Triune God who is three Persons in One Being. By forming such a close relation between the hypostatic union in the Person of Christ and the hypostatic union in Trinity, Torrance risks a danger of creating four persons in the Godhead by implicating hypostatic union as a union of persons instead of natures.

The existence of the three divine Persons, according to Torrance, indicates not only different modes of existence in their distinctiveness, but also hypostatic interrelations which belong intrinsically to the Triune

---

266 Torrance, *Reality and Evangelical Theology*, 117–118.
267 Torrance, *The Mediation of Christ*, 75.

Being that they coinhere in each other. It is thus the ontic relation between the divine Persons which defines what they are as Persons.[268] In general, Torrance employs the phrase *hypostatic union* to mean the union of two natures in Christ, however, it is easily applied to the union in Trinity when the innermost divine nature of the Triune God is addressed. Hypostatic union acts as a bridge that the Father is revealed himself through Christ, and Christ is revealed as the Son by the Father. Thus, we come to know the Father, the Son and the Holy Spirit, that God is three Persons in One Being and One Being in three Persons. This, according to Torrance, forms the basis of the understanding of the doctrine of *perichoresis* which is a refined form of thought that helps us to understand the mutual indwelling of Father, Son, and Spirit. It demonstrates that three Persons mutually indwell in one another and coinhere in one another while at the same time each remains distinct from one another.[269] Torrance accuses Luther of distorting the concept of *perichoresis* by transferring it from its applicable scope from Trinity to hypostatic union, and developing a notion of the coinherence of the divine and human nature and violating the distinction of two separate natures through the deification of Christ's humanity.[270] Unfortunately, Torrance himself is basically sharing a similar idea by assigning hypostatic union to both Trinity and the person of Christ. Since the hypostatic union of Trinity clearly entails the concept of *perichoresis*, when it is applied to the hypostatic union of two natures, it automatically evokes the idea of mutual coinherence and implies the communication between the divine nature and the human nature in the Person of Christ. The logical result is that it violates the Chalcedonian formula that each nature remains distinct from one another.

In the hypostatic union, we can come to realise not only empirical events, but also the deep meaning of reality, which is God Himself. The knowledge of the Father and the knowledge of the Son cannot be separated, for we cannot know the Son apart from the Father and the Father apart from the Son because the Son is of one and same nature and Being as the Father. As the fullness of the Father is in the Son, and the Son is

---

268   Torrance, *The Christian Doctrine of God*, 157.
269   Ibid., 102.
270   Torrance, *Space, Time and Incarnation*, 32.

the whole God.[271] Thus, the hypostatic union is the access point to the knowledge of God because it is both in God himself and in our creaturely existence. It is the place where God the Father reveals himself through his self-giving to us in Jesus Christ his Son within the human structures and conditions of time and space. And at the same time, the knowledge that God gives to us in his Son is from his own ontological being according to his divine nature. That is to say, it is the proper way to know the Father through the Son, and the knowledge of the Father is thus both godly and precise.[272] The knowledge of God in this way does not mean that we can comprehend God. God is infinite and boundless and cannot be comprehended by our limited human capacity. We cannot embrace all the knowing of God within our finite conceptions and definitions as God eludes the grasp of our minds. However, Torrance appeals to Hilary in arguing that God nevertheless leaves something of himself within our grasp, that we are able to believe, to apprehend, and to worship him.[273] It is through piety and godliness that the knowledge of God arises and takes shape in our mind and this knowledge is maintained through the experience of worship, prayer, holiness and godliness.[274] Torrance says, we can know God only if God brings us into communion with him in his inner relations of his own being, and this can be done only through the incarnate Son.[275] According to Torrance, in apprehending God, we do not mean that we can bring the totality of God into our comprehension, but it means that we know God as we are known of God in the sense that we are seized by his reality.[276]

The Son of God unites himself to human nature so completely that by living out his divine nature within our human life he reveals something that is of the most inner secret of his own divine life as the Son of the Father. By revealing to us his own nature as the Son, he also reveals the nature of the Father. Thus, according to Torrance, it is the conviction of the Nicene church that it is only through the incarnate Son that the true knowledge of God is revealed within the grasp of human under-

---

271 Torrance, *The Trinitarian Faith*, 52.
272 Ibid., 53.
273 Ibid.
274 Ibid., 54.
275 Ibid.
276 T. F. Torrance, *God and Rationality* (London: Oxford University Press, 1971), 22.

standing.[277] The focus on the mutual knowledge of God the Father and the Son, according to Torrance, should not detract from the reality and prominent role of the Holy Spirit in the Triune God. It is only through the communion of the Holy Spirit who is sent by the Father through the Son that we may actually partake in the relation of the Son to the Father.[278]

3.3.3. Hypostatic Union and Homoousion

According to Torrance, *homoousion* has an inseparable bond with the hypostatic union because the incarnation constitutes the epistemological centre as well as the ontological centre, that our knowledge of God derives from the centre in our world of time and space, and the centre in God himself. It is through the Word that we have cognitive access to God and may have real knowledge of him in himself as the Son who belongs to the innermost Being of God.[279] *Homoousion* is not a biblical term, however, Torrance says that it is still justified for the patristic fathers to employ this terminology in the Nicene Confession to safeguard the true identity of the incarnate Son that he is God, and through the Creed to prevent various heresies such docetism[280] and ebionitism[281].

---

277 Torrance, *The Trinitarian Faith*, 55.
278 Ibid., 56.
279 Torrance, *The Christian Doctrine of God*, 101.
280 Torrance rejects both docetism and ebionitism, he says that they approach the doctrine of Christ either from above or below. See Torrance, The Trinitarian Faith, 60. Docetic Christology does not take the body of Christ as real. The effect of this is to treat the human nature and the suffering of Christ as unreal, and it undermines the objective and historical reality of Christ. See Torrance, *The Christian Doctrine of God*, 113.
281 Ebionite Christology takes several different manifestations ranged from the idea that Jesus was only a great man, exalted in his teaching, might even be sinless, that he came to be regarded as God. Christ lived a perfect life and had a special relationship with God that he was adopted as his only Son. God raised Jesus to a position above any man or prophet. In essence, the doctrine starts with Jesus the man, a hero of mankind, and at his hightest point, man was made equal to God. See Torrance, *The Doctrine of Jesus Christ*, 63–64. However, Torrance argues that Chist's own claim does not lie in his humanity, but in the reality of his divine nature. Even though according to Ebionitism, Christ was exalted above all men or

122

The Nicene Council confesses that Jesus Christ is of one substance or Being with the Father through the usage of the word *homoousion*, that Christ is fully God and shares the same Being as the Father and thus equals to the Father. If anybody denies the divine nature of the Son, he denies that God is eternally and intrinsically Father,[282] because God is the Father to the Son; without the Son, there is no Father. The Son is of one and the same Being as God that he is God of God and Light of Light.[283] Thus, Torrance says that *homoousion* is the king-pin of the Nicene-Constantinopolitan Creed, without this ontic unity, there is no Mediator between God and man, and Jesus Christ has no role in the self-giving and self-revealing of the eternal God, [284] and everything will ultimately fall apart. Some heretics in the early church suggested to use the word *homoiousion* to describe the relation between the Son and the Father by indicating *similarity* rather than *sameness* in Being. Torrance argues that the only kind of similarity that could give saving substance to the words and deed of Christ is that he is really equal with God and of the same nature of God.[285] This type of argument is particular strong from the mouth of Athanasius that man remains mortal and unsaved if the Son is only a creature, and is not joined to God.[286] Unless Christ is God, he cannot save because only God can save. And this is exactly what the word *homoousion* states.

The doctrine of *homoousion* would allow us to enhance our knowledge of God by moving from the basic doxological level to the theological level, and from the theological level to the ontological level which reveals the innermost relations of God in himself.[287] At the first level, our knowledge of God is apprehended intuitively through our experience and worship. The second level allows us to engage in the apprehension of the general theological structures which underlie this experience, and

---

prophets, he still remains anything but a creature. See Torrance, *The Doctrine of Jesus Christ*, 63–64.

282 Torrance, *The Trinitarian Faith*, 124.
283 Torrance, *Reality and Evangelical Theology*, 112–113.
284 Torrance, *The Incarnation*, xi.
285 Ibid., xiii–xiv.
286 Athanasius, 'Against the Arians', in *Nicene and Post Nicene Fathers*, ed. Philip Schaff and Henry Wace, 4 (Peaboy, Mass.: Hendrickson, 1999), 2.69, 386.
287 Torrance, *The Christian Doctrine of God*, 95.

it brings a transition from our intuitive form of understanding to 'the economic Trinity'.[288] The transition to the highest ontological level involves a movement from a level of economic Trinitarian relations to the level of Trinitarian relations which is immanent in God himself and which lies behind and sustains the relations of the economic Trinity.[289] *Homoousion*, according to Torrance, is the central organizing truth that holds these two theological levels together. Instead of splitting between the economic Trinity and ontological Trinity, *homoousion* serves to bind them together,[290] and is referred to by Torrance as double reference.[291] Economically, we cannot read back into the eternal Life and Being of God of temporal existence in time and space, however, ontologically, we have to recognize that the mediating act of the Son and the mission of the Holy Spirit have an essential place within the very life of God.[292] If the self-revealing and self-giving of God in Jesus Christ in time and space has an essential place in the ontological Being, then the economic revelation of the Trinity is actually that of the ontological Trinity. What is read in temporal existence in the life of Christ has to be in the very life of the Triune God. The economic Trinity as revealed through the Son in time and space is in essence the eternal ontological Being of the Triune God. However, how is the economic Trinity differentiated from the immanent Trinity? Torrance admits that 'there is much here that we cannot, and will never, understand.'[293] That is to say, the double reference of *homoousion* is somehow a mystery because in reality, Torrance says, there are not two Trinities but only one Trinity.[294]

In the controversy of Arianism, *homoousion* is employed to guard against subordinationism or *homoiousion*, that Jesus Christ cannot be anything less than God because he is God. Thus, subordination is clearly excluded in the formulation of the concept of *homoousion*. How then can the economic subordination, which Torrance affirms,[295] be manifested in

---

288 Ibid., 91–92.
289 Ibid., 98–99.
290 Ibid., 98.
291 Ibid., 97.
292 Ibid.
293 Ibid.
294 T. F. Torrance, *Trinitarian Perspectives Toward Doctrinal Agreeement* (Edinburgh: T&T Clark, 1999), 79.
295 Torrance, *The Christian Doctrine of God*, 180.

the ontological equality of the Trinity? Unless the economic subordination of the Son is apart from the self-revelation of God which takes place within the very life of God, economic subordination cannot be substantiated. Unlike Torrance, Barth does not see that subordination in the form of obedience within the Trinity forms an unequal relation. Barth says that God is just natural to be lowly as to be high, to be little as to be great.[296] The humility of Christ is not something external to him but is grounded in the very Being of God, thus, Barth says that God is free and able to render obedience.[297] Indeed, Barth is suggesting a mutual submission within the Trinity, he says,

> We have not only not to deny but actually to affirm and understand as essential to the being of God the offensive fact that there is in God Himself an above and a below, a *prius* and a *posterius*, a superiority and a subordination. And our present concern is with what is apparently the most offensive fact of all, that there is a below, a *posterius*, a subordination, that it belongs to the inner life of God that there should take place within it obedience... Therefore we have to state firmly that, far from preventing this possibility, His divine unity consists in the fact that in Himself He is both One who is obeyed and Another who obeys.[298]

Barth, by refusing to recognize the transitory nature of economy, takes on a new idea of *homoousion* that *subordination* is part of its meaning . Torrance on the other hand maintains that subordination of Christ is only limited to his earthly mission.[299]

In the light of the Nicene fathers, the term *homoousion* is used to affirm the divine nature of the person of Jesus Christ that he shares the same substance or Being as the Father. The Nicene fathers, however, do not apply *homoousion* to affirm the human nature of Christ because clearly the human nature is never part of the eternal God. Unlike the concept of hypostatic union, *homoousion* does not extend beyond the divine nature of Christ. This is generally observed in Torrance writings. However, Torrance argues that *homoousion* is grounded in the reality of our Lord's humanity. He says,

---

296 Barth, *Church Dogmatics*, 4/1, 191.
297 Ibid., 193
298 Ibid., 200–201.
299 Torrance, *Trinitarian Perspectives Toward Doctrinal Agreeement*, 67.

the homoousion applies to the relation between the incarnate Son and God the Father. That is to say, it grounds the reality of our Lord's *humanity*, and of all that was revealed and done for our sakes by Jesus, in an indivisible union with the eternal being of God.[300]

Even though the human nature of Christ is not associated with the concept of *homoousion*, it is nonetheless the reason why the concept is to be developed that Christ is not only man, but he is also God. *Homoousion* sets the relation between the Father and the Son, and the Son through his hypostatic union of two natures sets a reality in humanity that he is one of them. Thus, *homoousion* cannot be separated from hypostatic union if there is any real meaning in our salvation in the Person of Christ because the main focus and purpose of *homoousion* in the confession is that it was set in a soteriological context.[301]

Torrance says that it is not the term *homoousion* that is significant, but the central issue that it signifies is important. However, due to the fact this term carries such weight that there is a danger of misunderstanding because 'The infinite and boundless God cannot be made comprehensible by a few words of human speech.'[302] The primary intention of the word *homoousion* is to guard against heresies and their gross misinterpretations. Thus, it should be regarded as an exegetical and clarificatory expression having to do with the semantic relation between the sign and the reality that it signifies. It is thus a guiding frame of the church in understanding the relation between Jesus Christ and God the Father.[303] Thus, *homoousion* is the ontological substructure upon which the Scripture is to be interpreted.[304] However, from a purely linguistic construct, Jenson says that *homoousion* carries two possible meanings which are both unacceptable. He says,

That two things are *homoousios* could mean that they are exactly the same one; applied to the Father and the Son, this would abolish their distinction. Or it could

---

300 Torrance, *The Trinitarian Faith*, 135.
301 Torrance, *The Christian Doctrine of God*, 94.
302 Torrance, *The Incarnation*, xii.
303 Ibid., xii–xiii.
304 Ibid., xii.

mean that both perfectly instantiate the same essence; applied to the Father and the Son, this would give us two gods.[305]

Thus, Torrance states that the word *homoousion* embodies two unique meanings, first, it carries a meaning of sameness in Being that the Son is same as the Father, and second it indicates a distinctiveness of the Father and of the Son in the One Being that it reflects the objective otherness in the Godhead.[306] The sameness does not give us two gods, Torrance quotes Athanasius in arguing that since the Son is the image of the Father, therefore, it must be understood the Father is the Being of the Son, and the Being of the Son is whole God.[307] Thus both the Son and the Father are in the Oneness of the Triune Godhead. The second meaning is less prominent in the confession, but it is equally important because it avoids linguistically what Jenson suggests, that it may abolish the distinction of the Father and the Son, and what historically, Macleod says: that it gives an impression of monarchianism[308], and that even Sabellius[309] used it. Macleod says,

> To make matters worse, the Council of Antioch (265/266) in condemning Paul of Samosata had explicitly rejected the word homoousion, on the ground that to attribute this title to God was to portray him as single and undifferentiated, at once Father and Son to himself.[310]

---

305 R. Jenson, *Systematic Theology*, 1 (New York: Oxford University Press, 1997), 103.

306 Torrance, *The Trinitarian Faith*, 125.

307 Ibid., 304.

308 It is a monotheism doctrine by denying personal distinctiveness of a divine Son and the Spirit in contrast to God the Father. It is also referred as Patripassianism or Sabellianism. See W. A. Elwell (ed.), *Evangelical Dictionary of Theology* (Grand Rapids, Mich.: BakerBaker, 1996), 727.

309 Macleod, *The Person of Christ*, 124. Sabellius in the third century tried to solve the problem of how to accept the deity of Christ and at the same time to maintain the Oneness of God. He achieved it at the expense of three persons in the Godhead. Each person is reduced to a mode or manifestation of the one God. Thus, it is a form of modalism, or is called modalistic monarchianism by emphasizing the primacy of the Father. The Son and the Spirit are simply temporal modes of the Father's self-revelation. See Douglas, 871.

310 Macleod, *The Person of Christ*, 124.

Thus, there exists a danger in the employment of the term *homoousion* if the second meaning of differentiation within the Oneness is omitted. Torrance avoids this pitfall by the inclusion of the meaning of otherness in the doctrine of *homoousion* because the Nicene fathers believed that the distinction between the Father and the Son is fundamental to the idea of *homoousion*. According to Torrance, the concept of *homoousion* is not restricted to the Son, it is also applied to the Holy Spirit. Though very little was said about the Holy Spirit at the Council of Nicea, however, the belief in the deity of the Holy Spirit belongs to the tradition of early church. Thus, in the subsequent Council of Constantinople, the Deity of the Holy Spirit was fully affirmed in the Confession that God the Father, the Son, and the Holy Spirit are all equal in honor, majesty and eternal sovereignty as three perfect Persons. Although the term *homoousion* was not employed in the Creed itself, the intention was there that the Holy Spirit is 'from the Father', and Torrance sees it as an equivalent to 'of one being with the Father'.[311] However, the *homoousion* applies to the Spirit shares a different manner to that of the Son because it applies specifically to the distinctive nature and personal reality of the Holy Spirit. When the *homoousion* is applied to the Son, the Son acts as an epistemic bridge between God and man that he is both the Being of God and the Being of man. Thus, in Christ the *homoousion* is inseparably related to the hypostatic union. However, the Spirit is not knowable in his own distinctive person in the same way as the Son who is an objective reality of existence in time and space. Unlike the two-natured incarnate Son, the Spirit is God of God and not man of man.[312] Thus, Torrance says the *homoousion* is applicable to the Holy Spirit similarly to the Son but also at the same time differently from the Son.

3.3.4. Hypostatic Union and Atonement

Hypostatic union and atonement, according to Torrance, cannot be disjoined from each other because throughout the whole life of Jesus, the hypostatic union and atonement involved each other in both redemption

---

311 Torrance, *The Christian Doctrine of God*, 96.
312 Ibid., 101.

and new creation.[313] Both are implied and interpenetrated in each other in the mediation of Christ. On one hand, atonement allows the removal of sin and guilt from humanity, on the other hand, hypostatic union makes it an ontological reality by actualizing it in our fallen humanity.[314] And through hypostatic union, Christ identifies with us. The work of atoning salvation does not take place external of Christ, but rather within himself.[315] Atonement carries a meaning of reconciliation because it is only through the act of atonement, we are able to have reconciliation with God in Christ. Through reconciliation, the fallen humanity is restored to the original relation between God and man prior to the Fall. However, according to Torrance, the scope of the whole life of Christ is itself an atonement which began with his virgin birth, entered active operation at his baptism and reached its culmination on the Cross,[316] and which transcends the ethical and legal relation into a deeper relation with God in which the forensic and condemnatory aspect of the Law is removed.[317] According to Torrance, the scope of Christ's atonement is not limited to the fallen humanity, it also applies to the whole universe of things, both visible and invisible.[318] By that, the fallen angels may also benefit from what Christ did on the Cross. However, it does not seem that Torrance has this idea in mind when he says that the effect of atonement extends beyond humanity to the whole creation, but rather to indicate that the whole creation will be reconciled with God through Christ's atonement. Nonetheless, this is a logical implication if the content of the creation is not specified. In fact, there are few discussions in Torrance's writings regarding the redeeming power of Christ on the fate of the fallen angels.

The atonement itself is a historical event which becomes timeless as Torrance portrays that Christ, as the living atonement, is eternally pre-vailing in his advocacy for man before God.[319] This brings in another

---

313   Torrance, 'The Atonement and the Oneness of The Church', 247–248; Torrance, *The Christian Doctrine of God*, 85.
314   Torrance, *The Mediation of Christ*, 76; Torrance, *The Doctrine of Jesus Christ*, 144.
315   Torrance, *The Trinitarian Faith*, 155.
316   Torrance, 'The Atonement and the Oneness of The Church', 252.
317   Torrance, *The Doctrine of Jesus Christ*, 177.
318   Torrance, *Space, Time and Resurrection*, 155.
319   Ibid., 55.

aspect of Christ's atonement that it is a continuous event and has an implication that Christ did not complete his mission on the cross. As a living atonement, Torrance renders Christ's saying on the cross 'It is finished' (John 19:30) meaningless. At best, it is only partially finished. However, this is consistent with Torrance's view of open-ended incarnation that the human nature of Christ remains with him forever, thus, the mission itself is never finished because the mark of the mission - Christ's humanity is carried into eternity. This is not uniquely a Torrance idea, Walvoord also believes that the hypostatic union will continue forever, and claims that the act of incarnation is not a temporary arrangement which ends with Christ's death and resurrection, it continues into eternity.[320]

There are several major atonement theories. The oldest is the 'ransom theory' that the death of Christ is viewed as a ransom paid to rescue men from the power of sin, death, and Satan. It carries an imagery that the Cross was described as a mousetrap baited with the blood of Christ[321] or a fish hook with Christ as the lure. Through Christ's atonement on the Cross, Satan was trapped and hooked. This theory was taken up by Gregory of Nyssa, and Torrance says that this kind of interpretation of Christ on the Cross is crass and has a deficiency in the moral requirement of God's nature,[322] and thus, must be rejected; however, Torrance regards that it may have value of truth in which the Cross of Christ represents God's defeat of evil,[323] and the analogy of ransom could also be able to illustrate the atoning exchange that Christ gave body for our body and his soul for our soul.[324] By rejecting the 'ransom theory', Torrance does not reject the idea of ransom in the understanding of the atonement; he sees that the death of Christ on our behalf is a representative death, a substitutionary death, in the form of a ransom by which we are delivered from the bondage of sin and the judgment.[325]

The second theory is the 'satisfaction theory' that was put forward by Anselm that Christ died on the Cross to satisfy the justice of God. This

---

320 Walvoord, 113.
321 V. Taylor, *The Cross of Christ, Eight Public Lectures*, (London: MacMillan, 1957), 71–72.
322 Torrance, *The Trinitarian Faith*, 178.
323 Torrance, *The Doctrine of Jesus Christ*, 166–167.
324 Torrance, *The Trinitarian Faith*, 165.
325 Torrance, *The Doctrine of Jesus Christ*, 176.

theory lays its emphasis on the divine requirements that must be met for our salvation.[326] Aulen refers to this theory as 'objective' atonement because God is the object of the Christ's atonement, and is reconciled through the satisfaction of God's justice.[327] The third theory is the 'forensic theory' of the Reformers that Christ suffered the judgment of God on our behalf. It is substitutionary in character. It emphasizes the idea that Christ did for us what we cannot do for ourselves.[328] Aulen calls this type 'subjective' atonement because it calls for a change taking place in humanity rather than in God.[329] He also proposes another theory – 'dramatic' atonement, which is similar to 'objective' atonement but differs from the 'objective' type in that the work of atonement or reconciliation from first to last a work of God himself alone. While the 'objective' type has its origin in God's will, but is carried out by Christ who made an offering to God as man and on man's behalf.[330] For 'dramatic theory', God is both the author and the object of the reconciliation that he is reconciled in the act of reconciling the world to himself.[331] This theory clearly minimizes the role of vicarious humanity of Christ that he acts in our capacity. Torrance sees that Christ's humanity holds the key to our salvation, and it is the vicarious humanity of Christ that is making the atoning exchange.[332] Other than these theories, Taylor says that some Greek Fathers also spoke of atonement as a work of deification, with its emphasis laid upon the sacrificial concepts.[333] It is clear in Athanasius' theology, the idea of deification plays a prominent role that 'For He was made man that we might be made God.'[334] Deification, as interpreted by Torrance, does not mean any change in human nature, but by which we are made to participate in divine Sonship.[335] Torrance shares similar idea in the concept of atoning

326 Taylor, *The Cross of Christ, Eight Public Lectures*, 72–73.
327 Aulen, 18.
328 Taylor, *The Cross of Christ, Eight Public Lectures*, 72–73.
329 Aulen, 18.
330 Ibid., 21–22.
331 Ibid., 72.
332 Torrance, *The Trinitarian Faith*, 4.
333 Taylor, *The Cross of Christ, Eight Public Lectures*, 73.
334 Athanasius, 'On The Incarnation', in *Nicene and Post Nicene Fathers*, ed. Philip Schaff and Henry Wace, 4 (Peaboy, Mass.: Hendrickson, 1999), 65.
335 Torrance, *Divine Meaning*, 369.

sacrifice that Christ is dealing with God on our behalf, he is our High Priest offering atoning sacrifice for sin and also at the same time fulfilling from man's side the obedience that brings the reconciliation between God and man and man and God. Thus, atonement according to Torrance is understood as the vindication of the Divine honour and also as the vicarious life of Christ in his obedience of man to God.[336] Torrance says that western fathers were more focused on the external forensic account of death of Christ as a judicial transaction in the transference of the penalty from the sinner to the sin bearer.[337] The eastern fathers emphasized more Christ's vicarious humanity that he united himself with us in our actual existence and that the atonement took place within the incarnate life;[338] thus, Christ is not only instrumental but also integral and essential in his atonement.[339]

In the modern era, Torrance's doctrine of atonement is heavily influenced by R.W. Dale and McLeod Campbell. The strength of Dale's theology, according to Torrance, is that he stresses the substitutionary work of Christ in his submission to divine judgment and in satisfaction for sin offered on the Cross, but there is a lack of the necessity of the vicarious life and obedience of Christ in the incarnation. In Campbell's teaching, on the other hand, he stresses Christ's vicarious life of the love of the Father without giving a major place to the conception of forensic satisfaction of divine justice in the sacrificial death of Christ on the Cross.[340] Thus, Torrance develops his own doctrine of atonement by integrating both strengths as a single account of atonement. It is not so much as balance between the two but to reach a real understanding of the atonement in Christ's obedient life and vicarious death.[341] Thus, it carries the concepts of representation and substitution that Christ does not only represent us in our response, but also his response has ontological bearing on us in our actual human being.[342] In the integration of his atonement doctrine, Torrance rejects several erroneous ideas of Campbell, these include the idea of vicarious punishment that what

---

336   Torrance, *The Doctrine of Jesus Christ*, 168.
337   Torrance, *The Mediation of Christ*, 50.
338   Torrance, *The Trinitarian Faith*, 161.
339   Torrance, 'The Atonement and the Oneness of The Church', 251.
340   Torrance, *The Doctrine of Jesus Christ*, 166–167.
341   Ibid.
342   Torrance, *The Mediation of Christ*, 90-91.

Christ suffered was not a punishment in essence[343] and the idea of universalism which caused Campbell to be deposed by the Church of Scotland in 1931.[344] However, Torrance still says that Campbell's idea has a value in his primary emphasis on the vicarious life of Christ in fulfilling the holy and forgiving love of the Father, even though he pays little attention to the idea of satisfaction. On the other hand, Torrance treasures Dale's idea by stressing the penal judgment and satisfaction before the wrath and satisfaction of God, which is close to the traditional Anselmic concept of atonement.[345]

Torrance believes that the vicarious offering of Christ is made for all mankind instead of only those who are elected. Thus, this idea of unlimited atonement created some tension within the student evangelical world during Torrance's student years.[346] Torrance deeply believes that Christ did not die for some, but for all humanity,[347] however, it does not necessarily mean that because Christ died for all so that all are saved. Contrary to the unlimited atonement, the limited atonement forms an important element in the traditional understanding of the five pillars[348] of the Reformed doctrines of Grace, and many Reformers see that these five pillars stand or fall together, as together they point to the one central truth that salvation is all grace.[349] However, Macleod says that Torrance tries to contrast the teaching of Calvinists unfavourably with the teaching of Calvin himself by arguing that he and Calvin share the same view.[350]

---

343 Taylor, *The Cross of Christ, Eight Public Lectures*, 73–74.
344 Ibid., 73.
345 Torrance, *The Doctrine of Jesus Christ*, 166–167.
346 McGrath, 26.
347 T. F. Torrance, *When Christ Comes and Comes Again* (Eugene: Wipf and Stock Publishers, 1957), 114.
348 The five pillars are generally referred to as: Total depravity, Unconditional election, Limited atonement, Irresistable grace, Perseverance of saints or simply TULIP. Boice calls it five points of Calvinism. See J. M. Boice, and P. G. Ryken, *The Doctrines of Grace* (Wheaton, Il.: Crossway, 2002), 29–32.
349 Ibid., 32.
350 D. Macleod, 'Dr T.F. Torrance and Scottish Theology: a Review Article', *The Evangelical Quarterly*, 72/1 (January 2000), 60-61. Torrance himself sees that based on his reading of Calvin's commentaries and the Institutes, he is convinced that Calvin's theological position is very different from the hardened Calvinism. See T. F. Torrance, *Calvin's Doctrine of Man* (London: Lutterworth Press, 1949), 7.

Macleod challenges Torrance on his quotation from Calvin's treatise, *Concerning the Eternal Predestination of God*, and says,

> The statement Dr Torrance cites is as follows: 'For this the common solution does not avail, that Christ suffered sufficiently for all, but efficiently for the elect.' The context, however, suggests that Calvin is in fact quoting this remark from Georgius[351] himself. His own comment follows: 'By this great absurdity, this work has brought great applause in his own fraternity, but it has no weight with me.'[352]

The main emphasis of Torrance's doctrine of atonement is clearly on the sufficiency of the atonement rather than the efficiency and efficacy of the atonement, and his idea of unlimited atonement has a tendency of leading to universalism which he fervently denies.[353] Torrance argues that if universalism is true, 'then every road whether it had the Cross planted on it or not would lead to salvation.'[354] That is to say, if universalism is true, the Cross becomes unnecessary in the salvation of mankind. However, his teacher, Barth does not seem to be enthusiastic in the outright rejection of universalism. In fact, many people accuse Barth of adopting universalism. Kent says that Barth in his later years defended the idea of universal salvation due to the idea of total adequacy of God.[355] Cassel sees that Barth just stops short of proclaiming universal salvation as God has extended unlimited love to all that all may be saved.[356] Goetz also sees that Barth is coming very close to affirming universal salvation as Barth's theology is characterized as the triumph of grace that it is a free substitution for mankind.[357] However, these are unfair criticisms of Barth who in fact is not accepting universalism, but

---

351 Calvin has an agrument with his adversary, Georgius, relating to I John 2:2, 'those who wish to exclude the reprobate from participation in Christ must place them outside the world.' See Macleod, 'Dr T.F. Torrance and Scottish Theology: a Review Article', 60.

352 Ibid., 60–61.

353 T. F. Torrance, 'Universalism or Election?', *Scottish Journal of Theology*, 2 (1949), 317.

354 Ibid., 312.

355 J. H. Kent, *The End of The Line* (London: SCM Press, 1982), 121.

356 P. Cassel, *Karl Barth on Revelation and God's Relationship to the World* <http:// people.bu.edu/wwildman/WeirdWildWeb/courses/mwt/dictionary/ mwt_themes_ 750_barth.htm> accessed 14 Oct 2004.

357 R. Goetz, *The Karl Barth Centennial: An Appreciative Critique* <http://www. religion-online.org/showarticle.asp?title=1> accessed 4 Sep 2005.

at the same time, he is not rejecting it. In his *Church Dogmatics*, Barth says,

> If we are to respect the freedom of divine grace, we cannot venture the statement that it must and will finally be coincident with the world of man as such (as in the doctrine of the so-called apokatastasis). No such right or necessity can legitimately be deduced. Just as the gracious God does not need to elect or call any single man, so He does not need to elect or call all mankind... But, again, in grateful recognition of the grace of the divine freedom we cannot venture the opposite statement that there cannot and will not be this final opening up and enlargement of the circle of election and calling.[358]

In regarding the circle of those saved, Barth argues that it is the divine freedom that governs. Thus, it is not possible to restrict the possibility of saving circle that whether it covers the whole human population or not. That is to say, it is an open possibility guided only by God's divine freedom of love. Thus, he does not accept nor reject universalism which is referred to as *apokatastasis*[359]. However, on the other hand, even though the Cross by itself is sufficient for the salvation of all mankind, and it is really up to God to determine how many that are to be saved,

---

358 Barth, *Church Dogmatics*, 2/2, 417–418.

359 Apokatastasis is a name given to a doctrine that teaches all free creatures will one day share in the grace of salvation. 359 See *Catholic Encyclopedia* <http://www.newadvent.org/cathen/01599a.htm>. The doctrine was explicitly taught by Gregory of Nyssa in his On the Soul and Resurrection, in which he says that the purpose of atonement is for God to attract souls to himself. Wickedness can be somehow refined into purity just like gold is refined from the dross, that the dross is consumed while the gold remains. Similarly evil is being consumed in the purgatorial fire. When a clay plastered on a rope is pulled through a narrow hole by force, the clay will be scraped off while the rope remains as it is. Thus, there is at the end, men are pulled towards God through some afflictions by separating it from evil. See Gregory of Nyssa, 'On the Soul and The Resurrection', in *Nicene and Post-Nicene Fathers*, ed. Philip Schaff & Henry Wace, 5 (Peaboy, Mass.: Hendrickson, 1999), 451. Thus, the punishment by fire is not an end in itself, but leading to the final communion to God. Every free will shall turn to God and shall be in God and evil exists no more. See Gregory of Nyssa, 'On the Soul and The Resurrection', 452. However, the doctrine of apokatastasis is not originated by Gregory of Nyssa, it is taken from Origen who teaches the final restoration of all intelligent creatures to communion with God. (Origen, 'De Principiis', in *Ante-Nicene Fathers*, ed. Alexander Roberts & James Donaldson, 4 (Peaboy, Mass.: Hendrickson, 1999), 6.6, 344–348.

however, in reality, Barth sees that the number of elect in Christ cannot be the totality of all men,[360] because clearly not all men in human history believed in Christ. Historical past is an unchanged reality, however, historical future is still an open possibility. Thus, Barth does not reject what is to be possible because he refuses to limit the scope of possibility within God's divine freedom of how many people are to be saved, it may well include everyone. However, Bettis comments that the possibility can never be the basis of a theological doctrine of universal salvation, and 'Barth fails to bridge the gap of divine possibility and a theological statement of its actuality.'[361] The idea of possibility is simply a human statistical concept, it would never have any divine meaning as all things in the past, present and future lay naked in God's eyes timelessly. Barth does not deny the possibility of universalism, however, he criticizes the argument of God's love as the premise of universalism. Barth rejects the definition of love in terms of what it does to men, Bettis says,

> To say that God is love because He saves men is to say that apart from men God would not be love. This is to say that God's essence is not self-defined, but is defined in relation to men.[362]

That is to say, God's love is preconditioned by his creation rather an attribute of his own Being. Barth argues that God is still love even if there are no men around for him to love.[363] Love should be defined by God himself rather by his creation. According to Barth, universalism is actually limiting God's love instead of extending his love because the love of God lies in the fact that God can give it freely rather than out of necessity.[364]

Barth encounters many criticisms of his unique neutral position on universalism. According to Bettis, Emil Brunner argues that Barth's definition of sovereign love of God destroys the meaning of human freedom.[365] The human decision of faith is determined by the actuali-

---

360 Barth, Karl, *Church Dogmatics*, 2/2, 421–423.
361 J. D. Bettis, 'Is Karl Barth A Universalist?', *Scottish Journal of Theology*, 20/1 (1967), 427.
362 Ibid., 428.
363 Ibid., 428–429.
364 Ibid.
365 Ibid., 424–425.

zation of God's love, and this inevitably and logically leads to universalism. 'The human decision of faith is simply an acknowledgment of that ontological reality; the decision itself has no bearing on one's salvation.'[366] Berkouwer says that the faith of man is elected through God's grace and love, and the unfaith of man is rejected through God's justice and wrath. This double decree preserves the freedom and power of God's love and at the same time the real meaning of the decision of faith.[367] Unfortunately, Berkouwer's double decree was rejected by Torrance.[368] Instead, Torrance proposes the doctrine of election to express the universal action of God's grace and at the same time retaining the personal elements of choice and decision.[369] However, Torrance's doctrine of election is different than that of the traditional Reformed idea that God 'chose us in him before the creation of the world' and 'he predestined us to be adopted as his sons through Jesus Christ' (Ephesians 1:4-5) that all believers have been eternally chosen and elected. According to Torrance, the election is driven by God's eternal love[370] and in the strictest sense, Christ himself is the election of God. Torrance says,

> It is not too much to say then, that the doctrine of the Deity of Christ is basically and really the same as the doctrine of election - for the fact that the eternal God himself has chosen to become Man in the Lord Jesus Christ means that the salvation of man rests on that divine choice or decision. Election is what it ultimately is, and means therefore, because God has chosen and willed to become man in the Lord Jesus Christ... Election means that God acts, that God executes his decision; and our election means that it is executed for us. The doctrine of election has been much misunderstood because it has not been thought of IN CHRIST.[371]

Torrance rejects the decree of predestination because it precedes the act of grace in Christ,[372] and does not see that predestination itself is an act of grace in Christ. That is to say, Christ himself is the one who is elected instead of individual believers, though he does not deny that we are

---

366 Ibid.
367 Ibid.
368 T. F. Torrance, 'Universalism or Election?', *Scottish Journal of Theology*, 2 (1949), 312.
369 Ibid.
370 Ibid. 314–315.
371 Torrance, *The Doctrine of Jesus Christ*, 144.
372 Torrance, 'Universalism or Election?', 315.

appropriated in the election of Christ. Thus, we are saved by the living act and grace of Christ, and not by some kind of dead predestination that was predetermined eternally in the past by God.[373] However, election does carry a meaning of some kind of predetermination in Christ because the shepherd has to know his flock. By rejecting both universalism and double predestination,[374] Torrance is in a difficult position to find a way out. He uses the idea of 'mystery of iniquity' to explain that God can choose all men, but only a few are saved, because those reprobates choose their final destiny in rejecting God's offer and his eternal love.[375] Thus, man instead of God makes the final decision on his salvation. This clearly contradicts Torrance's own doctrines on faith and election because God's election finally has to be determined by man, and man's faith is no longer gained by Christ on behalf of the unsaved. If this is true, according to Torrance, then it is far from being Good News for the sinner because if everything depends on him, he is utterly lost.[376]

On the one hand, Torrance says that man cannot be depended on, however, on the other hand, Torrance says that man chooses his own destiny because the effectiveness of the work of Christ is conditional upon the act of sinners, and they bear the ultimate responsibility. Torrance does not seem capable of untying this knot, and at the same time, he is moving towards universalism, he says,

> The amazing message of the Gospel is that Christ has chosen all men, died for all men. In that He died for all He has taken the judgment of all men upon Himself; thus in that He died all died.[377]

If Christ has chosen all men, and all men are saved, then this becomes the doctrine of universalism. However, according to Torrance, Christ is not able to make all those chosen to be realized in his salvation because those who are fallen outside the salvation are in reality the fault of their own instead of his election. Thus, it is man's own choice instead of his election by God that bears the cause of eternal punishment. The distinction of Berkouwer's belief from that of Torrance lies not in the

---

373 Ibid.
374 Ibid., 317.
375 Ibid., 316–317.
376 T. F. Torrance, *God and Rationality*, 58.
377 Torrance, 'Universalism or Election?', 316.

138

freedom of men to choose but in the freedom of God to choose, which is the basis of two divine decrees.[378]

In both atonement doctrines of Torrance and Barth, the attribute of the divine freedom of the love of God acts like a trump card, it can easily trump the omniscience of God in the understanding of the divine possibility. Torrance's view on God's love is so prominent in his sermon, universalism is almost in sight, he preaches,

> God has refused to let us (sinners) go. He has insisted on making Himself one of us, and one with us, in order to make our lost cause His very own, and so to restore us to Himself in love.[379]

If God refuses to let sinners go, who can pull himself out of God's hands? Torrance further says that even in a sinner's eternal punishment, God's hand of love will continue to grasp him there.[380] This carries a strong resemblance to Origen's thinking[381] that ultimately, everybody will be changed or purified by God's love, and the punishment will end. Thus, there exists a dualist thinking in Torrance's doctrine of atonement that what Christ chooses is different than what Christ actually saves. By rejecting both universalism and predestination, there is not much left in his dialectical theology without violating his own unitary structure.

3.4. Divine Nature, Space and Time

Incarnation has to be understood as God becomes man, however, Jesus Christ is not just man, he is essentially God.[382] According to Torrance's scientific approach, one knows things only under the constraint of their distinctive nature, since there is no likeness between the Creator and creature, God can be known only out of himself. Thus, in order to have

---

378   Bettis, 'Is Karl Barth A Universalist?', 426.
379   Torrance, *When Christ Comes and Comes Again*, 41.
380   Torrance, 'Universalism or Election?', 317.
381   Torrance sees that both Origen and Gregory Nyssa shared the idea of universalism that all humanity are finally saved by God. See Torrance, *The Trinitarian Faith*, 182.
382   Ibid., 150.

any scientific knowledge about God, God must reveal himself through his own nature, his divine nature. Since Jesus has the same divine nature as that of the Father, Jesus reveals God in his Act and Being.[383] Unless Christ is of the same nature and Being as the Father, he is not the self-revelation and self-communication of God. If Jesus does not share the same divine nature as the Father, there would be no identity between God and his revelation, mankind would have no access to the Father through the Son.[384] Torrance employs Athanasius' soteriological argument[385] that unless Christ is God by his nature, we are still unsaved because only God can save. If the incarnate Son is not fully God then he has no power and authority to forgive our sins, and his atonement on the cross has no ultimate and final validity, mankind is still in sin. If the incarnate Son and the Father are not one and the same Being, then we really do not know him. The Gospel becomes an empty mockery as men are still hopeless in their misery.[386] Christ's own claim to worship, according to Torrance, does not lie in his humanity but in his divine nature.[387] Torrance says,

> If the humanity of Christ is the guarantee that God's Salvation actually reaches men; the divinity of Christ is the guarantee that the action of Redemption in Jesus Christ is actually of God.[388]

Christ's divinity guarantees that the salvific act of Christ is actually of God. That is to say, the vicarious humanity of Christ has to be vindicated by his own divinity that he is God and he can save and forgive our sins. Torrance believes only God can forgive because human beings can never really forgive one another as we can never undo the wrongs. Even though we can forget it, we cannot cancel the guilt. Only God can forgive and undo our guilt.[389]

What is *divine nature*? Or more specifically, what is *nature*? Torrance does not seem to provide a clear answer. The uniqueness of *nature* in the

---

383   Ibid., 52.
384   Ibid., 133.
385   Torrance, *Trinitarian Perspectives Toward Doctrinal Agreeement*, 52.
386   Torrance, *The Trinitarian Faith*, 8.
387   Torrance, *The Doctrine of Jesus Christ*, 64.
388   Ibid., 140.
389   Ibid., 179.

understanding among *nature*, *person*, and *being* is not well established. However, Torrance does provide a good differentiation between *person* and *being*, or *hypostasis* and *ousia* in the concept of Triunity which is to be discussed in chapter 3. In the discussion in section 2.1.3., Torrance has a tendency to personalize *nature* as *person* by employing the theological concept *enhypostasia*, which is specially formulated for the understanding of the human *nature* of Christ, in the *personal* relation within the Trinity. Thus, he extends the meaning of *enhypostasia* beyond the *nature* of a person and creates an impression that the divine nature by itself is a person, that is to say, hypostatic union is a *person* imbedding in a *person*. This risks of creating two persons instead of two distinct natures in one person.

The fundamental understanding of *homoousion*, according to Torrance, is that God in himself is the same as God in Jesus Christ.[390] That is to say, Christ is the same as God according to his divine nature. In the understanding of Christ's divine nature, Torrance says that Calvin asserts the intrinsic consubstantiality of the Trinity, for the three divine Persons have one and the same spiritual Being.[391] Torrance quotes Athanasius,

> In each hypostasis the whole divine Nature is understood, it being assumed that each has his own subsistent property. The Father is wholly in the Son and the Son is wholly in the Father, as he himself declares: "I am in the Father, and the Father in me."[392]

That is to say, both Calvin and Athanasius believe that all three divine Persons have the same Being. Christ is divine due to his divine nature, thus, he is of the same Being as the Father. Torrance says,

> As there is only one Being of the Father, the Son and the Spirit, so the hypostatic reality of each of them is as eternal and perfect as that of the others. The three divine Persons do not share with one another their distinguishing properties as Father, Son and Holy Spirit, for they are personally other than one another, but they do share completely and equally in the one homogeneous Nature and Being of God.[393]

---

390 Torrance, *The Trinitarian Faith*, 133.
391 Torrance, *Trinitarian Perspectives Toward Doctrinal Agreeement*, 57.
392 Ibid.
393 Ibid., 132.

Christ does not only share the same *nature* of the Father, he is the very *Being* of the Father. That is to say, *nature* is not only the predicate of the subject or inherent property which is specific to the subject, it is the subject itself. Clearly, Torrance indicates that the divine *nature* of Christ is same as the *Being* of God, and the human *nature* is same as the contingent *Being* of man.[394] Thus, divine *nature* means divine *Being*, and human *nature* means human *Being*. *Being* could not be separated from *Person* according to Torrance interpretation of the concept of Triunity because *Being* is the essence of *Person*, thus, hypostatic union becomes a union of two *Beings*. Instead of two natures in one person, it becomes two Beings in one person, and creates a reverse to the conception of Triunity which is three Persons in one Being. Torrance may not agree with the conclusion,[395] however, it is a natural implication if *nature* is not precisely defined, especially if it is not clearly differentiated from *Person* and *Being*. There were two alternative definitions of *Person* for Torrance to consider, he says,

> The Boethian definition of person is a philosophical concept derived through logical analysis from Aristotelian and Neoplatonic notions of particular and general substance and rational nature. The Ricardine definition, however, is a theological concept reached by way of ontological derivative from the communion of Love in the Being of God between Father, Son, and Holy Spirit, who wholly interpenetrate and coinhere in one another in such a way that their personal distinctness as Father, Son, and Holy Spirit remains inviolate.[396]

It is clear that in the understanding of the relation of three Persons in the Triune Being, the essence of differentiation among three Persons lies in their relation to each other rather than substance because all three Persons share the same substance as the Being of God. Thus, Torrance holds that the relational aspect of the definition suggested by Richard of St. Victor is superior than that of Boethius, who suggests that it is the substance that makes a person unique. However, when the relational definition is applied to the hypostatic union, it is hardly sufficient to dif-

---

394   Torrance, *The Trinitarian Faith*, 123.
395   Torrance clearly says that the doctrine of the Trinity is one Being, three Persons, not one Nature, three Persons, thus, Being is not fully identical with Nature. See T. F. Torrance, *Theological Dialogue Between Orthodox and Reformed Churches*, 2 (Edinburgh: Scottish Academic Press, 1993), 119.
396   Torrance, *Reality and Evangelical Theology*, 43.

ferentiate *nature* from *Person* because the relation between *nature* and *Person* in the hypostatic union is different than that of *Person* and *Being* in Trinity. It would be beneficial if the Boethian definition is considered. Berkhof shares the Boethian definition of *nature* and *Person*, he says,

> The term "nature" denotes the sum-total of all the essential qualities of a thing, that which makes it what it is. A nature is a substance possessed in common, with all the essential qualities of such a substance. The term "person" denotes a complete substance endowed with reason, and, consequently, a responsible subject of its own action... A person is a nature with something added, namely, independent subsistence, individuality.[397]

The Boethian definition is by no means perfect, however, it provides a clearer differentiation between *nature* and *Person*. The human nature of Christ, according to Berkhof, is denoted by his human flesh; and the essential elements of human nature are a material body and a rational soul.[398] These elements together with an individuality form a person. Accordingly, the divine nature of Christ is spirit since God is a spirit. Unfortunately, the distinction between *nature* and *Person* is not well addressed in Torrance's writings.

In God's divine nature, according to Pannenberg, time always remains present to God. All things in the past and the future are present to God in their actuality.[399] That is to say, *I Am that I Am* is always referring to God's timeless eternal status that carries a human understanding of present moment. This is basically an Augustinian view of time that God's today is both yesterday and tomorrow.[400] However, Torrance extends its meaning to include *I Shall Be Who I Shall Be* that the self-existing God is ever-continuing in his Being,[401] thus a human aspect of future is also included in the understanding of the present reality of the self-living God with an intention to embrace the idea of God that he is dynamic in his divine nature. Torrance dislikes any idea that is static and mechanistic in nature, and he sees that Newtonian cosmological idea is particularly destructive because it is characterized

---

397 L. Berkhof, *Systematic Theology* (Grand Rapids, Mich.: Eerdmans, 1977), 321.
398 Ibid., 318.
399 W. Pannenberg, 'Eternity, Time and the Trinitarian God', *CTI Reflections*, 3 (1999), 50.
400 Augustine, *Confessions*, tr. R.S. Pine-Coffin (London: Penguin Books, 1961), 27.
401 Torrance, *The Christian Doctrine of God*, 235.

by absolute space and time, of which all contingent events are contained.[402] Torrance argues that Einsteinian theory of relativity does not only make space a relative concept, but also relativizes the concept of time. The concept of time which is no longer absolute is a bit difficult to understand, Hawking uses an example of a pair of twin brothers, one stays on earth and one goes to a space travel at nearly the speed of light. After a long period of time, when he returns to earth, he finds himself much younger than his twin brother. This is known as the twins paradox. However, it is only paradox if the absolute time is assumed because in the theory of relativity, there is no unique absolute time, but instead each has his own time according to where he is and how he is moving.[403] That is to say, both time and space can no longer be defined in strict Newtonian dimensions.

Torrance believes that the divine nature of the Person of Christ cannot be confined to the human idea of physical place, instead of being contained by time and space, the divine nature of Christ contains all.[404] That is to say, the humanity of Christ is contained by space and time, while his divinity contains space and time. It is paradoxical in nature that he both contains and is contained by time and space. Similarly, Barth says that Christ is the omnipresent, almighty, eternal and glorious One according to his divine nature, however, at the same time, he is not omnipotent and eternal, limited in space and time according to his human nature.[405] Thus, the concept of incarnation, according to Torrance, has to be understood in accordance with Christ's natures because space is a predicate of the occupant.[406] That is to say, the relational view of space and time is developed in accordance with the nature of the Creator who transcends all space and time and also in accordance with the nature of the creature subjected to space and time through the interaction in Jesus Christ. [407] Thus, the concept of space in the Nicene confession as understood by Torrance is basically closed from the side of human due to our limited physical existence, but is infinitely open on the side of God because the spatial formulation is defined in accordance with the

---

402 Torrance, *Theology in Reconciliation*, 268.
403 S. Hawking, *A Brief History of Time* (New York: Bantam, 1988), 33.
404 Torrance, *Divine Meaning*, 351.
405 Barth, *Church Dogmatics*, 4/1,184.
406 Torrance., *Divine Meaning*, 366.
407 Torrance, *God and Rationality*, 129..

interaction between God and man, eternal and contingent happening.[408] Space and time are functions of contingent events within the creation, and they serve as the bearers of its immanent order, that means, space and time are used by God as the medium of his interaction with nature. Through the reality of space and time, God confirms his eternal purpose through the incarnation of his Son.[409]

Torrance says his relational concept of space as quite different than that of Aristotelian form which is defined in terms of a containing vessel with an immobile absolute centre. The Aristotelian concept, according to Torrance, says that anything beyond the enclosed space as unthinkable and unintelligible. If God is intelligible, he must be finite.[410] Torrance argues that this is impossible for Christian theology because God is the transcendent Source of all rationality and has absolute priority over all space and time, and since God created the universe out of nothing, he also created space and time.[411] God himself is totally independent of his creation and infinitely exalted over space and time.[412] Time is in creation, however, creation is not in time because God is not contained by anything but rather that he contains everything.[413] Thus, space and time cannot be a container that contains its own creator. Rather, patristic theology, according to Torrance, believes in a relational and differential concept of space as a meeting place in the interaction between God and the world.[414] Interestingly, Torrance excludes Augustine from his approved list of patristic fathers in supporting a correct understanding of time and space because Torrance sees Augustine as promoting two kingdoms, the city of God and the city of man, and thus creating dualism by drawing a line between a kingdom that is located in heaven, and a kingdom that is located on earth; and these two kingdoms are so divided that they meet only tangentially.[415] In fact, Augustine is employing a

---

408 Torrance, *Divine Meaning*, 371.
409 Torrance, *God and Rationality*, 112.
410 Ibid., 123–124.
411 Ibid.
412 Torrance, *The Trinitarian Faith*, 89.
413 Torrance, *Space, Time and Incarnation*, 11–12.
414 Torrance, *God and Rationality*, 123–124.
415 Torrance, *Space, Time and Incarnation*, 33–34.

similar paradoxical idea in the concept of space that Christ in his divine nature is everywhere and he contains the heaven and earth.[416]

Kant sees space and time as a priori forms of intuition: the substance and causality are a priori categories of the understanding, which provide our possible empirical experience.[417] Torrance criticizes Kant as basically transferring absoluteness from God to man,[418] and if space and time are a priori forms of man's sensory perception, then the absolute centre lies in man himself and he is the fixed point in his self-understanding. This means that there cannot be any God outside of himself or independent of his consciousness.[419] Torrance sees no justification in the Kantian idea because the absoluteness of space and time has already been invalidated by the relativity theory of Einstein.[420] Theologically speaking, the created universe has to be open because, according to Torrance, our Creator has unlimited spontaneity and freedom in his creation.[421] Unfortunately, while on the one hand, Torrance rejects the concept of absolute space and time, on the other hand, he is accepting the absolute speed of light as suggested by Einstein's relativity theory and absolute temperature[422] which was developed by William Thomson in the nineteenth century. That is to say, though the universe is somehow unbound as perceived by Torrance, yet somehow, there exists at least a pair of unmoved references. In order to eliminate the so-called container notion of space, Torrance in reality introduces a different type of container concept through absolute light speed and absolute zero temperature. This contradicts his own criticism of the Newtonian idea of rigid absolutes in the foundation of science.[423] However, Torrance admits that there exists a difficult ambiguity in the Newtonian idea of space and time that Newton does admit that the whole universe cannot be explained only

---

416 Augustine, *Confessions*, 22–23.
417 Torrance, *Divine and Contingent Order*, 16.
418 Ibid.
419 Torrance, *Space, Time and Incarnation*, 44.
420 Torrance, *Divine and Contingent Order*, 16.
421 Torrance, *The Ground And Grammar of Theology*, 12.
422 Torrance, *God and Rationality*, 56. The absolute zero is a theoretical temperature at which the molecules of a substance have the lowest energy. See *Encyclopedia Britannica* (CD, 1998 standard edition).
423 Torrance, *Divine and Contingent Order*, 13.

in mechanical terms, it has to be interpreted by its relation to God. Torrance says,

> this correlation of the universe with God implied that it is finally an open system. This was very important for Newton, for it meant that the universe is not to be regarded as closed in upon itself, a consistent and complete system in itself, a system that is not finally self-explanatory.[424]

Thus, Torrance's criticism of the Newtonian container notion of space is not totally correct. In fact, the Newtonian ambiguity may well be the paradoxical truth which Torrance employs frequently in his theology. The most difficult problem in Torrance's defense of unbound space comes from the universally accepted natural law - the second law of thermodynamics. There are three basic principles in the natural law of thermodynamics. The first principle concerns the conservation of energy. The second principle or law states that a thermodynamic system can go in one direction only, it cannot be reversed. The second law was proposed by Rudolf Clausius in 1850 stating that heat cannot of itself pass from a cold to a hot body. A quantitative concept of entropy[425] was introduced as a indication of the dissipation of available energy, which is also an indicator of the disorder of a system. An energy source can only be dissipated when there exists a discrepancy between itself and the surrounding, when the energy source itself and the surrounding have the same level of energy, there can be no dissipation of energy. At a temperature of absolute zero, all movement of atoms ceases, and the disorder or entropy of such substance is zero. Thus, the third law of thermodynamics states that the entropy at the absolute zero temperature is zero, the most ordered possible state. That means all substances above absolute zero will have a positive entropy value that increases with temperature. When a hot body cools down, the surrounding air heats up. The combined entropy of the hot body and surrounding actually increases because the entropy increase of the surrounding air is greater than the

---

424 Torrance, *The Ground And Grammar of Theology*, 69.
425 'Entropy is a measure of the lack of order in the energy. There is no definite value of entropy for a given system (as there is for, say, mass), as entropy is a purely statistical measure. When there is zero entropy, all the energy can be used. As the entropy increases, available energy decreases until, with maximum entropy, no useful energy is available.' See S. Bleasdale, Entropy and the Universe <http:// www.chiark.greenend.org.uk/~sbleas/creative/ entropy> accessed 4 Dec 2005.

entropy decrease of the cooling hot body.[426] The second law of thermodynamics is a proved universal law of science which governs all processes with no known exception. One of the implications of the second law is that the whole universe is becoming more disorderly. Its total energy remains the same but it will be more evenly distributed, that means it has less energy to perform any more work, and the universe will die.[427] It is widely accepted in the scientific community that the entropy of the universe is increasing, that means the universe is becoming more random and disorderly.[428] Torrance himself admits that there is a natural inclination of nature 'to degenerate into states of disorder - the sort of the thing that every gardener knows only too well!'[429] The only reason that this happens is because the universe itself is a closed system and entropy increases in a closed system. Clearly, this scientific law contradicts Torrance's idea of open and unbound universe in his unitary outlook. This makes Torrance uneasy because he cannot selectively pick the theory of relativity and reject the second law of thermodynamics in pursuit of his unitary structure and the relational interpretation of space and time. Torrance argues that entropy cannot be merely equated with disorder, however, he realizes that the contingent order entails decay, decomposition and death, and these represent the dissolution of certain state of order.[430] Torrance admits that the increase in entropy works only in a closed system.[431] Since Torrance does not see the universe as a closed system, he speculates that there may be an emergence of some richer and complex forms of order to resist the ever increasing entropy.

---

426 *Encyclopedia Britannica* CD, 1998 standard edition.
427 H. M. Morris, *Many Infallible Proofs* (El Cajon, Cal.: Master Books, 1990), 237. Torrance himself also agrees that if the universe is only in itself, there is no exchange of matter and energy beyond the enclosed universe, the universe will be running towards a state of complete equilibrium and final death in accordance to the second law of thermodynamics. See Torrance, *Divine and Contingent Order*, 125.
428 The second law of thermodynamics is commonly used by apologists against the theory of evolution that through the evolution process a less complicated organism over time can naturally develop into a highly complicated organism such as man. That is to say, a disorder universe becomes more orderly, non-living elements develops into highly organized and structured intelligible creatures.
429 T. F. Torrance, 'The Concept of Order in Theology and Science', *The Princeton Seminary Bulletin*, 5/2 (1984), 132–133.
430 Torrance, *Divine and Contingent Order*, 120–121.
431 Ibid.

Torrance sees that the universe is still expanding, there is still a constant advance in overall order.[432] He tries to find a solution to enable him to account for the downward process of increasing entropy with the upward gradient of orderly development in the cosmos.[433] Morrison comments on these ideas,

> For example, the argument based on the laws of thermodynamics is sidestepped by postulating either: (a) a "steady-state" cosmology, in which continual evolution of matter out of nothing is supposedly taking place in some unknown region in space to offset the continual decay of energy which is observed everywhere in the known universe; or (b) an "oscillating-universe" cosmology, in which the present reign of decay in the universe is supposedly offset by alternate cycles of growth, during which all things are somehow re-energized. Neither of these theories is capable of proof, since the postulated rewinding of the universe takes place outside of those regions of space and time which can be experimentally observed. Such theories are at best, therefore, speculative suppositions. The Second Law, on the other hand, has been experimentally observed to be true wherever and whenever it can be tested, without exception. The Second Law is science; the theories which attempt to circumvent it are strictly fictions, conceivable perhaps, but never observed in real life.[434]

Interestingly, Torrance proposes similar ideas as that of 'steady-state universe' and 'oscillating universe', however, he sees that these theories collapse according to the scientific evidence.[435] According to Torrance, an open unbound universe is not necessarily an infinite universe. Thus, universe can be finite in time and space, yet it is unbound and open.[436] Torrance is facing a dilemma, on one hand, he has to agree based on the scientific evidence that there is persistent downward drag of entropy,[437] however, on the other hand, he tries to find ways to introduce a counterbalance to this increase of disorder. But the fact is, if there exists a counterbalance to the increase of entropy, the second law of thermodynamics could not be formulated in the first place. The existence of the second

---

432 Ibid., 126.
433 Ibid., 120–121.
434 Morris, 114.
435 Torrance, *The Ground And Grammar of Theology*, 70, 102.
436 Torrance apparently accepts the big bang theory that the universe comes from a singular source, and the universe is expanding at an acceleration greater than that of the gravitational pull among the celestial bodies. See Torrance, *The Ground And Grammar of Theology*, 101–102.
437 Torrance, *Divine and Contingent Order*, 126.

law is simply due to the observation of the increase of entropy in the universe. Thus, the second law does not help but rather dismantle Torrance's unitary structure of an open unbound universe.[438]

---

438 Torrance has been trying hard to come up with a scientific solution to this problem. In his *The Ground and Grammar of Theology*, he again argues that, based on the recent work of Ilya Prigogine and others, there must exist a higher level of open system that is characterised by a minimum of entropy, though our existing universe is actually an enclosed system. That is to say, there exists an open universe beyond our enclosed universe. Unfortunately, it is more a speculation or hypothesis than a scientific proven theory. This is a clear indication that Torrance is wrestling with the established law of thermodynamics and its implications. See Torrance, *The Ground And Grammar of Theology*, 141–142.

4. Triunity in Incarnation

It is of great importance that Torrance employs the Greek concept of *homoousion* to establish the reality that Jesus Christ is both God and man, and employs the concept of *Triunity* to establish that Christ is God and at the same time, he is the Son, the second Person in the One Being of God. Torrance sees that the doctrine of Trinity as the ultimate ground of theological knowledge of God because the very knowledge of God is grounded in the ultimate relations intrinsic to God's own Being.[1] The terms *Trinity* and *Triunity* are not found in the Scripture, however, it is a fundamental Christian concept that is nonetheless based on the revelation manifested by the Scripture. The doctrine of the Trinity, according to Torrance, is not to be interpreted as moving from the Three Persons to the One Being or from One Being to the Three Persons, but rather a dynamic movement of Trinity in Unity and Unity in Trinity.[2] Torrance's doctrine of Trinity is based on the teachings of Athanasius and the Constantinopolitan Confession,[3] and he realizes that Athanasius does not presuppose a precise definition of the relation between the three Persons and the one Being of God, but rather emphasizes the eternal consubstantiality of the three Persons and the self-revelation of God the Father which is given to us in Christ through the Holy Spirit.[4] The whole Being of the Father and the whole Being of the Son are mutually indwelling, inexisting and co-existing in one another.[5] The doctrine of Trinity formulated by Athanasius provides a consubstantial unity of three perfect co-equal enhypostatic Persons in the one indivisible Godhead.[6] Jesus Christ as the incarnate Son has a indissoluble hypostatic connection with

---

1   T. F. Torrance, *The Ground and Grammar of Theology* (Edinburgh: T&T Clark, 2001), 158–159.
2   T. F. Torrance, *Trinitarian Perspectives Toward Doctrinal Agreeement* (Edinburgh: T&T Clark, 1999), 113–114.
3   T. F. Torrance, *The Trinitarian Faith* (Edinburgh: T&T Clark, 2003), 340.
4   Torrance, *Trinitarian Perspectives Toward Doctrinal Agreeement*, 19.
5   T. F. Torrance, *The Christian Doctrine of God, One Being Three Persons* (Edinburgh: T&T Clark, 2001), 169.
6   Torrance, *The Trinitarian Faith*, 11.

the inner Life of the eternal God in Trinity.[7] Hilary, according to Torrance, affirms that there exists coinherence among the three divine Persons that each wholly contains the other without any diminishing in honor and glory.[8] Thus, God is distinguished in three Persons, and not three Gods as there is no division in the one Being of God, so that the Monarchia of the Father is not violated by the distinction of the three Persons.[9]

Torrance says that the term *Triunity* could better reflect the essence of *Trinity*, since it embodies the concept of Three Persons in One Being and One Being in Three Persons and the coinherent relationship between Trinity and Unity. *Triunity*, according to Torrance, defines the ultimate Triune nature and reality of God that Trinity is intrinsically and essentially a Unity, and the Unity is intrinsically and essentially Trinity.[10] Torrance's *Triunity* is a true reflection of the trinitarian theology of Gregory of Nazianzus who says,

> I cannot think of the One without immediately being surrounded by the radiance of the Three; nor can I discern the Three without at once being carried back to the One. When I think of the Three I think of him as a Whole... I cannot grasp the greatness of the One as to attribute a greater greatness to the rest. When I contemplate the Three together, I see but one Luminary, and cannot divide or measure out the undivided Light.[11]

Torrance sees that our knowing of God is in a circular movement from Unity to Trinity and from Trinity to Unity because we are unable to speak about the one Being without already speaking the three Persons, and to speak about the three Persons without assuming the knowledge of the one Being of God.[12] Although Trinity is plural in nature, Torrance finds that it is singular in essence; although Unity is a singular entity, Torrance realizes that it has three distinctive perspectives. The reality of Triunity is recognized because the self-revealing and self-giving God proclaims himself in the incarnation that he is Three Persons in One Being, and that the Son, the Father and the Holy Spirit all share the same

---

7   Torrance, *Trinitarian Perspectives Toward Doctrinal Agreeement*, 81.
8   Torrance, *The Christian Doctrine of God*, 169.
9   Torrance, *Trinitarian Perspectives Toward Doctrinal Agreeement*, 69.
10 Ibid., 25.
11 Gregory of Nazianzus quoted by Torrance, see *The Christian Doctrine of God*, 201.
12 Ibid., 173–174.

essence, oneness in Being. The one Being of God is not an abstract of an impersonal essence, but a living dynamic Being. Thus, Torrance suggests that both the one Being and Trinity can be referred to as *he*, though this reference may be linguistically difficult to both Greek and Latin theologians, however, he argues that this is essentially the evangelical and personal understanding of the one Triune God.[13]

Though all three Persons in the One Being are co-substantial and equal, there exists an order within the Triune God that God the Father is always first, God the Son second, and God the Holy Spirit third. This order, according to Torrance, is clearly reflected in the baptism that believers are baptized in the name of the Father, the Son, and the Holy Spirit. However, this priority of order or Monarchy of the Father does not indicate a priority or superiority within the Deity or among the three divine Persons, thus it does not disturb their complete equality.[14] The order only demonstrates the onto-relationship within the Deity that the Son is begotten of the Father and not vice versa, and this is the order manifested in the incarnation between the Father and the Son;[15] and this order is grounded in the irreversible relation between the Father and Son that the Father is regarded as the *Fons et Principium Deitatis*.[16] And the relationship among the three divine Persons is expressed by a theological conception of *perichoresis* which according to Torrace was a conception first used by an unknown theologian on the Trinity attributed to Cyril of Alexandria. It carries a meaning of a dynamic union and communion of the three divine Persons in one Being that they are mutually indwelling and inter-penetrating in one another without any commingling with one another and at the same time without any separation from one another in a onto-relationship. All three Persons are completely equal and identical in deity and power.[17] It is not a speculative concept, Torrance says, it expresses the soteriological truth of the identity between God himself and his saving grace in Christ.[18] *Perichoresis* indicates that the Trinity may only be known as a whole because as a whole that God makes himself known to us as three divine Persons. Torrance sees *perichoresis*

---

13   Torrance, *Trinitarian Perspectives Toward Doctrinal Agreeement*, 19.
14   Torrance, *The Christian Doctrine of God*, 201.
15   Ibid.
16   Torrance, *Trinitarian Perspectives Toward Doctrinal Agreeement*, 31–33.
17   Torrance, *The Christian Doctrine of God*, 170–171.
18   Ibid., 172.

as strengthening our understanding of the hypostatic distinction within the Trinity through the reciprocal relation with one another as Father, Son and Holy Spirit that all three together constitute the very communion of the one eternal God.[19] In Trinity, all three Persons are fully consubstantial, co-equal and co-eternal, however, each has his own distinct characteristics in relation to the other. The Persons are not just different modes of existence, but they are in substantive relations eternally immanent in the Being of God as God and constitutive of his indivisible Oneness as God.[20]

The incarnation, according to Torrance, is a demonstration of a complete coinherence in Being and Act between the Father and the Son. Torrance sees that there is a significant coordination among the three Persons in the economy of mankind that God's saving grace is operated by the Father, through the Son, and in the Holy Spirit.[21] That is to say, the saving activity is acted upon by all three divine Persons. They are not only Triune in Being, Torrance insists, but also Triune in Activity because God's Being and Activity completely interpenetrate each other. God is Being in Activity and Activity in Being. In other words, the three divine Persons always act together in both creation and redemption, and in every divine operation, and they act in such a way that their distinctive activities are always maintained in according to their distinctive otherness as three divine Persons. Torrance calls it *the perichoretic coactivity of the Holy Trinity.*[22] That is to say, each divine Person does not act independently but rather coordinatively with other divine Persons within the One Triune Godhead.

Historically, there are different ways of understanding the Holy Spirit especially about the procession of the Holy Spirit. The concept of *filioque* or so-called *double procession* drives a wedge between the East and West. The Western theologians, according to Torrance, hold that unless the Spirit proceeds from the Son as well as the Father, the Son is not regarded fully as God in the same sense as the Father. However, the Eastern theologians see the danger of creating two ultimate divine

---

19   Ibid., 175.
20   Torrance, *Trinitarian Perspectives Toward Doctrinal Agreeement*, 134.
21   Torrance, *The Christian Doctrine of God*, 195–196.
22   Ibid. 197–198.

Principles in God that the unity of the divine Monarchy is undermined.[23] In defending their position, according to Torrance, the Eastern theologians want to highlight the distinction between *procession* and *mission* in the teaching of Jesus according to the Gospel of John that the eternal *procession* of the Spirit from the Father is different than the historical *mission* of the Spirit from the Son, thus, *filioque* is denied.[24] For Athanasius, according to Torrance, the procession of the Spirit from the Father is related to the eternal generation of the Son from the Father which transcends the thoughts of men, and does not see that it is reverent to ask how the Spirit proceeds from God. Thus, Athanasius has no problem with *filioque*. However, Torrance argues that 'from the Father' according to Athanasius means 'from the being of the Father'.[25] Thus, procession is interpreted as a procession from the Being of God rather than from the Person Father in the Triune God. Torrance appeals to Calvin's idea that God is Spirit, thus the Holy Spirit is not only a distinct Person of the Being of God, but himself is the kind of Being that God is.[26] Torrance argues,

> any proper understanding of the procession of the Spirit must be of procession from the whole spiritual Being of God the Father which the Holy Spirit has entirely in common with the Father and the Son.[27]

By this argument, Torrance cleverly relocates the centre of the issue from the Person to the Being, and apparently solves the divisive problem by suggesting that the Holy Spirit proceeds not from God the Father but from God who is Father.[28] Thus, whether it is a single procession or a double procession, the emphasis is on the Being of God rather than the individual divine Persons. However, in his Auburn lectures, Torrance says,

> What is theologically significant about the expressions 'procession' or 'spiration', is that they speak of a distinctive relation of the Holy Spirit, in accordance with the

---

23   Ibid., 246, 337.
24   Ibid. 186.
25   Torrance, *The Trinitarian Faith*, 235–236.
26   Torrance, *Trinitarian Perspectives Toward Doctrinal Agreeement*, 25; Torrance, *The Christian Doctrine of God*, 191.
27   Ibid.
28   Torrance, *Trinitarian Perspectives Toward Doctrinal Agreeement*, 82–83.

nature of his particular Person, to the Father in comparison with and in difference from the distinctive relation of the Son to the Father.[29]

Procession, according to Torrance, indicates a relational aspect of divine actions of the divine Persons. Thus, it indicates an objective otherness rather than the intrinsic essence of the Triune God because it is a distinctive characteristic of an internal relationship within the three divine Persons rather than the whole Being of God. That is to say, procession by itself defines the relational aspect of Holy Spirit to the Father and to the Son rather than to the Being of God. In fact, there is no relational aspect between the divine Person and the Being of God because the Person himself is God. Thus, Torrance's solution confuses the intrinsic relation of the three divine Persons and does not really solve the issue of *filioque*.

4.1. Ousia and Hypostasis

The doctrine of Trinity cannot be unfolded unless the relation between *Person* and *Being* is addressed. According to Torrance, the Greek equivalent of *Person* is *hypostasis*, and *Being* is *ousia*. *Ousia* is understood as Being in its own internal relations, while *hypostasis* is understood as Being in its objective inter-relations. Torrance says,

> ousia was used to refer to the one being of the Godhead common to the three divine Persons, hypostasis was used to refer to them in their differences from one another and in their relations with one another in accordance with their particular modes of subsistence in God as Father, Son and Holy Spirit.[30]

In other words, *ousia* means subsistence of its own Being, and *hypostasis* means objective relation within its own being.[31] However, in earlier

---

29   Torrance, *The Christian Doctrine of God*, 193.
30   Torrance, *The Trinitarian Faith*, 219.
31   Ibid., 10.

days, these two terms shared very much the same meaning.[32] Torrance indicates that Athanasius understands both *ousia* and *hypostasis* as *Being*,[33] and in the Nicene Council, both terms in their simplest senses share similar meaning of very being or existence. Only when they are applied to the One Being and the Three Persons, they are differentiated from one another.[34] That is to say, the human language at the time was not yet developed conclusively to provide a definitive meaning to the word *Person* when it is used in the concept of Triunity. Torrance sees that there are two types of definition of *Person*, one is the Boethian notion of individual substance and the other is Richardine notion of eternal subsistent relations.[35] According to Boethius, the original meaning of the word comes from the mask worn by the Grecian actors in their acts of comedies and tragedies. It signifies a certain character that the actor is representing or playing on the stage. Thus, there is a certain mask for a king, a servant and so forth. And this is what the word *persona* represents.[36] The original intention of the Boethian definition is that in his treatise against Eutyches and Nestorius Boethius tries to differentiate *nature* from *person* that Christ is a person consisting of two natures.[37] He says that *nature* is a substrate of *person*, and that *person* cannot be predicated apart from *nature*. Since *nature* is defined by Boethius as either substances or accidents, and since a person cannot come into being among accidents, thus, person is properly applied to substances which can be either be corporeal or incorporeal, rational or irrational.[38] However, person cannot be affirmed of bodies that have no life (stone cannot be regarded as a person); or living things that lack sense (a tree); or living things which are dumb and not able to reason properly (a horse). In order to meet these requirements, only man, God, or angel are persons. Boethius further says that substances can be either universals or particulars, universal substances are those that are pre-

---

32 G. L. Prestige, *Fathers and Heretics* (London: Society for Promoting Christian Knowledge, 1940), 180–181.
33 Torrance, *Trinitarian Perspectives Toward Doctrinal Agreeement*, 15.
34 Ibid., 131.
35 Ibid., 49–50.
36 A. Boethius, *The Theological Tractates*, tr. H.F. Stewart and E.K. Rand (London: William Heinemann & Cambridge, 1962), 87.
37 Ibid., 77.
38 Ibid., 83.

dicated of individuals, and particulars are those which are never predicated of other things, and a person cannot in any case be applied to
universals, but only to particulars and individuals because there is no
person of a man, but only single persons of individuals such as Cicero or
Plato.[39] Boethius says,

> if Person belongs to substances alone, and these rational, and if every nature is a
> substance, existing not in universals but in individuals, we have found the definition
> of Person, viz.: "The individual substance of a rational nature."[40]

Thus, *the individual substance of a rational nature* becomes the classic
definition of a person in the Roman church.[41] In Boethian definition, the
Greek *ousia* is equivalent to the Latin *essence*, and *hypostasis* is equivalent to *substance*. Thus, Boethius says that Trinity is one *ousia*
(essence), three *hypostases (substances)*. However, at the same time, he
also sees that *nature* shares the same meaning as *Being* or *ousia*. Thus,
Boethius creates an ambiguity between *nature* and *Being* by claiming
nature is the specific property of any substance, and *person* is the
individual substance of a rational *nature*.[42] Torrance rejects this Boethian
definition of *person* because he sees it as a purely philosophical concept
derived from Aristotelian and Neoplatonic logical notions of particular
and general substance and rational nature.[43]

If it is not the substance, then what makes an individual person to be
distinctive from others? Torrance sees that Richard of St. Victor as
providing a theological concept of person which is derived from the
ontological relations of the three divine Persons within the Godhead, and
argues that the Richardine definition keeps each personal distinctness as
Father, Son, and Holy Spirit intact.[44] That is to say, the distinctiveness of
a person is determined by his relation with one another. Torrance says
that the concept of person as substantive relation was put forward by
Gregory of Nazianzus in contrast to the concept of *modes of Being*

---

39   Ibid., 85.
40   Ibid.
41   *Catholic Encyclopedia* <http://www.newadvent.org/cathen/11726a.htm> accessed
      6 Sep 2005.
42   Boethius, 93.
43   Torrance, *Reality and Evangelical Theology*, 43.
44   Ibid.; Torrance, *Trinitarian Perspectives Toward Doctrinal Agreeement*, 49–50.

developed by other Cappadocians and Didymus the Blind. *Ousia* is referred to as Being in its internal relations, *hypostasis* as Being in its objective relations.[45] Torrance believes that relations among the three divine Persons are not just modes of existence but hypostatic inter-relations that intrinsically belong to the Being of God. These relations are regarded as unchangeable, and these relations belong to what they are as persons. Thus, Torrance sees that person is an onto-relational concept.[46]

Calvin, according to Torrance, understands person as a *subsistence* or *hypostasis* dwelling in the Being of God, while each person is related to others yet himself is distinguished from others by a special feature of his own which itself cannot be transferred to others or shared with others.[47] However, at the same time, this *subsistence* is something different from Being, it is joined to Being by an indivisible nexus, yet itself is not to be equated with it. Torrance sees that when we consider the Father along with the Son, we should think of them in their relationship to each other as distinct Persons. However, when we speak of God, it applies no less to the Son, the Spirit than to the Father.[48] There exists a distinction between a divine Person and a divine Being that a Person should be spoken relatively, and the Being should be spoken absolutely. Calvin sees *subsistence (subsistentia)* or *hypostasis* is different from *Being (essentia)*; *subsistence* is referred as Being-in-relation, and *Being* is referred as Being-in-itself. Torrance says,

> In precise theological usage ousia now refers to being not simply as that which is but to what it is in respect of its internal reality, while hypostasis refers to being not just in its independent subsistence but in its objective otherness.[49] As Prestige expressed it, ousia denotes being in its 'inward reference', while hypostasis denotes being in its 'outward reference'.[50]

Torrance sees Calvin as adopting the eternal subsistent relations in God in defining the characteristic of subsistence according to the development of Augustine, Richard of St. Victor, Duns Scotus and John Major

---

45   Ibid., 70.
46   Torrance, *The Christian Doctrine of God*, 157.
47   Torrance, *Trinitarian Perspectives Toward Doctrinal Agreeement*, 69–70.
48   Ibid.
49   Torrance, *The Trinitarian Faith*, 130–131.
50   Ibid.

instead of the Boethian notion of individual substance which is adopted by Thomas Aquinas.[51] Etymologically, according to Prestige, the Latin *substantia* is an exact translation of the Greek *hypostasis*, however, he sees that the terms are not exactly identical. Prestige says,

'Substance' means an object consisting of some particular stuff; it has an inward reference to the nature of the thing in itself, expressing what logicians call a connotation. 'Object' means a substance marked off as an individual specimen by reason of its distinction from all other objects; it bears an outward reference to a reality independent of other individuals, and expresses what logicians call a denotation.[52]

That is to say, *substance* could carry a meaning of *ousia* when it is used inwardly, and carry a meaning of *hypostasis* when it is used outwardly.[53] To avoid confusion, Torrance adopts the Greek term *ousia* to refer to the one Being of the Godhead common to all three divine Persons, and *hypostasis* to refer to them in their differences from one another.[54] However, Gunton questions the validity and necessity of these two separate terms in defining the reality of Triunity, he says,

The two terms, accordingly, chiefly denoting terms, picking out different aspects of the one divine being. However, when it comes to connotation (to what the terms distinctly mean) should we differentiate between inner and outer in the way that Torrance does? He cannot intend the modalistic teaching that God is outwardly (in the persons) one thing, and inwardly, in his unified being another. But if not, what is the point of distinction between inner and outer? Do not being and person both refer to God both outwardly (in the economy) and inwardly (in the immanent Trinity)? Surely there is no relational being of God which is not that of the three persons in mutually constitutive perichoresis.[55]

Gunton argues that Torrance's usage of *ousia* and *hypostasis* may risk creating an inner reality and an outer reality of God that he is presented outwardly Persons and inwardly unified Being. Since God is inwardly and outwardly the same God, Gunton questions the necessity of se-

---

51 Torrance, *Trinitarian Perspectives Toward Doctrinal Agreeement*, 49–50.
52 Prestige, 181.
53 Ibid., 180.
54 Torrance, *The Trinitarian Faith*, 219.
55 C. Gunton, 'Being and Person', in *The Promise of Trinitarian Theology*, ed. Elmer M. Coyler (Lanham: Rowan & Littlefield Publishers, 2001), 128.

parating these two aspects which indeed are inseparable. Torrance suggests that Gunton misinterprets what he is saying, *ousia* is not simply an internal reality and *hypostasis* is not an independent subsistence but rather an objective otherness in differentiating one from the other in the Triune relationship of the three divine Persons.[56] Torrance particularly appeals to Prestige for his unique understanding of inward reference and outward reference. According to Prestige, a simple question of 'What is St. Mary's Church?' can have two possible answers. The first answer would give a physical location and an external appearance of the building so that one can recognize it if one is looking for it. It gives you the distinct and concrete fact. The second answer would tell you that it is a church building with an altar and a pulpit, it is not a shop nor a hostel, but a place of worship. This answer gives you the distinctive and significant fact. Thus, it is still the same building, however, two kinds of answer produce two different kinds of explanation.[57] Basically, it is two sides of the same coin.

According to Boethian definition, a thing to be an individual means that its substance cannot be further divided, thus, an individual is incommunicable, it is totally distinctive. However, this argument is only good for creaturely beings because each individual can be identified by his substance whether it is corporeal or incorporeal, however, when it comes to Triunity, all Persons basically share the same Being, thus the differentiation cannot come from its substance. The Richardine definition does seem to provide a better choice in differentiating the distinctiveness of the individual Persons without ever violating their sameness in the One Being. However, the relational notion of the definition of person is not without problem. Scotus argues that the relational *thisness* validates the principle of individuation, however, when it is applied to a subject, the subject must have already been individuated. Thus, Clark, according to Timothy, argues that *thisness* reflects the individuation, but itself does not cause individuation.[58] That is to say, relationship confirms an individual person but it does not cause the

---

56 T.F. Torrance, 'Thomas Torrance Responds', in *The Promise of Trinitarian Theology*, ed. Elmer M. Coyler (Lanham: Rowan & Littlefield Publishers, 2001), 316–317.

57 Prestige, 181–182.

58 C. Timothy, *A Defense of the Thomistic Definition of Person* <http://www.gocart.org/thesis.html> accessed 4 Nov 2003.

individuation of that person because that person must have been there already. If relationship is the only factor in defining a person, then, it would be difficult to argue that a statement is not a person when it is related to another statement, or an animal is not a person when it is related to another animal. The whole relational argument presupposes that an individual in relationship is a person, however, at the same time, it never defines what is a person? Torrance's usage of the Richardine definition in Triunity is relatively easy because God is well established as a rational Being according to the Boethian definition.

4.2. Economic Trinity and Immanent Trinity

In his self-giving and self-communication, God reveals himself in the person of Jesus Christ through the incarnation that he is Triune. The conception of *homoousion* employed by the church fathers affirms that the incarnate Son is the second Person in the Godhead. According to Torrance, it is through the incarnate Son who was born of the Virgin Mary, died on the Cross, risen from the death that we come to know the economic Trinity. It is then from the activity of the economic Trinity that we may know something about the activity of the ontological or immanent Trinity because the economy reflects the ontological reality of the Triune God.[59] That is to say, it is through the economic Trinity that we know the relation of the incarnate Son to the Father, and through love and prayer and worship, we know the interpersonal relation of God with us but also within God himself as Father, Son and Holy Spirit in his own Being.[60]

Though there is only one Trinity,[61] it has two very distinctive identities. Athanasius, according to Torrance, holds that the economic Trinity and immanent Trinity have to be clearly distinguished, at the same time, they cannot be separated from one another. If economic Trinity is separated from immanent Trinity, then it would bring into

---

59   Torrance, *The Christian Doctrine of God*, 198.
60   Torrance, *Trinitarian Perspectives Toward Doctrinal Agreeement*, 100.
61   Ibid., 79–80.

question whether God himself is the actual content of his revelation. If there is no real bond between the economic Trinity and the immanent Trinity, the saving events proclaimed in the salvation history of mankind are without any divine validity and lacking any ultimate divine truth. Torrance sees that economic Trinity and immanent Trinity overlap each other and belong to each other.[62] The Nicene concept of *homoousion*, according to Torrance, affirms that the economic Trinity is ontologically and epistemologically related to the immanent Trinity.[63] Thus, *homoousion* provides a clear distinction of two perspectives of Trinity and defines what may and may not be read back from God's economy in history to what he is eternally and inherently in himself.[64] Torrance calls this the double reference of *homoousion* because it refers to both the economic Trinity and the immanent Trinity. That is to say, something that belongs to the identity of the economic Trinity does not belong to the identity of the immanent Trinity. The concept of *homoousion* in the Nicene Confession is primarily soteriological.[65] It establishes the oneness between the incarnate Son and the Father, thus, the Trinitarian structure reflected in the confession of the early church fathers is basically addressing the economic Trinity instead of the immanent Trinity. The humanity of Christ is the main characteristic that differentiates the economic Trinity from immanent Trinity, because it is a created visible reality that is not part of the Trinity prior to the incarnation. It is only through the relation of *homoousion* that the economy is related to the ontology of the Triune God, that the incarnate Son shares the same essence as the eternal Logos who is in himself, entirely unconditioned by a reality other than himself, and thus totally independent of his creation.[66]

Even though we can speak of oneness between the economic Trinity and the immanent Trinity, we have to recognize the distinction between the two that elements in the incarnate economy cannot be read back into the eternal life of God in his eternal existence prior to the creation.[67]

---

62   Torrance, *The Christian Doctrine of God*, 7–8.
63   Ibid., 30.
64   Ibid., 97.
65   Torrance, *The Trinitarian Faith*, 148; Torrance, *Trinitarian Perspectives Toward Doctrinal Agreeement*, 62.
66   Torrance, *The Trinitarian Faith*, 89.
67   Torrance, *The Christian Doctrine of God*, 109.

Torrance warns that we must learn what is proper to read back into the immanent Trinity and what is not proper to read back.[68] He says,

> we may not read back into the eternal Life and Being of God the kind of temporal and causal connections that obtain in our creaturely existence in time and space, and yet the homoousion carries with it the recognition that the incarnation and the atoning mediation of the Son of God, together with the mission of the Spirit from the Father through the incarnate Son, have an essential place within the very Life of God.[69]

The economic Trinity is not fully identical with the immanent or ontological Trinity because though both share the essential oneness, each has its own distinctiveness.[70] The eternal Logos is eternally begotten of the Father[71] while the humanity of the incarnate Son is not part of the eternal Logos prior to creation. Even though the Creed insists that the one who was born of the Virgin Mary is the one who was born before all worlds, it is not saying that the humanity of the incarnate Son is pre-existent.[72] That is to say, the humanity could only be identified with Trinity in its economy. Torrance says,

> This means that we cannot but think of the incarnation of the Son as falling within the being and life of God - although, as we have had occasion to note, the incarnation must be regarded as something 'new' even for God, for the Son was not eternally man any more than the Father was eternally Creator.[73]

Torrance sees that the economic condescension of God in salvation is only of a temporal nature, and it is not identical with the abiding reality of God, that is to say, what is revealed in the incarnation does not change the fundamental concept of Being in respect of God.[74] The economic Trinity is a predetermined manifestation of the immanent Trinity in the history of salvation out of the freedom of God before the foundation of the world.[75] In Torrance's theological science, there exists a movement of knowledge from the level of economic Trinitarian relations in all that

---

68   Torrance, *Trinitarian Perspectives Toward Doctrinal Agreeement*, 85.
69   Torrance, *The Christian Doctrine of God*, 97.
70   Ibid.
71   Torrance, *Trinitarian Perspectives Toward Doctrinal Agreeement*, 118.
72   T. F. Torrance, *Divine Meaning* (Edinburgh: T&T Clark, 1995), 343–344.
73   Torrance, *The Trinitarian Faith*, 155.
74   Torrance, *Trinitarian Perspectives Toward Doctrinal Agreeement*, 85–86.
75   Torrance, *The Christian Doctrine of God*, 109.

164

God is toward us to the level of Trinitarian relations that God is eternally in his own Being. That is to say, our thought moves from the Trinity *ad extra* to the Trinity *ad intra* as we move from the lower level to the higher level, while the higher level controls the lower level.[76] The two identities of Trinity inevitably bring in two identities of *perichoresis*, the immanent *perichoresis* and economic *perichoresis*. The former applies to the Father, the eternal Son, and the Holy Spirit prior to the creation in their eternal communion of love,[77] and the latter applies to the Father, the incarnate Son, and the Holy Spirit in incarnation. This runs parallel to the two identities of relationship between the Father and the Son, one is the mutual relation of the eternal Son and the Father, and the other is the relation of the incarnate Son and the Father.[78] The former relation is demonstrated in the immanent Trinity, and the latter in the economic Trinity. Out of his overflowing love, according to Torrance, God freely created the universe in time and space. God was doing something utterly new and bringing into existence what did not exist before.[79] Though the incarnation is not necessary for God to be God,[80] he makes himself known in the economy of incarnation that he is God who is three Persons in One Being. Thus, the immanent *perichoresis* is related to the economic *perichoresis* through the concept of *homoousion*.[81] Gunton sees Torrance's homogeneous[82] view of the persons in the economy through the hypostatic relationship as ensuring that the move between economy and immanent Trinity is smooth.[83]

A number of recent Trinitarian theologians, according to Gunton, have denied the need for the distinction between the economic Trinity and the immanent Trinity.[84] Karl Rahner stresses that the economic Trinity is already the immanent Trinity because the basic event of the whole economy of salvation in the self-communication of God through

---

76   Torrance, *The Ground and Grammar of Theology*, 157–158.
77   Torrance, *The Christian Doctrine of God*, 221.
78   Torrance., *The Trinitarian Faith*, 58–59.
79   Torrance, *The Christian Doctrine of God*, 221.
80   Ibid., 108.
81   Torrance, *Trinitarian Perspectives Toward Doctrinal Agreeement*, 81.
82   By homogeneous, Gunton means that at the economic level, all three Persons have their full and equal deity. See Gunton, 'Being and Person', 120–121.
83   Ibid.
84   Ibid.,121–122.

the incarnate Son and the sending of the Spirit would not be really self-communication of God if the two-fold mission were not intrinsic to him. [85] Rahner's argument, according to Torrance, results in the conviction that in reality there is only one Trinity, and the Trinity *ad extra* and *ad intra* are identical.[86] Rahner does not see that the Scripture, even in the prologue of the Gospel of John, presents explicitly a doctrine of immanent Trinity. Thus, he says that the Trinity is a mystery of salvation, otherwise it would never have been revealed.[87] That is to say, Trinity is revealed simply for our salvation, and it is through our salvation that we know about Trinity. In our salvation, Jesus is revealed not simply God in general, but as the Son, the second divine person and he is man and only he is man. Rahner holds that it is the hypostatic union or the economic reality that defines Christ as the second Person, thus, the Trinity is the economic Trinity.[88] Rahner argues that the relation between the eternal Logos and the incarnate Son is more essential and intimate, and human nature is not a mask assumed from without but from within the eternal Logos that from the start it is the constitutive, real symbol of the Logos himself. Thus, human nature is the exteriorization of the Logos.[89] That is to say, human nature is never apart from the Being of God in his essence. [90] This leads to the formal thesis of Rahner's Trinitarian doctrine that the economic Trinity is the immanent Trinity, and the immanent Trinity is the economic Trinity.[91]

LaCugna goes further on Rahner's thesis by claiming that there is no distinction between the doctrine of the Trinity and the doctrine of the economy of salvation, there is only an essential unity of *oikonomia* and *theologia*.[92] She says, 'As for the nature of this unity, there cannot be a strict identity, either epistemological or ontological, between God and

---

85   Torrance, *Trinitarian Perspectives Toward Doctrinal Agreeement*, 100–101.

86   Ibid., 80.

87   K. Rahner, *The Trinity*, tr. Joseph Donceel (London: Burns & Oates, 1970), 21–22.

88   Ibid., 23–25.

89   Ibid., 32–33.

90   Torrance disagrees with Rahner and denies that somehow the humanity of Jesus existed before the Incarnation. See T. F. Torrance, 'The Pre-eminence of Jesus Christ', *The Expository Times*, 89 (October 1977-September 1978), 54.

91   Torrance, *Trinitarian Perspectives Toward Doctrinal Agreeement*, 100–101.

92   C. M. LaCugna, *God for Us* (San Francisco: HarperSanFrancisco, 1993), 221.

God for us.'[93] Gunton sees this as a clear denial of the need for a distinction between economic and immanent Trinity, or between God's historical act and his eternal being.[94] According to LaCugna, *oikonomia* is the concrete realization of the mystery of *theologia* in time, space, history, and personality, she says,

> Oikonomia is not the Trinity ad extra but the comprehensive plan of God reaching from creation to consummation, in which God and all creatures are destined to exist together in the mystery of love and communion. Similarly, theologia is not the Trinity in se, but, much more modestly and simply, the mystery of God.[95]

Instead of explaining Trinity as *ad extra* by referring to its unique manifestation in God's economy, LaCugna sees it as a salvation history which is in a close relation with the eternal being of God.[96] Thus, salvation history and the eternal being of God provide two aspects of the Trinity. In fact, the word *oikonomia* carries a meaning of economy,[97] thus, the economic aspect is nonetheless embedded in LaCugna's Trinitarian theology. The economic Trinity and the immanent Trinity, according to Torrance, are not two Trinities, but rather two relational aspects of one Trinity.[98] Both aspects cannot be separated from one another for they are locked together in God's threefold self-revelation and self-communication to us as Father, Son and Holy Spirit.[99] That means the concepts of God for us and God in himself are inseparable. Torrance criticizes Rahner for creating a confusion of movement of logical thought from one doctrine of the Trinity to another, and a movement of understanding and devotion from God's economic self-revelation in space and time to God's ontological self-revelation that he is eternally in his inner divine life. Torrace questions Rahner's statement that immanent Trinity is the necessary condition of the possibility of God's free self-communication, he asks,

---

93   Ibid.
94   Gunton, 'Being and Person', 121–122.
95   LaCugna, 223.
96   Ibid., 230.
97   *Catholic Encyclopedia* <http://www.newadvent.org/cathen/12213b.htm> accessed 14 Sep 2005.
98   Torrance, *Trinitarian Perspectives Toward Doctrinal Agreeement*, 79–80.
99   Torrance, *The Christian Doctrine of God*, 7.

Does this not involve a confusion between a necessary movement of thought (a logical necessity) and the kind of 'necessary' arising from the fact that God has freely and irreversibly communicated himself to us in the Incarnation once for all in such a way as to make any other possibility unentertainable by us?[100]

In response to Torrance's criticism of Rahner's idea, Gunton says that there is a distinction between the Being and the will of God that God is always the Triune God but he is not always creator because while the Son comes from his Being, the world is the product of his will. Gunton says that Torrance justifiably accuses Rahner of abstraction, an abstraction of confusing the order of knowing with the order of Being.[101] That is to say, Rahner confuses what we know logically of the economic Trinity and what Trinity is immanently in its own Being. However, Torrance still says positively in Rahner's argument that the self-communication of God to us in the Son and in the Spirit would not be a self-communication of God to us if what God is for us in the Son and the Spirit are not proper to God himself in his own intrinsic Being.[102] Thus, Torrance claims,

the Economic Trinity and the Ontological Trinity are identical, for there is only one divine Reality of God in himself and in his saving and revealing activity toward us in this world.[103]

Incarnation, according to Torrance, is the entry point that leads us to understand God in his inner ontological Triune Being through his economic condescension, and by means of *homoousion*, the economic Trinity and the immanent Trinity can be understood that they are 'one and the same'[104] because what God has revealed to us must be what God is in his very own Being.[105] Torrance says, if we take seriously that both the Logos and the activity of God are internal to the Being of God, we must hold that the economic condescension of God in revelation and salvation through Christ has opened up for us the knowledge of God in himself.[106]

---

100 Torrance, *Trinitarian Perspectives Toward Doctrinal Agreeement*, 79–80.
101 Gunton, 'Being and Person', 123.
102 Torrance, *Trinitarian Perspectives Toward Doctrinal Agreeement*, 80.
103 Torrance, *The Ground and Grammar of Theology*, 158.
104 T. F. Torrance, 'Introduction', in *The Incarnation: Ecumenical Studies in the Nicene-Constantinopolitan Creed A.D. 381*, ed. T. F. Torrance (Edinburgh: The Handsel Press, 1981), xx.
105 Torrance, *Reality and Evangelical Theology*, 24.
106 Torrance, *Trinitarian Perspectives Toward Doctrinal Agreeement*, 85–86.

Torrance thus creates an impression that economic Trinity is so closely linked to the immanent Trinity that these two are somehow the same and identical. This triggers some concerns from Gunton that Torrance tends to identify the economic Trinity with the immanent Trinity.[107] Gunton says that Torrance follows the footstep of Barth's great treatise on the Trinity that if revelation is truly God's self-revelation, then what we know of him must be that of him in his own eternal Being.[108] Though Torrance does tend to link the economic Trinity very closely with the immanent Trinity, it would probably be his poor usage of words that creates the confusion. Nonetheless, Torrance admits that we will never be able to fully understand this two-fold Trinity.[109]

4.2.1. Subordination

It is difficult to dispute that in the Scripture, there are many passages that indicate the subordination of the incarnate Son to the Father. Professor Gunton uses examples from the fourth Gospel and I Corinthians 15:24-28 to show that the Son obeys the Father, does the Father's work, and will hand over the kingdom to the Father.[110] These are all solid evidences that the Son serves the Father, and he subordinates himself to the Father. In response to these subordinational ideas, Torrance claims that the statement 'My Father is greater than I' has to be interpreted economically or soteriologically instead of ontologically.[111] Torrance argues that this is also the understanding held by Gregory Nazianzen, Cyril of Alexandria and Augustine. In other words, Torrance says,

> the subordination of Christ to the Father in his incarnate and saving economy cannot be read back into the eternal personal relations and distinctions subsisting in the Holy Trinity.[112]

107 Gunton, 'Being and Person', 130.
108 Ibid.,123.
109 Torrance, *The Christian Doctrine of God*, 97.
110 Gunton, 'Being and Person', 120–121.
111 Torrance, *The Christian Doctrine of God*, 180.
112 Torrance, *Trinitarian Perspectives Toward Doctrinal Agreeement*, 67.

Torrance clarifies that in Calvin's theology of Trinity, there is no ontological priority of one Person over the other, it has to do only with the order of relations which they have with one another within the unity of the Godhead.[113] There exists a principle of order that is to be observed that the Father is considered first, then the Son from Him and the Spirit from both. However, this order exists prior to the incarnation.[114] Thus, the order is independent from the economic subordination and is rooted in the eternity of God himself. Hence, there is no indication of inferiority to the Father in respect of Christ's Being. Subordination is seen as an economic phenomenon related only to Christ's human existence, and which cannot be read back into Trinity.[115] Since Trinity is purely divine, and all three Persons are sharing full equality among them in One Being, thus there can be of no subordination of the Son to the Father in the realm of divine nature. Torrance says,

> Of far-reaching importance is the stress laid by The Agreed Statement[116] on the 'Monarchy' of God, or the one ultimate Principle of Godhead, in which all three divine Persons share equally, for the whole indivisible Being of God belongs to each

---

113   Ibid., 65–66.

114   Ibid., 71.

115   'In relation to what Gunton says about economic subordination of the Son, that is, I believe, properly to be understood of the incarnate Son, but may not be read back into the eternal Godhead unless one operates with the altogether dubious idea that the Father is the "cause" of the being of the Son, as both Basil and Gregory Nyssen held, a notion which Gregory of Nazianzus rightly rejected in line with the teaching of Athanasius.' See Torrance, *Thomas Torrance Responds*, 316.

116   'On 13 March 1991, there was issued in Geneva a "Joint Statement of the Official Dialogue between the Orthodox Church and the Word Alliance of Reformed Churches' announcing that an "Agreed Statement on the Holy Trinity" had been reached.' The Agreed Statement features doctrinal consensus on (1) One Being and Three Persons must be understood in a personal way, that both Being and Persons are understood as personal. (2) One indivisible Being of God belongs to each of the three Persons as it belongs to all Persons. (3) Procession of the Spirit from the Father must be understood according to the principle that each Person is perfectly and wholly God. The Procession of the Spirit should be understood as that the Spirit is proceeding from the Being of God instead of the Person of the Father. (4) The doctrine of Trinity is neither approached from the Three Persons to the One Being of God, nor from the One Being of God to the Three Person, but rather it is approached from the dynamic Triunity of God as Trinity in Unity and Unity in Trinity. See Torrance, *Trinitarian Perspectives Toward Doctrinal Agreement*, 110–114)

of them as it belongs to all of them. This is reinforced by a deepened understanding of the way in which the three divine Persons indwell, interpenetrate and contain one another, while remaining what they are in their different properties and distinctness as Father, Son and Holy Spirit. Any notion of subordination in the Trinity is completely ruled out, as is any notion of degrees of Deity among the divine Persons.[117]

Any notion of subordination within the Trinity is clearly ruled out by Torrance as he indicates that subordination is an economic property which cannot be carried into the eternal relation in the immanent Trinity. While Christ was a God-man on earth, he subordinated himself to the Father. This is to say that his human nature assumes subordination, thus, there existed a time when subordination was not. Since subordination is a predicate of his humanity, it entails all properties of human nature. Thus, every aspect of Christ's human life forms an inseparable part of his subordination, which includes his suffering, emotion, weakness, mortality, will and obedience. Subordination in the form of submission and obedience is manifested through Christ's human life from his very birth to death and resurrection.[118] His vicarious humanity brings us back from disobedience to obedience, from defiance to love. Christ subordinates his own human will to the will of the Father as Jesus praying in Gethsemane, 'Not my will, but thine be done.'[119] Christ in his subordination has to learn obedience by the things he suffered, as the incarnation itself is a suffering and humiliation. He grew up within our bondage and ignorance, shared human anguish and weakness, and faced human temptations.[120] These are all to be interpreted economically instead of ontologically because subordination itself is an economic phenomenon.

Torrance's view on subordination is undoubtedly different from that of his teacher Karl Barth who sees that subordination does not only belong to the economy of the Triune God, but it is also intrinsic to the Triune Being. Gunton understands that in Barth's theology, the economic subordination is read up into the eternal Trinity and becomes an immanent equality of Being. Thus, Barth can say on the basis of his Christology, according to Gunton, it is as godlike to be humble as to be

---

117   Ibid., 112.
118   T. F. Torrance, *Theology in Reconstruction* (London: SCM Press, 1965), 155.
119   T. F. Torrance, *When Christ Comes and Comes Again* (Eugene: Wipf and Stock Publishers, 1957), 42–43; Torrance, *Theology in Reconstruction*, 126.
120   Ibid., 132.

exalted, and both elements of commanding and obeying exist within the immanent Trinity.[121] Subordination is no longer an economic activity but an ontological attribute of the divine Person. Barth says, 'In His mode of being as the Son He fulfils the divine subordination, just as the Father in His mode of being as the Father fulfils the divine superiority.'[122] That is to say, the nature of the eternal Son to be submissive is no different than that of the Father to be superlative. Barth sees that God reveals to us just as natural to be lowly as it is to be high,[123] thus, to be subordinate is simply a virtue that the divine possesses. The humility of Christ is not something that is extrinsic to Christ, but rather it is intrinsic to the very Being of Christ because humility is grounded in the Being of God. Barth says that since

> God is in Christ, if what the man Jesus does is God's own work, this aspect of the self-emptying and self-humbling of Jesus Christ as an act of obedience cannot be alien to God. But in this case we have to see here the other and inner side of the mystery of the divine nature of Christ and therefore of the nature of the one true God – that He Himself is also able and free to render obedience.[124]

It is out of God's own will that he renders obedience as an exercise of his freedom to choose and act. Thus, humility is not something apart from God, but rather it is a demonstration of his freedom as manifested in the obedience of Christ to the Father. Barth affirms that it is essential to God that he is both an above and a below, a superiority and a subordination, that is to say, Barth believes that God is both the one who is obeyed and the one who obeys.[125] However, this is not a mutual subordination, the Son is always subordinating to the Father, and this forms an intrinsic relation within the Trinity. Thus, Barth is projecting the economic Trinity onto the immanent Trinity by equating what is happening in the salvation history as what is immanently in God himself.

Athanasius, according to Torrance, argues that in order to take the complete humanness of Christ seriously, we must include all human affections proper to human nature of Christ, which include weakness,

121   Gunton, 'Being and Person', 120–121.
122   Barth, *Church Dogmatics*, 4/1, 209.
123   Ibid., 191.
124   Ibid., 193
125   Ibid., 200–201.

anxiety, agitation, passion, ignorance, sentient characteristics of human beings, otherwise, all his salvific act 'for our sakes', 'on our behalf' and 'in our place' would be meaningless.[126] According to Athanasius, these are all part of the economic condescension of the Son to be our Saviour, and by no means that his economic activities and affections indicate any subordination of the Son ontologically.[127] Christ's divinity in his own ontological Being is by no means in any subordinating situation. In rebuking Arians who

> searched the Scriptures for passages referring to the weakness, poverty, lowliness and servile status of Christ, such as Philippians 2:9 f., and passages which spoke of him as obeying, praying, worshipping God and sharing with us our infirmities, such as Hebrews 3:1 f., in order to establish their argument as to the creaturely nature of Christ.[128]

Athanasius claims that all these should be understood in terms of the economic condescension of Christ. That is to say, his human prayer, his human receiving of divine blessing, his obedience and the whole of his becoming flesh belong only to his human economy that he undertook for our sake.[129] Athanasius clearly sets the boundary that humanly properties remain to be human, Christ's divinity remains unchanged, and there is no interchange between these two natures and no mix-up of properties. Torrance agrees that economic properties, historical events, and Christ's human affections cannot be projected into the eternal Being of God. He says,

> when the Creed speaks of the historical events in the experience of the Incarnate Son, in suffering and death and resurrection and identifies him with the One through whom all things were made, it is not projecting historical happening into the eternal Being of God.[130]

Torrance goes further by saying that even though Christ assumes a human body, shares our physical space, he remains whatever he ever was, and operates beyond human concept of space and time that he is on earth

---

126 T. F. Torrance, *Theology in Reconciliation* (Eugene: Wipf and Stock Publishers, 1996), 152.
127 Ibid., 151.
128 Ibid.
129 Ibid.
130 T. F. Torrance, *Divine Meaning* (Edinburgh: T & T Clark, 1995), 343–344.

and at the same time he is in heaven. Since space is a predicate of the occupant, it has to be determined and understood according to the nature of the occupant. Thus, the divine nature of Christ cannot have the same space-relation with the Father as we creatures have, otherwise, he would not be God. [131] Unfortunately, this particular economic property is confused by Torrance's own unitary view of Act and Being that Christ's economic suffering becomes an ontological suffering of God. [132] However, at the same time he claims that suffering is an economic property, he says,

> In other words, the subjection of Christ to the Father in his incarnate economy as the suffering and obedient Servant cannot be read back into the eternal hypostatic relations and distinctions subsisting in the Holy Trinity. [133]

Torrance does not seem consistent in addressing two distinct natures of Christ such that his economic property can be distinguished from his ontological property, his economic existence distinguished from his ontological reality. Depending on the doctrinal topic he is discussing, Torrance tends to switch between the economic subordination and ontological subordination. When Torrance is addressing Christ's earthly activities, he clearly indicates that the subordination is limited to his economic existence. However, when he is addressing the doctrine of Trinity, especially the suffering of Christ, an economical property suddenly penetrates into the ontological Being and becomes an ontological reality. Thus, Gunton warns that economic subordinationism has to be strictly distinguished from ontological subordinationism. [134]

4.2.2. Impassibility and Immutability

Impassibility and immutability are regarded as two untouchable doctrines of the early Christian church. [135] These classical conceptions were

---

131 Ibid., 366.
132 Torrance, *The Christian Doctrine of God*, 249.
133 Ibid., 180.
134 Gunton, 'Being and Person', 120–121.
135 J. Y. Lee, *God Suffers For Us* (The Hague: Martinus Nijhoff, 1974),1-2; B. R. Brasnett, *The Suffering of The Impassible God* (London: Society For Promoting

similarly reflected in the 1646 Westminster Confession of Faith that God is 'invisible, without body, parts, or passions, and immutable' (2:1) and The Thirty-Nine Articles of 1571 that God is 'without body, parts, or passions' (Article 1). In general, the doctrine of impassibility carries a meaning that God is not affected by human passions,[136] thus he is not subject to suffering and pain as that of human. Lee sees that the terms *passibility* and *impassibility* are used to designate the capacity or incapacity of God to experience suffering.[137] Suffering however is different than pain. Pain, according to Lee, is defined as a physical sensation bound to the body, since God is a Spirit, thus it is irrelevant to attribute pain to God. Suffering, according to Lee, is defined within a loving relationship bound to time.[138] Torrance does not see that pain is any different than suffering as both are used metaphorically to indicate suffering in his writings. McWilliams gives a more restrictive definition that impassibility is defined as not capable of being affected or act upon.[139] However, the main focus is still God's capacity to suffer. Tertullian in his treatise against Marcion highlights that because we have passions, thus we think that God must have the same passions. He argues that when we read the physical metaphors of God such as his right hand, eyes and feet from the Scripture, we do not confuse these *anthropomorphisms* with those of human beings.[140] Thus similarly when we read of *anthropopathisms* or figurative expressions of God's passions, we also do not believe that God shares the same human passions.[141] Tertullian claims that our human sensations are corruptible and could not belong to God who is incorruptible due to his divine essence.[142] That is to say, God does not share corruptible human passions. Gregory of Nyssa says that human life has two limits, one is the start of our life and the other is the

---

Christian Knowledge, 1928), 1; W. McWilliams, *The Passion of God* (Macon: Mercer University Press, 1985), 10, 13.

136 D. W. Bercot (ed.), *A Dictionary of Early Christian Beliefs*, (Peaboy, Mass.: Hendrickson, 1998), 313.

137 Lee, 4.

138 Ibid., 4–5.

139 McWilliams, 4.

140 Tertullian, 'Against Marcion', in *Ante-Nicene Fathers*, ed. Alexander Roberts & James Donaldson, 3 (Peaboy, Mass.: Hendrickson, 1999), 310.

141 Ibid.

142 Ibid.

end of our life, and heavenly passionlessness is preserved for us for both ends by God who is himself passionless.[143] In other words, human passion does not exist prior to our birth and it is a temporal attribute which would disappear by the end of our life on earth. Gregory firmly believes that God is both impassible and changeless.[144] According to Athanasius, God is faithful to his words that he remains the same and unchanging, even if we believe not, he is still faithful because he cannot deny himself.[145] Thus, Athanasius sees the unchangeness is closely related to his faithfulness. However, Athanasius also sees that God cannot change because change belongs to bodies in the creation, he says, 'the change is in the things which afterwards came to be, and not in God.'[146] That is to say, change happens in creation, the creator remains unchangeable. Athanasius in his *Defence of the Nicene Definition* says that Christ's divine nature is fully unchangeable and immutable because that is the essence of the Father.[147] All human properties such as hungry, thirsty, suffering, according to Athanasius, can only attribute to the flesh of Christ.[148] The human passions of the body, though belong to Christ, Athanasius insists that they do not touch him in his deity.[149] That is to say, the deity of Christ remains impassible.[150] Though the doctrines were widely assumed in the early Christian church, it was not totally unchallenged. The patripassianist controversy in the third century highlighted the opposing views of God's impassibility.[151]

---

143 Gregory of Nyssa, 'Letter to Eustathia, Ambrosia, and Basilissa', in *Nicene and Post-Nicene Fathers*, ed. Philip Schaff & Henry Wace, 5 (Peaboy, Mass.: Hendrickson, 1999), 544.

144 Ibid.

145 2 Timothy 2:13

146 Athanasius, 'Against the Arians', in *Nicene and Post Nicene Fathers*, ed. Philip Schaff and Henry Wace, 4 (Peaboy, Mass.: Hendrickson, 1999), 4.15, 439.

147 Athanasius, 'Defence of The Nicene Definition', in *Nicene and Post Nicene Fathers*, ed. Philip Schaff and Henry Wace, 4 (Peaboy, Mass.: Hendrickson, 1999), 5:23, p. 165.

148 Athanasius, 'Orations Against The Arians', in *The Christological Controversy*, ed. Richard A. Norris (Philadelphia: Fortress, 1980), 3:31, 89.

149 Ibid., 90.

150 Ibid., 93.

151 Patripassianism is a kind of monarchianism which believes that it is the Father who became incarnate, was born of a virgin, the Father Christ cosuffered with the human Jesus and died on the cross. See McWilliams, 12–13, and Elwell, 727.

While God is impassible and immutable, yet there are difficulties as seen by Mozley in the language of the Scripture in God's love and wrath. Mozley says that for behind any action of God there must be something which explains the action, and this something is necessarily connected with the feeling-tone in God. At least, the Cross does not reveal an apathetic God. Thus, he argues that beyond a certain point, the orthodox theology could not go.[152] Brasnett in his *The Suffering of the Impassible God* argues that God can be both passible and impassible, and this is not necessarily contradictory that it cannot be true in both cases. He argues that God is passible because he wills to suffer, and he is impassible because he wills only the good, thus he is impassible to the moral evil.[153] God suffers because he is good, and pain is an inevitable result of goodness, thus, Brasnett says, 'a creator God who refused to bear pain for the good of his creatures would be less than good.'[154] Thus, Brasnett sees suffering as an attribute of God, however, this would risk God of becoming evil because evil is the source of the suffering. Karl Barth, according to Torrance, believes that the immutable and impassible concept of God will devastate Christian life and work,[155] because impassibility would detach God from our life on earth. Barth says that God has a close interaction with his creatures and especially his incarnate Son. In the humiliation of his Son, God the Father suffers. Barth says,

> This is that primarily it is God the Father who suffers in the offering and sending of his Son in his abasement, The suffering is not his own, but the alien suffering of the creature, of man, which he takes to himself in the Son. But he does suffer it in the humiliation of his Son with a depth with which it never was or will be suffered by any man - apart from the One who is his Son.'[156]

Suffering, according to Barth, is not intrinsic to God himself, it is an alien nature of the creature, however, it becomes his own when God became man. That is to say, the impassible God becomes passible in the person of Jesus Christ. Torrance shares Barth's idea and argues that if the one who suffered for us was mere man, then we are not in fact

---

152   J. K. Mozley, *The Impassibility of God* (Cambridge: Cambridge University, 1926), 174–175.
153   Brasnett, 90–92.
154   Ibid., 92.
155   Torrance, *Trinitarian Perspectives Toward Doctrinal Agreeement*, 4.
156   Torrance, *The Christian Doctrine of God*, 249.

redeemed. Unless it is God who suffered in Christ, then we cannot be saved because only God can be our savior,[157] and only God can bear our burden and forgive our sins in and through Jesus Christ.[158] Torrance argues that if God is merely impassible, then he has not made room for himself in our agonized existence, and if he is merely immutable, then he has neither place nor time for frail evanescent creatures in his unchanging existence.[159] McWilliams sees that the crucial component in the affirmation of divine suffering is to resolve the problem of human suffering.[160] Unless God suffers, he cannot solve our suffering. Unless we know that God suffers with us, we can have no consolation in our suffering. Impassibility and immutability, according to Torrance, are simply scholastic concepts of dualistic Augustinianism that God is apart from the world.[161] Torrance sees God as invariant in love but not impassible, constant in faithfulness but not immutable.[162] Though God is not subject to the human passions, he is not untouched by human sufferings. The sufferings of Christ are not extrinsic but intrinsic to his very divine nature.[163] God is not apathetical to the pain and suffering of his human creatures, his heart goes out for them in redemptive sympathy as Torrance appeals to Moltmann's idea of God's passibility.[164] In Moltmann's theology of the cross, he says that we know God through his suffering rather than his glory, the theology of the cross must come ahead of the theology of hope. God does care, understand, and feel for our pains. Moltmann challenges traditional understanding of the apathetic God and asks,

> The Old Testament speaks often of the wrath of God. But if the apathetic God neither loves or hates, how can he then be wrathful? How can he be interested in the history of his people on earth? How can he have compassion on Israel's suffering?[165]

---

157   Ibid., 247–248.
158   T. F. Torrance, *The Doctrine of Jesus Christ* (Eugene: Wipf and Stock Publishers, 2002), 153.
159   T. F. Torrance, *Space, Time and Incarnation* (London: Oxford University Press, 1969), 75.
160   McWilliams, 5–6.
161   Torrance, *Trinitarian Perspectives Toward Doctrinal Agreeement*, 82.
162   Torrance, *Space, Time and Incarnation*, 75.
163   Torrance, *The Trinitarian Faith*, 185.
164   Torrance, *The Christian Doctrine of God*, 248.
165   J. Moltmann, 'The Crucified God', *Theology Today*, 31/1 (April 1974), 11.

Moltmann believes that God does not only participate in our suffering but also make our suffering into his own.[166] In becoming man, God the Son himself does not only enter into the finitude of man but also into the situation where he is abandoned by God the Father. Thus, the Father suffers the loss of his Son, and the Son suffers in the abandonment by the Father. On the cross, Moltmann argues that a rupture tears through God himself because the suffering of abandonment lies intrinsically in God himself.[167] Unless God is capable of suffering, according to Moltmann, God is not capable to love.[168] That is to say, suffering is a manifestation of God's love. Thus, Moltmann argues that because God loves, then, God must also be capable of suffering. An impassible God, according to Moltmann, 'is capable of neither love nor feeling.'[169] Thus, in Moltmann's theology, our sufferings are consoled by God's suffering. Rahner, however, sees differently, he says, 'it does not help me to escape from my mess and mix-up and despair if God is in the same predicament.'[170]

Torrance however hesitates to go all the way in Moltmann's direction that God is passible and he suffers for us in his own Being. Torrance sees that there is an ambiguity in the concept of impassibility and immutability because on one hand God is not moved by anything outside of himself that he does not suffer of anything other than himself, on the other hand, it does not mean that God does not move himself or he is incapable of divine passion.[171] Torrance believes that according to the classical doctrine of impassibility God is not subject to any human passions, thus God is opposed to all suffering and pain, and is not moved or swayed by anything other than himself.[172] Torrance makes it clear in his writings that he has no intention to challenge the patristic conceptions adopted at Chalcedon or in the terminology of Leo's Tome that the mystery of the God-man is embedded in the negatives of impassibility

---

166 Ibid., 15.
167 Ibid., 14–16.
168 J. Moltmann, *History and the Triune God* (London: SCM Press, 1991), 123.
169 Ibid.
170 Karl Rahner argument quoted by Moltmann in Jurgen Moltmann's *History and the Triune God*, 122.
171 T. F. Torrance, *Divine and Contingent Order* (Edinburgh: T&T Clark, 1998), 6.
172 Torrance, *The Christian Doctrine of God*, 248.

and immutability,[173] and God is intrinsically impassible in his own nature.[174] However, at the same time, Torrance does not see that God is locked up in his self-isolation that he cannot be touched with our human feelings, pains and hurts. Torrance believes that God can act freely and passionately to interact with us because he is the ever living and loving God who graciously determines himself for us as our God and savior.[175] If God is utterly unchangeable and impassible, Torrance argues, then there exists no ontological bond between his transcendent reality and the Lord Jesus Christ who loved us and gave himself for us, and there is no place for our human prayer or any expectation that it will be answered because God is so remote and impassible.[176]

Torrance admits that logically passibility and impassibility exclude one another, however, he argues that it must be understood soteriologically and dynamically for its co-existence that God is both suffering and not suffering.[177] Soteriology has an effect of setting aside the static notions of God's being in favor of God's free movement of love that he enters into relations with others and establishing reciprocal relation with them. That is to say, passibility has to be understood as a temporal event that it actualizes in time and space, however, impassibility by itself is not of temporal nature, it is the eternal characteristic of the divine nature of God and cannot be defined by time. Torrance recognizes that he is in a paradoxical situation, thus he says, we have to understand passibility and impassibility in a paradoxical relation.[178] On one hand, Torrance says that God is impassible in the sense that he remains eternally and changelessly the same, on the other hand, God is passible that he in fact became so in taking upon himself the form of a servant. The conjunction, according to Torrance, is as incomprehensible as the mode of the union of two natures in Christ.[179] Here again, Torrance employs his dialectical approach to absorb two opposite ideas without ever addressing the unbridgeable discrepancies.

---

173   T. F. Torrance, 'The Atonement and The Oneness of The Church', *Scottish Journal of Theology*, 7 (1954), 247.
174   Torrance, *The Christian Doctrine of God*, 248.
175   Ibid., 4.
176   Ibid., 254.
177   Torrance, *The Trinitarian Faith*, 185.
178   Torrance, *The Christian Doctrine of God*, 249–250.
179   Ibid., 249–250.

4.2.2.1. Dynamic Constancy

Torrance believes that God can act freely and passionately to interact with us because he is the ever living and loving God who graciously determines himself for us as our God and savior.[180] God is eternally new and constantly surpasses himself in all that he does, and this infinite mobility and newness are based on the constancy of God that he always remains the same mighty living God. Torrance sees that God is immutably free, free to become one of us in our creaturely existence and to enter into the depths of our misery and alienation, yet at the same time, remains what he is always.[181] That is to say, God is free to suffer in Christ. God is not totally immutable because he could act and make changes while he himself remains in his eternal unchanging life. Thus, in the New Testament, God has revealed himself through his creating and saving acts in Jesus Christ.[182] That is to say, mutability is extrinsic to God in his creation while immutability is intrinsic to God in his own Being. Immutability, according to Torrance, is to be understood as God's permanent faithfulness that he is absolutely reliable. God's immutability is a living immutability instead of immobility that he is able to act out of his freedom in his divine constancy.[183] There exists a dynamic of newness in his intrinsic unchangeableness that God is a divine Being and at the same time a divine becoming.[184] *I am who I am*, according to Torrance, implies *I will be who I will be* because the nature of God's eternal life is not immobile but continually self-moving. God's eternal life is continually new and carries within it the eternal purpose of God's love, moving uninterruptedly toward its perfect fulfillment.[185] Though Calvin sees that *I am that I am* carries a meaning of *I will be what I will be*, yet it is of the same force as the present because it designates the perpetual duration of time.[186] The future and present are in fact the same time, the future is not ahead of present in the eyes of God. According to Pan-

---

180   Ibid., 4.
181   Ibid., 239.
182   Ibid., 236.
183   Ibid., 244.
184   Ibid., 237.
185   Ibid., 235, 240.
186   J. Calvin, 'Commentaries on The Four Last Books of Moses', in *Calvin's Commentaries*, 2 (Grand Rapids, Mich.: Baker, 2003), 73.

nenberg, Augustine sees nothing changeable in God because there is no past which is no longer, nor future which is not yet, but only present. Pannenberg says,

> Our contemporary exegesis, of course, told us to read that phrase "I shall be who I shall be". This changes the point and deprives Augustine's argument of its most important evidence. There is future to God, then, and he will show himself to be what he will be. In other words, he is free and unrestricted in his actions. This is a far cry from the timeless identity of "I am who I am".[187]

The timeless identity of *I am that I am* is interpreted by Torrance as a timely human identity in order to bring in continual newness of God in the future. However, according to Augustine, this newness is already embodied in the timeless identity of *I am that I am*. Pannenberg says, 'in the trinitarian life the present is never separated from the future and the past because of the unity of the eternal life they share.'[188] In the Trinitarian life, there is no past or future. That is to say, what happened in the past is not old, what will happen in the future is not new, everything is present to God. Newness is a human idea, it is simply not applicable to God. When it is applied to God, then either God is humanized, or newness is divinized. However, Torrance does not see there is any conflict between the unchanging constancy of God and the movement and activity of God toward the fulfillment of his eternal purpose. He argues that in the incarnation, the eternal became time that the divine Being is also a divine Becoming. This does not mean, according to Torrance, God becomes other than what he eternally is or he passes over from becoming into Being something else, but rather he continues to be what he always is and ever will be in the living movement of his eternal Being.[189]

4.2.2.2. Communicatio Idiomatum

According to Torrance, God is free to feel for our suffering that he is taking our hurt and pain into himself.[190] He denies that God is merely

---

187 W. Pannenberg, 'Eternity, Time and the Trinitarian God', *CTI Reflections*, 3 (1999), 51.
188 Ibid., 58.
189 Torrance, *The Christian Doctrine of God*, 242.
190 Torrance, *Space, Time and Incarnation*, 74.

impassible because he has made room for himself in our agonized existence, and claims that God is invariant in love but not impassible.[191] Torrance sees it as a paradox that we must think of God as impassible that he is not subject to the passions of creaturely existence, but on the other hand, he is not untouched by the suffering of his people. Torrance suggests that impassibility and immutability of God refer to the eternal tranquility and serenity of God in his transcendence over all the changes and chances, all the pain and violence, of our world, that God is able to move himself and his is not devoid of passion and love.[192] That is to say, God maintains his eternal tranquility while he suffers in our sufferings, he maintains his faithfulness while he makes changes. Torrance says,

> we cannot think of the sufferings of Christ as external to the Person of the Logos. It is the very same Person who suffered and who saved us, not just man but the Lord as man; both his divine and his human acts are acts of one and the same Person.[193]

Torrance argues that since the person suffers, then, both humanity and divinity of Christ must suffer at the same time because if he who suffered for us was mere man, we are not in fact redeemed. It was Christ as God who suffered, and he suffered for us to redeem mankind from their suffering and to redeem suffering in mankind.[194] Since there is the perfect oneness of his human nature and divine nature, we cannot say that Christ suffered only in his humanity and not in his divinity.[195] Since the Son suffers, the Father and the Spirit also suffer with the Son in their own distinctive hypostatic realities.[196] That is to say, the human nature of Christ penetrates into his divine nature that the suffering is no longer limited to the humanity of Christ, but it moves into the divinity of Christ. This clearly violates the fundamental Chalcedonian formula that there exists no movement between the two natures of Christ. The uniqueness of the two natures are highlighted in the Chalcedonian Confession that the person Jesus Christ is known of

---

191   Ibid., 74.
192   T. F. Torrance, *The Ground And Grammar of Theology* (Edinburgh: T&T Clark, 2001), 65.
193   Torrance, *The Trinitarian Faith*, 185.
194   Torrance, *The Christian Doctrine of God*, 247–248.
195   Ibid., 252.
196   Ibid., 253.

two natures, without confusion, without conversion, without severance, and without division; the distinction of the natures being in no wise abolished by their union, but the peculiarity of each nature being maintained, and both concurring in one person and hypostasis.[197]

In criticizing the Lutheran concept of communicatio idiomatum, Torrance charges that Lutherans transferred the concept of *perichoresis* from the Trinity to the hypostatic union and so developed a notion of coinherence of the divine and human natures that risked the deification of Christ's humanity.[198] Unfortunately, Torrance is making the same mistake in his acceptance of the idea of possibility that human attributes such as suffering are transferred from the human nature of Christ to the divine nature of Christ by arguing that if humanity of Christ suffers, then deity of Christ must also suffer. A non-existent passion which was alien to God in his eternal Being is now a predicate of God. It is true that Christ is both impassible and passible, immutable and mutable. However, these two characteristics are unique to his two distinctive natures, and there is absolutely no interchange between these two natures in the person of Jesus Christ. In becoming man, God does not change but remains ever one and the same without ceasing to be what he eternally was and is and ever will be in himself.[199] Torrance confuses the human economy with divine reality and contradicts his own argument that human economy such as subordination can never be read back into the eternal Being. By taking earthly experience into the ontological Being, Anders says that it creates a *retroactive* effect on God's primary relationship to himself, he says, 'God affects the world and is affected by his experiences of the world to the point that the economic Trinity can be understood as actually taken up into the immanent Trinity.'[200] That is to say, God must relate to the creation in order to exist and God is no longer free not to relate to the world as he is influenced by the world in his very Being of existence. If God really suffers in his own Being, Anders says,

---

197 P. Schaff, *History of The Christian Church*, 3 (Grand Rapids, Mich.: Eerdmans, 1995), 745–746.

198 Torrance, *Space, Time and Incarnation*, 32.

199 Torrance, *The Christian Doctrine of God*, 238.

200 P. Anders, *Divine Impassibility and Our Suffering God* <http://www.modern reformation.org/mr97/julaug/mr9704impassibility.html> accessed 20 Jan 2003.

It would no longer be possible to say that there was a time when God did not suffer, and then in freedom God chose to suffer; when suffering is associated with his intrinsic being and "divinized" or "eternalized," it is not accurate to talk of it in temporal terms... when suffering takes on an eternal and perpetual significance by virtue of its incorporation into the immanent Trinity, it can no longer be said that there was a time before when it was not and a time after when it is. When suffering is taken into the being of God, it always and everlasting is.[201]

When suffering is incorporated into the Being of God, God suffers eternally and perpetually. He is a suffering God because suffering becomes an attribute of his Being, and God can no longer free from suffering. An eternal suffering God cannot redeem mankind from suffering because he himself is eternally attached to suffering. Both Torrance and Moltmann are making similar mistakes by projecting human experience and relation onto God, and twist an econo-relation into an onto-relation that God is impacted by his economy in human history.

4.2.2.3. Reciprocity

Many think that if love is stripped of passion, it is a lesser kind of love. If God is love, then God must be passionate like us.[202] In order for God to love, he must have the opportunity to be loved. Thus, the fundamental presupposition of the argument of God's passibility is that God as the ultimate reality is essentially love.[203] It carries a conviction that God could not be so closely associated with the world without sharing the pain and suffering of the world.[204] Thus, God to be God is by making himself vulnerable within the relationship with us.[205] Dennis Ngien says,

> An almighty God who cannot suffer is poverty stricken because he cannot love or be involved. If God remains unmoved by whatever we do, there is really very little point in doing one thing rather than the other. If friendship means allowing oneself to be affected by another, then this unmoved, unfeeling deity can have no friends or be our friend.[206]

201 Ibid.
202 P. R. Johnson, *God Without Mood Swings* (2000) <http://www.spurgeon. org/~phil/articles/impassib.htm> accessed 20 Feb 2006.
203 Lee, 175.
204 Mozley, 176.
205 Johnson, *God Without Mood Swings*
206 D. Ngien, 'The God Who Suffers', *Christianity Today* 3 (February 1997) <http:// www.biblical-theology.com/miscellaneous/suffer.htm> accessed 1 Feb 2006.

According to Torrance, incarnation reflects the interaction between God and this world, that God can feel our human suffering in such a way that our suffering creates a reciprocal effect on him because God is the kind of God who creates a personal reciprocity of love between himself and us.[207] There are two types of reciprocal love, one is intrinsic to God and the other is between God and his creatures. The former is a onto-relation in reciprocal loving within the three Persons and is expressed through the theological expression of *perichoresis*. The reciprocity belongs to what they are each hypostatically in themselves as divine Persons in their self-giving to one another and receiving from one another.[208] God's love is not that of solitary inactive or static love, it is a dynamic movement of reciprocal loving within the eternal Being of God,[209] thus, love cannot be anything less than the Trinitarian reciprocal relation. The latter is a personal reciprocity between God and man in the communion of love.[210] God who listens to our prayers, according to Torrance, involves a two-way movement between God and man, and this movement is reciprocal in nature which is patterned upon the reciprocal relation between the Son and the Father.[211] That is to say, the Trinitarian reciprocal relation is extended by Torrance to include the relation between God and man that we share similar reciprocity as that of the Trinitarian Being.[212] God himself then becomes vulnerable in this reciprocity of love that he may be hurt. This is exactly what Moltmann is proposing that 'The more one loves, however, the more vulnerable one becomes.'[213] Love according to the modern human idea is reciprocal in nature, thus the love between God and man must be also reciprocal. However, the Scripture teaches that God's love always moves in one direction, that is, it moves from God to man. That is to say, our reciprocal response to the love of God does not change or influence his love towards us. Torrance affirms that God's love is not conditioned by the incarnation or the salvation history of mankind because the love of God does not have a temporal beginning,

207   Torrance, *Trinitarian Perspectives Toward Doctrinal Agreeement*, 3.
208   Torrance, *The Christian Doctrine of God*, 166.
209   Ibid., 5.
210   Torrance, *Trinitarian Perspectives Toward Doctrinal Agreeement*, 3.
211   T. F. Torrance, *The Mediation of Christ* (Exeter: Paternoster Press, 1983), 22.
212   Torrance, *The Christian Doctrine of God*, 6.
213   Moltmann, 'The Crucified God', 17.

it is as eternal as his very Being.[214] That means, the love of God cannot be determined by mankind in human time and space, it is beyond the reciprocity of man. That is to say, God's love towards mankind is not conditioned by the reciprocity of man. God loves us because he loves, not because we respond to his love, because his loving is the primary act of his Being.[215] Thus, God's love is always active, never passive. This creates a paradox because on one hand, God's love is always active disregarding how we respond to his love, on the other hand, Torrance sees that there exists a personal reciprocal relation of love between God and man that God shares our suffering, God suffers because we suffer. Thus, Torrance claims that God loves us more than what he loves himself.[216] Since God's love by itself is perfect, how can God love us more than what is already perfect? Phillip Johnson highlights the important problem of the reciprocity of passions, he says,

> If His creatures can literally make Him change His mood by the thing they do, then God isn't even truly in control of His own state of mind. If outside influences can force an involuntary change in God's disposition, then what real assurance do we have that His love for us will remain constant? That is precisely why Jeremiah cited God's immutability and impassibility as the main guarantee of His steadfast love for His own: "It is of the Lord's mercies that we are not consumed, because his compassions fail not" (Lamentations 3:22). God Himself made a similar point in Malachi 3:6: "For I am the Lord, I change not; therefore ye sons of Jacob are not consumed."[217]

Undoubtedly, some see that God's love can change God himself. Ngien says, 'God suffers because God wills to love'.[218] That is to say, unless God suffers, he could not love. If that is true, since love is eternally in God himself, does that mean suffering is also eternally in himself prior to the creation? If not, how can God suffer in his own Triune communion of love? Anders sees that both Moltmann and Ngien are simply bringing the economic properties of the Triune God into the very Being of God immanently. Impassibility does not mean that God does not have affections, it simply means that he is not subject to involuntary passions,

---

214 Torrance, *The Christian Doctrine of God*, 210.
215 Ibid., 244–245.
216 Ibid., 215.
217 Johnson, *God Without Mood Swings*.
218 Ngien, *The God Who Suffers*.

and his affections are always active and never passive.[219] That is to say, God's love and affection towards us is never determined by our reciprocal response. Thus, God's love is not defined by its vulnerability but by its ontological reality of what God is eternally.

4.3. Open Ended Incarnation

In the Incarnation, Torrance sees the divine nature and the human nature of Christ as really and eternally united into oneness of the God-man, a real Mediator between God and man.[220] This seems to be the prevailing theological view that 'the union of humanity with deity in the person of Christ is indissoluble and eternal.'[221] In patristic writings, Athanasius points out that after having fulfilled his human economy, the incarnate Son sits at the right hand of the Father. Torrance further expounds that the union between the incarnate Son and the Father is more than a transient episode in time, but rather ontologically and eternally real in the Triune God.[222] Thus, the incarnation itself is not a temporary event but rather a permanent reality. Torrance argues that by seeing incarnation as a temporal economy would undermine the co-eternity and co-equality of the three divine Persons. That is to say, the temporal identity of the second Person as the incarnate Son does not share the same equality and eternity as the other two Persons. Torrance appeals to the confession of the Council of Constantinople that Christ's kingdom shall have no end, and there is one power, one lordship and one kingdom, and which is the kingdom of Christ. This, according to Torrance, serves as the recognition of the finality and the everlasting nature of the saving economy in the

---

219   Johnson, *God Without Mood Swings*.
220   Torrance, *Theology in Reconstruction*, 130.
221   A. H. Strong, *Systematic Theology* (Old Tappan, N.J.: Fleming H. Revell, 1976), 698; R. L. Dabney, Lectures in Systematic Theology (Grand Rapids, Mich.: Zondervan, 1976), 550–553.
222   Torrance, *The Trinitarian Faith*, 308; Torrance, *Trinitarian Perspectives Toward Doctrinal Agreeement*, 13.

incarnate Son who reigns forever.[223] Torrance also appeals to the Nicene Creed and claims that

> Jesus Christ and God are not to be separated, and therefore it affirms belief in the one Lord Jesus Christ who will come again with glory to judge the quick and the dead, and whose Kingdom shall have no end. That is to say, the oneness of being between Jesus Christ and God that characterized the incarnation is not something of merely temporary duration in the economy of salvation: it is a final reality enduring endlessly into eternity.[224]

That is to say, the incarnation is essentially an eternal union of divine nature and human nature that the eternal Son is forever changed into the incarnate Son.[225] The hypostatic union of God and man, according to Torrance, is the union of the eternal Word of God with the humanity of Jesus, which is eternal and never-ending.[226] In the incarnation, God became man without ceasing to be God, Torrance argues that similarly in his ascension Christ became God without ceasing to be man, he says,

> so in his ascension we have to think of Christ as ascending above all space and time without ceasing to be man or without any diminishment of his physical, historical existence.[227]

Christ's humanity will remain with him in heaven, and the same incarnate Son will come again to make all things new. If the incarnation is of temporal nature, then the one to come again will not be the one crucified on the cross.[228] That is to say that the human nature of Christ is forever carried into eternality in the divine Person and shares the same ontological status as the Godhead. The everlasting humanity of Christ will not only come again and rule his eternal kingdom, according to Torrance, he will serve as a living atonement, Torrance says, 'he emerges as the living Atonement eternally prevailing in its advocacy before God and eternally availing in its propitiation for man with God.'[229] This implies that the atonement is a not accomplished event, but rather an ongoing

---

223 Torrance, *The Trinitarian Faith*, 274–275.
224 Torrance, *The Incarnation*, xv.
225 Torrance, *Theology in Reconstruction*, 130.
226 Torrance, *The Doctrine of Jesus Christ*, 195.
227 Torrance, *Space, Time and Resurrection*, 129.
228 Torrance, *The Trinitarian Faith*, 274–275.
229 Torrance, *Space, Time and Resurrection*, 55

event. Thus, Christ at the right hand of God in heaven continues the very work which he came here to do.[230] That is to say, the incarnation is still in progress, and the saving work has not been done on the Cross. This challenges the effectiveness and sufficiency of Christ's atonement on the Cross that it still needs a continual maintenance by the incarnate Christ or by a Man who sits on the throne of the universe.[231]

In many of his writings, Torrance clearly indicates that the incarnation itself is a mission.[232] A mission that God sent His Son to the world to save the world, and Torrance says that Christ mission does not return to God void but accomplished. If a mission has a starting point, a mission must have its ending. Incarnation, according to Torrance, is a unique evangelical mission that has its completion in Christ's resurrection, he says,

> in a real sense the Resurrection might well be said to be the completion of the Incarnation. Consequently if in one way the Incarnation means the end of all history, yet in another way it means the proper fulfilment of it – in and through the mighty Word of God incarnate in Christ.[233]

That is to say, resurrection is both the completion of the incarnation and fulfillment of God's saving act in the history of mankind. In fulfilling his unique evangelical mission, Torrance says, Christ's supreme mission is carried on through the subordinate mission of his disciples.[234] Regarding the ministry of the church, Torrance says,

> The ministry of the Church is in no sense an extension of the ministry of Christ or a prolongation of certain of His ministerial functions. That is the view that leads to very wrong notions of Eucharistic Sacrifice as an extension of Christ's own priestly sacrifice in the Eucharist, and to wrong notions of priesthood as the prolongation of His Priesthood in the ministry: and behind it all lies the notion of the Church as an extending or prolonging of the Incarnation, and sometimes, as in certain Roman expositions, there even lurks the heretical idea of the reincarnation of Christ in the Church through the Spirit regarded as the soul of the Church.[235]

---

230 Torrance, *The Doctrine of Jesus Christ*, 192.
231 T. F. Torrance, *When Christ Comes and Comes Again* (Eugene: Wipf and Stock Publishers, 1957), 154.
232 Torrance, *Space, Time and Resurrection*, 63.
233 Torrance, *The Doctrine of Jesus Christ*, 78.
234 Torrance, *The Trinitarian Faith*, 285–286.
235 T. F. Torrance, *Royal Priesthood* (London: Continuum T&T Clark, 2003), 37.

If the church is not the extension of Christ's ministry, then the incarnation as the supreme mission must have been accomplished, then it is no longer an ongoing event or to be prolonged indefinitely. However, incarnation as a mission completed contradicts Torrance's own theological idea of open-ended incarnation that Christ's self-oblation in his humanity remains forever before God.[236] There is an inconsistency in Torrance's idea that Christ's human economy is fulfilled yet his humanity remains, or in other words, an evangelical mission is accomplished on the Cross, yet the mission related humanity drags on. This open-ended incarnation contradicts his own understanding of the economic Trinity and the immanent Trinity that what is proper and what is not proper to read back into the Being of God[237] because what happened in the economy of God is not the same as what is God eternally himself. Subordination can only be part of the economic Trinity because it is related to the human economy, and according to Torrance, it cannot be read back into the immanent Trinity. Since the humanity of Christ is the very essence of the subordination, and if subordination cannot be read back into the ontological reality of the Triune God, then humanity cannot be read back into the eternal reality of the Triune God. Since subordination is a temporal event, the humanity of Christ must also be a temporal event. If the humanity of Christ is carried forward into eternality in God, then Christ as the second Person in the Trinity will forever be subordinate to the Father, and this would shatter the doctrine of the co-equality of the three divine Persons that Torrance wants to maintain. Thus, if Torrance really sees the incarnation as a human economy as he says in his writings, then it must be of temporal nature. According to Thomas Aquinas, Christ's human nature is a sort of tool of his divine nature, its usage is only in the hand of the user, not in itself.[238] Thus, the tool cannot be identified with the tool user forever, its existence is for a purpose in human time and space. Torrance has a tendency to identify the humanity of Christ as an inseparable element of the everlasting God in his eternal existence.

---

236 Torrance, *Space, Time and Resurrection*, 115.
237 Torrance, *Trinitarian Perspectives Toward Doctrinal Agreeement*, 87–88.
238 Aquinas, Thomas, *Summa Theologiae*, ed. Timothy McDermott (Allen, Tx.: Christian Classics, 1991), 316.

Torrance realizes that the dominant theological concept of the eternal kingdom of God is that it is to be administered by the Son throughout the world until its very end, then Christ will hand it over to the Father.[239] The kingdom of Christ then becomes the kingdom of God. For the reign of Christ, Torrance says that Calvin has dated its commencement from the period of the building of the temple after the seventy years of exile, and ending at his second coming on the last day.[240] Thus, Calvin assigns a fixed duration to the kingdom of Christ that it does not last forever. Calvin comments,

> But Christ will then restore the kingdom which he has received, that we may cleave wholly to God. Nor will he in this way resign the kingdom, but will transfer it in a manner from his humanity to his glorious divinity, because a way of approach will then be opened up, from which our infirmity now keeps us back. Thus, then Christ will be subjected to the Father. because the vail being then removed, we shall openly behold God reigning in his majesty, and Christ's humanity will then no longer be interposed to keep us back from a closer view of God.[241]

By transferring his humanity to his divinity, according to Calvin, there is a strong implication that the humanity of Christ finally comes to an end, and his humanity will no longer be interposed between God and us. Unfortunately, Torrance is reluctant to accept Calvin's idea and claims that Calvin is not always lucid in the language he uses, and interprets it as that Christ 'continues to wear our humanity, but in such a way that we see Him in the full glory and majesty of Godhead.'[242] It seems that there is a clear distortion of Calvin's intention that the humanity of Christ is no longer an element in the relation between God and man after the transfer of the kingdom because the Son at that time is no longer an incarnate Son, he is again the eternal Son by detaching from his temporal humanity. In fact, Calvin may well suggest that there will be a transfer of the kingdom from the incarnate Son (humanity) to the eternal Son

---

239 T. F. Torrance, *Kingdom and Church* (Eugene: Wipf and Stock Publishers, 1996), 76; this idea is shown up in Thiessen's Systematic Theology, see H. C. Thiessen, *Lectures in Systematic Theology* (Grand Rapids, Mich.: Eerdmans, 1977), 515.
240 Torrance, *Kingdom and Church*, 117.
241 Calvin, John, 'Commentary on The Epistles of Paul the Apostle to The Corinthians', in *Calvin's Commentaries*, 20/2 (Grand Rapids, Mich.: Baker, 2003), 32–33.
242 Torrance, *Kingdom and Church*, 137–138.

(divinity) and this signals the end of the incarnated humanity. Prior to the transfer of the kingdom, Calvin indicates that Christ had already given up his mortal body when he ascended into heaven.[243] However, it is not known whether the transformed human body or humanity was still with Christ in his ascension, Calvin does not provide a clear answer. Calvin's idea that the humanity of Christ will finally come to an end is also mentioned in the patristic writings of Hilary of Poitiers and Marcellus of Ancyra.[244] In his work *On The Trinity*, Hilary says that Christ will deliver the kingdom to God the Father when the authorities are abolished, death conquered, and enemies subdued, and God shall be all in all, by that time, Hilary says,

> no trace of the nature of His earthly body may remain in Him. Although before this time the two were combined within Him, He must now become God only; not, however, by casting off the body, but by translating it through subjection; not by losing it through dissolution, but by transfiguring it in glory.[245]

The humanity in the last day, according to Hilary, is not totally detached from the eternal Son, but rather it is somehow absorbed into his divinity; and thus makes it, according to Grillmeier, completely incorruptible, eternal, and spiritual.[246] Marcellus shares a similar view that Christ's human economy will come to an end after the last judgment, and Christ will hand over the rule to God the Father,[247] he says,

> Now I believe the divine scriptures, that there is one God and that his Logos came forth from the Father so that 'all things' might be made 'through him' (John 1.3). But after the Day of Judgement and the rectification of all things and the conquest of

---

243 Calvin, John, 'Commentaries on The Prophet Daniel', in *Calvin's Commentaries*, 13 (Grand Rapids, Mich.: Baker, 2003), 42, 44.

244 'Marcellus, bishop of Ancrya, in Galatia, noted for the part he took in the Synod of Ancyra (314-315), held at the end of the persecution of Maximin, made himself conspicuous at the Council of Nicea (325) by his homoousian views, and was upheld by Athanasius and the whole Western Church.' See J. Strong, and J. McClintock, *Cyclopdeia of Biblical, Theological, And Ecclesiastical Literature*, 5 (Grand Rapids, Mich.: Baker, 1981), 734.

245 Hilary of Poitiers, 'On the Trinity', in *Nicene and Post-Nicene Fathers*, ed. Philip Schaff & Henry Wace, 9 (Peaboy, Mass.: Hendrickson, 1999), 11.40, 214.

246 Marcellus of Ancyra quoted by Grillmeier Aloys, *Christ in Christian Tradition*, 1 (Atlanta: John Knox Press, 1975), 291.

247 Ibid., 399.

every hostile power, 'then he himself will be subject to the one who has subjected everything to him' (I Cor. 15. 15.28, 24), the God and Father, so that the Logos may again be in God what he was earlier before the beginning of the world.[248]

That is to say, in the incarnation, God assumed humanity to become the incarnate Son. After the final judgment, the incarnate Son returns to his original status as the eternal Son. Thus, the incarnation as a human economy finally ends. The very characteristic of the incarnation is the humanity of Christ, if the humanity of Christ lasts forever, the incarnation lasts forever. Thus, in Torrance's theology, the incarnation that has its starting moment in the human history is always ongoing. In other words, Christ's evangelical mission will remain unaccomplished forever.

---

248 Marcellus of Ancyra quoted by Grillmeier, 292.

5. Incarnation is The Revelation

Gunton comments that Barth's theology is centered essentially on the theology of revelation, while Torrance's theology is centered on the concept of *homoousion*.[1] Torrance disagrees and asserts that he is no less committed to revelation than Barth, and his doctrine of *homoousion* underscores his commitment to God's self-revelation in the incarnation.[2] In Torrance's theology, the incarnation is regarded as the pinnacle of God's revelation: God reveals himself in his own Being and Act in the person of Jesus Christ so that we may know him in a true and accurate way.[3] It is only through the Son that we are able to understand God as the Almighty Creator,[4] and to know him as the Father and the Holy Spirit.[5] Brunner sees the whole of the Scripture as concerned with the divine revelation, even though there is no explicit mention of the revelation.[6] The word *revelation* carries a meaning of the unveiling of something hidden.[7] According to Vincent, in classical Greek, *revelation*, used as a verb, is to uncover something such as the head or the body, however, its religious sense is unknown to the heathens.[8] In the biblical sense, Brunner says that in addition to the meaning that something hidden is made known or a mystery is unveiled, *revelation* carries a double signature of absoluteness and personal character that it is the

1   C. Gunton, 'Being and Person', in *The Promise of Trinitarian Theology*, ed. Elmer M. Coyler, (Lanham: Rowan & Littlefield Publishers, 2001), 118.

2   T. F. Torrance, 'Thomas Torrance Responds', in *The Promise of Trinitarian Theology*, ed. Elmer M. Coyler, (Lanham: Rowan & Littlefield Publishers, 2001), 315.

3   T. F. Torrance, *The Trinitarian Faith* (Edinburgh: T&T Clark, 2003), 3.

4   Ibid., 7.

5   Ibid., 8.

6   E. Brunner, *Revelation and Reason* (London: Student Christian Movement Press Ltd., 1947), 21.

7   M. R. Vincent, *Word Studies in the New Testament*, 2 (Peaboy, Ma.: Hendrickson Publishers, 1984), 405; J. Baillie, *The Idea of Revelation in Recent Thought* (London: Oxford University Press, 1956), 19.

8   Vincent, 406.

absolute manifestation of something that is absolutely concealed.[9] The unveiledness is especially emphasized by Barth who sees revelation as the self-unveiling of God who according to his nature cannot be unveiled to man.[10] However, the *unveiling* has a reserved qualification that God in his self-revelation to man is still hidden. The hiddenness of God, Barth argues, is due to the fact that the Creator is totally distinct from his creation that he does not belong to the realm of human knowledge, thus we cannot know directly about God. God is hidden from us because he is the Holy One, we are not able to see him even indirectly with our corrupted eyes.[11] In his own nature, God cannot be unveiled, thus, God takes on our human form in order to reveal to us.[12] Thus, according to Torrance, Barth sees the revelation in Jesus as indeed the most complete veiling of God's incomprehensiblity.[13] However, at the same time, by taking up our form, God assumes our language, world and humanity so that we can hear with our human ears, see with our eyes.[14]

According to Barth, the actuality of the incarnate revelation is that God has not only created a world different from himself, he also becomes a creature himself for human beings created by himself. Thus, it establishes a reciprocal relationship between himself and his creatures. And man is called and enabled by God's revelation to put this reciprocity into practice.[15] Torrance adopts Barth's idea that revelation creates a reciprocity between God and man, and by revealing himself to man God summons answer from man.[16] Torrance says that we do not know God in abstract, but in a relation which he has established in the revelation between God and man. We thus know God because he has made himself known in the revelation. Torrance argues that we cannot construct the

9   Brunner, *Revelation and Reason*, 23.
10   K. Barth, *Church Dogmatics*, tr. by G.T. Thomson, 1/1 (Edinburgh: T&T Clark, 1963), 368.
11   Ibid.
12   Ibid.
13   T. F. Torrance, *Karl Barth: An Introduction To His Early Theology, 1910–1931* (London: SCM Press, 1962), 44.
14   Barth, *Church Dogmatics*, 1/1, 399.
15   K. Barth, *Church Dogmatics*, tr. G.W. Bromiley & T.F. Torrance, 2/1 (Edinburgh: T&T Clark, 1964), 58.
16   T. F. Torrance, *Reality and Evangelical Theology* (London: InterVarsity Press, 1999), 85.

knowledge of God outside this God-man revelation and relation.[17] He says,

> the reciprocity created by the movement of divine revelation takes the form of a community of reciprocity between God and man established in human society, which then under the continuing impact of divine revelation becomes the appropriate medium of its continuing communication to man.[18]

God's self-revelation in the person of Jesus Christ is established in human history and communicated to us in our human form, so that we can apprehend the truth according to our human existence. Thus, revelation is not an event that is operated tangentially to human existence and history, but rather within human existence and history. The revelation is not an isolated incident in human history, according to Torrance, because God has a long history of dialogue with Israel. Israel plays an important role in the mediation of revelation,[19] and through Israel God's self-revelation provides humanity with permanent structures of thought and speech for the apprehension of that revelation.[20] Unfortunately, God's self-giving and self-communicating to the people of Israel is not an easy and painless process. Israel, as the chosen medium of his self-revelation to mankind, was brought upon intensive suffering in its relations with other peoples due to its conflict with God's holiness, mercy and truth.[21] In the midst of all these sufferings, according to Torrance, God was preparing the final mediation such that the divine revelation could be faithfully responded to by man. In the fullness of time, God became man so that the divine revelation and the faithful response that it calls for were indivisibly united and fulfilled in the person of Jesus Christ.[22]

---

17   T. F. Torrance, *God and Rationality* (London: Oxford University Press, 1971), 31.
18   Torrance, *Reality and Evangelical Theology*, 86.
19   T. F. Torrance, *The Mediation of Christ*, (Exeter: Paternoster Press, 1983), 17.
20   Ibid., 27. Torrance mentions that the Holy Scriptures have only a time-conditioned significance, thus, it is transient in nature. Nonetheless, Torrance says that there are structures of biblical thought and speech found in the Old Testament which have permanent structure.
21   Ibid., 18.
22   Ibid., 18–19.

In the revelation, according to Torrance, God is not revealing something about God, but God reveals himself in such a way that the revealed and the revealer are one and same,[23] because God who reveals himself in Jesus Christ is not something other than himself but his very own self.[24] Thus, the content of the revelation is God himself instead of truths about God such as is suggested in propositional revelation. Packer argues differently, he says that Christ and apostles, all spoke of God's words to men in the form of statement and inference, argument and deduction. He says,

> God's word in their mouths was propositional in character. Christ and apostles regularly appealed to Old Testament statements as providing a valid basis for inferences about God, and drew from them by the ordinary laws of grammar and logic conclusions which they put forward as truths revealed there.[25]

Torrance on the other hand sees God's self-revelation as relational and personal, and cannot be reduced to an abstract idea projected out of human consciousness.[26] However, at the same time Torrance does not deny that God also reveals himself to the people of Israel in the Old Testament.[27] Torrance says,

> In his desire to reveal himself and make himself knowable to mankind, he selected one small race out of the whole mass of humanity, and subjected it to intensive interaction and dialogue with himself in such a way that he might mould and shape this people in the service of his self-revelation.[28]

In the Old Testament, God's self-revelation is through his Act rather than his Being. Thus, it is difficult to reject the idea that revelation may be propositional in nature. In Torrance's theology, God's self-revelation in Christ is identical with himself, and in Christ, God communicates to us in such a way that authentic knowledge of God is embodied in our humanity that it can be communicated to us and understood by us. Ac-

---

23   T. F. Torrance, *The Christian Doctrine of God* (Edinburgh: T&T Clark, 2001), 22.

24   T. F. Torrance, *The Doctrine of Jesus Christ* (Eugene: Wipf and Stock Publishers, 2002), 101.

25   J. I. Packer, *Fundamentalism and the Word of God* (Grand Rapids, Mich.: Eerdmans, 1958), 93.

26   Torrance, *The Christian Doctrine of God*, 22.

27   T. F. Torrance, *The Trinitarian Faith* (Edinburgh: T&T Clark, 2003), 247–248.

28   Torrance, *The Mediation of Christ*, 16.

cording to Torrance, Christ is the complete revelation of God to man, and the perfect correspondence on man's part to that revelation.[29] That is to say, revelation is not only an act from God to man but also an act from man to God because the humanity of Christ is the very substance of the revelation,[30] and through his obedience, Christ provides a concrete action of mediation between God and man.[31]

In Barth's theology, the doctrine of revelation precedes the doctrine of Trinity in the sense that revelation is regarded as the ground of the doctrine of Trinity.[32] We know that God is Triune because he reveals to us in the person of Jesus Christ. Unless we know the Son, we cannot know the economic reality of the Triune God. Torrance says that without the incarnate Son, we are unable to know the Almighty. By knowing the Son, we know the Father, and the relation of the Son to the Father, according to Torrance, is the very essence of the Gospel. And in the incarnation, God reveals himself to us as Father, Son and Holy Spirit, three Persons in One Being. It is only when we know God the Father in and through his Son who is his very own Being, then we may know him in a true and accurate way, that is to say, we know God in accordance with his divine nature.[33]

Torrance believes that Christ as revealed in the incarnation is a guarantee that God is like him, and in Christ we can have real knowledge of God because God and Christ are one.[34] That is to say, God is really like Jesus because there exists a mutual and exclusive relation between him and the Father.[35] Torrance argues that if what God reveals to us in Jesus Christ is not the same as what God is in himself, then there exists no identity between God and his revelation, and there is no access to the Father through the Son, and we are left completely in the dark about God.[36] That is to say, God would be an absolute blank for us if the Son is

---

29   Torrance, *The Christian Doctrine of God*, 1; T. F. Torrance, *Theology in Reconstruction* (London: SCM Press, 1965), 129.
30   Ibid., 130.
31   Ibid., 130–131.
32   Barth, *Church Dogmatics*, 1/1, 382.
33   Torrance, *The Trinitarian Faith*, 3.
34   Torrance, *The Doctrine of Jesus Christ*, 101.
35   A. E. McGrath, *T.F. Torrance: An Intellectual Biography* (Edinburgh: T&T Clark, 1999), 74.
36   Torrance, *The Trinitarian Faith*, 133.

not eternally inherent in him because we cannot know God through a divided Son. A divided Son is like a light that does not shine, or a fountain without water.[37] If the Son is not God himself, according to Torrance, then God is utterly unknowable because no creature can mediate any authentic knowledge of God.[38] If there is no oneness between the revelation of God and God himself, the revelation is unable to reveal God in his own Being because God himself is detached from the revelation. Only when the Son is identical to God in being in the incarnate revelation, then we are able to know the Father through our knowledge of the Son in his human existence. Thus, Torrance says that Athanasius accesses the knowledge of God strictly through the Son because Athanasius believes that in beholding the Son, we see the Father, and in our knowledge of the Son, we access the knowledge of the Father because the Son is the proper offspring from his Being.[39] Likewise, we also access our knowledge of the Spirit from our knowledge of the Son.[40] Barth insists that there is no knowledge of God apart from the incarnate revelation,[41] and Torrance agrees that there is no God apart from the one revealed in the person of Jesus Christ because God does not hide behind the back of Jesus Christ. Any revelation other than that of the incarnation would undermine the necessity and uniqueness of God's revelation, thus, Barth and Torrance argue that if knowledge of God can be achieved independently apart from Christ, then man can dictate the knowledge of God.[42] Pannenberg comments that the root of Barthian revelational theology is the self-revelation of God. If God has totally and decisively revealed in the decisiveness of the Christ event, then he cannot in consistency also reveal in other events.[43] Pannenberg says,

---

37   Ibid., 133–134.
38   Ibid., 133.
39   Ibid., 8.
40   Ibid.. 11.
41   T. F. Torrance, *Space, Time and Resurrection* (Edinburgh: T&T Clark, 1998), ix–x.
42   McGrath, 179.
43   W. Pannenberg, *Revelation As History*, tr. David Granskou (New York: Macmillan, 1968), 6.

A multiplicity of revelation implies a discrediting of any particular revelation, for then the form of the divine manifestation is no longer the singularly adequate expression of the revealer.[44]

This gives a good reason why Barth refuses natural theology because self-revelation of God restricts the scope of divine revelation, and makes incarnation as the revelation. Inclusion of natural theology would inevitably jeopardize the Barthian concept of self-revelation, thus, Barth is extremely reluctant to accept Torrance's request in his late years to consider natural theology as part of God's revelation, he would only see it as something that is 'impossible' but nonetheless 'exists'.[45] The incarnate revelation is so unique, according to Barth, that God does not only reveal himself, he reconciles himself with us in the person of Jesus Christ, thus, the incarnate revelation is itself the reconciliation.[46] Torrance believes that both revelation and reconciliation operate together in the saving acts of God, each acts simultaneously in a movement from above to below and a corresponding movement from below to above. The downward movement of the divine revelation is met with the upward movement of reconciliation through the vicarious humanity of Jesus Christ.[47]

According to Torrance, the content of revelation cannot be discovered through our minds but must be given through divine initiative.[48] We cannot detach the knowledge of God from the fact that God in his freedom of grace gives us knowledge of himself, and so makes it a predicate of us.[49] Torrance says that strictly speaking, the knowability of God can only be predicated of God himself, and it may be predicated of man only through his grace of self-giving.[50] In the theology of Torrance, revelation is the covenant of grace because Christ himself is the divine

---

44   Ibid.
45   T. F. Torrance, 'The Problem of Natural Theology in The Thought of Karl Barth', *Religious Studies*, 6 (1970), 121, 125.
46   Torrance, *The Christian Doctrine of God*, 33.
47   R. S. Anderson, 'Torrance as a Practical Theologian', in *The Promise of Trinitarian Theology*, ed. Elmer M. Coyler, (Lanham: Rowan & Littlefield Publishers, 2001), 166; Torrance, 'Thomas Torrance Responds', 322.
48   T. F. Torrance, *Theological Science* (Edinburgh: T&T Clark, 1996), 27.
49   bid., 206.
50   Ibid.

covenant[51] and at the same time, he identifies himself as the revelation.[52] Christ is the divine covenant because he represents both sides of the covenant through his divinity and vicarious humanity.[53] Christ is the revelation because he himself is the content of the revelation and is identical with the revelation which he mediates.[54] Thus, revelation signifies the covenant of grace. According to Torrance, the covenant of grace embraces not only man but the whole of creation in a covenanted correspondence that God creates a world utterly distinct from himself, yet assume it into a close relation with himself that it may reflect his glory.[55] The revelation is seen as the primacy of grace of God who turns toward the world. It is not the world that is attracted towards God but rather God acts upon the world.[56] Torrance says that the whole implication of revelation 'is just this, that in it we have a movement of God in the direction of men, and not a movement of men in the direction of God.'[57] And this movement from God to man is the foundation of the covenant of grace because it is God's sole grace toward man that we are able to know him and enter into a covenantal relation with him.[58] This relation is only possible in the person of Jesus Christ who himself is God's grace to us.[59] In the incarnate revelation, Christ identifies himself both as the giver and the gift in the fulfillment of the covenant of grace,[60] thus, the covenant of grace cannot be interpreted apart from Christ's self-revelation.

In order to make revelation really revelation to man, Torrance says that the Word of God must come to man in his ruined situation that he takes upon himself all the ideas and language of man. The Word who was in the beginning with God became flesh, and tabernacled among

---

51   T. F. Torrance, *Divine Meaning* (Edinburgh: T&T Clark, 1995), 100.
52   Torrance, *The Mediation of Christ*, 19.
53   T. F. Torrance, 'One Aspect of the Biblical Conception of Faith', *The Expository Times*, 68 (October 1956 - September 1957), 113.
54   Torrance, *The Mediation of Christ*, 19.
55   Torrance, *Theological Science*, 68.
56   Ibid., 67.
57   Torrance, *The Doctrine of Jesus Christ*, 74.
58   Torrance, *Theological Science*, 68.
59   Ibid. 155; T. F. Torrance, *The Doctrine of Grace in The Apostolic Fathers* (Eugene: Wipf and Stock Publishers, 1996), 20–21.
60   Torrance, *Theological Science*, 68; Torrance, *Reality and Evangelical Theology*, 14–15.

men in the person of Jesus Christ. Incarnation is regarded by Torrance as the final and definitive form of revelation to man.[61] The revelation of Truth is so unlimited and inexhaustible that there is infinite fullness of his reality that lies beyond our limits of contingent being and experience. However, the revelation is not an unintelligible mystery, it opens wide our knowledge and experience.[62] That is to say, God is both knowable and unknowable in his incarnate revelation that on one hand he is infinite and inexhaustible, on the other hand, he avails himself for us to know him within our intellectual capacity. Many understand revelation as mystery, a mystery that cannot be unveiled. This mystery plays a prominent role in Torrance's revelational theology that God is revealed through his concealment. Torrance says,

> God reveals himself to us in such a way as still to be veiled from us in the infinite depths of his ultimate Being, for he does not surrender his transcendence or sovereign freedom but remains the absolute Lord of what he reveals and of our knowing of him. Thus in a strange way God is known by us in not being known, or known in such a way that our knowing of him rebounds back from the Holiness and Majesty of his Being, for what we may know of him through Christ and in the Spirit we cannot master and capture within the brackets of our explicit theological constructs.[63]

That is to say, there exists a paradoxical relation in God's revelation that he reveals to us through his concealment, that God is known to us by not being known. Downing says that the Christian revelation is a manifestation of a mystery which by itself is incomprehensible, a mystery cannot lose its hiddenness even when it is revealed.[64] If the mystery is not revealed, how is there a revelation? The writers of both the New Testament and the Old Testament, according to Downing, do not have much use of the word *revelation*, and the New Testament canon itself records no revelation.[65] Pannenberg agrees that there is no passage in the New Testament that has God revealing himself. He says that God continually reveals something or someone but never precisely himself.[66] There were many appearances of Yahweh reported in the Old Testament,

---

61   Ibid., 87.
62   Ibid., 141.
63   Torrance, *The Christian Doctrine of God*, 81.
64   G. F. Downing, *Has Christianity a Revelation* (London: SCM Press, 1964), 11.
65   Ibid., 16, 283–284.
66   Pannenberg, *Revelation As History*, 8.

according to Pannenberg, these are manifestations instead of revelations because they do not involve the disclosure of the essence of God himself.[67] Downing argues that God cannot be known without very heavy qualification on how much we know about the incomprehensible God. Thus, he says that revelation provides a knowledge that no one knows exactly[68] and claims that 'Jesus on the cross in fact "reveals" nothing; he just demands our still confused and inarticulate faith and obedience.'[69] It is true that we do not know the incomprehensive God through his self-revelation, however, we cannot say that we do not know the person of Christ who reveals himself in the incarnation that he is the Son of God. This paradox, according to Tillich, is not a real paradox because revelation includes cognitive elements. Tillich says,

> Revelation of that which is essentially and necessarily mysterious means the manifestation of something within the context of ordinary experience which transcends the ordinary context of experience. Something more is known of the mystery after it has become manifest in revelation. First, its reality has become a matter of experience. Second, our relation to it has become a matter of experience. Both of these are cognitive elements. But revelation does not dissolve the mystery into knowledge.[70]

Through our cognitive capacity, we are able to know more about the revealed objective reality, however, at the same time, our knowledge is limited by our human capacity that God still remains an infinite mystery. The revelation by itself does not penetrate the mystery and unfold it. In the revelational theology of Barth and Torrance, there exist two types of cognitive knowledge, the revelational knowledge of the historical event and knowledge of the self-revealed God in his own being. The first type is that the revelation must be recognized by the knower, otherwise the revelation remains hidden in the history.[71] The second type is that the revelation is recognized, yet the objective reality remains hidden. Barth says,

---

67   Ibid., 9.
68   Downing, 285–285.
69   Ibid., 290.
70   P. Tillich, *Systematic Theology*, 1 (Welwyn, Herts: James Nisbet & Co., 1963), 121.
71   Torrance, *God and Rationality*, 155; Torrance, *The Mediation of Christ*, 28; McGrath, 134; Torrance, *Theological Science*, 134.

we must not overlook the fact that in revealing Himself in this way, He also conceals Himself. He reveals His glory to faith, which sees it in this hiddenness. He reveals it in that it makes itself knowable to faith in spite of and in this hiddenness.[72]

The truth is revealed to those who have faith, hidden from those who do not, and for those who have faith, God is still hidden in his revelation. Torrance explains that when God gives us access to the knowledge of himself, he does so within the human conditions and capacities that we may be able to apprehend;[73] thus, according to Hilary, we are not ignorant of him, however, at the same time, we cannot describe him.[74] Both Gregory of Nazianus and John Calvin, according to Torrance, agree that we cannot know what God is because his essence is utterly incomprehensible, however, this does not mean we may not know God himself.[75] Through his incarnate revelation, we may know what kind of God he is in accordance with his saving acts.[76] Since he has actually made himself known to us in the person of Jesus Christ, thus, he has made us known personally as Father, Son and Holy Spirit.[77] That is to say, through the incarnate revelation, we come to know God who is Triune in nature. Since the Being of God is intrinsically incomprehensible, thus, Torrance says that instead of asking *what God is*, we should ask *what kind of God he is*, and sees that the latter question is in accordance with the incarnate revelation.[78] That is to say, we may know God through his self-revelation according to our limited human cognitive capacity, however, at the same time we have to recognize that God himself in his revelation is beyond our cognitive capacity.

Torrance believes that we do not know God by acting on him, but by being acted upon by him because God is only known through God as he reveals himself in his incarnate Son.[79] If there is a real knowledge of God, Torrance sees that there must be an incongruence between God as the known and man as the knower, but if that knowledge is to take place

---

72   Barth, *Church Dogmatics*, 2/1, 55.
73   Torrance, *The Trinitarian Faith*, 52.
74   Ibid., 53.
75   T. F. Torrance, *Trinitarian Perspectives Toward Doctrinal Agreement* (Edinburgh: T&T Clark, 1999), 37.
76   Ibid., 38.
77   Ibid., 37.
78   Ibid., 41–42.
79   Torrance, *Theological Science*, xix.

then it must rest on the reality and grace of the Object known, to have its reality acting upon us. Barth, according to Torrance, insists that in the knowledge of God we cannot raise questions as to its reality from an external position.[80] Thus, revelation is not an extension of our natural knowledge. Torrance says,

> Revelation must be thought of as the approach of reality to man, not as approach of man to reality. The latter is discovery, the former is a divine communication... Christianity does not set out from anything positive within man; it sets our from something positive that comes to man, and comes from beyond. Man is sought and found; he does not seek and find. We are concerned with a movement of God to man; not a movement of man to God.[81]

We know God because we are known by God, unless God comes to seek us, we are unable to know him. Torrance calls this *the logic of grace* because the truth comes to us in accordance with his grace,[82] it is purely a movement of God to man. Thus, revelational theology is not an independent human activity based upon human reason and experience,[83] but rather it breaks down the autonomous structure of human reasoning that the revealer in the revelation is in fact the Lord of our knowledge.[84]

5.1. Revelation and History

There are many different views on the relationship between revelation and history. In general, they can be classified in two categories, the subjective view and the objective view. The general characteristic of the subjective view is that revelation is revelation only when it is recognized, received or interpreted by the knower; of the objective view is that revelation is independent of the knower, it has its own objective reality. Of the subjective view, the knower determines whether a historical event

---

80   T. F. Torrance, *Space, Time and Incarnation* (London: Oxford University Press, 1969), 54.
81   Saying of Torrance quoted by McGrath, 135.
82   Torrance, *Theological Science*, 206.
83   McGrath, 135.
84   Torrance, *Theological Science*, 131.

is a divine revelation. Baillie says that in subjective view of historical revelation,

> the receiving is as necessary to a completed act of revelation as giving it. It is only so far as the action of God in history is understood as God means it to be understood that revelation has place at all. The illumination of the receiving mind is a necessary condition of the divine self-disclosure.[85]

Unless the individual is illuminated, he cannot recognize revelation in any of the historical events. There are two variations of the subjective view, the first one is referred to as revelation *in* history by Erickson in his *Christian Theology*.[86] This view is represented by Ernst Wright who insists that the Scripture is simply a recital of historical events. The knowledge of God is understood as inferences[87] drawn from the way that God has acted in history. One such inference is the doctrine of divine grace through the election of his people. The concept of God is thought of not in terms of Being and essence, but rather of his acts. Wright argues that divine grace cannot be explained, it could only be inferred and accepted in faith according to the acts of God in history. The divine election serves as the essence of the existence of the people of Israel simply because God loves her. Thus, the historical revelation is interpreted through this knowledge of election. Wright says,

> The being and attributes of God are nowhere systematically presented but are inferences from events. Biblical man did not possess a philosophical notion of deity whence he could argue in safety and 'objectivity' as to whether this or that was of God.[88]

Wright detaches the Being of God from the historical acts of God that the Being of God serves only as an interpretation of the acts of God in history. The objectivity of the historical event becomes a subjective interpretation. The knowledge of God lies in the inference rather than the actual history. Thus, the revelation is within the history however, it is not

---

85   J. Baillie, *The Idea of Revelation in Recent Thought* (London: Oxford University Press, 1956), 64.

86   M. J. Erickson, *Christian Theology* (Grand Rapids, Mich.: Baker, 1985), 182.

87   According to Wright, inference is an interpretation of an event. See G. E. Wright, *God Who Acts* (London: SCM Press, 1952), 50.

88   Ibid., 57

equated with the history.[89] Erickson sees an inconsistency in Wright's approach that Wright on the one hand finds concepts of God's Being and essence in Scripture, yet at the same time, he insists that biblical writers did not think in terms of Being and essence but of acts and history.[90] If the Scripture does not present God in his Being and essence, how then can the people of God know about God's Being and essence. Erickson charges that Wright is using a twentieth-century presupposition to control the interpretation of biblical events.[91]

Dodd shares a similar idea to that of Wright, though he sees it slightly differently. Dodd sees that history as written in the Scripture bear witness to the revelation of God. The Scripture itself affirms a series of events happened, in which God revealed himself in action for the salvation of man.[92] History is seen as the medium of God's self-revelation in action.[93] However, not every historical event could be regarded as the self-revelation of God, though in general, God's action may be discovered anywhere in the history.[94] Thus, when Dodd speaks of history as the self-revelation of God, he is thinking not of bare occurrences, but of the rich concreteness of events.[95] Thus, revelation of God is reflected in its historical meaning based on human interpretation. Dodd admits that the element of interpretation would open doors to all the fallacies of human mind, but the attempt to rule out any interpretation is by itself a false interpretation.[96] Interpretation of any event is necessary; without it, it has no historical importance. Thus, interpretation of the historical events gives the meaning of the event and which makes it a revelation of God to man. However, if divine revelation is based on the individual interpretations of historical events, then, there is simply no meaningful objective theology.

A second subjective view is revelation *through* history that God has worked within history, manifesting himself to man. Historical events should not be identified with revelation, they are merely the means

---

89 Erickson, 183.
90 Ibid.
91 Ibid.
92 C. H. Dodd, *History and the Gospel* (London: Hodder & Stoughton, 1964), 11–12.
93 Ibid., 15.
94 Ibid., 18.
95 Ibid., 21.
96 Ibid., 73.

through which revelation comes.[97] Erickson explains this neo-orthodox view,

> Truth is personal, not propositional. Revelation is something that *happens*, not something that *is*. Thus, when the neoorthodox speak of revelation, they have in mind the *process* as opposed to the *product* of revelation (what is said or written about it), and the *revealing* as opposed to what is *revealed*. The historical event and, for that matter, the account of it are not the revelation... Revelation comes through occurrences of history, but not as them.[98]

Barth is a representative of this neo-orthodox view. According to both Barth and Torrance, revelation is understood as an objective unveiling of God, and itself is not a revelation until it is recognized and received as revelation.[99] However, this process of recognition is not acquired by the knower through human virtues, but is given by God through his grace. Revelation is an event in which the Word of God is addressed to men and it subverts the natural approach of man by challenging the autonomy of the human mind.[100] That is to say, revelation is historical, however, a historical event may not be a revelation. Torrance takes up Barth's interpretation of the reality of history that historical happenings are not necessarily perceived as revelations. Barth says,

> Millions in the ancient East may once have heard the name *Yahweh* and sometime or other have seen His temple. But this historical element was not revelation. Thousands may have seen and heard the Rabbi of Nazareth. But this historical element was not revelation. Even the historical element at the resurrection of Christ, the empty grave regarded as an element in event, that might possibly be fixed, was certainly not revelation. This historical element, like everything historical, is admittedly susceptible of an even highly trivial interpretation.[101]

Though the history in reality has revealed itself, its significance may not be recognized as what it should be by us. Brunner shares a similar idea that unless we recognize the significance of the historical event, we do not see revelation. He says, 'Jesus Christ is not "revelation" when He is

---

97 Erickson, 183–184.
98 Ibid. 185.
99 Torrance, *God and Rationality*, 155; Torrance, *The Mediation of Christ*, 28; McGrath, 134; Torrance, *Theological Science*, 134.
100 McGrath, 134; Torrance, *Theological Science*, 131.
101 Barth, *Church Dogmatics*, 1/1, 373.

not recognized by anyone as the Christ, just as He is not the Redeemer if He does not redeem anyone.'[102] History is revelation, according to Barth, only when it gives a concrete relation to concrete men.[103] That is to say, when the historical event is recognized as the revelation, it becomes an effective meeting between God and man, and establishes a relationship between God and man.[104] Revelation is a relation rather than an abstract idea that is projected out of our human consciousness.[105] Torrance argues that in order for the revelation to be intelligible and communicable for mankind, it has to be embodied within the human structure. That is to say, in the words of Colyer, 'God's self-revelation to humanity includes a social coefficient[106] as part of its embodiment with our creaturely human reality.'[107] The incarnate revelation, according to Torrance, is actualized within the conditions of our creaturely existence, that is to say, it is within the historic medium of human thought and speech.[108]

In Torrance's revelational theology, the significance of an objective event does not only lie in the event itself, but rather on how it is perceived and received. Torrance sees an inseparable relation between the mental and the physical, the actions of agents and the events of nature.[109] That is to say, the revelation as perceived in our minds cannot be detached from the objective historical events. Torrance says,

> The inside and the outside of historical events cannot be separated without distortion in our understanding of them, for the thoughts do not occur in a physical vacuum, and the physical facts cannot be considered in detachment from the purposeful actions of agents if we are to remain within the field of historical inquiry.[110]

---

102 Brunner, *Revelation and Reason*, 33.
103 Barth, *Church Dogmatics*, 1/1, p. 374.
104 Ibid., 381.
105 Torrance, *The Christian Doctrine of God*, 22.
106 Torrance defines social coefficient as a social cultural capacity of human life. See T. F. Torrance, *Reality and Scientific Theology* (Edinburgh: Scottish Academy Press, 1985), 102–103.
107 E. M. Colyer, *The Nature of Doctrine in T.F. Torrance's Theology* (Eugene: Wipf & Stock, 2001), 135.
108 Torrance, *Reality and Evangelical Theology*, 85.
109 Torrance, *Theological Science*, 317.
110 Ibid., 319.

Torrance says that unless we are acted upon by God, we are unable to distinguish the historical fact of divine intervention than any other historical facts.[111] Incarnation is a historical event, unlike any other historical events, it is laden with divine Word so that we are able to encounter the Son of God.[112] In order to make this encounter meaningful and personal, according to Torrance, we need an act of discernment beyond common historical observation and rationality to acknowledge God's revelation in history,[113] we need to penetrate into the inner happening of the historical events in order to apprehend the meaning and significance of events. Incarnation as a historical event is not a fact without a meaning nor a meaning without a fact.[114] However, its meaning can only be obtained through faith.[115]

One important reason why both Barth and Torrance share the idea that historical events are revelational only if they are recognized by the knower, according to Erickson, is that they both bear the burden of historical criticism. By adopting a Barthian doctrine of revelation, Erickson argues that revelation could allow for any amount of historical criticism. He says that criticism works on the historical events, and since historical events are not necessarily revelations, it is thus safeguarded from corrosive effect of historical criticism.[116] It is evident in their writings, Barth and Torrance are struggling with historical criticism. One important feature of their passiveness is that, according to Kent, Barth does not answer the questions raised by the historical critics about the narratives of the resurrection, but instead, Barth asserts that they described an event which is beyond the reach of historical research or description.[117] Historical criticism clearly places a great burden on Barth that he on one hand accepts the authority of the revelation as presented in the Scripture, but on the other hand, he faces difficulties in addressing historical problems tabled by the critics. Thus, he argues that historical revelation cannot be attested on the basis of general concept of historical

---

111   Ibid., 322–323.
112   Ibid., 323.
113   Ibid., 325.
114   Ibid., 333.
115   Ibid., 325.
116   Erickson, 185.
117   J. H. Kent, *The End of The Line* (London: SCM Press, 1982), 124.

truth.[118] He says that history related to revelation must mean that there is no court of reference above it by which it could be inspected as a fact.[119] Torrance on the other hand takes a more positive view on the historicity of the biblical events, he claims that if our doctrine of Trinity is detached from God's self-revelation in history, it is nothing but a speculative projection.[120] Torrance says that we cannot interpret the biblical events merely theologically 'as if it could be done apart from history, for that would mythologize and docetize it, and then we would have nothing to interpret.'[121] However, at the same time, Torrance realizes the difficulties as presented by the New Testament historical critics on the accounts of resurrection. Torrance offers no arguments in defending the historicity of these apparent discrepancies in the narratives. Thus, Torrance gives an impression of insufficient support to the historicity of the narratives in the Gospels. Coyler comments,

> the New Testament record may not be literally historical in its details regarding the chronology of the events of Easter morning or the exact words Jesus said. But that is neither the way natural memory (with its in-depth structures) operates, nor is it of real consequence for Christian theology and faith, for what is important is the fact that Jesus did rise on Easter (leaving the tomb empty) and the significance of resurrection for Christian faith and theology. And for Torrance, the fact and significance of resurrection have a quite literally unforgettable character that was indelibly impressed upon the memory of the Apostles and the early Christian community in such a way that, in spite of inaccuracies regarding the details, what is of real consequence has been faithfully and adequately preserved in the New Testament witness.[122]

If the historic self-revelation of God as documented in the Scripture is inaccurate, then, the historicity of the self-revelation of God is also in jeopardy because there is no intrinsic evidence other than what is recorded in the Scripture. Since in traditional ecclesiastical formulation, revelation is identified with the written word of Scripture, thus the action of God in history has the revelational status.[123] Torrance believes that since we get to the original events only through the subjectivity of

---

118   Barth, *Church Dogmatics*, 1/1, p. 375-378.
119   Ibid.
120   Torrance, *Trinitarian Perspectives Toward Doctrinal Agreement*, 81.
121   T. F. Torrance, *Space, Time and Resurrection* (Edinburgh: T&T Clark, 1998), 94.
122   Colyer, *The Nature of Doctrine in T.F. Torrance's Theology*, 67.
123   J. Baillie, 62.

others, so we have to allow for coloring and misrepresentation of the facts through them.[124] If the Scripture is less than perfect, then revelation itself as revealed in the history is also less than truly historical. Thus, Torrance's hermeneutics plays an important part in his understanding of historical revelation that historical events are not necessarily revelations because human history is detached from revelation due to the imperfection of the Scripture.[125]

Erickson refers to the objective view of historical revelation as revelation *as* history.[126] This view is championed by Wolfhart Pannenberg that God has acted in history and that events are actually revelation of God. The whole history of mankind, not only the salvation history, is regarded as a revelation of God. By doing so, Erickson says, Pannenberg has virtually obliterated the distinction between general and special revelation.[127] However, Erickson sees this view as more close to biblical witness, he says,

> Moreover, Jesus maintained that there was an objective revelation associated with historical events. Thus he said in response to Philip's request to be shown the Father, "He who has seen me has seen the Father" (John 14:9). Furthermore, Jesus placed responsibility upon those who had heard him (and had also seen his miracles): "He who has ears to ear, let him hear" (e.g. Matt. 11:15)... Thus he seemed to be saying that the historical events actually were revelation. For that matter, the psalmists and prophets speak as if they and the people of Israel had actually seen the works of God (e.g., Ps. 78).[128]

If what Jesus says is not metaphorical, then, history does reveal objectively. There is no distinction between the works of God as his self-revelation and the others as offering no such revelation, Temple says,

> Unless all existence is a medium of revelation, no particular revelation is possible... Either all occurrences are in some degree revelation of God, or else there is no such revelation at all; for the conditions of the possibility of any revelation require that there should be nothing which is not revelation. Only if God is revealed in the rising

---

124 Torrance, *Theological Science*, 313.
125 Torrance, *Divine Meaning*, 10.
126 Erickson, 186.
127 Ibid.
128 Ibid., 186–187.

of the sun in the sky can He be revealed in the rising of a son of man from the dead.[129]

If nature itself is not regarded as the revelation of God, then, there is no revelation. Pannenberg believes that revelation should not be understood in terms of supernatural disclosure, but in terms of the comprehensive whole of reality.[130] That is to say, revelation should be understood in history as an objective reality rather than subjective religious experience. According to Pannenberg, in the Scripture there exists no proof of God's direct self-revelation of which God reveals himself in terms of his essence to us, thus he argues that there exists only indirect[131] self-revelation as a reflex of his activity in history.[132] That is to say, God reveals himself indirectly to us through the totality of history which witnesses the speech and activity of God. A major thesis of Pannenberg's doctrine of revelation is that the historical revelation is open to anyone who has eyes to see, and it has universal character. Pannenberg says,

> We are ordinarily urged to think of revelation as an occurrence that man cannot perceive with natural eyes and that is made known only through a secret mediation. The revelation, however, of the biblical God in his activity is no secret or mysterious happening. An understanding that puts revelation into contrast to, or even conflict with, natural knowledge is in danger of distorting the historical revelation into a gnostic knowledge of secrets.[133]

Pannenberg refuses to accept that revelation is only in the eyes of beholder. He argues that what God does in the history is to prove his deity to all people, not just his chosen people.[134] This view seems to match quite nicely with Torrance's realist theological science that history

---

129 Saying of William Temple quoted by J. Baillie, 70–71.
130 Pannenberg, *Revelation As History*, ix.
131 According to Pannenberg, 'The distinction between direct and indirect communication is not therefore dependent on whether the communication requires a mediator or not. It is not a question of mediateness or immediateness in the act of communication, but whether the content of a communication can be linked in a direct or indirect way with its intention.' It is like that we participate in revelation only by mediation of the prophetic and apostolic witness. See Pannenberg, *Revelation As History*, 15.
132 Ibid., 13.
133 Ibid., 135.
134 Ibid., 135–136.

carries its own intelligibility and reality.[135] That is to say, history that serves as a bearer of God's contingent order is able to reveal the reality of God in his creation. In this sense, the objectivity of history is independent of the subjectivity of man. Torrance is in a dialectical situation that he tries to mediate between Barthian revelational theology and his own theological science. Torrance's movement towards the acceptance of natural theology as part of the revelation suggests that he is no longer as restrictive as that of Barth.

Carl Henry charges that the doctrine of revelation of Barth and Torrance is simply a personal but non-cognitive confrontation of man, and which eliminates its external and objective features by concentrating solely on an internal divine confrontation. Thus, he regards Torrance's doctrine on revelation existential or paradoxical rather than rational in nature. [136] If revelation is merely a perspective-altering event, it can provide no basis for distinguishing rational from irrational or moral from immoral perspectives.[137] Henry says that

> The theological reluctance to return to objective revelation divinely given in external historical acts interpreted in turn by the divinely inspired writers of Scripture resulted in part from the impact of positivistic philosophy upon religious beliefs. Radical secularism presumed to explain nature and history comprehensively by naturalistic categories; the only remaining role for God was therefore restricted to something internal in man.[138]

History that serves as a medium, according to Henry, has nothing to do with biblical revelation because revelation itself is strictly a mental conception that the knowledge of God is issuing from the mind and will of God, and addressing to the mind and will of human beings.[139] Thus, Henry says, revelation

> involves primarily an activity of consciousness that enlists the thoughts and bears on the beliefs and actions of its recipients. To restrict God's disclosure either to divine

---

135 Torrance, *Theological Science*, 331.
136 C. Henry, *God, Revelation and Authority*, 3 (Waco, Texas: Word Books, 1979), 248–249.
137 Ibid., 251.
138 Ibid., 252.
139 Ibid.

self-revelation, or to *cosmic* revelation, or to *historical* revelation, in express contrast to a divine disclosure of truths and information, is an arbitrary modern view.[140]

That is to say, revelation is not restricted to any medium. It is simply a cognitive knowledge issued by God and received by man. John Baillie says that all valid knowledge, all apprehended truth, in a sense, may be regarded as revelation because he sees knowledge as an activity of the human mind.[141] This mental recognition apart from history makes the recognition subjective and to certain degree abstract. Torrance clearly rejects this separation of mental from physical in the recognition of divine revelation.[142]

5.2. Revelation and Old Testament

The essence of Torrance's theology is Christology, and the central piece of his doctrine of Christology hinges on the Act and Being of God manifested in the person of the incarnate Son. Thus, incarnation is regarded by Torrance as the revelation, and Christ serves as the controlling centre of this full and final self-revelation of God, which constitutes the reality and substance of God's self-revelation.[143] Though Israel is regarded as God's elected way of mediating knowledge of himself to the world, it only serves as a medium rather than the content of the revelation. It is not Israel but rather Christ in Israel that serves God's self-revelation.[144] According to Barth, the God of Israel as revealed in the Old Testament was somehow hidden, God only revealed his name to the people.[145] *I am that I am (ehyeh asher ehyeh)* as revealed in Exodus 3:14 is the sole response of God to mankind regarding his name in the Scripture, and countless biblical scholars have tried to explicate this puzzling three-word Hebrew name. Cross says that both

---

140   Ibid., 248.
141   J. Baillie, 19.
142   Torrance, *Theological Science*, 317.
143   Torrance, *The Mediation of Christ*, 32.
144   Ibid.
145   Barth, *Church Dogmatics*, 1/1, 365.

Ehyeh, the first person form, and *Yahweh*, the third person form, are regarded as acceptable alternate forms of the revealed name of God.[146] Freedman says that even though there is no consensus, the structure and etymology of the word *Yahweh* is generally thought to be a verbal form derived from the root of *Ehyeh*,[147] and which according to Cross, is a causative imperfect of the Canaanite-Proto-Hebrew verb *to be*. The connecting word *asher* carries a meaning of *who, what, which, when, where, how*, or *because*.[148] Thus, the name is generally rendered as *I am that I am*. However, in the ancient Hebrew language, there was no past, present, or future tense, it had only imperfective and perfective indicators of time.[149] Thus, *Ehyeh asher ehyeh* could be rendered in a present or a future mode. In Torrance's theology, *Ehyeh asher ehyeh* is rendered as both *I am who I am* and *I shall be who I shall be*.[150] However, Calvin argues that the verb *to be* is in the future tense, and it should be rendered as *I will be what I will be*, but it has the same force as the present.[151] Cross suggests the verb carries a meaning of *to cause to be* or *to create*. Though the Massoretes read *Ehyeh asher ehyeh* as *I am he who exists* or *I am he who endures*, it may be well suited if it is rendered as *I create what I create* or *I am the creator*.[152] It is plausible, according to Brueggemann, that the entire Exodus narrative is an exposition of the name *Ehyeh asher ehyeh*.[153] Rabbi Joseph Telushkin sees the name as carrying a meaning that God reveals himself through his actions that he is what he acts. The name also establishes a relation with individuals in a personal and private way that one can experience.[154] Seitz says that what God reveals to Moses is not a proper name like Jim or Sally, rather it is

---

146 F. M. Cross, *Canaanite Myth and Hebrew Epic* (Cambridge, Mass.: Harvard University Press, 1973), 68.

147 G. J. Botterweck, and Helmer Ringgren, *Theological Dictionary of The Old Testament* (Grand Rapids, Mich.: Eerdmans, 1974), 500.

148 S. Kostelnik, *The Name of God: Revealed!* <http://members.nuvox.net/~on.roz/God/name/ revealed.html> accessed 12 Dec 2005.

149 *Wikipedia* <http://en.wikipedia.org/wiki/I_am_that_I_am> accessed 12 Dec 2005.

150 Torrance, *The Christian Doctrine of God*, 235.

151 J. Calvin, 'Commentaries on The Four Last Books of Moses', in *Calvin's Commentaries*, 1 (Grand Rapids, Mich.: Baker, 2003), 73.

152 Cross, 61–68.

153 W. Brueggemann, *Theology of The Old Testament* (Minneapolis: Fortress, 1997), 124.

154 J. Telushkin, *Biblical Literacy* (New York: William Morrow, 1997), 101.

the most personal revelation of God's own character.[155] God's name involves something that he will be or become or something that has not yet been manifested. Seitz sees that the name carries three important meanings, the first is to give the privilege to Moses of the knowledge of his name that he could state it to the people of Israel; the second is to let Moses know that he is the God of his ancestors, the God of Abraham, Isaac, and Jacob; the third is that he will deliver the people of Israel from the bondage through his presence with them.[156] At the time of Exodus 3:14, Seitz says that God's name was not known to the people of Israel as he is about to make himself known through his mighty deliverance.[157] Athanasius says that the name *Ehyeh* (*I am*) indicates that God is One and Only and First, there is no God apart from the One that is revealed to Moses,[158] and the Son shares the same essence as the Father in the oneness of the Being of God.[159] Augustine understands that the name carries the very essence of God that he is the supreme existence, and all other things owe their existence entirely to him.[160] That is to say, all our existence is contingent upon him who gives the meaning of our existence. Since God is the supreme existence, Augustine argues that he is unchangeable because the supreme existence cannot be changed.[161] Thus, according to Athanasius and Augustine, the name of God reflects the very nature of God.

The name *I am that I am*, according to Barth, indicates a refusal of any other name, and itself is a name that no one can repeat, and thus it recalls the hiddenness of the revealed God. Barth believes that in the Old Testament God did not reveal himself to his people, he only revealed his name to his people in such a way that his name was realised in the

---

155 C. Seitz, 'The Call of Moses and the "Revelation" of the Divine Name', in *Theological Exegesis*, ed. Christopher Seitz and Kathryn Green-McCreight (Grand Rapids, Mich.: Eerdmanns, 1999), 154.

156 Ibid., 151–159.

157 Ibid., 158–159.

158 Athanasius, 'Against the Arians', in *Nicene and Post Nicene Fathers*, ed. Philip Schaff and Henry Wace, 4 (Peaboy, Mass.: Hendrickson, 1999), 3.23.6, 397.

159 Ibid., 4.1, 433.

160 Augustine, 'On Christian Doctrine' in *Nicene and Post-Nicene Fathers*, ed. Philip Schaff, 2 (Peaboy, Mass.: Hendrickson, 1999), 531.

161 Augustine, 'The City of God', in *Nicene and Post-Nicene Fathers*, ed. Philip Schaff, 2 (Peaboy, Mass.: Hendrickson, 1999),12.2, 227.

covenant with his people.[162] Thus, the knowledge of the name *Yahweh* means to be partner in the covenant founded by *Yahweh*.[163] The Old Testament serves no self-revelation of God himself, but only serves as a mere shadow of the final revelation in the person of Jesus Christ, and itself will dissolve in the incarnate revelation.[164] The only true deity can only be learned from what took place in Christ.[165] Thus, the Old Testament to Barth, according to Berkouwer, is not really revelation, it is only an expected revelation pointing towards the revelation.[166] In other words, Jesus Christ is the revelation, alone and exclusively.[167] The Old Testament serves as a provisional witness to Christ and the New Testament serves as its fulfillment.[168] That is to say, the self-revelation of God in the Old Testament does not have its substance and meaning unless it is interpreted as a pointer to the incarnation because Christ is the fulfillment of the revelation of God in himself. Torrance sees God's self-revelation in the person of Jesus Christ as not only fulfilling but also at the same time transcending and relativizing the historical dialogue of God with Israel.[169] The historical dialogue of God with Israel indicates that God's self-revelation does not enter into the history of mankind without trace. Torrance says,

> for the Word of God spoken to man did not operate in a vacuum but penetrated human existence in the particular life and history of one people elected as the instrument for the actualization of God's revelation in humanity and separated as a holy nation in whose midst God dwelt in an intimate way through the presence of His Word. The covenant relationship between God and Israel which this set up was a particularization of the one covenant of grace which embraced the whole of creation and constituted its inner bond and ground, and therefore carried in it the promise of a final universalization of God's revelation in which His Word would bring light and salvation to all the peoples of mankind and indeed a new heaven and a new earth.[170]

---

162 Barth, *Church Dogmatics*, 1/1, p. 365.
163 Ibid.
164 Ibid., 365, 367.
165 Barth, *Church Dogmatics*, 4/1, 177.
166 G. C. Berkouwer, *General Revelation* (Grand Rapids, Mich.: Eerdmans, 1955), 24.
167 Ibid.
168 Barth, *Church Dogmatics*, 4/1, 170-171.
169 Torrance, *Reality and Evangelical Theology*, 93.
170 Torrance, *God and Rationality*, 147.

Though God reveals himself in the history of Israel, however, the revelation is not completed and fulfilled till God himself is actualized in the human form in the incarnation. [171] Thus, Israel is seen as the particularization of God's revelation in an actualized sense and the universalization of the covenant of grace with the people of Israel in a proleptic sense. [172] According to Torrance, God makes himself known in the historical acts and events of the Old Testament. That is to say, the knowledge of God as revealed in the Old Testament is not an object of abstraction which is acquired through necessary truths of reason, but rather a historical Being, a living God who comes into living contact and fellowship with his people. [173] Calvin, according to Torrance, sees the name of God *I am that I am* as expressing God's Being. [174] However, Torrance holds that the concept of God's Being is not fully expressed in the Old Testament, he believes that only the incarnate Son can reveal God's act and Being in oneness. There is no such actuality in the Old Testament. [175] The Old Testament by its very nature points beyond itself toward the saving acts of God in the incarnation. [176] Torrance says,

> Thus in the Old Testament we have really the Word of God, but it is a Word in promissory form, not which is itself actualised in humanity or among actual human beings in history... In Jesus Christ, however, we do have not only the Word but the Word made flesh, not only revelation of God but such a complete and final revelation that it is itself actually God himself. [177]

In the Old Testament, according to Torrance, the God of Judaism[178] is so utterly transcendent that he is ineffable, unnameable and unknowable, so that anyone who claims to have a knowledge of God in himself is rejected with horror as impiety. Thus, Torrance claims that God does not give mankind access to any knowledge of himself in his own eternal

---

171   Ibid., 149.
172   R. S. Anderson, *Historical Transcendence and the Reality of God* (Grand Rapids, Mich.: Eerdmans, 1975), 120.
173   Torrance, *The Doctrine of Jesus Christ*, 5.
174   Torrance, *Trinitarian Perspectives Toward Doctrinal Agreement*, 51.
175   Torrance, *The Doctrine of Jesus Christ*, 133–134.
176   Ibid.
177   Ibid.
178   Torrance does not provide a clear definition on Judaism, however, it seems that he refers to the religious belief of the people of Israel in the Old Testament.

being.[179] There can be no knowledge of God in his internal relations, but only knowledge of him in his external relations in the Old Testament.[180] That is to say, God is knowable only in his external relation with the people of Israel of what he says and acts, and these acts and words do not express or articulate God's own internal relation. In the New Testament, however, according to Torrance, we are given access to himself through the person of Jesus Christ so that we may know him in the inner relations of his Being as Father, Son, and Holy Spirit,[181] because it is the Son who reveals the Father, rather than the Father revealing the Son through the prophets.[182] According to Torrance, revelation is not some vague and inarticulate awareness of God projected out of the human consciousness, but an intelligible, articulate revealing of God by God whom we are enabled to apprehend through the creative power of his Word addressed to us.[183] Thus, God's self-revelation can only be realized through his Act and Being within the conditions of our creaturely existence and in our human form.

Torrance sees the New Testament as a continuation of the Old Testament which God revealed himself through the law and prophets.[184] The knowledge of God as revealed in the incarnation cannot be detached from what had been revealed in the Old Testament, but rather intensifies and interiorises the Fatherhood of God in his unique relation to the Son.[185] In the Old Testament, according to Torrance, God proclaimed himself as the creator of heaven and earth, he made himself known as God and Saviour through servants and prophets within the special covenant relation.[186] The knowledge of God was communicated to the people of Israel through a mediator such as Moses.[187] When God re-

---

179 Torrance, *The Trinitarian Faith*, 117.
180 Ibid., 66.
181 Torrance, *Trinitarian Perspectives Toward Doctrinal Agreement*, 128.
182 Torrance, *The Trinitarian Faith*, 7.
183 Torrance, *Reality and Evangelical Theology*, 85.
184 T. F. Torrance, *Theology in Reconciliation* (Eugene: Wipf and Stock Publishers, 1996), 28.
185 Torrance, *The Christian Doctrine of God*, 55.
186 Ibid., 14.
187 T. F. Torrance, *When Christ Comes and Comes Again* (Eugene: Wipf and Stock Publishers, 1957), 173.

vealed to Israel, he revealed indirectly through his servants.[188] Thus, there was a barrier between God and his people that God made himself known to man of his divine will but withheld himself from man, otherwise, man would be consumed by his divine majesty.[189] However, in the New Testament according to Torrance, God reveals to us directly and personally in the person of Jesus Christ in accordance with what he really is in himself.[190] Thus, Torrance sees that God revealed himself indirectly to and through the people of Israel in the Old Testament, and reveals himself directly to us in the person of Jesus Christ in the New Testament.[191]

Torrance on one hand argues that we can really know God in the person of Jesus Christ, the incarnate revelation serves as the complete and final revelation of God, on the other hand, he tries to harmonize the three-fold revelation of God as Father, Son and Holy Spirit with the one Lord God revealed in the Old Testament. He claims that the true knowledge of God can only be found in Israel even though there exists a barrier between God and man in the Old Testament. He argues that the Old Testament at the time of Jesus Christ was the only Scripture that Jesus had, and Jesus clearly showed his reverence for the Scripture as utterly holy and inviolable. Jesus had no hesitation in referring faith to the self-revelation of God in the Old Testament. Thus, according to Torrance, Israel serves as a unique revelation to mankind.[192] Torrance says that God's presence and power were accessible to his people within the covenant relations in the Old Testament. God also had his personal interaction with Abraham, Moses, or Samuel. However, at the same time, Torrance argues that God did not make himself personally accessible to them, he was hidden behind his mighty acts or revelation and salvation.[193] That is to say, God had personal relationship with his people, however, the personal relationship is not personal enough as compared to that of the New Testament. In other words, the people in the New Testament has a closer relationship with God than those in the Old Testament.

---

188   Ibid., 173–174.
189   Torrance, *Space, Time and Resurrection*, 97.
190   Torrance, *The Christian Doctrine of God*, 14.
191   Torrance, *Reality and Evangelical Theology*, 11.
192   Torrance, *The Christian Doctrine of God*, 67–68.
193   Ibid., 68.

Torrance insists that if we really know God, then we must know him in accordance with his Triune nature.[194] Only the incarnate Christ can provide us accurate and precise knowledge of God because he is the perfect and proportionate image of God.[195] Even though there are mediators in the Old Testament such as Moses who spoke with God face to face, they do not have such a close relation with God that they can come to know him directly in himself as we do in the person of Jesus Christ.[196] Torrance believes that it is the fatherhood of the God as revealed in the incarnate Son that determines how we are to understand God as Almighty Creator, and not the other way round.[197] That is to say, unless we know the Son, we do not know the Father. The Father-Son relationship, according to Torrance, takes a place of primacy and centrality in the Christian understanding of God.[198] Unless we know God as Triune Being, we do not really know God. If it is true, then, the knowledge of God as acquired by the people of Israel in the Old Testament and the knowledge of God acquired by us in the New Testament are essentially different. However, if Moses served the same God as we know in the New Testament, what makes his knowledge of God different from us? Even if there is a difference, does it matter in our relation with God? It seems Torrance is equating personal relationship with the knowledge of the revelation: the more accurate the knowledge of God, the closer is the relation with God. But a young child may have a very close relationship with his mother without knowing much about his mother, while an adult child may have a poor relationship with his mother however he knows more about his mother. There is a danger in Torrance's theology of revelation that the relationship between God and man is determined by the knowledge of God through the incarnate revelation, this would deny the authenticity of personal relation between God and his chosen people prior to the incarnation, and also would jeopardize the saving activity of God in the Old Testament. According to Torrance, the knowledge of God through Christ is essentially the knowledge of God's saving activity, and it is through the redeeming

---

194 T. F. Torrance, *The Ground And Grammar of Theology* (Edinburgh: T&T Clark, 2001), 148.
195 Torrance, *The Trinitarian Faith*, 63.
196 Ibid., 66.
197 Ibid., 7.
198 Ibid.

activity of Christ that we come to know him.[199] Thus, the knowledge of God through his self-revelation is related directly to our salvation. If God is not known according to his Triune nature, according to Torrance, we do not really know God. This would put God's chosen people in the Old Testament outside of his saving grace because they did not know God in himself. If God's self-revelation in the Old Testament serves as a pointer to the incarnation, then the pointer itself must also be recognized as the revelation because unless the pointer and the reality share the same essence, the Old Testament revelation stops short of the true revelation and lacks the redeeming power. Torrance believes that it is the same Holy Spirit who spoke to the people of God through prophets in the Old Testament and speaks to us through Christ in the New Testament.[200] If the people of God in both the New Testament and the Old Testament receive the saving grace from the same Spirit, then, they must know and acknowledge the same God. The incarnation gives us a clearer picture of God in his own being, however, it does not make the divine revelation in the Old Testament deficient.

In the Old Testament, according to Torrance, God did not reveal himself in his own being, this does not mean that Christians can bypass the Old Testament because it provides a divine framework within which the New Testament is to be interpreted. It is based on the foundation of the one Lord God in the Old Testament that Christian knowledge of God rests and takes shape.[201] It is under the light of the Old Testament that the early Christians interpreted the incarnation that Jesus Christ is the anointed Messiah, the Lamb of God who had come to bear the sins of the world.[202] However, at the same time, the New Testament is seen by Torrance as the unfolding of the Old Testament to its full significance.[203] The New Testament serves as the reinterpretation of the Old Testament.[204] Thus, Torrance interprets the Scripture as a whole in the light of the incarnation.[205] Torrance does not deny the importance of the Old Testament, however, he does not deal with it in the same force as that of

---

199   Torrance, *The Doctrine of Jesus Christ*, 16.

200   Torrance, *The Trinitarian Faith*, 247.

201   Torrance, *The Christian Doctrine of God*, 69.

202   Torrance, *The Doctrine of Jesus Christ*, 5.

203   Torrance, *The Christian Doctrine of God*, 69.

204   T. F. Torrance, *Theology in Reconstruction* (London: SCM Press, 1965), 144.

205   Torrance, *Space, Time and Resurrection*, 5.

the New Testament. In order to make sense of the Old Testament revelation, according to Torrance, all major revelations in the Old Testament have to be Christologically interpreted, so that the shadowy prefigurements of redemption under the old covenant are guided by the final truth of redemption through the sacrifice of Christ in the new covenant.[206] The importance of the New Testament thus supercedes that of the Old Testament because the former is regarded as the fulfillment of the latter.[207] Langford says,

> A basic question needs to be asked: does Torrance mean to take all Scripture as equal? Obviously, formally, all Scripture is equally amenable to God's power. But we are asking an historical question. Is all Scripture equal?[208]

Langford questions the un-equality of the New Testament and the Old Testament in Torrance's treatment of God's self-revelation. He says that if the Scripture is taken seriously, then both the Old Testament and the New Testament should have the same revelational status. Torrance's idea of incarnation as the supreme divine revelation clearly creates an unbalance between the Old Testament and the New Testament. Morrison criticizes that Torrance belittles the revelation of God in the Old Testament.[209] Carl Henry comments that in the divine revelation, there should be no discontinuity between the Old Testament and the New Testament, that the latter is not superior than the former, but rather both serve as a single self-revelation of God that what God reveals himself in the New Testament is not different than what he revealed in the Old Testament. Henry says,

> The Christian church has insisted from the outset on the essential unity of Old and New Testaments, emphasizing that the Old Testament bears an indispensable testimony to Jesus Christ, and that the New Testament – albeit in terms of fulfillment – expounds no salvation other than that which is implicit and explicit in the Old Testament.[210]

---

206 Torrance, *The Trinitarian Faith*, 172.
207 Torrance, *Theology in Reconstruction*, 144.
208 T. A. Langford, 'T.F. Torrance's Theological Science: A Reaction', *Scottish Journal of Theology*, 25 (1972), 162–163.
209 J. D. Morrison, *Knowledge of the Self-Revealing God in The Thought of Thomas Forsyth Torrance* (New York: Peter Lang, 1997), 269–270.
210 C. Henry, *God, Revelation and Authority*, 3 (Waco, Texas: Word Books, 1979), 101.

The incarnation is unique in the sense that God reveals himself in the person of Jesus Christ, however, at the same time, this unique revelation is somehow embedded in the revelation of the Old Testament, thus God's self-revelation in the Old Testament shares the same degree of accuracy and truthfulness as that of the New Testament. In the Old Testament, Merrill says that God revealed more than just his name as what is suggested by Karl Barth, God revealed his essence and Being in terms of anthropomorphic and anthropopathic forms, and also manifested his attributes and character.[211] The Triune identity may be less prominent in the Old Testament than that of the New Testament, yet it is not totally unfound in the Old Testament without any traces or references.[212] It is true that the Trinitarian concept is more explicitly laid out in the New Testament, yet it is also implicitly revealed in the Old Testament. It is difficult to deny that the conceptual idea of Trinity was embedded in the revelation of the Old Testament. The Holy Spirit revealed himself very early in the creation (Genesis 1:2) and the Word was also manifested in the well-known words of Psalm 110:1 'The Lord says to my Lord' that he is the Lord of the universe in differentiating himself from the Lord God Father. Augustine says, 'we are utterly unable to doubt that Christ is announced in this Psalm.'[213] And this Christ, according to Augustine, 'is with the Father, invisible and incorruptible, because He is His Word, and His Power, and His Wisdom, and God with God, through whom all things were made.'[214] Augustine does not see Christ revealed in the Old Testament as a foreshadow any different than the Christ revealed in the New Testament. The Psalm 110:1, according to Athanasius, claims that even before Christ became man, 'he was King and Lord everlasting, being Image and Word of the Father.'[215] Thus, the incarnate revelation differs from that of the Old Testament only in the degree of clarity but not in essence. That means,

---

211   E. H. Merrill, 'A Theology of The Pentateuch', in *A Biblical Theology of The Old Testament*, ed. Roy B. Zuck (Chicago: Moody, 1991), 66.

212   N. Kassulke, 'The Doctrine of the Trinity in the Old Testament', *Theologia*, 5/2 (winter 2003). <http://www.wls.wels.net/publications/theologia/vol5no2> accessed 10 Feb 2006.

213   Augustine, 'On the Psalms', in *Nicene and Post-Nicene Fathers*, ed. Philip Schaff, 8 (Peaboy, Mass.: Hendrickson, 1999), 541.

214   Ibid., 542.

215   Athanasius, 'Against the Arians', vol. 4, discourse 2, 15.13, 355.

the God who was known by Moses is the same God who is known by Torrance. There is no difference in the essence of God's self-revelation to both.

5.3. Revelation and Knowing God

One of the most heated discussions of Torrance's theology is probably related to his doctrine of revelation on how the knowledge of God is acquired in his self-revelation. According to Torrance, God is utterly ineffable and incomprehensible to creaturely men due to his infinite greatness and majesty which exceed our human capacity to understand. There is a great gulf between the Creator and creature that creature is unable to comprehend its Creator. However, God himself has chosen to make himself known to mankind through his love by becoming incarnate in the historical person Jesus Christ, to reveal knowledge about himself both economically and ontologically. By becoming one of us, God makes it possible for men to understand him in human language. Thus, the incarnation makes the invisible visible and the incomprehensible comprehensible within the capacity of human being.[216] According to Torrance, there are two aspects of knowledge of God. One is knowable, and the other is incomprehensible. The knowable is based on the human capacity, the incomprehensible is beyond human capacity. Torrance, by referring to Calvin, says,

> While God is infinitely exalted above what we can ever conceive of him of ourselves, he nevertheless makes himself known to us through a twofold movement of revelation in which he lifts us up above the world and descends to us far beneath his own exaltedness, lisping to us, as it were, in words that we can grasp but that are not limpid expressions of what God is like so much as accommodations of his knowledge of this kind is, it is not to be confused with 'comprehension', for it is a kind of knowledge that surpasses all understanding, since the divine Reality that our minds embrace by faith in this way is infinite.[217]

---

216 Torrance, *The Trinitarian Faith*, 32–33.
217 Torrance, *The Christian Doctrine of God*, 11.

Even for the knowable knowledge which lies within the conceptual framework of the subject, it is still unknowable if the subjectivity of the subject has not been acted upon by the objectivity of the object. Thus, the knowledge of God can only be explained through the power of the Holy Spirit.[218] It is only through the Holy Spirit, according to Torrance, that we may know and believe in Jesus Christ, and it is only through the Holy Spirit that we are made free to receive and apprehend God's self-revelation and believe in the utterly astonishing truth announced to us, that in Jesus Christ God himself has become one of us in space and time.[219] That is to say, without the mediating power of the Holy Spirit, this knowledge of God revealed in the incarnation is lost. We cannot attribute the knowledge of God to ourselves, it is God's act upon us even though it is our knowledge of him. The knowledge is explicable only from the side of God who participates freely in his self-knowledge.[220] Torrance believes that it is the miraculous act of the Holy Spirit who creates in us the ability to know God beyond all human capacities and at the same time does not suppress our rational and critical powers.[221] Human rationality, according to Torrance, is a gift endowed by God that we are able to understand, to investigate, and to interpret the reality of his creation.[222] Our rationality is independent yet contingent upon God's own uncreated and transcendent rationality.[223] When God reveals himself in incarnation, he reveals to us in modes of rationality which he has conferred upon us in the creation.[224] However, this endowed rationality by itself, according to Torrance, is not able to realize the ultimate reality because the knowledge of God requires 'a change in the logical structure of our consciousness.'[225] It is a breach of our logic so that our thinking can act in accordance with the objective movement.[226] That is to say, the knowledge of God has to be attained beyond the human logical connections, and this requires a decision beyond logic in a Kierkegaardian 'leap

218   Torrance, *God and Rationality*, 22.
219   Torrance, *The Christian Doctrine of God*, 62–63.
220   Torrance, *God and Rationality*, 166.
221   Ibid., 168.
222   Torrance, *The Ground And Grammar of Theology*, 5.
223   Ibid., 55.
224   Ibid., 1.
225   Torrance, *Theological Science*, 154.
226   Ibid., 153–154.

of faith'.[227] Torrance insists that God can only be known through faith, he says,

> the God and Father of Jesus Christ is to be known through faith creatively called forth from people in response to the thrust of its intrinsic truth upon them and in sharp antithesis to what they had believed about God before.[228]

It is precisely in faith we are grasped by the ultimate reality and in faith we are freed from imprisonment of our own preconceptions and errors.[229] Barth, employs a similar idea in his understanding of the objective movement in the knowing of God. Faith, according to Barth, is beyond all human ideas and every positive religious achievement. There is no assured possession of faith, it is always a leap into the darkness of the unknown, a flight into empty air.[230] Barth's view does not indicate any certainty in the leap, it is a leap into the unknown. However, Torrance does not see Kierkegaard's leap as a leap into uncertainty or the unknown, but rather a leap of reason. Can this leap be rational? Torrance argues that it is rational because it is 'the activity of reason in obedient reaction to the action of the Truth'.[231] However, Hepburn thinks differently and argues that if man is compelled to accept Jesus' authoritative words about himself and about God, then, verification and explanation become unnecessary and irrelevant.[232] Because faith itself cannot be reasoned or rationally justified, Hepburn sees the leap itself as basically irrational.[233] Purves sees Torrance as operating a fideism[234] because there is no independent tribunal that one can appeal to regarding

---

227 Ibid., 154.
228 Torrance, *The Christian Doctrine of God*, 19.
229 T. F. Torrance (ed.), Belief *in Science and in Christian Life: the Relevance of Michael Polanyi's Thought for Christian Faith and Life* (Edinburgh: Handel Press, 1980), 3.
230 K. Barth, *The Epistle to the Romans*, tr. Edwyn C. Hoskyns (London: Oxford University Press, 1975), 96.
231 Torrance, *Theological Science*,154.
232 R. W. Hepburn, *Christianity and Paradox* (New York: Pegasus, 1968), 22.
233 Ibid.
234 Fideism is the view that faith takes precedence over reason. The word is often used as a term of abuse to designate a view considered by a critic to be a form of irrationalism. Kierkegaard is often cited as fideist. See C. S. Evans, *Pocket Dictionary of Apologetics & Philosophy of Religion* (Downer Grove, Il.: InterVarsity Press, 2002), 45.

the knowledge of God in the singularity of Jesus Christ. Carl Henry says that both Barth and Torrance fail to recognize that our mental judgment is also a divine gift of God, and thus should be regarded as a proper way by which man is to know God.[235] Henry sees Torrance as overstressing the deformity of human reason in the knowledge of God by disregarding the general revelation that confronts human reasoning. By denying the human logic in knowing God, Henry argues that nonsense can be regarded as divine truth.[236] That is to say, if our knowledge of God is based on the breach of our human logic which entails the law of contradiction, then we can say nothing about the objective knowledge of God because there is no application of human reasoning, and nonsense may become divine truth. Henry has made an important observation that many can claim to receive divine truth, however, if there is no sound reasoning in discerning the truth received, there is no way to differentiate many so-called truths from the ultimate truth in the world. Langford makes similar observation that in Torrance's doctrine of revelation, there is not enough provision for 'affective, volitional, or active dimensions of the response of the total man to God in Christ.'[237] This may devalue the participation of the total man in faith because, according to Langford, the dominant character of faith is its rationality and not its obedience.[238] In other words, obedience has to be discerned by one's own rationality in order to make it what it is. Molnar sees Torrance as refusing to establish any logic bridge between the world and God or between our thoughts and God's Being.[239] That is to say, there is no inferential[240] argument that can be developed from the created intelligibility to God's uncreated intelligibility even though God is revealed himself in the person of Jesus Christ. The gap could only be bridged by the non-inferential[241] faith

---

235 Henry, 171.

236 Ibid., 218.

237 Langford, 158.

238 Ibid.

239 P. D. Molnar, 'God's Self-Communication in Christ: A Comparison of Thomas F. Torrance and Karl Rahner', *Scottish Journal of Theology*, 50/3 (1997), 291.

240 Inferential beliefs are those which depend logically on a battery of interconnected concepts. See R. F. Thiemann, *Revelation and Theology*, (Notre Dame, Ind.: University of Notre Dame Press, 1985), 41.

241 Non-inferential beliefs are established independent of any conceptual framework, i.e., by direct relation to the objects they represent. See Thiemann, 41.

through obedience. Unfortunately, the claim of the knowledge of God is not the monopoly of Christianity if human rationality is disallowed to participate. Henry does not deny that there is a deficiency in the human rationality to know the truth, however, he believes that Divine Truth works through human rationality instead of apart from or independent of human rationality. Henry argues that if man cannot know the truth through his own rationality, then he cannot be held accountable for his personal rejection of the revelation because he is basically immune to the revelation,[242] he says,

> If the imago Dei on the basis of divine creation includes categories of thought and forms of logic ample to the knowledge and service of God, and if the fall of man has not destroyed man's rationality, it need not at all be the case, contrary to Torrance, that in God's free disclosure of the rational divine Word "we are face to face with a Reality which we cannot rationally reduce to our own creaturely dimensions" (Theological Science, p. 54)[243]

That is to say, Henry believes that human being does have the capacity to know God through the rational mind given by God, provided that the mind is enlightened by God.[244] Unfortunately, Henry does not give the necessary details of how the mind is enlightened by God, and this may well lie in the objective grace of God. Regarding Henry's criticism, Torrance responds,

> His (Carl Henry) whole position rests on the divine inspiration of logic, and the nominalist identity of truth with the terms that refer to the truth. Moreover it rests on an immense error in which he thinks that logic refers to the relation between terms and reality, when it has to do with the relation of statements to one another or the relations of ideas consistently with each other.[245]

Much of the disagreement, according to Morrison, lies in two different views of human rationality in relation to the self-revelation of God. Henry sees logic not as an invention but as a discovery, and objectivity is

---

242 Henry, 220.
243 Ibid., 222.
244 Ibid., 271.
245 It is a response to Morrison by Torrance on Henry's criticism. See Morrison, *Knowledge of the Self-Revealing God in The Thought of Thomas Forsyth Torrance*, 255.

only possible within the logic framework in which humans participate.[246] For Torrance, rationality and objectivity are related to the nature of the object, and the object's internal structure and intelligibility can only be revealed and acknowledged by the object. True rationality must follow the proper object's mode of rationality. Thus, Henry is accused by Torrance of taking the logic as divine in his argument. In fact, Henry does believe that human rationality is a divine endowment from God. In Torrance's response, Henry is accused as a nominalist because he is perceived by Torrance as separating the Word from God by focusing both Scripture and Jesus Christ as the Word of God. However, Torrance sees Scripture only to be the apostolic and human witness or pointer to the Word or Truth of God.[247] Torrance also argues that logic does not necessarily mean that it has to be established between the term and reality, it can also be between statements or ideas. Unfortunately, Torrance does not explain how the logical connection between statements can discern the reality of truth if human reason is excluded. Both Torrance and Barth, according to Klinefelter, see that autonomous human reason is a diseased form of rationality, it loses touch with reality by turning itself inward by satisfying its own requirement rather than bearing relation to the objective reality upon which it reasons.[248] Torrance's knowledge of God, according to Klinefelter, is neither subrational nor irrational but rational in the sense that it involves the conformity of our reason to intelligible realities and is our capacity for objectivity.[249] There are two notions of objectivity in Torrance's theology, according to Ferre, the first is the ordinary objectivity based on human rationality of logical principles and reasoning, and second is the true objectivity. The true objectivity is the capacity for the mind to be conformed to its object.[250] Ferre says that when the Word of God confronts man in his own self-revelation, there manifests the supreme instance of the incompatibility of ordinary objectivity of human reason

---

246 Ibid., 268–269.
247 Ibid.
248 D. S. Klinefelter, 'God and Rationality: A Critique of the Theology of Thomas F. Torrance', *The Journal of Religion*, 53 (1973), 119; Torrance, *Theological Science*, 26.
249 Klinefelter, 118.
250 F. Ferre, *Language, Logic and God* (London: Eyre & Spottiswoode, 1962), 80–81.

with true objectivity of genuine rationality.[251] When God reveals himself to man, man tries to fit the new Object into his existing patterns of ordinary objectivity, Torrance says,

> But reason is unable to subdue this Divine Subject-Object to ordinary objectivity (i.e. to its own subjectivity) for that would not be behaving in terms of the Object... Therefore reason, in order to be truly rational, must suspend its ordinary urge to objectivity, and find its true objectivity in the Divine Person who cannot be subdued to a mere object or resolved into the conclusion of a philosophical argument. This is the trouble with our reason that it is habituated to subduing objects to its own subjectivity.[252]

Torrance argues that unless we suspend our subjective rationality and let the objectivity of the object to act upon us, we could not come to realize the objective reality. In regarding to the belief of the objective reality, Torrance sees that there are two types of belief - implicit and explicit. Pascal claims that in order to make an explicit definition, we have to presuppose another set of terms, however, to define these terms, we would have to presuppose still other terms.[253] Thus, Torrance says,

> it is impossible to operate only with explicit propositions or definitions, for whenever we seek to define the meaning of something in precise terms we have to make use of other terms which for this purpose must themselves remain undefined.[254]

That is to say, explicit belief has to be based on some kind of implicit belief, and implicit belief somehow remains undefined. Similarly Polanyi, according to Torrance, points out that we are unable to reach a formal definition without referring to some undefined or implicit beliefs.[255] Thus, in our explicit belief, we rely on our implicit belief, and undefined knowledge. However, this 'implicit knowledge become more fully known as we rely on it in making an explicit definition.'[256] That is to say, explicit belief is justified by implicit belief, and implicit belief is

---

251 Ibid.
252 T. F. Torrance, 'Faith and Philosophy', *Hibbert Journal* 47/3 (1949), 243-244.
253 T. F. Torrance, 'The Framework of Belief', in *Belief in Science and in Christian Life: the Relevance of Michael Polanyi's Thought for Christian Faith and Life*, ed. T.F. Torrance (Edinburgh: Handsel Press, 1980), 18.
254 T. F. Torrance, 'The Deposit of Faith', *Scottish Journal of Theology*, 36 (1983), 1.
255 Torrance, 'The Framework of Belief', 18.
256 Ibid.

clarified by explicit belief. Though our implicit beliefs and explicit beliefs bear on each other in a circular way, Torrance does not see that it is trapped in a vicious circle of our own subjectivity. Torrance believes that our beliefs, whether explicit or implicit, are based on ultimate or fundamental belief that is linked to the objective pole in reality even though these ultimate beliefs are irrefutable as well as unprovable, as Polanyi argues.[257] Since we cannot offer independent demonstration of these ultimate beliefs, Torrance holds that the only way is to have responsible self-criticism.[258] That is to say, the objectivity of the reality is determined through the subjectivity of the knower in his self-criticism. It is up to the knower to determine what is and what is not the objective knowledge that is forced upon him. However, if that is the case, then the subject can determine the knowledge of the object rather than the object determines the knowledge of the object itself. Torrance denies that the subjectivity of the knower alone can discern the knowledge of the objective reality without first affirming the validity of the ultimate belief of the incarnate revelation that Jesus Christ is the Son of God. Klinefelter asks that if the knowledge of God is acquired from proper philosophical inquiry, why there is an arbitrary reliance on Christian revelation to control all epistemological questions?[259] That is to say, Torrance has set the presupposition that Christian revelation is the foundation for the source of any valid knowledge of God. Macquarrie warns that Torrance's idea of objective reality can easily be abused with human reasoning.[260] That is to say, if we take revelation simply based on what it claims without proper evaluation by human reasoning and conscience, then, there is no way to discern wheat from chaff, or truth from superstition.

Morrison sees Torrance's knowledge of God as based on his epistemological foundationalism: the upper stories of Torrance's thinking are supported by the lower stories or foundations which are given.[261] Thiemann also calls Torrance a foundationalist because Torrance's rational

---

257 Ibid., 18–19.
258 Ibid., 19.
259 Klinefelter, 121.
260 J. Macquarrie, *Twentieth-Century Religious Thought* (London: SCM Press, 1963), 334–335.
261 Morrison, *Knowledge of The Self-Revealing God in The Thought of Thomas Forsyth Torrance*, 65–66.

knowledge of God is based on the intuition[262] which signifies the in-dubitable and incorrigible causally imposed knowledge.[263] Torrance rebuts that since intuition is related to an ultimate belief, thus it can only be sensed but not proved; and also this intuition is necessary in all orderly scientific thinking and activity.[264] That is to say, according to Torrance, intuition is related to our experience and points to an objective reality beyond ourselves. Even though Torrance rejects the kind of mechanization of knowledge that is found in many forms of found-ationalism,[265] and argues that human rationality plays an important part in human understanding and knowing,[266] yet his revelational knowledge is nonetheless based on some foundational beliefs that cannot be validated or violated by human reason. And these foundational beliefs can only be instilled in us through the mediating power of the Holy Spirit.[267] Thus, according to Thiemann, in Torrance's doctrine of re-velation man is simply a vessel which cannot act on its own in judging the validity of God's self-revelation. He says,

> Torrance's defense of revelation's self-evidence and his correlative denial of the contribution of the human subject to knowledge of God is reminiscent of the problem which plagued Karl Barth in his Epistle to the Romans. A position which stresses both God's sovereign transcendence and his knowability is hard pressed to give an account of how we can come to know such a God. Barth's solution (of which Torrance's position is an updated version) is to grant God's Spirit the mediating power to bring divine object and human object together. The Spirit of God dwells within the believing interpreter and bestows the capacity to know the unknowable.

---

262 According to Torrance, there is no logical bridge between our ideas and experience, we have to use an intuitive mode of apprehension based on the inherent intelligible features in nature if we are to grasp the elementary principles in the nature. It is posteriori knowledge based on the revelation of the objective reality. It is non-inferential in nature and cannot be deduced from observations. See Torrance, 'The Framework of Belief', 9.

263 Torrance, 'Thomas Torrance Responds', 331; E. M. Colyer, 'A Scientific Theological Method', in *The Promise of Trinitarian Theology*, ed. Elmer M. Coyler, (Lanham: Rowan & Littlefield Publishers, 2001), 228–229.

264 Torrance, 'Thomas Torrance Responds', 331.

265 Colyer, 'A Scientific Theological Method', 228-229; T. F. Torrance, *Christian Frame of Mind: Reason, Order, and Openness in Theology and Natural Science* (Colorado Springs: Helmers & Howard, 1989), 45.

266 Ibid., 45.

267 Torrance, *The Christian Doctrine of God*, 62–63.

But God's Spirit is finally not the human subject but the "not-I" which dwells within. Thus "I" know God only insofar as I conform my subjectivity to the power of the Spirit; only as the God within knows the God without can true interpretation take place. Human subjectivity then becomes nothing more than the vessel through which God knows himself.[268]

In the process of knowing God, human subjectivity is lost and taken over by the Holy Spirit. Thus, the knowledge of God is in fact God knows God himself independent from human rationality. Our human mind is just a vessel for the Spirit to work through. However, Torrance insists that our faith through the mediation of the Holy Spirit is an act of rational understanding because our minds are opened to grasp what is beyond their natural power and at the same time, can freely acknowledge the objective reality based on its divine nature and self-evidence.[269] Faith, according to Torrance, is a movement of response in which there are elements of freedom and compulsion, however, they are corresponding to the mutual involution of Word and Event in God's self-revelation in Jesus Christ.[270] That is to say, God cannot be recognized other than what he is known in accordance with his incarnate revelation. The historical actuality and reality of Jesus Christ and of his divine authority demands full recognition that he is the Son of God.[271]

Thiemann sees faith as always a bestowed gift of God. The knowledge of God is not a natural human possession, but a new possibility granted through the graciousness of God. Thus, it is God's prevenience of grace that renders us the knowledge of God. Thiemann argues that the doctrine of revelation in Torrance's theology runs against the doctrine of God's prevenience.[272] Torrance's doctrine of revelation, according to Thiemann, is the epistemological foundationalism to provide theoretical justification for Christian belief in God's prevenience. This foundationalism, according to Thiemann, relies on an incoherent notion of non-inferential intuition as the means of asserting the priority of God's gracious reality.[273] The essence of the argument that Thiemann

---

268 Thiemann, 42.
269 Torrance, *God and Rationality*, 155.
270 Ibid.
271 Ibid.
272 Thiemann, 2–3.
273 Ibid., 7.

presents is that a revelational theologian such as Torrance who does not believe that the prevenience of God's grace is sufficiently enough for our salvation but rather assumes that God's revelation must be conformable to universal standards of rationality. Thiemann says,

> In order to maintain the absolute prevenience of grace, they argue, revelation must be conceived as the "impossible possibility" granted to the believer in a "moment of crisis." Revelation shatters the autonomous structure of human reason and communicates that which lies beyond reason's grasp...Torrance's argument moves in deft dialectical fashion. On the one hand he boldly asserts the absolute autonomy and prevenience of God's revelation. On the other hand he argues that theology's acceptance of that autonomy is perfectly rational and scientific.[274]

According to Thiemann, in Torrance's revelational theology, rational interpretation takes place only as we subordinate our subjectivity to God's objectivity, and allow God to be his own interpreter.[275] This rational normative interpretation of God's revelation, according to Thiemann, is Torrance's employment of the absolute prevenience of God's grace, and sees that this is the basic theological conviction that cannot be undermined by any account of theology's rationality. However, at the same time Torrance's argument for rationality contradicts his claims of absolute grace.[276] Thiemann questions how Torrance's theological science can be a rational discipline if human subjectivity is consistently denied.[277] That is to say, human rationality and subjectivity by itself cannot recognize the divine knowledge, unless it is objectively influenced and acted upon by God. Thus, Yeung does not see Torrance's theological science as a scientific discipline but rather a religion of faith because revelation simply cannot be recognized through human rational inquiry.[278] Torrance says,

> Apart from space and time nature would be indeterminable and unintelligible, for it would have no sequences or patterns of change and no series of continuous coherent structures and would thus be incapable of any kind of meaningful formalization. It is to space and time, therefore, that we have to look for the determine and intelligible

---

274   Ibid., 32–33.
275   Ibid., 37–38.
276   Ibid.
277   Ibid.
278   Personal discussion with professor Jason Yeung of China Graduate School of Theology (Hong Kong), 2005.

medium within which God makes Himself known to us and within which our knowledge of Him may be formed and grounded objectively in God's own transcendent rationality.[279]

Jesus Christ enters the realm of determination and intelligibility. Yeung argues that this is the realm of conditional and experiential nature, so the Word of God is no longer non-inferential. Thus, it has to be treated as the object of science.[280] And every science, according to Torrance 'presumes that the object it investigates is accessible and amenable to rational interpretation.'[281] Our rational interpretation is definitely inferential. However, unless God interacts with us, Torrance says, 'it is impossible for us as men on earth and in history to have any understanding of God or to say anything about Him.'[282] Thus, unless God imposes his self-revelation upon us and interacts with us on the experiential level, we would not be able to understand the revelation in the realm of time and space. That is to say, our minds have to conform to the mind of God in order to see what God reveals. The key weakness of Torrance's revelational theology, according to Yeung, is the non-inferential statement of revelation by trying to maintain human rationality at the expense of God's prevenient grace.[283] It is in fact difficult to maintain both inferential knowledge from human rationality and non-inferential knowledge from religious faith. Thiemann says,

> In order to recognize an experience as revelatory one must possess a general concept of the form X is a reliable symptom of Y. But to admit that is to grant that the 'revelatory' experience yields knowledge precisely because it can be integrated into a conceptual framework. But that in turn is a denial of the non-inferential quality of revelatory experience![284]

Our revelatory experience is based on our conceptual framework of inferential propositions, but by doing that, we automatically deny the non-inferential quality that Torrance is stressing upon through his

---

279 Torrance, *Space, Time and Incarnation*, 61.
280 J. H. K. Yeung, *Being and Knowing: An Examination of T.F. Torrance's Christological Science* (Hong Kong: Jian Dao, 1996), 91.
281 Torrance, *Theological Science*, 29-30.
282 Ibid., 294.
283 Yeung, 91–92.
284 Thiemann, 42.

epistemological inversion that the object acts on the subject through the encountering of the reality.[285] According to Torrance, the utter lordship of the Object takes precedence in our inquiry. That is to say, all knowledge of God has its reference from a centre in God and not in ourselves. Thiemann sees that Torrance's defense of revelation collapses when he appeals to non-inferential knowing of God apart from an inferential human conceptual framework. Thiemann says,

> How can we claim to have knowledge of God? If we bring God into a context dominated by our categories and concepts, we treat him as if he were simply another object among the many objects we know through rational schematization. If we set God outside that framework and allow him to create his own conditions and content of knowledge, then we cannot say how it is that we know him. The former option denies God his divinity; the latter denies us our humanity.[286]

Thiemann argues that if we know God through our inferential conceptual framework, then we do not really know God because God cannot be defined by human concepts; however, if we know God apart from our inferential framework, then we are unable to recognize him because he is outside of our conceptual capacity. Thiemann sees that Torrance's very argument of extraordinary cause as violating the pattern of reasoning which precedes it. Non-inferential belief of the epistemological foundationlists, according to Thiemann, undermines the whole pattern of inference.[287] Thiemann argues that God's grace must stand at the center of human life, however, when God's grace is conceived under the category of revelation, then grace becomes an extraordinary aspect of human life.[288] That is to say, if our knowledge of God is grounded on his revelation and not on his prevenient grace, grace becomes another aspect of human life rather than a gift of God. Thiemann's argument is simply that if our salvation is purely grounded in the prevenient grace of God, then our knowledge of God has everything to do with God's gracious act, and has nothing to do with human rationality. Our salvation does not depend on how rational we are, but rather how gracious God is.

---

285 Torrance, *Theological Science*, 131.
286 Thiemann, 42–43.
287 Ibid., 45–46.
288 Ibid., 48.

In summary, Torrance's doctrine of revelation is mediated between human rationality and divine enlightenment. On one hand, Torrance argues that our human inquiry of the objective reality is a rational endeavor, on the other hand, he insists that without faith, we cannot know God. There exists no compromising position in between as he rejects Thiemann's idea of God's prevenient grace as the source of our non-inferential knowledge, and Henry's idea of human reason in our inferential knowledge of God. It is like an analogy that light is always there, but unless our eyes are opened, we cannot see the light. Torrance argues that if we conform ourselves to the objectivity of the light, then we can see the light, however, at the same time, we are unable to open our eyes without God's help. Thus, if we see the light, it is because God opens our eyes. I have to agree with Yeung that Torrance's argument on human rationality is superficial, the real essence of his doctrine of revelation is hinged on faith which by itself is totally beyond the scope of rationality. It is purely by God's grace that we come to know him in his incarnate revelation.

6. Kenosis

The doctrine of kenosis could be regarded as one of the most debatable theological issues in the history of Christianity. The idea of kenosis is based on several Scriptural passages such as Philippians 2: 6-11, II Corinthians 8:9 and John 17:5. The word *kenosis* is derived from the verb *ekenosen* used in Philippians 2:7, which is rendered in the New International Version as "*made* himself *nothing*", and in the American Revised Version as "*emptied* himself". The word is also found in Romans 4:14, I Corinthians 1:17; 9:15, and II Corinthians 9:3; and carries a meaning of *no value, emptied, deprive* or *prove hollow*. Kent and others, in regards to Philippians 2, comment,

> Although the text does not directly state that Christ emptied himself "of something," such would be the natural understanding when this verb is used. Furthermore, the context has most assuredly prepared the reader for understanding that Christ divested himself of something.[1]

The understanding of this self-emptying concept is extremely difficult, especially about what was Christ emptying of? Many theories have been proposed to address this something. Bruce comments,

> The diversity of opinion prevailing among interpreters in regard to the meaning of the principal passage bearing on the subject of Christ's humiliation – that, namely, in the second chapter of Paul's Epistle to the Philippians – is enough to fill the student with despair, and to afflict him with intellectual paralysis.[2]

It is indeed not an exaggeration to suggest that kenosis is not a theological idea that can be grasped easily. Traditionally, many see that Christ as putting on a veil to mask his divine glory in his earthly mission, he does not give up any of his divine attributes, and remains as God.[3] Some argue that kenosis is not about the possession of the divine

---

1   H. Kent Jr., C. Vaughan, and A. Rupprecht, *Philippians, Colossians, Philemon* (Grand Rapids, Mich.: Zondervan, 1996). 31.

2   A. B. Bruce, *The Humiliation of Christ* (Grand Rapids, Mich.: Eerdmans, 1955), 8.

3   Common view of Patristic fathers, see discussion in section 5.1.

attributes but rather the use of those attributes,[4] others argue that he has given up some minor attributes which are not essential to his divine nature.[5] Some suggest that Christ has depotentiated himself to become a man, losing all his divine attributes,[6] others argue that kenosis is only restricted to his human nature, there is nothing to do with his divine nature, thus, the Philippians 2:6-11 passsage is interpreted as an anthropological hymn instead of an incarnational hymn.[7] Some would prefer to talk about kenosis as *state*, heavenly *state* and earthly *state*, which can be switched back and forth.[8] Torrance sees the so-called kenotic theory as ultimately a theory of how God and man can be conceived together in the historical person of Jesus Christ.[9]

The understanding of kenosis depends very much on the interpreter's theological position. Those taking the top down view would inevitably uphold the divinity of Christ that he has to remain God in its entirety, any change would violate that Christ is truly God. Those taking the bottom up view would like to argue that Christ lives a human life, he experiences the same difficulties as ours and shares with us the same sufferings, he grows up in both physical and mental capacities as us, thus he sets a perfect human example for us to follow. They believe that Christ loves us so much that he is willing to forsake his divinity and become a man. Torrance's theology on kenosis is basically rooted in patristic tradition while at the same time sympathetic to some modern ideas.

---

4   Thiessen is a representative of this view. See H. C. Thiessen, *Lectures in Systematic Theology* (Grand Rapids, Mich.: Eerdmans, 1977), 296.

5   This is the view of Thomasius, see discussion in section 5.2.

6   This is the view of Gess, see discussion in section 5.2.

7   See George Howard's essay on Philippians 2:6-11, 'Phil 2:6-11 and the Human Christ', Catholic Biblical Quarterly, 40 (1978), 377.

8   This is the view of Berkhof. See L. Berkhof, *Systematic Theology* (Grand Rapids, Mich.: Eerdmans, 1977), 328.

9   T. F. Torrance, *The Doctrine of Jesus Christ* (Eugene: Wipf and Stock Publishers, 2002), 110.

6.1. Patristic Tradition of Kenosis

In his formulation of the doctrine of kenosis, Torrance relies on the interpretations of the patristic fathers such as Cyril of Alexandria, Athanasius, Hilary, and Origen. According to Torrance, Cyril argues that the verb *ekenosen* should not be understood in a literal sense of emptying out of one receptacle into another, but rather a powerful expression of utter abasement or humiliation of becoming nothing. It means that Christ empties himself or puts off his divine glory and takes on the humble form of a servant.[10] That is to say, Cyril interprets kenosis as the veiling of Christ's divinity, the acceptance of a human disguise.[11] The essence of the self-emptying, according to Cyril, is the humility of Christ that he humbles himself to become one of us by taking up human weaknesses. However, Torrance emphasizes that in accordance with Cyril Christ does not cease to be God.[12] Unless he who suffers for us is God himself, Torrance claims, we are not redeemed.[13] That is to say, in order for us to be saved, Christ has to be God and he is eternally equal to the Father and equally unchangeable as the Father, there is no change to his deity in the mystery of the incarnation.[14] Thus, according to Torrance, Cyril argues that the act of self-emptying does not imply that Christ empties his divine content but rather makes our humanity his own by assuming the form of a servant under the yoke of the law.[15] That is to say, the self-emptying is not a subtraction but rather an addition.[16] Torrance says,

> Far from implying any emptying of divine content out of the Son of God the Incarnation was interpreted to import an adding to what he ever was in making our humanity his own and in assuming the form of a servant under the yoke of the law; and far from implying any depreciation or diminishing of human nature it was interpreted to mean not only the upholding and preserving of it in its integrity as human but the completing and perfecting of it in an enriched relation to God by a

---

10   T. F. Torrance, *Theology in Reconciliation* (Eugene: Wipf and Stock Publishers, 1996), 161.

11   R. Lucien, *Christ the Self-Emptying God* (New York: Paulist, 1997), 74–75.

12   Torrance, *Theology in Reconciliation*, 161-162, 175.

13   T. F. Torrance, *The Trinitarian Faith* (Edinburgh: T&T Clark, 2003), 159.

14   Lucien, 74–75.

15   Torrance, *Theology in Reconciliation*, 161–162.

16   Ibid., 162.

process which Cyril called 'transelementing', that is, not a transubstantiation but a transformation of it as through the Spirit it is made to participate in the renewed and sanctified humanity in Christ.[17]

That is to say, Torrance believes that Cyril's interpretation does not only maintain the divinity of Christ, it also transforms the humanity of Christ. Christ's self-emptying is a voluntary act of God out of his own freedom of love, and this voluntary act entails humiliation because God wants to form an indissoluble union in the person of Jesus Christ that he allows economically the measures of humanity to prevail over himself.[18] Christ's abasement includes all facets of his human existence whether it is moral or mental experiences.[19] According to Torrance, Cyril's doctrine of kenosis has to be interpreted in accordance with the economic nature of the incarnation.[20]

Most ancient fathers do not believe that Christ abandons his omniscience when he assumes humanity. However, there are mysterious sayings of Christ concerning the timing of the judgment in Matthew 24:36 and Mark 13:32.[21] Does the person Jesus Christ know the time of the judgment?[22] Does he give up his omniscience when he assumes humanity? Hilary, according to Torrance, sees Christ's ignorance as essentially an economic property which he experiences for our sakes in sharing our human growth and development in his childhood. And by taking up our place, Christ is able to lift us up to his place in communion

---

17   Ibid., 161–162.

18   Ibid., 164.

19   Ibid., 173, 180.

20   Ibid., 177–178.

21   F. J. Hall, *The Kenotic Theory Considered With Particular Reference to its Anglican Forms and Arguments* (New York: Longmans, 1898), 10.

22   Powell gives a list of possible interpretations: (a) That Christ was giving pre-eminence to the Father in know this secret. He knew it Himself only as the Father knew it. (b) Although He knew as God, He did not as Man. (c) He knew not the time as fixed, since it is determined conditionally only. (d) As Head of His Body, the Church, He knew not. (e) "The Son" is not used personally, but as standing for His adopted people. (f) He knew both as God and Man, but not as commissioned to reveal it. (g) He knows the time, but not practically, since He has not yet executed the judgment. (h) The "day and hour" means the absolute blessedness of seeing God as He is. He did not possess this knowledge as Man. (i) He knew in His human mind, but not by its powers. See Hall's footnotes, 10-11.

with God.[23] Though Christ experiences human limitations, he nonetheless is able to transcend our natural weaknesses and rise above our
creaturely ignorance in his kenosis.[24] Hilary's argument, according to
Torrance, is based on the reality of the human nature of Christ that 'The
words and acts of Christ are words and acts in his human nature, yet they
are words and acts of One who did not cease to be God even in his
kenosis.'[25] That is to say, Torrance believes that Hilary's theology on
kenosis[26] has to be interpreted in accordance with the two-fold nature of
Christ that the reality of the human nature of Christ cannot violate the
reality of the divine nature of Christ.[27] Similarly, Athanasius argues that
there is no ignorance in the divine nature of Christ; he says, 'let them
hear that there is no ignorance in the deity but that not knowing is, as has
been said, proper to the flesh.'[28] That is to say, as far as Christ is the
Logos, he knows all things even before their origination. A particular
feature of the assumed humanity as seen from Athanasius is that the

---

23 T. F. Torrance, *Divine Meaning* (Edinburgh: T&T Clark, 1995), 405.
24 Ibid.
25 Ibid., 406.
26 In the theology of Hilary of Poitiers, it is paramount that Christ is none other than
    God himself and is equal to the Father. Christ has been sealed in the form of God
    and which is an image of all that God possesses. Though Christ takes the form of a
    servant, he remains God. He empties himself through obedience, and though he is
    in the form of God, he takes the form of a servant. As a servant, he is obedient unto
    death. Hilary argues that by being in the form of God does not make Christ less
    than God. Christ is styled in the likeness of the invisible God in order that we may
    understand by his exercise of the power that he has divine nature. However, as the
    incarnated Son of God, Christ humbles himself and is found as man in the form of
    a servant. Hilary sees kenosis as putting on physical form of man, and putting down
    his invisible form of God, however, the divine nature remains in him. That is to
    say, in the act of self-emptying, Christ trades his appearance from the form of God
    to the form of man. In Hilary's theology, the word form carries a distinctive and
    different meaning than nature. Christ is the very nature of God while He empties
    himself the form of God and takes on the form of a servant. According to Hilary,
    the form of God is no different than the glory of God. That is to say, Christ puts
    down his eternal glory in his act of self-emptying which itself is an act of
    obedience. See Hilary of Poitiers, 'On the Trinity', in *Nicene and Post-Nicene
    Fathers*, ed. Philip Schaff & Henry Wace, 9 (Peaboy, Mass.: Hendrickson, 1999),
    150-151, 173-174.
27 Torrance, *Divine Meaning*, 406.
28 Athanasius, 'Orations Against The Arians', in *The Christological Controversy*, ed.
    Richard A. Norris (Philadelphia: Fortress, 1980), 97.

humanity of Christ incorporates the ignorance of men, so that he might redeem humanity from its imperfections, and cleanse and offer it to the Father.[29] According to Torrance, Athanasius' view is supported by both Gregory of Nazianus and Gregory of Nyssa that ignorance is essential to Christ's humanity.[30] Ignorance is just as essential to Christ's self-abasement as his physical limitations, and all of these are simply predicated of his incarnate reality.[31] Torrance says,

> It was an economic and vicarious ignorance on our Lord's part by way of a deliberate restraint on his divine knowledge throughout a life of continuous kenosis in which he refused to transgress the limits of the creaturely and earthly conditions of human nature. As the Word or Mind of God become flesh Jesus Christ was the incarnate wisdom of God, but incarnate in such a way as really to share with us our human ignorance, so that we might share in his divine wisdom... Unless the Son of God had assumed the whole nature of man, including his ignorance, man could not have been saved.[32]

Unless Christ shares our ignorance, we would not have been saved. That is to say, even though Christ is all knowing, he sometimes presents himself ignorant of divine knowledge for our sake in accordance with his human nature. It is Cyril of Alexandria, according to Torrance, who develops the soteriological approach of Athanasius most fully. Cyril, according to Torrance, encounters a problem of how to harmonize Jesus' real human growth from ignorance to knowledge with his divine nature. Cyril is forced to say that while Christ is subjected himself to our human ignorance, he is nevertheless ignorant of nothing because he divinely partakes of the wisdom of the Father. Torrance does not see Cyril as taking a dualist view of Christ's two natures, but rather perceiving that Christ acts both divinely and humanly according to his incarnate reality.[33] Ignorance does not necessarily indicate a deficiency in character, but rather a characteristic of a true human being that he does not know everything. Torrance says,

---

29   Torrance, *The Trinitarian Faith*, 186–187; Athanasius, 'Orations Against The Arians', 97.
30   Torrance, *The Trinitarian Faith*, 186–187.
31   Ibid.
32   Ibid., 187.
33   Torrance, *Theology in Reconciliation*, 165.

Though conceived by the Holy Spirit and born of the Virgin Mary, Jesus was yet born in the womb of a sinner, within the compass of our sinful flesh. As the Son of Adam he was born into our alienation, our God-forsakenness and darkness, and grew up within our bondage and ignorance, so that he had to beat his way forward by blows, as St Luke puts it, growing in wisdom and growing in grace, before God as well as before man.[34]

The humanity of Christ is not endowed with infinite wisdom, he has to learn obedience by the things he suffers and gains wisdom as he grows up. Torrance uses the genealogy of Jesus recorded in the Gospel of St. Matthew to show that the Incarnate Son is really one of us that he makes the generations of humanity his very own.[35] Torrance says 'this Jesus who as bone of our bone and flesh of our flesh is of one and the same being with us',[36] he shares the same being and substance as human being, and is constrained under the same physical limitations. Christ assumes the manner of man and lives in the form of a servant.[37]

Jesus Christ as a historical person is physically bounded in time and space, how can he maintain his omnipresence which is part of his divine attribute? Since Christ does not give up any of the divine attributes in his act of self-emptying, then, if he is God then he must be here and everywhere. Torrance appeals to Origen in saying that even though God assumed human life in the person of Jesus, the one who was in the beginning with God and who was himself God does not leave the place where he was, Christ does not leave his throne.[38] That is to say, God is not moving from one place to another in a way that he is emptying one place and filling up another place, but rather Christ is everywhere that he is with the Father and at the same time he is with us on earth. Christ's presence is not contained within a bounded space. Self-emptying does not mean that the Son empties something out of a receptacle, but rather that he assumes a body in addition to his deity that Christ is wholly present in the body he assumes, and yet wholly everywhere in

34 T. F. Torrance, *Theology in Reconstruction* (London: SCM Press, 1965), 132.

35 T. F. Torrance, *The Mediation of Christ* (Exeter: Paternoster Press, 1983), 50.

36 T. F. Torrance, 'Introduction', in *The Incarnation: Ecumenical Studies in the Nicene-Constantinopolitan Creed A.D. 381*, ed. T. F. Torrance (Edinburgh:The Handsel Press, 1981), xviii.

37 T. F. Torrance, *Space, Time and Resurrection* (Edinburgh: T&T Clark, 1998), 84.

38 Torrance, *Divine Meaning*, 355–356.

accordance with his divine nature.[39] The fundamental point of Origen's thought, according to Torrance, is that when God becomes man by assuming a human body, partaking in our physical space, he remains whatever he was. The spatial concept has to be interpreted from the side of God's active and controlling occupation of bodily existence and place. Torrance says,

> Space is a predicate of the Occupant; it is determined by his agency, and is to be understood in accordance with his nature. He cannot therefore have the same space-relation with the Father as we creatures have; otherwise he would be quite incapable of God.[40]

Since Christ is both God and man, thus, the concept of space has to be interpreted both physically and metaphysically because the concept of space is a predicate of its occupant, that means, the space has to be defined by its occupant. Torrance further illustrates with an example of our salvation in the notion of space that even though we are bounded by the confinement of evil, we may ascend to heavenly places without leaving our physical location on earth. Thus, according to Torrance, salvation means

> to have our place on earth opened out to the kind of place where Christ is; to be saved means to be brought to share in the fullness of God and thus to reach true magnitude and space of mind in communion with him.[41]

That means the concept of space is no longer restricted by purely physical dimension. Even though we are physically bounded, our mind can travel to locations beyond our physical restrictions. That is to say, humanly speaking, our mind can be here and there at the same time. Similarly, Athanasius says that while God becomes human, he is not bounded by his body but rather he masters his body. That is to say, God is not only in the body but he is everywhere. Even though he is born of the virgin, he does not suffer any change nor has his glory diminished. He becomes a creature, yet at the same time he sustains the whole

---

39   Ibid., 361.
40   Ibid., 366.
41   Ibid., 363.

248

creation.[42] According to Torrance, Athanasius believes that God comes to the world and at the same time he remains present with the Father. That is to say, the Son is fully present with us in time and space, and yet remains with the Father.[43] The humanity of Christ is simply an economic form which he takes in the condescension.[44] According to Athanasius, there are things that belong to Christ's divine nature, and things that belong to his human nature. Athanasius argues, according to Torrance, we must apply all human properties and limitations properly to Christ's human nature.[45] However, at the same time, Athanasius rejects any subordinationism in the doctrine of the Son.[46] All human weaknesses and limitations belong to Christ's flesh, and the miraculous works are done through the flesh by Christ's deity which is within the flesh.[47] Christ is God clothed in human flesh, and the act of self-emptying is seen as a reflection of his human nature in the totality of Christ as a person. The assumption of humanity in the form of a servant, according to Athanasius, forms the basic understanding of Christ's act of self-emptying. Thus, early church fathers believe that it is the assumption rather than the subtraction that gives the correct interpretation of the doctrine of kenosis.[48] Kenosis and all its associated limitations are

---

42   Athanasius, 'Incarnation of the Word', in *Nicene and Post Nicene Fathers*, ed. Philip Schaff and Henry Wace, 4 (Peaboy, Mass.: Hendrickson, 1999), 45.

43   Torrance, *Divine Meaning*, 364.

44   Torrance, *The Trinitarian Faith*, 83.

45   Torrance, *Theology in Reconciliation*, 152.

46   Ibid., 151.

47   Athanasius, 'Orations Against The Arians', 89.

48   There were many fathers who affirmed this principle. Chrysostom says that Christ's deity remains the same; he is the pre-existent Logos. The self-emptying, according to Chrysostom, means that Christ takes on what he was not, the form of a servant, made in the likeness of men. Though Christ is made flesh, he remains God, see Chrysostom, 'Homilies on Philippians', *Nicene and Post-Nicene Fathers*, ed. Philip Schaff, 13 (Peaboy, Mass.: Hendrickson, 1999), 213-214. Tertullian sees that in accordance with normal human perception when one takes up another form, he is losing something that is part of him initially. Thus, when Christ takes up humanity, it is naturally to imply that he would have ceased to be God. However, God is different from human, thus kenosis cannot be understood purely in accordance with human nature. God can continue his divinity even after he takes up humanity. Tertullian cites that in the Old Testament that angels took up the form of man, and interacted with human beings; Abraham washed their feet (Genesis 18), and Lot was rescued from the Sodomites by their hands (Genesis 19). Even though these

related only to the economic aspect of the incarnation. Torrance adopts this traditional patristic understanding that Christ remains what he was, he takes what he was not.[49]

6.2. Modern Kenotic Ideas

The seed of modern kenoticism, according to Hall, is sown by Martin Luther due to his interpretation of *communicatio idiomatum* by imparting divine attributes to the manhood of Christ.[50] This deviation from the catholic tradition, according to Torrance, is due to the receptacle notion of space which is of immense importance to Lutherans for it is their way of asserting the reality and actuality of the Son of God in our human

---

angels are inferior to God, they are still able to remain angels after being changed into human bodily form. Thus, according to Tertullian, the Creator has no problem of keeping his fully divine status in becoming a man. The kenotic verse does not change the divinity of Christ, but it simply adds the form of humanity similar to what the angels did in the Old Testament, see Tertullian, 'On the Flesh of Christ', in *Ante-Nicene Fathers*, ed. Alexander Roberts & James Donaldson, 3 (Peaboy, Mass.: Hendrickson, 1999), 523. According to Origen, Christ exists eternally with the Father and he acts as a servant to the Father in the creation. When he becomes man, Origen sees that Christ divests his glory in the act of self-emptying. When the Son becomes man, the eternal glory of the Son is concealed in his act of self-emptying. Even though Christ is a man, Origen argues that he remains God as who he was. The Father is the origin and source of the Son, yet the Son was never created. Christ is the image of the invisible God, and the purpose of the image is to demonstrate to us the fullness of his deity. The Father is called omnipotent, thus the Son is also called omnipotent. He and the Father are one. However, in becoming man, Christ divests his divine majesty. In essence, Origen does not want to deviate from the orthodox teaching that Christ is God and his divine nature remains with him during his earthly mission. However, at the same time, his glory and majesty are somehow hidden in his earthly mission. See Origen, 'De Principiis', in *Ante-Nicene Fathers*, ed. Alexander Roberts & James Donaldson, 4 (Peaboy, Mass.: Hendrickson, 1999), 240, 245-250, 270, 281; Origen, 'Commentary on Matthew', in *Ante-Nicene Fathers*, ed. Allan Menzies, 9 (Peaboy, Mass.: Hendrickson, 1999), 465.

49   Torrance, *Theology in Reconciliation*, 161–162.
50   Hall, 13.

existence that the whole Son is contained in the historical Jesus and communicated to us in the Eucharist.[51] Luther's interpretation of Eucharist is especially troublesome to the Reformers, he insists that 'this is my body' is the physical substance of the Lord's body when we partake in the Eucharist. His literal interpretation of the text clearly drives a wedge between the Swiss and German reformers. Luther's belief in consubstantiation in reality is fairly close to the Roman doctrine of transubstantiation which he condemns. Is the body of Christ really in the Eucharist, and if so, why? This is a debate among the Lutherans that leads to the ubiquitarian controversy. Melanchthon, Luther's lieutenant, tries to maintain that Christ's body is not in the Eucharist because Eucharist is performed and received everywhere, and is impossible for the physical presence of the Lord's body to be everywhere at the same time. Any physical matter is bounded by time and space. Thus, Luther's unique interpretation of the *communicatio idiomatum* plays a guiding principal in this debate. Brenz says,

> the attributes of the divine nature had been communicated to the humanity of Christ which was thus deified. If deified, it was everywhere, ubiquitous, just as His divinity, and therefore really present in the Eucharist.[52]

In order to have the omnipresence of Christ's body in the Eucharist, the divine attribute of Christ is somehow downloaded to the manhood of Christ. Thus, the very principle of the Chalcedonian formula that the two natures of Christ are distinct and non-confused is violated. The Lutheran doctrine of *communicatio idiomatum*, according to Torrance, has transferred the concept of *perichoresis* from the Trinity to the hypostatic union and thus damaged the demarcation of divine and human by the deification of Christ's humanity.[53] The concept of *perichoresis* involves a dynamic union and communion of the three divine Persons such that they are mutually indwelling and inter-penetrating in one another, while the doctrine of hypostatic union affirms a clear distinctiveness of two unique natures that cannot be intermingled with one another. When the

---

51 T. F. Torrance, *Space, Time and Incarnation* (London: Oxford University Press, 1969), 30.

52 *Catholic Encyclopedia* <http://www.newadvent.org/cathen/15117a.htm> accessed 1 Dec 2005.

53 Torrance, *Time and Incarnation*, 32.

concept of *perichoresis* is transferred to the hypostatic union, it creates a movement or interchange between two unique natures. The result of this change, according to Torrance, leads to the depotentiation of divine properties of Christ in the understanding of kenosis by the German theologians.[54] Depotentiation, according to Torrance, is the extension of a human receptacle to contain the divine.[55]

According to Torrance, the theology of Calvin emphasizes the ubiquity of Christ that while he is born of the virgin's womb, he has never left heaven or the governance of the cosmos that he created.[56] That is to say, Christ is acting on earth and at the same time he is ruling in heaven. This conception is important in maintaining Christ's full divinity as God, because anything less than that would make him less than what he was originally in the Triune Godhead. The incarnation, according to Torrance, involves the whole Son of God who is wholly present in the body he assumed, and also wholly everywhere in accordance with his divine nature.[57] However, Calvin's idea is interpreted by Lutherans, according to Torrance, that in the incarnation only part of the Logos is contained in the baby of Bethlehem and there is something left behind in heaven or left *outside*, hence, it is so-called *Calvinist Extra*.[58] The rejection by the Lutherans, according to Barth, is because they could see in it a Nestorian separation of the divine and human natures, thus, Lutherans believe that for Christ to fill the whole world (Ephesians 4:10), it has to be also said of the man Jesus as such on the basis of his union with the Logos.[59] Torrance sees a benefit in the Lutherans' intention to maintain the fullest possible incarnation that the Logos as a whole becomes the person of the historical Jesus, there is nothing left behind, and demonstrate the completeness of Christ's incarnation. However, at the same time he makes it clear that the rejection of *Calvinist extra* creates many difficulties and argues that Lutherans are operating with a receptacle view of space that kenosis carries a meaning

---

54 Ibid., 36.
55 Torrance, *Space, Time and Resurrection*, 125.
56 Ibid., 124.
57 Torrance, *Divine Meaning*, 361.
58 Torrance, *Space, Time and Resurrection*, 124.
59 K. Barth, *Church Dogmatics*, tr. G.W. Bromiley and T.F. Torrance, 4/1 (Edinburgh: T&T Clark, 1957-1975), 181.

of emptying the Son of God into a containing vessel.[60] That is to say, the Son is contained by the space rather than the space being contained by the Son. Calvin on the other hand argues that Christ has not given up his omnipresence, he only divests his glory intermittently while he is on earth.[61] Self-emptying, according to Calvin, means that Christ lays aside his glory in the view of men, not by lessening it, but by concealing it.[62]

Some have traced the modern kenoticism to Count Zinzendorf, a pioneer of pietism, who sees much of Christ life on earth as a human phenomenon.[63] However, Luther had already laid down the foundation for the depotentiation of Christ's divine attributes through his doctrine of *communicatio idiomatum*. Thomasius, Gess, and others in the nineteenth century made a paradigmatic shift in the interpretation of the self-emptying of God by depotentiating the divine attributes of Christ, so that God becomes more like a historical man. Torrance sees these thoughts as being basically developed within the framework of the receptacle idea with philosophical touch ups. [64] Bruce comments that the Lutheran conception of the hypostatic union demands one of two things, either the infinite should come down to the finite or that the finite should be raised to the infinite. So, he sees that old Lutherans took the latter way and encountered many difficulties; thus, the modern Lutherans give up the ancient path of God's majesty and strike the new path of kenosis, that incarnation is understood as the *self-limitation* of the Son of God.[65]

Gottfried Thomasius was born in the period of modern criticism that the intellectual minds were preoccupied with the quest of the historical Jesus. He wants to show that it might be possible to think of the two-natured Christ of faith as the historical Jesus.[66] In order to maintain the unity of Christ, Thomasius sees that there cannot be a twofold mode of

---

60   Torrance, *Space, Time and Resurrection*, 124.
61   J. Calvin, 'Commentaries on The Prophet Daniel', in *Calvin's Commentaries*, 13 (Grand Rapids, Mich.: Baker, 2003), 42.
62   Ibid.
63   R. J. Tapia, *The Theology of Christ: Commentary* (New York: The Bruce Publishing Company, 1971), 409.
64   Torrance, *Space, Time and Incarnation*, 46.
65   Bruce, 138–139.
66   Colin Brown, Jesus *in European Protestant Thought 1778-1860* (Durham: The Labyrinth Press, 1985), 254.

being, a double life, a double consciousness;[67] that is to say, the divine consciousness and the human consciousness cannot exist side by side in the historical person of Jesus. He argues that the historical Jesus has a gradual natural human development instead of the divine consciousness because if during the time of Jesus' natural development of life, he remains fully unlimited, knows everything in timeless intuition, there would exist a duplication of consciousness and activity that would destroy the truth of the infant consiousness and natural development.[68] He says that when the eternal Son of God gives himself over into the form of human limitation, he limits himself to the spatio-temporal existence under the conditions of a human development.[69] The assumption of the human nature, according to Thomasius, entails the self-limitation of God the Son in the form of divesting his divine mode of Being in favor of the human creaturely form of existence. However, it is not a surrender of divine ego, but nevertheless, a divesting of a higher form of existence.[70] In the person of Jesus Christ, there is only one unitary movement, experience and devclopment of life because there exists only one ego, one divine-human personality.[71] That is to say, two natures could not form two personalities within the same ego, there exists only one personality which is both divine and human. Thus, Thomasius suggests that in kenosis, Christ maintains his immanent divine attributes such as absolute power[72], truth, holiness and love. These attributes are inseparable from the essence of God and stay with the Son in his incarnation. However, as the incarnate Son, he divests his so-called relative atributes of omnipotence, omniscience, omnipresence. Thomasius suggests that the incarnate Son waives claim to the possession of all

67   G. Thomasius, 'The Person of the Mediator', in *God and Incarnation In Mid-Nineteenth Century German Theology*, ed. tr. Claude Welch, (London: Oxford University Press, 1965), 47.
68   Ibid., 53–54.
69   Ibid., 47–48.
70   Ibid., 49–50.
71   Ibid., 58–59.
72   According to Thomasius, absolute power is different from omnipotence. Absolute power means the freedom of self-determination while omnipotence means absolute power in the world. He claims that Christ did not actively rule the world at the same time he walked on earth as man. See Thomasius, 69-70.

these relative attributes.[73] According to Bruce, in Thomasius' theory, the consciousness of Christ is human, he has the same content and conditions as ours. The only difference between Christ and us is that he is not originally born out of the human nature but rather born into it in order to work out of it and through it into a complete divine-human person.[74] However, Thomasius' theory does not disturb the immanent Trinity because the relative attributes are not essential to the being of God himself.[75] In addition to Thomasius, others such as Konig, Daelitzsch, and Kahnis all share a similar view that relative attributes or economic attributes do not necessarily belong to God for him to be God. These attributes are related to God's essence in creation. Since creation is come by the will of God and thus these attributes can be abandoned by the same will, their abandonment does not violate divine immutability. Thus, the essential attributes of God such as absolute power, absolute truth, absolute holiness, and absolute love can be revealed more perfectly in the incarnation by emptying his relative attributes.[76]

In stressing pietism, Wolfgang Gess elevates the importance of Christ's humanity at the expense of his divinity. In becoming a full human being, according to Gess, Christ depotentiates himself of all his divine attributes, and even ceases his eternal consciousness on earth and his duty of maintaining the cosmos.[77] Bruce says that Gess lays stress on three scriptural representations of the incarnation that Christ is an outgoing Son from the Father, he is a descent from heaven, and he becomes flesh. Gess understands the first representation as an exit that the eternal Son is out of the intimacy of his communion with the Father. The exit though not totally dissolves the indwelling of the Father, Son and Spirit, it suspends the influx of the eternal life of the Father to the Son, thus, the Son ceases to have life in himself. Gess understands the descent from heaven to signify the humiliation. Christ transits from a state of equality with God into a state of dependence, and in doing so, he lays aside his eternal glory that was with him prior to the incarnation. In becoming man, Christ does not only give up his economic attributes, but

---

73 Ibid., 70.
74 Bruce, 142–143.
75 Ibid.
76 Hall, 16.
77 L. Berkhof, *Systematic Theology* (Grand Rapids, Mich.: Eerdmans, 1977), 327; Brown, 253.

also his immanent attributes of God. He suffers the extinction of his eternal self-consciousness, he only regains it gradually through human growth and development.[78] Bruce challenges that in accordance with Gess' full depotentiation of divine attributes, 'A capability of sinning must be ascribed to Christ, otherwise the reality of His humanity is denied.'[79] Thus Gess' theory of kenosis, according to Bruce, amounts to a metamorphosis of the Logos into a man. Bruce argues that it is not possible for a divine Being to extinguish himself in the process of self-emptying.[80] The kenotic theory of Gess reflects the extreme view of modern kenoticism that divinity is totally pushed out from the person of Jesus Christ. According to Hall, this radical view is shared by Gaupp, Schmieder, Reuss, Godet and others that God becomes a man with only human soul and body.[81] Hall says,

> The ancient heretic, Apollinaris, had said that the Logos took the place of a rational soul in Christ. These writers, on the other hand, brought forward the idea of conversion, metamorphosis, in the place of substitution. Hofmann says the Logos "remains Who He was, though He ceased to be what He was." The "form of God" was changed into the form of a servant." The Divine functions of the Word were left in the Father's hands until resumed by the Word at His glorification. Godet says that omnipotence gave place to obedience, omniscience to the ignorance of a learner, omnipresence to circumscribed bodily presence, immutable holiness to a liability to temptation and power to sin, infinite love to finite and progressive love, and consciousness of Divine Sonship to possession of bare personality and progressive consciousness.[82]

In between Thomasius and Gess, there are a variety of many different views.[83] Ebrard agrees with Gess that the Son in becoming man gives up his eternal consciousness and assumes a human life, thus, the whole

---

78   Bruce, 144–145; J. McClintock and J. Strong, *Cyclopedia of Biblical, Theological, and Ecclesiastical Literature*, 5 (Grand Rapids, Mich. Baker, 1981), 45.
79   Bruce, 148.
80   Ibid., 148–149.
81   Hall, 15–16.
82   Ibid.
83   Alex Bruce classifies modern kenoticism into four distinct types: (1) the absolute dualistic type, (2) the absolute metamorphic, (3) the absolute semi-metamorphic, and (4) the real but relative. Of the first, Thomasius may conveniently be taken as the representative; of the second, Gess; of the third, Ebrard; and of the fourth, Martensen. See Bruce, 138.

person is reduced to a human soul. However, he argues that it is not a loss, but rather a disguise of his divinity, that God exchanges his eternal manner of Being with a temporal manner of Being in assuming flesh.[84] According to Ebrard, Bruce says,

> The kenosis does not mean that Christ laid aside His omnipotence, omnipresence, and omniscience; but that He retained these in such a way that they could be expressed or manifested, not in reference to the collective universe, but only in reference to particular objects presenting themselves to His notice in time and space.[85]

That is to say, Christ's economic attributes could be manifested only to selected people in selected times and places. Ebrard maintains that Christ has only one human life center, Martensen on the other hand postulates two non-communicating life-centers. In addition to the human life center, Christ is also in the bosom of the Father that he continues to function in the Trinitarian life and remains as the creator and sustainer of the cosmos.[86] Thus, Martensen says that Christ lives a double life. As the deity Christ, he works in his divine capacity, and as the human Christ, he works in his depotentiated capacity. This clearly gives an impression that Martensen is creating two Christs, one in heaven and one on earth. He fervently denies that he is advocating two Christs, and claims that there is no new second Son to the Trinity.[87] Martensen says that in becoming man, God has renounced his majestic glory and shared a limited form of human consciousness, however, at the same time, the Son also comes into the full possession of his divine glory because Martensen argues that for love is never in full possession until it can fully communicate, and Christ's omnipotence is demonstrated when he overcomes all hearts.[88] In Christ's human form, all divine attributes are no longer infinite and unbounded, it is to be embodied in the attributes of human nature. Instead of the omnipresence, we have blessed omnipresence; instead of the omniscience, we have the divinely human wisdom; instead of the omnipotence, we have the infinite power of love.[89]

---

84   Berkhof, 327; Bruce, 153–154.

85   Ibid.

86   Berkhof, 328.

87   H. Martensen, *Christian Dogmatics*, tr. William Urwick (Edinburgh: T&T Clark, 1898), 267.

88   Ibid., 266.

89   Ibid., 267.

In general, there are two rival schools of thought in the modern kenoticism – Giessen and Tubingen. Torrance sees the rivalry as the unavoidable result of the Lutheran conception of receptacle that the incarnation is thought of the self-emptying of Christ into the receptacle of a human body, and claims that their attempts to solve this problem is either by the renunciation of certain properties of the divine nature or if not able to separate, by the concealment in order to preserve the form of the human receptacle.[90] The Giessen theologians suggest that while Christ is on earth, his divine attributes are temporary suspended so to leave room for human growth. However, the Tubingen theologians argue that the divine attributes are simply concealed during his earthly mission.[91] Barth comments that while both parties want to maintain the intactness of the eternal Logos in the state of his earthly humiliation, it is the Lutheran presupposition of the divinization of Christ's humanity that creates the controversy, and says that 'The thesis of Giessen derived from a concern at the threatened Docetism of the Tubingen anti-thesis.'[92] Barth believes that the divine nature of Christ does not suffer any change and thus does not cease anything in the incarnation. Christ's deity is not altered because the deity of God is unalterable. Barth argues, 'Any subtraction or weakening of it would at once throw doubt upon the atonement made in Him. He humbled Himself, but He did not do it by ceasing to be who He is.'[93] Barth is adamant that unless Christ is God, he cannot save us. The intention of both schools is good, according to Barth, because they 'want to clear away the difficulties of the traditional teaching and make possible a "historical" consideration of the life of Jesus.'[94] However, Barth argues that if Christ born of a manger and crucified on the Cross is not wholly God, then what else can we say about the reconciliation of the world with God in the humiliated One?[95] Barth says,

> In Himself He was still the omnipresent, almighty, eternal and glorious One, the All-Holy and All-Righteous who could not be tempted. But at the same time among us

---

90 Torrance, Space, Time and Incarnation, 36.
91 Hall, 13-14.
92 Barth, Church Dogmatics, 4/1, 181.
93 Ibid. 180.
94 Ibid. 183.
95 Ibid.

and for us He was quite different, not omnipresent and eternal but limited in time and space, not almighty but impotent, not glorious but lowly, and open to radical and total attack in respect of His righteousness and holiness. His identity with Himself consisted strictly in His determination to be God, our God, the Reconciler of the world, in this inner and outer antithesis to Himself.[96]

According to Barth, there is no loss of any divine attributes in Christ himself, thus, kenosis is basically a concealment, and this concealment is made out of God's freedom for his condescension, and it does not involve any loss or diminution or alteration of God's Being.[97] The concealment is only restricted to men because it is the humanity of Christ that conceals the glory of the Logos, the Godhead is still in Christ.[98] Concealment, according to Barth, is not a dishonor, instead, he is truly honored in this concealment.[99] In becoming man, the Logos gives himself, however, he does not gives himself away, he remains to be God.[100]

There are many voices objecting these modern kenotic theories particularly the depotentiation of Christ's divine nature. Packer flatly rejects these theories, claiming it as purely speculation without any Scriptural support.[101] Berkhof understands that the advocates of the kenotic theory have a desire to do full justice to the integrity of the manhood of Christ by stressing his self-denial and self-sacrifice,[102] but he sees the theory as based on the pantheistic conception that God and man are not so absolutely different but that the one can be transformed into the other, and charges that kenoticists cross the absolute line of demarcation.[103] Against the loss of divine attributes proposed by the modern kenoticists, Packer finds that the Scripture provides a lot of evidences (Matthew 28:18, 20; John 21:17; Ephesians 4:10) supporting the omnipresence, omnipotence and omniscience of the risen Christ, and denies that the self-emptying of Christ refers to Christ's divine attribute

---

96   Ibid., 184.
97   Ibid., 180.
98   Ibid.
99   Ibid., 188.
100 Ibid., 185.
101 J. I. Packer, *Knowing God with Study Guide* (London: Hodder & Stoughton, 1993), 66.
102 Berkhof, 327.
103 Ibid., 328.

and power because it has an implication that Christ is less divine than what he was originally. [104] Thiessen agrees with Packer that Christ repeatedly asserted his divine knowledge that he 'knew all men' and 'knew what was in a man.' (John 2:24-25). As for his power, Christ rebuked the wind, cured the sick, cast out demons and raised the dead; all these can only be performed by the power of Christ's own Deity. [105] Unlike miracles performed by Moses, Christ never referred his miraculous power to any source outside of himself because he himself was the source. As for his omnipresence, according to John 3:13, it clearly indicates that the Son of Man in his earthly life was not confined to earth because he was also in heaven.[106] Thiessen rejects the kenotic theories that Christ emptied himself of his relative divine attributes.[107] The problem of the modern kenotic theories, according to Tapia, is that it appears 'to give us a story of a temporary theophany, in which He who formerly was God changed Himself temporarily into man, or exchanged His divinity for humanity.' [108] Berkouwer says, 'The kenosis-theory, rather than an elucidation of the dual nature doctrine, violates and dissolves it.'[109]

Since the early days of the Christian church, immutability had been taught by the patristic fathers. At Nicea, Jesus Christ is confessed as the second Person of the Triune God, who shares the same substance with the Father and his Being is eternal. Many also conclude that the Nicene formula automatically stresses the unchangeableness of the divine nature of Christ.[110] The self-emptying as understood by the modern kenoticists clearly involves some changes in Christ's divine attributes, and this would violate the concept of God's immutability. Berkhof argues, based on Malachi 3:6 and James 1:7, that immutability is the very idea of God.

104   Packer, *Knowing God with Study Guide*, 67.
105   H. C. Thiessen, *Lectures in Systematic Theology* (Grand Rapids, Mich.: Eerdmans, 1977), 295.
106   Ibid., 296.
107   Ibid.
108   Tapia, 409.
109   G. C. Berkouwer, *The Person of Christ* (Grand Rapids, Mich.: Eerdmans, 1977), 30.
110   Richard, 79.

Berkhof says, "Absoluteness and mutability are mutually exclusive; and a mutable God is certainly not the God of Scripture."[111]

However, the God in the Old Testament is full of compassion and love, it is difficult if not impossible for the Israelites to think of their God as impassive and immutable. Jonah's story is probably a clear example to demonstrate how God could change his mind and not destroy the sinful city of Nineveh after its inhabitants repented their sins. Hezekiah's sickness in II Kings 20 is another example to show that God did change his mind. After proclaiming the immediate death of Hezekiah by prophet Isaiah, God showed his compassion towards Hezekiah by giving him another fifteen years to live. Edwards suggests that there are actually two independent views of God's immutability. One is that God does not change with respect to his goodness or righteousness. This view should not be confused with the second view that God does not change in any conceivable respect whatsoever.[112] He sees that the second claim does not have any biblical basis and simply a claim based on Greek philosophy of divine perfection.[113] Richard shares similar understanding that it was the Greek fathers who brought in the Greek concept that God is immutable by accepting the proposition that if God changes at all, then God can only change for worse, 'since we cannot suppose God to be deficient either in virtue or beauty...God is the unmoved mover.'[114] Though there is no actual mentioning of immutability as an attribute of the Triune God in the Nicene Creed in either the 325 AD draft or the 381 AD draft,[115] its implication is strong that God is immutable. It is better to understand immutability in the light of God's attributes and its presentation. The divine attributes of God do not change, however, God can change how it is presented. In the stories of Jonah and Hezekiah, God clearly demonstrated his unchanging love and compassion towards his people; however, the divine solutions were presented differently than what were told. Thus, one can still argue against modern kenotic theories based on the doctrine of immutability.

---

111 Berkhof, 328.
112 R. Edwards, 'The Pagan Doctrine of the Absolute Unchangeableness of God', *Religious Studies*, 14 (1978), 306.
113 Ibid.
114 Richard, 75.
115 P. Schaff, *History of the Christian Church*, 3 (Grand Rapids, Mich.: Eerdmans, 1995), 668-669.

One of the main objections to the modern kenotic theories is that who was holding the cosmos together while Christ was on earth. Colossians 1:7 clearly indicates that it is 'in him all things hold together.' If Gess' theory is correct, then 'for a certain period of history the world was let loose from the control of the Creative Word.'[116] Since the cosmos was still in order, Christ must have been in full control and exercised his divine power and authority. Thus, there must have no change to his deity in performing his cosmic function while he was on earth.

6.3. Exegesis of Philippians

Philippians 2:6-11 is probably the most important passage in the analysis of the kenoticism. This passage is commonly referred to as the Christ hymn, and is widely regarded as a hymn independent of Philippians and was quoted by Paul in his epistle.[117] The hymn consists of mainly two portions, the first portion (v. 6-8) describes Christ's abasement, and the second portion (v. 8-11) his exaltation. Byrne claims that beyond this general twofold structure, there are a great variety of different inter-pretations of the details.[118] Patristic fathers consistently interpreted the passage in the sequence of pre-existent Logos, earthly humiliation and heavenly exaltation. While kenosis touches the humanity of Jesus, it does not affect the pre-existent Logos.[119] The Patristic analysis excludes any possibility of the interpretation of Philippians 2 that it would indicate any movement from God to Jesus.[120] That is to say, there is no change in the

116 Tapia, 409.
117 B. Byrne, 'The Letter to The Philippians', in *The New Jerome Biblical Commentary*, ed. Raymond E. Brown, Joseph A. Fitzmer, and Roland E. Murphy (Upper Saddle River, N.J.: Prentice Hall, 1990), 794; C. Robbins, 'Rhetorical Structure of Philippians 2:6-11', *The Catholic Biblical Quarterly*, 42, 1980, 73; G. Howard, 'Phil 2:6-11 and the Human Christ', *Catholic Biblical Quarterly*, 40 (1978), 368; P. Schoonenberg, 'The Kenosis or Self-Emptying of Christ', *Concilium* 11 (1966), 28.
118 Byrne, 794.
119 Richard, 73.
120 Ibid., 82.

divine nature of Christ when he becomes man. Some, however, find it difficult to understand the divine aspect of the passage if the divine nature is unchanged. It is easier to understand kenosis in a human term if the divinity is excluded from the passage. Therefore, it is important to know whether the passage refers to the action of a pre-existent Being who empties himself or simply a human Jesus who acts in his human capacity. If it is the pre-existent Being who empties himself, then some aspects of divine nature must be involved in the action of self-emptying. If it is only the human nature of Christ who empties himself, then what is the role of his divine nature? In his interpretation of the hymn, Torrance sees that since Christ is living as both divine and human, he has a dark side and a light side, that is, Christ has a side of humiliation and at the same time a side of exaltation. Thus, Torrance does not see that humiliation has to precede his exaltation because both happen all through his incarnate life.[121] The hymn, according to Torrance, represents the almighty condescension as well as the self-humiliation of the Son of God that he wants to be one with us in our contingent being.[122]

Many biblical scholars see that the hymn reflects the Adam-Christ topology that Christ is spoken as the second Adam who has reversed the decision of the first Adam.[123] Regarding the Adam-Christ parallel, Hurst says 'The central issue to be decided is whether the act of Adam is contrasted with the act of the heavenly Christ or with that of the human Jesus.'[124] Those who take the anthropological approach would press on the Adam-Christ parallel and argue that 'being made in human likeness' and 'found in appearance as a man' would evoke the account of man's creation in Genesis that man is made in God's image and likeness. Therefore, the pre-existence of Christ is not necessarily envisioned in the passage.[125] As well, the final exaltation in the passage is simply a post-resurrection exaltation of Christ while he was still on earth as a human being. Howards says

---

121 Torrance., *Space, Time and Resurrection*, 46–47.

122 Torrance, *Divine and Contingent Order*, 135.

123 Howard, 'Phil 2:6-11 and the Human Christ', 373; L. D. Hurst, 'Re-enter the Pre-existent Christ in Philippians 2:5-11?', New Testament Study, 32 (1986), 449.

124 Ibid.

125 Howard, 'Phil 2:6-11 and the Human Christ', 377.

that the exaltation of Christ in the hymn of Phil 2:6-11 refers not to his later heavenly coronation, since this in no way is demanded by the text, but to his earthly post-resurrection glory.[126]

Athanasius takes a similar approach regarding the hymn, and asks what need is there that he should humble himself, as if to seek something which he had already? Athanasius believes that the passage does not refer to his eternal deity, he says,

> it might be plain that 'humbled' and 'exalted' are spoken of His human nature; for where there is humble estate, there too may be exaltation; and if because of His taking flesh 'humbled' is written, it is clear that 'highly exalted' is also said because of it.[127]

Thus, the humiliation of Christ, according to Athanasius is addressed to his humanity that he becomes flesh and takes the form of a servant.[128] Schoonenberg suggests that kenosis applies to Christ only after his birth in his human existence, and dismisses the possibility that the self-emptying has anything to do with the divine nature of God in the in-carnation except it is a choice made by Jesus during his earthly ministry. He admits, however, that it is not an act of Christ's human nature alone.[129] Those who take the incarnational approach would argue that though there may be a parallel between Christ and Adam, but to interpret every parallel detail of Christ by the experience of Adam is not war-ranted.[130]

In his interpretation of the Christ hymn, Torrance basically takes the incarnational approach that it is the eternal Logos who becomes man. He argues that in the Pauline text, there is no reference to indicate that Christ empties something or anything out of himself, but is emptying himself from one form *(morphe)* into another. That means, Christ does not set aside certain attributes.[131] According to Torrance, the meaning of *morphe* does not refer to the eternal substance but rather it is construed in the

---

126 Ibid., 381.
127 Athanasius, 'Against the Arians', in *Nicene and Post Nicene Fathers*, ed. Philip Schaff and Henry Wace, 4 (Peaboy, Mass.: Hendrickson, 1999), 330.
128 Ibid., 377.
129 Schoonenberg, 32.
130 Hurst, 454.
131 T. F. Torrance, *The Doctrine of Jesus Christ*, 109.

sense of external image, physical form, which nevertheless corresponds to an internal nature.[132] Torrance says,

> The Christ who was eternally with God and in the *morphe* of God emptied himself out of that *morphe* into another *morphe*, namely the form of a servant. There is nowhere any indication in the text that Christ is spoken of as having emptied anything out of himself; rather that he emptied himself out of his divine magisterial form and came among men, the Eternal Christ *incognito* in the humble form of a servant. Nevertheless, this form of a servant was real; it was not docetic; it was a form which did really correspond to the act and reality of the inhabitant of the Form.[133]

In assuming human flesh, Christ takes on the form of man which entails all human physical limitations because *morphe* refers to the volitional side of the external form.[134] That is to say, by assuming the form of a man, Christ assumes the fashion or habit of a man,[135] and this does not only mean that Christ share some likeness or resemblance with us, it also means that Christ takes up our actual form of existence.[136] *Morphe*, according to Torrance, is similar to a garment: Christ in the incarnation puts off the garment of his divine majesty and puts on the garment of humility.[137] While Christ is emptying from his divine *morphe* into his earthly *morphe*, he does not change in essence or consubstantiality with the Father.[138] That is to say, Christ takes the humble form of a servant in order to conceal his dignity and divinity.[139] The expression 'in the likeness of men', according to Torrance, does not mean to be in the appearance of superficial likeness, but in the concrete likeness of men that he shares the same human limitations and weaknesses.[140] Thus, Christ puts on a visible form by emptying out his eternal invisible form. However, Torrance at the same time also sees that *form* deals essentially with the essence of Godhead. By appealing to Athanasius, Torrance

---

132 Ibid., 57.
133 Ibid.
134 Ibid., 109.
135 Ibid.
136 Torrance, *The Trinitarian Faith*, 153.
137 Torrance, *The Doctrine of Jesus Christ*, 109.
138 Ibid.
139 Ibid., 57.
140 Ibid., 109.

argues that since the Son is the image of Father, it must be understood that the Godhead of the Father is the Being of the Son, he quotes,

> And this is the meaning of "who being in the form of God" and "the Father in me". Nor is this Form of God merely partial, but the fullness of the Father's Godhead is the being of the Son, and the Son is whole God... For the propriety of the Father's being is the Son... the Form of the Father's Godhead is the Son.[141]

The *form* is not a partial and relational identity of the Godhead, but rather it is the full identity. That is to say, claiming to be in the *form* of God is to mean that Christ is not only like God but rather he is identical to God and he is God. If Torrance sides with Athanasius on the meaning of *form*, he contradicts himself that the *form* carries a meaning of only relational feature but not essential identity of Godhead because if *form* carries a meaning of the full essence of Godhead, then, clearly, according to Torrance, Christ cannot empty his own Godhead.[142] Torrance tries to mediate dialectically between the doctrine of Trinity and the doctrine of kenosis. When he stresses the divinity of Christ who is Being in the *form* of God in his doctrine of Trinity, he emphasizes the very essence of the Father and the fullness of the Godhead of which the word *form* signifies; however, when he applies it to the humility of Christ in the *form* of a servant in his doctrine of kenosis, it becomes something that Christ can simply empty himself out of.

6.4. Torrance's Theology of Kenosis

Torrance is not mistaken in his writings that while Logos becomes man, he does not give up his divine nature.[143] Christ lives within our physical and historical existence without leaving the throne of the universe.[144] The Son is the Father's image, according to Torrance, has to be understood that the Godhead and propriety of the Father is the Being of the Son, that

---

141 Torrance, *The Trinitarian Faith*, 304.
142 Torrance, *The Doctrine of Jesus Christ*, 109.
143 Torrance, *The Trinitarian Faith*, 55, 184.
144 Torrance, *Space, Time and Resurrection*, 132.

266

the Son is fully God.[145] Christ lives out his divine life within our human life. Though he shares our human nature, he remains God and his divine nature is fully intact. However, at the same time, the self-emptying according to Torrance does not mean the eternal Son empties something out of himself, but instead God empties himself out of heaven onto earth and out of eternity into time and yet at the same time without ceasing to be eternal or whatever he was.[146] Self-emptying, according to Torrance, has a meaning of sharing in our creatureliness, littleness, and ignorance.[147] However, he does not indicate whether Christ shares our disease and sickness. In his appeal to Cyril, Torrance sees that the humanity of Christ entails physical imperfections and limitations.[148] Human imperfections would inevitably indicate disease and sickness. The Roman doctrine of kenosis disallows certain physical corruptions such as disease in order to maintain the dignity of Christ. The corruption of the body is seen as the destroying power of sin,[149] thus, Christ cannot be seen to be circumvented by evil. In the incarnation, Christ takes on himself not only the form of man which entails all physical limitations but also the form of a servant which is seen as an act of self-abasement and humiliation by adopting the servile condition in our state under the slavery of sin. Torrance sees that Christ is not like a servant, but rather he is a real servant, an actual form of existence which he takes over from the 'lump of Adam'.[150]

When the eternal Logos becomes incarnate, Torrance says, his self-emptying is inevitably a concealment of his divine power. Even though Christ's divine power is restricted by the creaturely reality, he could still operate it in accordance with the divine will through healing and re-creation.[151] Thus, in additional to a line of the concealment of God, according to Torrance, there is also a line of the unveiling of God in Christ's transfiguration, healing and miracles.[152] If the crucifixion

145 Torrance, *The Trinitarian Faith*, 304.
146 Torrance, *The Doctrine of Jesus Christ*, 110.
147 Torrance, *The Trinitarian Faith*, 55.
148 Ibid., 187.
149 *Catholic Encyclopedia* <http://www.newadvent.org/cathen/08617a.htm> 3 Dec 2005.
150 Torrance, *The Trinitarian Faith*, 153.
151 Torrance, *Space, Time and Resurrection*, 56.
152 Ibid., 57.

represents the low point of Christ's concealment, then the resurrection represents the high point of Christ's unveiling that he is the Son of God.[153] Just as humiliation and exaltation are involved one another, veiling and unveiling are also mutually involved one another in his incarnate life.[154]

While the Son is living on earth, according to Torrance, he is not in the condition of his transcendent glory as the eternal Son of which he had with the Father before the world was.[155] As creatures, we cannot look upon the naked glory of God because if we look upon the pure holiness of God, we would die. Torrance argues that no man has seen God and lived. However, we can look upon the glory of God in a veiled way through Christ. The very essence of Christ's veiledness is his grace towards us because unless Christ veils his glory in his self-humiliation, we are unable to see God.[156] Thus, the self-emptying entails a concealment of his glory in human time and space.[157] Only when Jesus is raised from the death and ascended to the throne of God Almighty, he regains the full glory that he had with the Father before the world was.[158] That is to say, the self-emptying in the form of concealment of his glory ends in his resurrection.

Torrance argues that if we are faithful to the nature of Christ as fully God and fully man then we must respect the fact that men are in time and space, and God remains transcendent in time and space. Thus, one needs to work with a relational view of space and time differentially or variationally related to God and to man. Unless we think in this way, we cannot really think the incarnation without falsifying it.[159] That is to say, one cannot employ creaturely time and space to explain the transcendence of God that he is everywhere. Torrance tries to accommodate the *Calvinist Extra* in his theology of kenosis by introducing relational aspects of time and space. According to Torrance, kenosis is not a subtraction of divine properties but an addition of human properties because

153   Ibid.
154   Ibid.
155   Ibid., 84.
156   Torrance, *The Doctrine of Jesus Christ*, 110.
157   Ibid., 35.
158   T. F. Torrance, *When Christ Comes and Comes Again*, 25; Torrance, *The Doctrine of Jesus Christ*, 187.
159   Torrance, *Space, Time and Resurrection*, 126.

268

according to the Pauline concept of kenosis, Paul does not indicate any contraction or self-limitation of God's infinite being but rather demonstrates Christ's self-abnegating love in the inexpressible mystery of abasement that he freely takes upon himself for our sake.[160] Thus, Torrance maintains a very important element of Patristic kenoticism that Christ does not cease to be God when he becomes man, and he does not leave the throne of the universe while he is on earth.[161]

Torrance believes that unless Christ assumes the whole nature of man which includes human ignorance, man could not have been saved.[162] That is to say, unless Christ is fully identified with us, he cannot represent us in his atonement, that he dies for our sins in exchange for our salvation. However, that does not mean Christ is ignorant. Christ's ignorance is only economic and vicarious in nature, that is to say, Christ deliberately restrains 'his divine knowledge throughout a life of continuous kenosis in which he refused to transgress the limits of the creaturely and earthly conditions of human nature.'[163] When Paul writes to the Corinthian church, he says, 'that though he was rich, yet for your sakes he became poor, so that you through his poverty might become rich.' (II Corinthians 8:9) Christ was rich and becomes poor so that we might become rich, according to Torrance, plays an important part in the understanding of the humiliation of Christ. Christ's poverty reflects his act of self-emptying. Torrance says that Paul's proclamation carries a meaning that Christ comes to the world and lives among us in the humble form of a servant in order to reveal himself to us in a way that we may really know him. It also has another meaning that the Lord of heaven stoops down to our lowliness by setting aside his glory so that our weak eyes may behold the lowly Jesus and through him we may be lifted up to know him in his deity and glory.[164] That is to say, his glory is seen through his lowliness and humility in the form of a servant. Unless he comes down to our lowliness and stoops to enter our frail mortal flesh, we would not be able to be delivered from sin and death.[165] Thus, he empties himself in exchange for our fullness in him.

---

160 Torrance, *Trinitarian Perspectives Toward Doctrinal Agreement*, 153.
161 Torrance, *The Trinitarian Faith*, 184.
162 Ibid., 187.
163 Ibid.
164 Torrance, The *Doctrine of Jesus Christ*, 112.
165 Ibid.

In general, Torrance's doctrine of kenosis follows the patristic tradition that the self-emptying of Christ does not involve any de-potentiation of his divine attributes but only that his eternal glory is temporarily concealed while he is on earth. It is not the subtraction of Christ's divine attributes but rather the addition of his humanity that forms the foundation of Torrance's doctrine of kenosis. However, the patristic idea of concealment is not without problem, concealment is an act of *self-limitation* which is similar in nature to all kenotic theories that Christ voluntarily gives up his attributes or makes himself less in divine power or makes himself less visible. The divine glory is actually God's attribute, the idea of concealment does not eliminate the implication that the incarnate Christ is still somehow less than what he was originally with the Father. Thus, Thiessen says the idea of laying aside his divine glory through concealment is much like the theory of modern kenotic theologians.[166] Disregarding which way one looks at the Christ hymn, incarnational or anthropological, only half of the person of Christ or one of his two natures is addressed but not both. This somehow is also evident in Torrance's kenotic theology that he emphasizes that Christ is both humiliated and exalted at the same time during his earthly sojourn, and argues that kenosis has to be interpreted in accordance with his two natures that he is both God and man. That is to say, Christ is omnipotent, omnipresent, and omniscient in accordance with his divine nature; and Christ shares human weakness, limitation, ignorance in accordance with his human nature. Thus, Torrance is interpreting kenosis dialectically in accordance with two *natures* of Christ. However, both patristic fathers and modern kenotic theologians are struggling with how to interpret Christ's humiliation in accordance with the *person* of Jesus Christ. Since Christ is an individual, a person who does not have two personalities or split personality, it is difficult to understand how he can be omniscient and at the same time ignorant. An individual person is the totality of all his predicates, thus, a person either knows or does not know, he cannot argue that one side of his personality knows and the other side of his personality does not know. This is exactly what the patristic fathers were struggling with Christ's ignorance, as an individual person, either he knows or he does not know. The conclusion according to Athanasius and Cyril is that Christ as an individual person, the totality of all his

---

166   Thiessen, 297.

predicates including his two unique natures, is all knowing. There is a danger in Torrance's theology that it creates a sense of split personality or two voices in the person of Christ that it is the *nature* rather than the *person* that is treated as an individual in his dialectical interpretation of kenosis. This is basically the fundamental issue that the modern kenoticists are struggling with.

7. Conclusion

Torrance's incarnational theology is mainly molded by his teacher, Karl Barth, who insists that there cannot be any relevant revelations other than that of the incarnation. Otherwise, it would simply undercut the significance and the necessity of the earthly mission of the incarnate Son. Thus, Barth adamantly rejects natural theology in his doctrine of revelation. The significance of Barth's position is that only Jesus Christ is God in his own Being and Act, and only he can offer the reconciliation of God to man and man to God. There is no other way that we can be redeemed except through the Mediator Jesus Christ. Barth's idea affects at least two important aspects of Torrance's doctrine of incarnation: the role of revelation in the Old Testament and the role of natural theology in the knowing of the personal God. Torrance agrees with Barth on the former, but rejects Barth's idea of natural theology in his later years. Torrance argues fervently that we may really know God in truth only as we access the Father through the Son. Unless we know the Son, we do not know the Father. Torrance's idea implies that the God who was known by Moses is different from that of Torrance since all the prophets, saints in the period of the Old Testament did not know the incarnate Son. He does not treat the revelation in the Old Testament as that of the New Testament, his hermeneutics is skewed towards the incarnate revelation. However, he is willing to accommodate natural theology within revealed theology. Thus, Torrance accepts the significance of creation as a pointer to objective reality though it may not be as clear and precise as that of the incarnation, and he affirms that in doing so it has its apologetic value. If nature is allowed to play its part in the divine revelation, then God who revealed himself as *I am that I am* in the Old Testament must also be regarded a divine revelation in human history.

However, in Torrance's theology, the revelation of God in the Old Testament is by no means comparable to that of his Son in the incarnation. On one hand, Torrance adopts Barth's idea of the Old Testament revelation, but on the other hand, he dislodges the dummy of natural theology in Barth's doctrine of revelation. By doing so, Torrance is in essence destroying the very basis of Barth's doctrine of creation and redemption, which makes his own incoherent. The very essence of Barth's revelational argument is that there is no revelation other than the incarnation, thus both natural theology and the Old Testament revelation could not be regarded as revelation. If one of the two non-revelations is accepted as part of the revelation, then Barth's theological argument of the supreme incarnational revelation becomes incoherent. Though Torrance claims that Barth finally accepts his idea of natural theology, it is obvious that Barth is extremely reluctant to accept this 'impossibility'. Without revising his own position on the Old Testament revelation in parallel to that of the natural theology, Torrance's theology of incarnation is less consistent than that of Barth because the supreme divine incarnate revelation cannot be undermined by either natural theology or the Old Testament revelation.

In his theology of knowing God in the incarnate revelation, Torrance approaches the issue from two different and opposite poles. On one hand, he argues from the perspective of rationality that the ultimate objective can be known through scientific inquiry in accordance with the nature of the object; on the other hand, he argues that it is the faith of Christ that we may know God. If the knowledge can be obtained rationally by the subject, then, there is no need for faith. If the subjective knowledge is acquired by the object, then, the scientific inquiry is useless. Torrance does not provide any compromise position between these two opposite poles; thus, it raises objections from both camps arguing for either human rational subjectivity or God's prevenient grace. Torrance's theological science in reality does not provide much apologetic thrust in the defense of Christian faith since there exists minimal common scientific ground acceptable to both Christians and non-believers. He could only argue philosophically on the presupposition of the ultimate belief, which by itself is beyond human capacity to validate. His overall theology of incarnation is characterized by his employment of presuppositions and dialectics. Torrance's presuppositional objectives in his theological science work well within the community of faith; however, it would be difficult to argue outside the community because theology in general is not regarded as science in a way that everyone follows the same inquiry would arrive at the same conclusion. Einstein is a good example of this so-called scientific inquiry in that he remains detached from the personal God while he is characterized by Torrance for his objective pursuit of scientific inquiry. In his dialectical theology, Torrance employs a mainly Kierkegaardian approach that two opposite ideas are pulled together to form a unitary structure without a higher level of synthesis or addressing the obvious mismatches. In his employment of dialectics, either he would use it to harmonize dualistic elements into a unitary structure or he would utilize it to pull two unbridgeable opposite poles together to form a dialectic unity when each side has its own strength. Torrance's dialectics is in fact a substitute for the dualism that he rejects. All dualistic elements are integrated into his unitary structure dialectically. The main reason for his frequent use of dialectics is his emphasis on the unity of the incarnate Son that his Act cannot be separated from his Being, anything that Christ has done has to be related to him ontologically because he himself is the content of his Act. His criticism of dualism is also sometimes misleading by highlighting only half of the picture. This is particularly true in his criticism of Aristotelian dualism and Newtonian dualism that if one looks closely, according to Torrance, the dualistic elements are actually closely related to each other, they do not marginally meet at a tangential point. In fact, according to Torrance, dualism is simply a strange kind of dialectics.[1] Dualism is also embodied in his hermeneutics wherein the authority of the Scripture lies in what it signifies rather than its own words. The Scripture is only divine in the truth that it points to, but the text itself may be erroneous. Thus, the text is regarded human, only the truth presented by the text is divine. This is indeed a dualism in which the words are detached from its reality.

Torrance's doctrine of Trinity is essentially patristic, and he owns his theological concepts very much to the Nicene fathers especially Athanasius[2], and the Constantinopolitan and Chalcedonian confessions. Though he is greatly influenced by Barth in his doctrine of revelation, he is less so in his doctrine of Trinity. In the case of subordination, Torrance differs significantly from his teacher by stressing the co-equality of the Son with the Father. However, Torrance's theology is not wholly patristic; he makes certain modifications based on modern theological

1   T.F. Torrance, 'Karl Barth and The Latin Heresy', *Scottish Journal of Theology*, 39 (1986), 468.
2   T.F. Torrance, 'The Doctrine of the Holy Trinity according to St. Athanasius', *Anglican Theological Review*, 71/ 4 (1989), 395–405.

ideas. Torrance does not fully agree with Karl Rahner, however, he is drawn closer to Rahner's full integration of the economic Trinity and the immanent Trinity. Moltmann is seldom mentioned in Torrance's writings; however, Moltmann's theology of the Cross creates a great emotional disturbance in Torrance's understanding of the divine suffering of God. Pulled by both patristic ideas and modern thoughts, Torrance tries to mediate between these two poles dialectically as he admits that passibility and impassibility are logically impossible for mediation because each excludes the other.

One of Torrance's significant theological contributions is his refinement of the concept of *homoousion* which provides a good connection to his doctrine of Triunity. In other words, his doctrine of Triunity is grounded on his doctrine of *homoousion*. We know God as Three Persons in One Being, and One Being in Three Persons because we know the Mediator who is both God and man. Jesus Christ serves as the Mediator because he has the same divine nature as God. The doctrine of *homoousion* thus enables us to enhance our knowledge of God by moving from the experiential level to the theological level that we are able to know the innermost relation of God in himself. Torrance's idea of *homoousion* embodies two unique meanings of sameness and distinctiveness that all divine Persons share the same Being, while each Person is distinctive from others. The idea of subordination is automatically excluded in Torrance's doctrine of *homoousion* because the essence of the doctrine is hinged on the equality of the divine Persons that Christ cannot be anything less than God, and it also serves as a double reference to bind the economic Trinity and the immanent Trinity together.

Torrance provides a careful conceptual analysis in identifying the distinction between the inward reference and the outward reference relating to the characteristics of *ousia* and *hypostasis* that *ousia* is understood as Being in its own internal relation, while *hypostasis* is understood as Being in its objective inter-relations. With his detailed analysis, Torrance further bridges the gap between the Eastern theologians and Western theologians on the thorny issue of *filioque*. He cleverly positions God the Father as an inward reference rather than an outward reference, that is to say, the Holy Spirit proceeds not from God the Father but from God who is Father. This is indeed a creative move by Torrance to solve the age-old problem in bringing the Eastern Church and the Western Church together. Unfortunately, the procession itself is clearly a relational distinction in defining the objective otherness within the Triune God. That is to say, the distinction of the procession is referenced to the *Person* not the *Being*, thus, it does not help in his ecumenical endeavour.

It is unfortunate that in Torrance's writings, the concept of *nature* is somehow excluded from his scope of analytical studies. There exists occasions in his writings that he extends the hypostatic relation within the Triune God to that of the non-confused distinctive natures within the person of Jesus Christ. The concept of *perichoresis* is somehow applied to the two natures of Christ, and Torrance has a tendency of regarding each distinctive nature as having its own individuality which exists within the person. Thus, in his interpretation of kenosis, he can claim all divine properties in accordance with Christ's divine nature and all human properties in accordance with Christ's human nature without giving full account of how these two natures together give one unitary movement in the individual person of Jesus Christ. Though his kenotic idea is basically patristic, he somehow misses a crucial point in the argument of Thomasius' kenotic theory that there exists only one unitary movement, experience, and development of life of Jesus because in him, there is only one ego and one divine-human personality. Torrance's dialectic way of interpretation avoids the very struggle of the kenotic controversy of how to interpret the dualistic nature of Christ in a unitary movement of an individual person. The modern kenoticists try to interpret the self-emptying from the perspective of an individual *person*, an incommunicable entity; while Torrance and some patristic fathers try to see it purely from the perspective of dual *nature* disregarding the internal mechanism of how does this dual *nature* produce a unitary outward movement in this unique *person*. Thus, the kenoticists are concerned about the individual *person*, while Torrance is focusing on the distinctive *natures* of the person. Nonetheless, the doctrine of kenosis, according to Torrance, is an inexpressible mystery.[3]

The doctrine of open-ended incarnation which is related to the humanity of Christ is not exactly part of Torrance's doctrine of *homoousion* which deals mainly with the divinity of Christ that Christ shares the same essence as the Father. The idea itself is not unique to Torrance,

---

3   T.F. Torrance, *Trinitarian Perspectives Toward Doctrinal Agreement* (Edinburgh: T&T Clark, 1999), 153.

Strong and Dabney both teach a similar concept that the union of humanity with deity in the person of Christ is indissoluble and eternal. However, the idea that the kingdom of Christ at the end of the world will be handed over by Christ to the Father, according to Torrance, is the prevalent theological concept which he rejects. Torrance sees the humanity of Christ in its finality quite different from the view shared by Calvin.

Though Torrance affirms that the incarnate Son is both God and man, however, his emphasis is more on the vicarious humanity of Christ that he shares our full humanity including our corrupted human nature in order to save the fallen humanity in him, through him, and by him. Christ does not only assume our corrupted human nature, he also becomes one of us, and thus, he is identified with us individually and corporately. Torrance's doctrine of vicarious humanity gives a profound understanding of Athanasius' principle of 'the unassumed is the unhealed'. However, Torrance's idea that Christ actually assumes our fallen human nature is unnecessary; it creates more problems than benefits.

In his doctrine of atonement, Torrance suggests that it consists of two important concepts of representation and substitution. By representation, Christ satisfies the justice requirement of God; by substitution, Christ makes an ontological exchange that his humanity substitutes for our humanity. Thus in the atonement, Christ is one of us and acts on behalf of us. These two elements are in fact quite complementary to each other, and give a fuller picture of the concept of atonement. Though Torrance claims to follow his Reformed tradition, he makes significant deviations. This is particularly evident in his rejection of the doctrine of predestination. This may possibly be due to his missionary zeal and background. Torrance is undeniably a great theologian of our times as seen with his depth and breath of the knowledge of the patristic era and the modern period as well as his knowledge concerning the subjects of humanity and science.

Bibliography

Achtemeier, P. Mark, 'The Truth of Tradition: Critical Realism in The Thought of Alasdair MacIntyre and T.F. Torrance', *Scottish Journal of Theology*, 47/3 (1994), 355–374.

Achtemeier, Paul J., Joel B. Green and Marianne Meye Thompson, *Introducing the New Testament: Its Literature and Theology* (Grand Rapids: Eerdmans, 2001).

Anders, D. Peter, *Divine Impassibility and Our Suffering God* <http://www.modern reformation.org/mr97/julaug/mr9704impassibility.html> accessed 20 Jan 2003.

Anderson, Ray S, *Historical Transcendence and the Reality of God* (Grand Rapids, Mich.: Eerdmans, 1975).

Aquinas, Thomas, *Summa Theologiae*, ed. Timothy McDermott (Allen, Tx.: Christian Classics, 1991).

Athanasius, 'Against the Arians', in *Nicene and Post Nicene Fathers*, ed. Philip Schaff and Henry Wace, 4 (Peaboy, Mass.: Hendrickson, 1999), 303–447.

__ 'Defence of The Nicene Definition', 150–172.

__ 'On the Incarnation', 31–67.

__ 'Orations Against The Arians', in *The Christological Controversy*, ed. Richard A. Norris (Philadelphia: Fortress, 1980).

Audi, Robert (ed.), *The Cambridge Dictionary of Philosophy* (2nd edn, Cambridge: Cambridge University Press, 1999).

Augustine, *Confessions*, tr. R.S. Pine-Coffin (London: Penguin Books, 1961).

__ 'On Christian Doctrine' in *Nicene and Post-Nicene Fathers*, ed. Philip Schaff, 2 (Peaboy, Mass.: Hendrickson, 1999), 519–597.

__ 'On the Psalms', vol. 8.

__ 'The City of God', vol. 2, 1–511.

Aulen, Gusaf, *Christus Victor*, tr. A.G. Hegert (London: Society for Promoting Christian Kowledge, 1937).

Babcock, William S., review of T.F. Torrance, *Theological Science* (New York: Oxford University Press, 1969), in *Theology Today*, 28 (April 1971 - January 1972), 116–118.

Baillie, Donald, M., *God Was In Christ* (London: Faber and Faber Limited, 1960).

Baillie, John, *The Idea of Revelation in Recent Thought* (London: Oxford University Press, 1956).

Barr, James, *The Semantics of Biblical Language* (Eugene: Wipf & Stock, 1961).

Barth, Karl, *Church Dogmatics*, tr. G.W. Bromiley and T.F. Torrance (Edinburgh: T&T Clark, 1957-1981).

__ *Church Dogmatics*, tr. G.T. Thomson (Edinburgh: T & T Clark, 1957–1981).

__ 'No! Answer to Emil Brunner', in *Natural Theology* (Ann Arbor, Mich.: University Microfilms, 1959), 67–128.

___ *The Epistle to the Romans*, tr. Edwyn C. Hoskyns (London: Oxford University Press, 1975).

Battaglia, Anthony, review of T.F. Torrance, *Transformation and Convergence in the Frame of Knowledge* (Grand Rapids: Eerdmans, 1984), in *Theology Today*, 41/1 (April 1984), 493-495.

Bercot, David W., *A Dictionary of Early Christian Beliefs* (Peaboy, Mass.: Hendrickson, 1998).

Berkhof, L., *Systematic Theology* (Grand Rapids, Mich.: Eerdmans, 1977).

Berkouwer, G., C., *General Revelation* (Grand Rapids, Mich.: Eerdmans, 1955).

___ *The Person of Christ* (Grand Rapids, Mich.: Eerdmans, 1977).

Bettis, Joseph D., 'Is Karl Barth A Universalist?', *Scottish Journal of Theology*, 20/1 (1967), 423–436.

Bleasdale, Sebastian, *Entropy and the Universe* <http://www.chiark.greenend.org.uk/~sbleas/creative/ entropy> accessed 4 Dec 2005.

Bloesch, Donald G., *Essentials Of Evangelical Theology*, 2 vols (n.p.: Prince, 1998).

Blomberg, Craig, *The Historical Reliability of the Gospels* (Leicester: Inter-Varsity Press, 1987).

Boethius, Anicius, *The Theological Tractates*, tr. H.F. Stewart and E.K. Rand (London: William Heinemann & Cambridge, 1962).

Boice, James M. & Ryken, Philip G., *The Doctrines of Grace* (Wheaton, Il.: Crossway, 2002).

Bonhoeffer, Dietrich, *Christ The Center* (New York: Harper & Row, 1966).

Botterweck, G. Johannes, and Helmer Ringgren, *Theological Dictionary of The Old Testament* (Grand Rapids, Mich.: Eerdmans, 1974).

Boyd, Frank Mathews, *The Kenosis of The Lord Jesus Christ* (San Fransico: Frank M. Boyd, 1947).

Brasnett, Bertrand R., *The Suffering of the Impassible God* (London: Society for Promoting Christian Knowledge, 1928).

Briggs, Charles Augustus, *The Incarnation of the Lord* (New York: Charles Scribner's Sons, 1902).

Brown, Colin, *Jesus in European Protestant Thought 1778–1860* (Durham: The Labyrinth Press, 1985).

Brown, Raymond E., Joseph A. Fitzmer, and Roland E. Murphy (eds.), *The New Jerome Biblical Commentary*, (Upper Saddle River, N.J.: Prentice Hall, 1990).

Bruce, A.B., *The Humiliation of Christ* (Grand Rapids, Mich.: Eerdmans, 1955).

Brueggemann, Walter, *Theology of The Old Testament* (Minneapolis: Fortress, 1997).

Brunner, Emil, 'Nature and Grace', in *Natural Theology* (Ann Arbor, Mich.: University Microfilms, 1959), 15–64.

___ *Revelation and Reason* (London: Student Christian Movement Press Ltd., 1947).

Bultmann, Rudolf, *Modern Theology: Selections from Twentieth-Century Theologians*, ed. E.J. Tinsley (London: Epworth Press, 1973).

Buntin, Charles T., *The Empty God* <http://www.bible.org/page.asp?page_id=657.> accessed 4 Sep 2005.

Burrell, David B., review of T.F. Torrance, *Divine and Contingent Order* (New York: Oxford University Press, 1981), in *Theology Today*, 39/1, (April 1982), 325-327.

280

Buzzard, Anthony F., 'Some Questions About the Chalcedonian Christology of Karl Barth', *A Journal from the Radical Reformation*, 5/2 (Winter 1996), 31–43.

Byrne, Brendan, 'The Letter to The Philippians', in *The New Jerome Biblical Commentary*, ed. Raymond E. Brown, Joseph A. Fitzmer, and Roland E. Murphy (Upper Saddle River, N.J.: Prentice Hall, 1990).

Caird, G.B., *New Testament Theology*, ed. and completed by L.D. Hurst (Oxford: Clarendon, 1995).

Calvin, John, 'Commentaries of The Epistle to The Romans', in *Calvin's Commentaries*, 19 (Grand Rapids, Mich.: Baker, 2003).

__ 'Commentaries on The Four Last Books of Moses', vol. 2.

__ 'Commentaries on The Prophet Daniel', vol. 12–13.

__ 'Commentary on The Epistles of Paul the Apostle to The Corinthians', vol. 20.

__ *Institutes of the Christian Religion*, tr. Henry Beveridge <http://www.reformed. org> accessed 1 Sep 2005.

Cassel, Paul, *Karl Barth on Revelation and God's Relationship to the World* <http://people.bu.edu/wwildman/WeirdWildWeb/courses/mwt/dictionary/mwt_themes_75 0_ barth.htm> accessed 14 Oct 2004.

Catholic Encyclopedia <http://www.newadvent.org> accessed 15 Jan 2005.

Chrysostom, 'Homilies on Philippians', in *Nicene and Post-Nicene Fathers*, ed. Philip Schaff, 13 (Peaboy, Mass.: Hendrickson, 1999), 181–255.

Clark, Gordon Haddon, *The Incarnation*, (Trinity Foundation, 1988).

Clark, Timothy D.B., *A Defense of The Thomistic Definition of Person*, <http://www.gocart.org/thesis.html> accessed 12 Jan 2004.

Colyer, Elmer M., *The Nature of Doctrine in T.F. Torrance's Theology* (Eugene: Wipf and Stock Publishers, 2001).

__ (ed.), *The Promise of Trinitarian Theology* (Lanham: Rowan & Littlefield Publishers, 2001).

Come, Arnold B., review of G.W. Bromiley and T.F. Torrance (trs.), *Church Dogmatics: Index Volume* (Edinburgh: T&T Clark, 1978), in *Theology Today*, 35/4 (January 1979), 499–502.

Comstock, W. Richard, review of T.F. Torrance, *The Ground and Grammar of Theology* (n.p.: University Press of Virginia, 1980), in *Journal of The American Academy of Religion*, 52/1 (March 1984), 190–191.

Cranfield, C.E.B., *The Gospel According to Saint Mark* (Cambridge: Cambridge University Press, 1959).

Cross, Frank Moore, *Canaanite Myth and Hebrew Epic* (Cambridge, Mass.: Harvard University Press, 1973).

Cullmann, Oscar, *Christ and Time*, tr. Floyd V. Filson (London: SCM Press, 1971).

Cushman, Robert E., 'Is the Incarnation a Symbol?', *Theology Today*, 15/2 (July 1958), 167–182.

Cyril of Alexandria, 'The Third Letter of Cyril to Nestorius', in *Christology of the Late Fathers*, ed. Edward R. Hardy (Philadelphia: The Westminster Press, 1954), 349-358.

Dabney, Robert L., *Lectures in Systematic Theology*, (Grand Rapids, Mich.: Zondervan, 1976).

Davis, Leon, *The Trinity in the Old Testament*, <http://www.biblicalresources.org/cms/printer_48.shtml> accessed 23 Nov 2005.

Dodd, C.H., *History and the Gospel*, (London: Hodder & Stoughton, 1964).

Douglas, J.D., *The New Internation Dictionary of the Christian Church* (revised edn, n.p.: Regency Zondervan, [1986]).

Downing, Gerald F., *Has Christianity a Revelation?* (London: SCM Press , 1964).

Dyson, A.O., review of T.F. Torrance, *Theological Science* ([New York]: Oxford University Press, 1969) and *Space, Time and Incarnation* ([New York]: Oxford University Press, 1969), *Theology* 74/607, (January 1971), 270–271.

Edwards, Rem, 'The Pagan Doctrine of the Absolute Unchangeableness of God', *Religious Studies*, 14 (1978), 305–313.

Einstein, Albert, 'Religion and Science', *New York Times Magazine*, (9 November 1930).

__ *The Human Side*, ed. Helen Dukas and Banesh Hoffman (n.p.: Princeton University Press, 1979).

Elwell, Walter A. (ed.), *Evangelical Dictionary of Theology* (Grand Rapids, Mich.: Baker, 1996).

Encyclopedia Britannica CD (1998 standard edition).

Erickson, Millard J., *Christian Theology* (Grand Rapids, Mich.: Baker, 1985).

Evans, C. Stephen, *Pocket Dictionary of Apologetics & Philosophy of Religion* (Downers Grove, Ill.: InterVarsity Press, 2002).

Fackre, Gabriel, review of T.F. Torrance, *Reality and Evangelical Theology* (Philadelphia: Westminster, 1982), *Theology Today*, 39/1, (April 1982), 449–453.

Ferre, Frederick, *Language, Logic and God* (London: Eyre & Spottiswoode, 1962).

Ford, David F., review of T.F. Torrance, *The Trinitarian Faith. The Evangelical Theology of the Ancient Catholic Church* (Edinburgh: T&T Clark, 1988), *Scottish Journal of Theology* 43 (1990), 263–267.

Fredriksen, Paula, *From Jesus To Christ* (New Haven and London: Yale University Press, 2000).

Goetz, Ronald, *The Karl Barth Centennial: An Appreciative Critique* <http://www.religion-online.org/showarticle.asp?title=1> accessed 4 Sep 2005.

Gray, Bryan J., 'Towards Better Ways of Reading The Bible', *Scottish Journal of Theology*, 33 (1980), 301–315.

Gregory of Nazianzus, 'To Cledonius The Priest Against Apollinarius', in *Nicene and Post-Nicene Fathers*, ed. Philip Schaff and Henry Wice, 7 (Peaboy, Mass.: Hendrickson, 1999), 439–443.

Gregory of Nyssa, 'Letter to Eustathia, Ambrosia, and Basilissa', in *Nicene and Post-Nicene Fathers*, ed. Philip Schaff & Henry Wace, 5 (Peaboy, Mass.: Hendrickson, 1999), 542–545.

__ 'On The Soul and The Resurrection', 430–468.

Grieve, Val, *Verdict on the Empty Tomb* (n.p.: Church Pastoral Society, 1976).

Grillmeier, Aloys, *Christ in Christian Tradition*, 1 (Atlanta: John Knox Press, 1975).

Habermas, Gary R., *The Historical Jesus: Ancient Evidence For The Life of Christ* (Joplin, Missouri: College Press, 1996).

Hall, Francis Joseph, *The Kenotic Theory Considered With Particular Reference to its Anglican Forms and Arguments* (New York: Longmans, 1898).

282

Harrison, F. Everett, Geoffrey W. Broniley, and Carl F. Henry, *Wycliffe Dictionary of Theology* (Peaboy, Mass.: Hendrickson Publishers, 1999).

Hawking, Stephen, *A Brief History of Time* (New York: Bantam Books, 1988).

Hebblethwaite, Brian, *The Incarnation - Collected Essays in Christology* (Cambridge: Cambridge University Press, 1987).

Hebert, Gabriel, '"Faithfulness" and "Faith"', *Theology* 58 (1955), 373–379.

Heltzel, Peter, *Thomas Torrance* <http://people.bu.edu/wwildman/WeirdWildWeb/courses/mwt/dictionary/mwt_themes_785_torrance.htm#top> accessed 8 Oct 2004.

Hendry, G.S., 'The Exposition of Holy Scripture', *Scottish Journal of Theology*, 1 (1948), 29–47.

Hengel, Martin, *Acts and the History of Earliest Christianity*, tr. John Bowden (London: SCM Press, 1979).

__ *Earliest Christianity* (London: SCM Press, 1986).

Henry, Carl, *God, Revelation and Authority*, 3 (Waco, Texas: Word Books, 1979).

Hepburn, Ronald W., *Christianity and Paradox* (New York: Pegasus, 1968).

Heppe, Heinrich, *Reformed Dogmatics*, tr. G.T. Thomson (Grand Rapids, Mich.: Baker Book House, 1978).

Hesselink, I. John, 'A Pilgrimage in the School of Christ - An Interview With T.F. Torrance', *Reformed Review*, 38/1 (Autumn 1984), 49–64.

Hilary of Poitiers, 'On the Trinity', in *Nicene and Post-Nicene Fathers*, ed. Philip Schaff & Henry Wace, 9 (Peaboy, Mass.: Hendrickson, 1999), 40–234.

Howard, George, 'Notes and Observations: On The "Faith of Christ"', *Harvard Theological Review*, 60 (1967), 459–465.

__ 'Phil 2:6-11 and the Human Christ', *Catholic Biblical Quarterly*, 40 (1978), 368–387.

__ 'Romans 3:21-31 And The Inclusion of The Gentiles', *Havard Theological Review*, 63 (1970), 223–233.

Hurst, L.D., 'Re-enter the Pre-existent Christ in Philippians 2:5-11?', *New Testament Study*, 32 (1986), 449–457.

Irving, Edward, *Collected Writings of Edward Irving*, ed. G. Carlyle, 5 (London: Alexander Strahan, 1865).

Jenson, Robert, *Systematic Theology*, 1 (New York: Oxford University Press, 1997).

John of Damascus, 'Exposition of the Orthodox Faith', *Nicene and Post-Nicene Fathers*, ed. Philip Schaff & Henry Wace, 9 (Peaboy, Mass.: Hendrickson, 1999), 1-101.

Johnson, Phillip R., *God Without Mood Swings* (2000) <http://www.spurgeon.org/~phil/articles/impassib.htm> accessed 20 Feb 2006.

Kassulke, Nathan, 'The Doctrine of the Trinity in the Old Testament', *Theologia*, 5/2 (Winter 2003) <http://www.wls.wels.net/publications/theologia/vol5no2> accessed 10 Feb 2006.

Kent, John H., *The End of The Line* (London: SCM Press, 1982).

Kent Jr., Homer A., Curtis Vaughan, and Aurther Rupprecht, *Philippians, Colossians, Philemon* (Grand Rapids, Mich.: Zondervan, 1996).

Kierkegaard, Soren, *The Essential Kierkegaard*, ed. Howard V. Hong and Edna H. Hong (Princeton, N.J.: Princeton University Press, 2000).

Klinefelter, Donald, S., 'God and Rationality: A Critique of the Theology of Thomas F. Torrance', *The Journal of Religion*, 53 (1973), 117–135.

Kostelnik, Solomon, *The Name of God: Revealed!* <http://members.nuvox.net/~on.roz/ God/name/ revealed.html> accessed 12 Dec 2005.

LaCugna, Catherine Mowry, *God for Us* (San Francisco: HarperSanFrancisco, 1993).

Ladd, George E., *A Theology of The New Testament* (Grand Rapids: Eerdmans, 1993).

Langford, Thomas A., 'T.F. Torrance's Theological Science: A Reaction', *Scottish Journal of Theology*, 25 (1972), 155–170.

Lee, Jung Young, *God Suffers For Us* (The Hague: Martinus Nijhoff, 1974).

Leo, 'The Tome of Leo', in *Christology of the Late Fathers*, ed. Edward Hardy (Philadelphia: The Westminster Press, 1954), 359–365.

Lovejoy, Arthur Oncken, *The Revolt Against Dualism* (La Salle, Il.: Open Court Publishing, 1960).

__ *The Great Chain of Being* (New York: Harper & Row, 1960).

Lucien Richard, *Christ the Self-Emptying God* (Mahwah, N.J.: Paulist, 1997).

Mackey, James Patrick, *The Christian Experience of God as Trinity* (London: SCM Press, 1983).

Mackintosh, H.R., *The Doctrine of The Person of Jesus Christ* (Edinburgh: T. & T. Clark, 1912).

__ *Types of Modern Theology - Schleiermacher to Barth* (London: Nisbet and Co., 1937).

Macleod, Donald, *The Person of Christ* (London: InterVarsity Press, 1998).

__ 'Dr T.F. Torrance and Scottish Theology: a Review Article', *The Evangelical Quarterly*, 72/1, (January 2000), 57–72.

Macquarrie, John, *Twentieth-Century Religious Thought* (London: SCM Press, 1963).

Martensen, H., *Christian Dogmatics*, tr. William Urwick (Edinburgh: T&T Clark, 1898).

Martin, Ralph P. and Brian J. Dodd, *Where Christology Began: Essays on Philippians 2* (Louisville, Ky.: Westminster John Knox Press, 1998).

McDowell, Josh, *A Ready Defense*, compiled by Bill Wilson (Nashville, Tenn.: Thomas Nelson, 1993).

McGrath, Alister E., *T.F. Torrance, An Intellectual Biography* (Edinburgh: T&T Clark, 1999).

McIntyre, John, *The Shape of Christology* (London: SCM Press, 1966).

McWilliams, Warren, *The Passion of God* (Macon: Mercer University Press, 1985).

Merrill, Eugene H., 'A Theology of The Pentateuch', in *A Biblical Theology of The Old Testament*, ed. Roy B. Zuck (Chicago: Moody, 1991), 7–88.

Molnar, Paul D., 'God's Self-Communication in Christ: A Comparison of Thomas F. Torrance and Karl Rahner', *Scottish Journal of Theology*, 50/3 (1997), 288–320.

Moltmann, Jurgen, *History and the Triune God*, (London: SCM Press, 1991).

__ *The Crucified God* (Minneapolis: Fortress, 1993).

__ 'The Crucified God', *Theology Today* 31/1 (April 1974), 6–18.

__ *Theology of Hope* (Minneapolis: Fortress, 1993).

Monsma, Peter Halman, *Karl Barth's Idea of Revelation* (Somerville, N.J.: Somerset Press, 1937).

Moreland, J.P., *Scaling the Secular City: A Defense of Christianity* (Grand Rapids, Mich.: Baker, 1987).

Morison, Frank, *Who Moved The Stone?* (Grand Rapids, Mich.: Zondervan, 1958).

Morris, Henry, M., *Many Infallible Proofs* (El Cajon, Cal.: Master Books, 1990).

Morrison, John D., 'Heidegger, Correspondence Truth and the Realist Theology of Thomas Forsyth Torrance', *The Evangelical Quarterly*, 69/2, (April 1997), 139–155.

__ *Knowledge of The Self-Revealing God in The Thought of Thomas Forsyth Torrance.* (New York: Peter Lang, 1997).

__ review of T.F. Torrance, *The Trinitarian Faith* (Edinburgh: T&T Clark, 1988), in *Calvin Theological Journal*, 25/1 (April 1990), 119–122.

__ 'Scripture as Word of God: Evangelical Assumption or Evangelical Question?', *Trinity Journal*, 20/2 (Fall 1999), 165–190.

__ 'Thomas Forsyth Torrance's Critique of Evangelical (Protestant) Orthodoxy', *The Evangelical Quarterly*, 67/1, (January 1995), 53–69.

Moule, C.F.D., 'The Biblical Conception of "Faith" (Contributions and Comments)', *The Expository Times*, 68 (October 1956 - September 1957), 157, 222.

Mozley, J.K., *The Impassibility of God* (Cambridge: Cambridge University Press, 1926).

Muller, Richard A, 'Karl Barth and The Path of Theology Into The Twentieth Century: Historical Observations', *The Westminster Theological Journal*, 51/1 (Spring 1989), 25–50.

__ review of T.F. Torrance, *Transformation and Convergence in the Frame of Knowledge: Explorations in the Interrelations of Scientific and Theological Enterprise* (Grand Rapids: Eerdmans, 1984), in *The Westminster Theological Journal*, 47/1 (Spring 1985), 136–140.

Murray, John, *The Epistle to the Romans*, 1 (Grand Rapids: Eerdmans, 1968).

Neidhardt, Walter J., *Thomas F. Torrance's Integration of Judeo-Christian Theology & Natural Science: Some Key Themes* <http://www.asa3.org/ASA/PSCF/1989/PSCF6-89Neidhardt.html> accessed 18 Oct 2004.

New Hart's Rules (Oxford: Oxford University Press, 2005)

Newton, Issac, *Newton's Principia*, tr. Andrew Motte. Berkeley (Cal.: University of California Press, 1947).

__ *Twelve Articles on Religion* <http://www.newtonproject.ic.ac.uk/texts/keynes009_n.html> accessed 12 Dec 2005.

Ngien, Dennis, 'The God Who Suffers', *Christianity Today* 3 (February 1997) <http://www.biblical-theology.com/miscellaneous/suffer.htm> accessed 1 Feb 2006.

__ *The Suffering of God: According to Martin Luther's 'Theologia Crucis'* (Vancouver, BC.:Regent College Publishing, 2005).

Norris, Frederick W., 'Mathematics, Physics and Religion: A Need For Candor and Rigor', *Scottish Journal of Theology*, 37 (1984), 457–470.

Norris, Richard A., *The Christological Controversy* (Philadelphia: Fortress Press, 1980).

Origen, 'Against Celsus', in *Ante-Nicene Fathers*, ed. Alexander Roberts and James Donaldson, 4 (Peaboy, Mass.: Hendrickson, 1999), 395–669.

__ 'Commentary on Matthew', in *Ante-Nicene Fathers*, ed. Allan Menzies, 9 (Peaboy, Mass.: Hendrickson, 1999), 412–512.

__ 'De Principiis', in *Ante-Nicene Fathers*, ed. Alexander Roberts & James Donaldson, 4 (Peaboy, Mass.: Hendrickson, 1999), 239–382.

Packer, J. I., *Fundamentalism and the Word of God* (Grand Rapids: Eerdmans, 1958).

__ *Knowing God with Study Guide* (London: Hodder & Stoughton, 1993).

Palma, Robert J., 'Thomas F. Torrance's Reformed Theology', *Reformed Review* 38/1 (Autumn 1984), 2–45.

Pannenberg, Wolfhart, 'Eternity, Time and the Trinitarian God', *CTI Reflections*, 3 (1999), 48–61.

__ *Jesus God and Man*, tr. Lewis Wilkins & Duane Priebe (London: SCM Press, 1968).

__ *Revelation As History*, tr. David Granskou (New York: Macmillan, 1968).

Philip Schaff, *History of the Christian Church* (Grand Rapids: Eerdmans, 1995).

Picard, R.W., *Newton - Rationalizing Christianity, or Not?* <http://web.media.mit.edu/~picard/Newton.html> accessed 6 Jan 2005.

Plantinga, Alvin, and Nicholas Wolterstorff, *Faith and Rationality: Reason and Belief in God* (London: University of Notre Dame Press, 1986).

Pohle, Mgr Joseph, *Christology: A Dogmatic Treatise On The Incarnation* (St. Louis, Mo.: B. Herder, 1925).

Pratz, Gunther, *The Relationship between Incarnation and Atonement in the Theology of Thomas F. Torrance* <http://home.apu.edu/~CTRF/articles/1998_articles/pratz.html> accessed 18 Oct 2004.

Prestige, G. L., *Fathers and Heretics* (London: Society for Promoting Christian Knowledge, 1940).

Rahner, Karl, *The Trinity*, tr. Joseph Donceel (London: Burns & Oates, 1970).

Ramsey, Ian, *Christian Empiricism* (London: Sheldon Press, 1974).

Reimarus, Hermann S., *Reimarus: Fragments*, ed. Charles H. Talbert (Philadelphia: Fortress Press, 1970).

Richard, Lucien, *Christ the Self-Emptying God* (New York: Paulist, 1997).

Richey, Alban, *The Incarnation and The Kenosis* (New York: James Pott, 1898).

Robbins, Charles J., 'Rhetorical Structure of Philippians 2:6-11', *The Catholic Biblical Quarterly*, 42, 1980, p. 73–82.

Robinson, D.W.B., *Justification and the Faith of Jesus* <http://www.presenttruthmag.com/ archive/XLIV/ 44-3.htm> accessed 1 Nov 2004.

Robinson, John A.T., *The Human Face of God* (Philadelphia: Westminster Press, 1973).

Rowe, J. Nigel, *Origen's Doctrine of Subordination: A Study in Origen's Christology* (Berne & New York: Peter Lang, 1987).

Schaff, Philip, *History of The Christian Church* (Grand Rapids: Eerdmans, 1995).

Schoonenberg, Piet, 'The Kenosis or Self-Emptying of Christ', *Concilium* 11 (1966), 27–36.

Schweitzer, Albert, *The Quest of the Historical Jesus*, ed. John Bowden (Minneapolis: Fortress Press, 2001).

Scotus, John Duns, *God and Creatures - The Quodlibetal Questions*, tr. Felix Alluntis and Allan B. Wolter (New York: Princeton University Press, 1975).

Seitz, Christopher, 'The Call of Moses and the "Revelation" of the Divine Name', in *Theologica Exegesis*, ed. Christopher Seitz and Kathryn Greene-McCreight (Grand Rapids, Mich.: Eerdmanns, 1999), 145–161.

Siemens Jr. and F. David, 'Two Problems With Torrance', *Perspectives on Science and Christian Faith*, 43/2 (June 1991), 112–113.

Spring, Kenneth, R., and Michael W. Davidson, *Light: Particle or a Wave?* <http://micro.magnet.fsu.edu/primer/lightandcolor/particleorwave.html> accessed 27 Dec 2004.

Strawbridge, Gregg, *Karl Barth's Rejection of Natural Theology or An Exegesis of Romans 1:19-20* <http://www.wordmp3.com/gs/barth.htm> accessed 3 Jan 2005.

Strong, Augustus H., *Systematic Theology* (Old Tappan, N.J.: Fleming H. Revell, 1976).

Strong, Edmund Linwood, *Lectures on The Incarnation of God* (London: Longmans, Green, 1920).

Strong, James & John McClintock, *Cyclopdeia of Biblical, Theological, And Ecclesiastical Literature* (Grand Rapids, Mich.: Baker, 1981).

Tapia, Ralph J., *The Theology of Christ: Commentary* (New York: The Bruce Publishing Company, 1971).

Taylor, Vincent, *The Atonement in New Testament Teaching* (London: The Epworth Press, 1958).

__ *The Cross of Christ: Eight Public Lectures* (London: MacMillan, 1957).

Telushkin, Joseph, *Biblical Literacy* (New York: William Morrow, 1997).

Temple, William, *Nature, Man and God* (London: MacMillan, 1964).

Tertullian, 'A Treatise on the Soul', in *Ante-Nicene Fathers*, ed. Alexander Roberts & James Donaldson, 3 (Peaboy, Mass.: Hendrickson, 1999). 181-235.

__ 'Against Marcion', 269–428.

__ 'On the Flesh of Christ', 521–544.

The Cambridge Dictionary of Philosophy (2nd edn, Cambridge: Cambridge University Press, 1999).

Thiemann, Ronald, F., *Revelation and Theology* (Notre Dame, Ind.: University of Notre Dame Press, 1985).

Thiessen, Henry C., *Lectures in Systematic Theology* (Grand Rapids: Eerdmans, 1977).

Thomasius, Gottfried, 'The Person of the Mediator', in *God and Incarnation In Mid-Nineteenth Century German Theology*, ed. tr. Claude Welch (New York: Oxford University Press, 1965), 31–101.

Thomsen, Dietrick E., review of T.F. Torrance, *Christian Theology and Scientific Culture* (New York: Oxford University Press, 1981), in *Theology Today*, 39/1 (April 1982), 314–321.

Tillich, Paul, *Systematic Theology*, 1 (Welwyn, Herts: James Nisbet & Co., 1963).

Timothy Clark, *A Defense of the Thomistic Definition of Person* <http://www.gocart.org/thesis.html> accessed 4 Nov 2003.

Torrance, T.F., 'A Study in New Testament Communication', *Scottish Journal of Theology*, 3 (1950), 298-313.

__ '"The Substance of The Faith": A Clarification of The Concept in The Church of Scotland', *Scottish Journal of Theology*, 36 (1983), 327–338.

__ *Calvin's Doctrine of Man* (London: Lutterworth Press, 1949).

__ 'Calvin's Sermons. 1. The Mystery of Godliness, And Other Selected Sermons. 2. The Deity of Christ and Other Sermons', *Scottish Journal of Theology*, 5 (1952): 424–427.

__ *Christian Frame of Mind: Reason, Order, and Openness in Theology and Natural Science* (Colorado Springs: Helmers & Howard, 1989).

287

__ *Conflict and Agreement in the Church. Vol. 1: Order and Disorder* (London: Lutterworth Press, 1959).

__ *Conflict and Agreement in the Church. Vol. 2: The Ministry and the Sacraments of the Gospel* (London: Lutterworth Press, 1960).

__ *Divine and Contingent Order* (Edinburgh: T&T Clark, 1998).

__ *Divine Meaning: Studies in Patristic Hermeneutics* (Edinburgh: T&T Clark, 1995).

__ *Einstein and God* <http://www.ctinquiry.org/publications/torrance.htm> accessed 1 Mar 2005.

__ *Expository Studies in St. John's Miracles* (London: James Clarke & Co., 1938).

__ 'Faith and Philosophy', *Hibbert Journal* 47/3 (1949), 237–246.

__ *God and Rationality* (London: Oxford University Press, 1971).

__ 'Hermeneutics According to F.D.E. Schleiermacher', *Scottish Journal of Theology* 21 (1968), 257–267.

__ 'Introduction', in *A Dynamic Theory of the Electromagnetic Field*, ed. T.F. Torrance (Edinburgh: Scottish Academic Press, 1982).

__ 'Introduction', in *Belief in Science and in Christian Life: the Relevance of Michael Polanyi's Thought for Christian Faith and Life*, ed. T.F. Torrance (Edinburgh: Handsel Press, 1980), xiii–xvii.

__ 'Introduction', in *The Incarnation: Ecumenical Studies in the Nicene-Constantinopolitan Creed A.D. 381*, ed. T. F. Torrance (Edinburgh:The Handsel Press, 1981), xi–xxii.

__ 'John Philoponos of Alexandria Sixth Century Christian Physicist', *Texts And Studies* 2 (1983), 261–265.

__ 'Justification: Its Radical Nature and Place in Reformed Doctrine and Life', *Scottish Journal of Theology*, 13 (1960), 225–246.

__ 'Karl Barth and The Latin Heresy', *Scottish Journal of Theology*, 39 (1986), 461–482.

__ *Karl Barth, Biblical and Evangelical Theologian* (Edninburgh: T&T Clark, 1990).

__ *Karl Barth: An Introduction to His Early Theology 1910-1931* (London: SCM Press, 1962).

__ *Kingdom and Church* (Eugene: Wipf and Stock Publishers, 1996).

__ 'One Aspect of the Biblical Conception of Faith', *The Expository Times*, 68 (October 1956 - September 1957), 111–114.

__ 'Phusikos Kai Theologikos Logos, St Paul and Athenagoras at Athens', *Scottish Journal of Theology*, 41 (1988), 11–26.

__ 'Realism and Openness in Scientific Inquiry', *Zygon*, 23/1 (March 1988), 159–169.

__ *Reality and Evangelical Theology: The Realism of Christian Revelation* (Downers Grove: InterVarsity Press, 1999).

__ *Reality and Scientific Theology* (Edinburgh: Scottish Academic Press, 1985).

__ review of B.B. Warfield, *The Inspiration and Authority of the Bible* (n.p.: The Presbyterian and Reformed Publishing Company), in *Scottish Journal of Theology*, 7 (1954), 104–108.

__ review of C.R.B. Shapland (introduction & notes), *The Letters of Saint Athanasius and Notes* (n.p.: Epworth, 1951), in *Scottish Journal of Theology*, 5 (1952), 205–208.

288

___ review of Heinrich Heppe, *Reformed Dogmatics, set out and illustrated from the sources*, tr. G.T. Thomson (n.p.: Allen and Unwin, u.d.), in *Scottish Journal of Theology*, 5 (1952), 81–85.

___ review of Oscar Cullmann, *The Earliest Christian Confessions*, tr. J.K.S. Reid (n.p.: Lutterworth, n.d.), in *Scottish Journal of Theology*, 5 (1952), 85–87.

___ review of T.H.L. Parker, *The Oracles of God: An Introduction to the Preaching of John Calvin* (n.p.: Lutterworth, n.d.), in *Scottish Journal of Theology*, 1 (1948), 212–214.

___ review of William Robinson, *The Biblical Doctrine of the Church* (St. Louis, Missouri: The Bethany Press, n.d.), in *Scottish Journal of Theology*, 4 (1951), 433–437.

___ *Royal Priesthood* (London: Continuum T&T Clark, 2003).

___ 'Science, Theology, Unity', *Theology Today*, 21/2 (July 1964), 149–154.

___ 'Scientific Hermeneutics, According to St. Thomas Aquinas', *The Journal of Theological Studies*, 13 (1962), 259–289.

___ *Space, Time and Incarnation* (London: Oxford University Press, 1969).

___ *Space, Time and Resurrection* (Edinburgh: T&T Clark, 1998).

___ 'The Atonement and The Oneness of The Church', *Scottish Journal of Theology*, 7 (1954), 245–269.

___ 'The Biblical Conception of "Faith"', *The Expository Times*, 68 (October 1956 - September 1957), 221–222.

___ *The Christian Doctrine of God, One Being Three Persons* (Edinburgh: T&T Clark, 2001).

___ 'The Christian Doctrine of Marriage', *Theology*, 56 (1953), 162–167.

___ *The Christian Frame of Mind: Reason, Order, and Openness in Theology and Natural Science* (Colorado Springs: Helmers & Howard, 1989).

___ 'The Church in an Era of Scientific Change - 2', *The Month*, 6/5 (May 1973).176–180.

___ 'The Church in an Era of Scientific Change', *The Month*, 6/4 (April 1973),136–142.

___ 'The Concept of Order in Theology and Science', *The Princeton Seminary Bulletin*, 5/2 (1984), 130–139.

___ 'The Deposit of Faith', *Scottish Journal of Theology*, 36 (1983), 1–28.

___ *The Doctrine of Grace In the Apostolic Fathers* (Eugene: Wipf and Stock Publishers, 1948).

___ *The Doctrine of Jesus Christ* (Eugene: Wipf and Stock Publishers, 2002).

___ 'The Doctrine of Order', *The Church Quarterly Review*, 160 (1959), 21–36.

___ 'The Doctrine of the Holy Trinity According to St. Athanasius', *Anglican Theological Review*, 71/4 (1989), 395–405.

___ 'The Framework of Belief', in *Belief in Science and in Christian Life: the Relevance of Michael Polanyi's Thought for Christian Faith and Life*, ed. T.F. Torrance (Edinburgh: Handsel Press, 1980), 1–27.

___ *The Ground And Grammar of Theology* (Edinburgh: T&T Clark, 2001).

___ *The Hermeneutics of John Calvin* (Edninburgh: Scottish Academic Press, 1988).

___ 'The Legacy of Karl Barth (1886-1986)', *Scottish Journal of Theology*, 39 (1986), 289–308.

__ *The Mediation of Christ* (Exeter: Paternoster Press, 1983).

__ 'The Mission of The Church', *Scottish Journal of Theology*, 19 (1966), 129–143.

__ 'The Pre-eminence of Jesus Christ', *Expository Times*, 89 (October 1977-September 1978), 54–55.

__ 'The Problem of Natural Theology in The Thought of Karl Barth', *Religious Studies* 6 (1970), 121–135.

__ 'The Roman Doctrine of Grace From The Point of View of Reformed Theology', *The Eastern Churches Quarterly*, 16/1, (1964), 290–312.

__ (ed.), *The School of Faith: The Catechisms of the Reformed Church* (London: James Clarke & Co. Limited, 1959).

__ *The Trinitarian Faith* (Edinburgh: T&T Clark, 2003).

__ *Theological Dialogue Between Orthodox and Reformed Churches*, 2 (Edinburgh: Scottish Academic Press, 1993).

__ *Theological Science* (Edinburgh: T&T Clark, 1996).

__ *Theology in Reconciliation* (Eugene: Wipf and Stock Publishers, 1996).

__ *Theology in Reconstruction* (London: SCM Press, 1965).

__ 'Thomas Torrance Responds', in *The Promise of Trinitarian Theology: Theologians in Dialogue with T.F. Torrance*, ed. Elmer M. Coyler (Landam, Md.: Rowman & Littlefield, 2001), 303–340.

__ *Trinitarian Perspectives Toward Doctrinal Agreement* (Edinburgh: T&T Clark, 1999).

__ 'Truth and Authority: Theses on Truth', *The Irish Theological Quarterly*, 34/3 (July 1972), 215-242.

__ 'Ultimate Beliefs and The Scientific Revolution', *Cross Currents*, 30/1, (Spring 1980), 129–149.

__ 'Universalism or Election?', *Scottish Journal of Theology*, 2 (1949), 310–318.

__ *When Christ Comes and Comes Again* (Eugene: Wipf and Stock Publishers, 1957).

Van Beeck, Frans J. '"This Weakness of God's is Stronger" (1 Cor. 1:25): An Inquiry Beyond the Power of Being', *Toronto Journal of Theology*, 9/1 (1993), 9–26.

Vincent, Marvin R., *Word Studies in the New Testament* (Peaboy, Ma.: Hendrickson Publishers, 1984).

Walker, Andrew, 'Interview with Professor Thomas F. Torrance', in *Different Gospels* (London: Hodder & Stoughton, 1988), 42–54.

Walvoord, John F., *Jesus Christ Our Lord* (Chicago: Moody Press, 1969).

Weinandy, Thomas G., *Does God Suffer?* <http://www.arsdisputandi.org/publish/articles/000023/ article.htm> accessed 3 May 2005.

Wikipedia < http://en.wikipedia.org> 4 Jan 2006.

Witherington III, Ben, *Paul's Letter to the Romans* (Grand Rapids, Mich.: Eerdmans, 2004).

Wright, G. Ernest, *God Who Acts* (London: SCM Press, 1952).

Yeung, Jason H.K., *Being and Knowing: An Examination of T.F. Torrance's Christo-logical Science* (Hong Kong: Jian Dao, 1996).

Zahrnt, Heinz, *The Question of God*, tr. R.A. Wilson (New York: Harcourt, Brace & World, 1969).